Advanced
Credit Risk Analysis

Wiley Series in Financial Engineering

Advanced Credit Risk Analysis

Financial Approaches and Mathematical Models to Assess, Price, and Manage Credit Risk

Didier Cossin
and
Hugues Pirotte

JOHN WILEY & SONS, LTD

Chichester · New York · Weinheim · Brisbane · Singapore · Toronto

Other Wiley Editorial Offices

John Wiley & Sons, Inc., 605 Third Avenue,
New York, NY 10158-0012, USA

WILEY-VCH Verlag GmbH, Pappelallee 3,
D-69469 Weinheim, Germany

Jacaranda Wiley, Ltd., 33 Park Road, Milton,
Queensland 4064, Australia

John Wiley & Sons (Asia) Pte, Ltd., 2 Clementi Loop #02-01,
Jin Xing Distripark, Singapore 129809

John Wiley & Sons (Canada), Ltd., 22 Worcester Road,
Rexdale, Ontario M9W 1L1, Canada

Library of Congress Cataloging-in-Publication Data

Cossin, Didier.
    Advanced credit risk analysis : financial approaches and mathematical models to assess,
price, and manage credit risk / Didier Cossin and Hugues Pirotte.
        p. cm. — (Wiley series in financial engineering)
    Includes bibliographical references and index.
    ISBN 0-471-98723-9 (cased)
    1. Credit—Management. 2. Risk management. 3. Financial management. I. Pirotte,
Hugues. II. Title. III. Series.
    HG3751.C67   2000
    332.7—dc21
                                                            99–057861

British Library Cataloguing in Publication Data

A catalogue record for this book is available from the British Library

ISBN 0-471-98723-9

Typeset in 10/12pt Times from the author's disks by Dobbie Typesetting Limited, Tavistock, Devon
Printed and bound in Great Britain by Biddles Ltd, Guildford and King's Lynn
This book is printed on acid-free paper responsibly manufactured from sustainable forestry,
in which at least two trees are planted for each one used for paper production.

To Cathie and Laurence

Contents

Acknowledgements

We thank the many academics who have worked or are working in the field of credit risk and whose research has made such a book possible. Their names can be found throughout the present work. We are especially grateful to Felipe Aparicio Acosta, Jamil Baz, Carliss Baldwin, Carlo Broggi, Guy Coughlan, Michel Crouhy, Sanjiv Das, François Degeorge, Jean Dermine, Jérôme Detemple, Athanasios Episcopos, Kenneth Froot, Helyette Geman, Rajna Gibson, Tomas Hricko, Van Son Lai, Hayne Leland, Scott Mason, Robert C. Merton, Garry Rayner, Eduardo Schwartz, Suresh Sundaresan, Agim Xhaja as well as to the following companies: KMV, Riskmetrics, Tradition, JPMorgan, and others not named here for confidentiality reasons.

We are also grateful for the help of the John Wiley team: Sally Smith, Lewis Derrick, Ben Earl and all the others involved in making this a successful venture (including some met at conferences and who showed dedication to the book even before its presence on the shelves).

Last, but not least, personal support from our partners and families was fantastic.

Although we have thoroughly checked the materials presented here, some mistakes may possibly remain. Please send any comment to: Didier.Cossin@hec.unil.ch

You can also refer to the book's web site for errata.

1
Introduction

Credit risk, or the risk of default, has always been a major topic of concern for banks and other financial intermediaries, and any agent committed to a financial contract for that matter. While the concern for the possible default of a counterparty on an agreed-upon financial contract is centuries old, modern techniques and models have arisen in the last few years that help master the problem. These advanced models and techniques are the topic of the present book. This volume aims at giving a synthesis of the many advanced models that are currently available. It will offer the tools that can help banks, financial intermediaries in general, corporates, investors, and many other economic agents obtain better pricing and better management of the credit risk exposures they are facing.

While it is true that the concern for default is centuries old, it is also true that the sheer magnitude and complexity of the problem have increased tremendously in the recent past.

First, the recent explosion of the financial markets have made a classical problem a world-wide behemoth. Derivatives alone have grown to a market of $33 trillion in the US alone (source: Office of the Comptroller of the Currency (OCC), March 1999, Notional Value), a market that dwarfs the largest stock markets in the world (New York Stock Exchange's biggest day ever, 19 October, 1987, had a volume of $21 billion). Over-the-counter (OTC) derivatives represented 88% of this volume during the first quarter of 1999 (while exchange traded derivatives represented just 12%). But OTC instruments, that have the advantage of being customizable to clients' needs, do present credit risk. Add to this the classical credit risky markets of fixed income, either public debt or corporate loans, that are themselves worth multi-trillions of dollars, and all sorts of other financial contracts (financial guarantees, etc.). The sheer size of the credit risk market has become mind-boggling, and grows fast as OTC instrument use grows much faster than those of exchange traded ones.

Second, while the credit risk market growth is impressive, its growth in complexity comes close to matching its growth in size. Credit risk on OTC derivative instruments is certainly more complex to understand than credit risk on a corporate loan. Consider for example a plain-vanilla interest rate swap. The credit risk bears on the net of the payments rather than on the notional. Credit risk in swaps is also two-sided as the swap may have negative or positive value for each of the concerned parties during its lifetime. It is also path dependent in the sense that once a party has defaulted, the other party's exposure has been cancelled.

In practice, collateralization or credit lines, as used frequently, will also affect the credit risk. And finally, netting agreements will affect the true exposure in nontrivial ways (see discussion on credit risk of derivatives for more details). Therefore a typical derivative instrument such as the interest rate swap contract has many more dimensions to consider in credit risk than a traditional corporate loan.

Third, credit risk targeted instruments have arisen recently that make credit risk both more manageable and easier to price, but at the same time require an increased sophistication. Credit derivatives in particular — such as credit default swaps, credit spread options, total return swaps, etc. — are filling a new space in the financial markets, reaching a notional value of $191 billion in the US only during the first quarter of 1999 (source: OCC data).

These three facts have led to an increased focus on credit risk, both from the practitioners' side and from the researchers' side. New models have been discovered, sometimes based on classical financial theory paradigms (such as contingent claim analysis or option pricing theory). These new models tend to substitute (but sometimes just complete) older, more traditional approaches to credit risk analysis and management based on actuarial methods.

For example, up until recently, management of credit risk was mostly done by credit risk departments that helped assign standardized credit limits to the different counterparties. Such credit limits take into account only cursorily the evolution of the risk considered or the real impact of instruments that have become more and more complex.

As their risk management systems become more sophisticated with respect to market risk, financial institutions become more aware of the weakness of their credit risk exposure calculation and of the need to value this exposure, rather than ration it through credit lines.

At the same time, the most sophisticated players in the field have started trading credit risk derivatives that by themselves allow for a better management of credit risk exposures. These credit risk derivatives also require some form of pricing. An easy arbitrage-free pricing on the basis of a simple instrument such as a bond cannot always be done. Competitive pressure thus gives the most advanced players a nice comparative advantage.

Hence both the need for better credit risk management and for a better understanding of new instruments coming to the markets require the help of good theories of credit risk pricing.

Many theoretical developments have indeed appeared in this field during the last few years. The goal of this book is to thus present the current trends in advanced models of credit risk pricing and credit risk management. We stress the logic of theoretical models, from the structural and from the reduced-form kind, their applications and extensions rather than the traditional actuarial methods. A major difficulty of actuarial methods is their complete dependence on historical data. They consist in fitting expectations of default to default data of the past. Their results are thus not necessarily coherent with the evolution of fundamentals across time. It is well known, for example, that fitting by taking an average of call values on past data, even calculating call values on expectations of stock values based on historical averages of stock prices, will not give rational call prices.

Instead an arbitrage-free theory of option pricing has been developed that relates call prices to current market variables. One can from thereon differentiate between the model(s) proposed and the estimates of the variables calculated to look for mistakes and approximation in call prices. Similarly, a rational theory of credit risk based on financial economics was developed as early as 1974 as an application of contingent claim analysis. This provides the basis for a modern theory of credit risk. The model of Merton (1974) gave birth to the so-called "structural models" of credit risk. It also inspired a different line of models, the so-called reduced-form models, to pursue arbitrage-free pricing in a less complete but possibly more practical manner. These two major streams, their extensions, and the financial engineering they led to in order to fit real securities are the topic of Part One of the book. Empirical difficulties (notably considering recovery rates and default probabilities) lead us to propose a new model in Part Two of the book. While credit risk pricing has attracted the full attention of the researchers, practitioners faced with the difficulty of pricing credit risk have preferred to mitigate the problem via practical solutions, notably collateralization and marking-to-market. We propose in Part Three of the book mathematical models that help determine optimal collateralization and marking-to-market policies. Part Four of the book is devoted to modern credit risk management issues. We cover notably the modern credit risk management tools that remain based on traditional actuarial methods, but implement them with sufficient dynamics to provide some interesting answers. And we pay attention to the current structuring techniques available with credit derivatives. This last section precedes general conclusions and appendices that the reader may find of special use.

1.1 FREQUENTLY USED NOTATION

1.1.1 Miscellaneous Remarks

1. In Part One it is usually understood that the starting time of the contract is time 0, unless it is defined differently. Therefore, the time to maturity, τ, is equal to the maturity itself, T.
2. Time subscripts indicate the time at which the function is evaluated. However, in partial differential equations, it is common to indicate partial derivatives also with subscripts. A warning will be specified whenever this is the case.

1.1.2 The Latins and the Greeks

This is the particular notation that is being used for most parts of the book unless otherwise specified. Special parts as collateralization that are a whole mathematical issue by themselves have their own notation because of their complexity which makes it difficult to apply the standard notation.

The Latins

B	Barrier level standing for the threshold value.
cs	Credit spread.
$\delta_0\,(V, T)$	Expected dividend stream at time 0, paid out from the assets value of the firm and up to T.
d_1	From the Black and Scholes option pricing formulation:

$$= \ln\left[\frac{S/Ke^{-rT}}{\sigma\sqrt{T}}\right] + \frac{1}{2}\sigma\sqrt{T},$$

under a flat-term structure of interest rates.

d_2	$d_1 - \sigma\sqrt{T}.$

D	Debt market value.
F	Face value of debt.
K	Exercise price of the standard Black and Scholes option.
h	Intensity rate of default used in reduced-form approaches.
L	Loss rate at default used in reduced-form approaches.
$N(\cdot), \Phi(\cdot)$	Cumulative standard normal distribution.
$n(\cdot), \phi(\cdot)$	Standard normal probability density.
$P_t(T)$	Price of a riskfree zero-coupon or discount bond, at time t with maturity T.
r	Short-term interest rate.
$R(T)$	Interest rate for a maturity T resulting from a term structure model of stochastic interest rates.
E	Equity: shareholder's market value or stock price.
T	Maturity of any contract.
v	Total market value of the firm.
V	Market value of the assets of the firm.
y	Yield on a corporate bond.

The Greeks

β	Continuous payout rate.
γ	Volatility parameter for the term interest rate spread.
δ	Continuous dividend rate.
ϑ	Volatility parameter for the long-term interest rate.
λ	Generic notation for the risk premia.
μ	Drift parameter of the dynamics of the assets value of the firm.
ξ	Equivalent to μ but once adjusted for the risk premia λ.
ρ	Correlation parameter. Subscripts denote the variables on which correlation applies.
σ	Generic notation for the volatility parameter in the diffusion processes. In particular, σ_v stands for the volatility of asset changes.
τ	Stands for the time to maturity or to the default event. In the latter case it is denoted as τ_b.
ϕ and φ	Recovery parameters on the values in the event of default.

1.1.3 Common Acronyms

AOA	Absence of opportunities of arbitrage.
APR	Absolute priority rule.
CIR	Cox, Ingersoll and Ross literature.
DF	Default frequency (KMV Corporation[1] methodology).
EDP	Expected default probability.

---

[1] Corporation founded by two academic professors, Stephen Kealhofer and Oldrich Vasicek, and John MacQuown, which has developed a methodology for credit risk management and which has participated in the elaboration of CreditMetrics methodology of JP Morgan and others.

DD   Distance-to-default (KMV Corporation methodology).
LGD   Loss given default.
PDE   Partial differential equation.

1.2 REFERENCES

OCC website: `http://www.occ.treas.gov/`
Bank for International Settlements, August 1996, *International Banking and Financial Market Developments*, 41 pp.

Part One
Credit Risk Pricing

2
Introduction to Modern Credit Risk Pricing

Most of the classical literature on credit risk tends to bear on traditional actuarial methods of credit risk (see Caouette et al., 1998 for a survey of these; see also for a critical approach Duffee, 1995a,b). Although these methods are widely used in banks, they present some difficulties. The basic principle of this type of approach is to estimate the probability of default (or of rating downgrade) and to estimate (often independently) the value of the contract at possible default times.

Rating agencies are standard sources for default probabilities. Techniques used to forecast default probabilities for individual firms are described in Altman et al. (1977). Methodologies have evolved from the calculation of mortality rates to the calculation of rating category migration probabilities. These probabilities (usually organized in so-called transition matrices) consist in the probabilities of downgrade and upgrade by rating category. These calculations are now frequently used by professionals.

As stressed by Duffee (1995a), end users tend to develop Monte Carlo simulations without taking into account the uncertainties in the models used to generate the estimates. Second, they rarely take into account the correlation among probabilities of default and estimates of possible losses. These correlations certainly affect the results. One can expect, for example, exposures linked to derivatives to rise with the volatility of the markets. But it is also at such a time that probabilities of default will arise. Unfortunately, historical correlations are difficult to obtain empirically. Some try to overcome this difficulty by using advanced analysis methods such as neural networks (see, for example, Tripi and Turban, 1996).

Third, these types of models often fail to consider the impact of the total portfolio of the institution considered on the upper bounds of credit losses associated with a single instrument or portfolio of instruments. By neglecting correlation effects, they thus obtain results that are not only based on simple replication of historic conditions but also that do not support the experience of the institution itself.

Many of the recent advances in this area are trying to address the portfolio issue, either at a practical and descriptive level of the portfolio of credit risks in a firm (for example with the help of CreditMetrics™), or at a more theoretical level to try and find a Markowitz type of efficient frontier with credit risks. Credit-risky returns have the particularity of not presenting the statistical properties necessary to apply the Markowitz framework (lognormality), and alternative models of an efficient frontier have thus to be found (see, for example, Altman and Saunders, 1996).

Nonetheless, as explained and illustrated below, all these methods face the major difficulty of being strongly dependent on historical estimates of credit risk dynamics. They are still a useful basis of information to start from, but financial theory has now provided us with more powerful analytical tools.

Modern credit risk analysis, on the other hand, is in the line of the continuous development of financial research on the integration of uncertainty. Broadly speaking, the investor faces risks that have been categorized as market risks, credit risk, country risk, and operational risk. Modern appraisal of credit risk follows directly from the advances that have been made for the management of market risks. To understand why the latter has been such a preoccupation in modern finance, let us introduce some chronology about market risks, their development, and the needs that have increased with respect to them.

Market risks integrate interest rate risk, exchange rate risk, and stock market risk. Interest in market risks began first with the development of stock exchanges and banking systems in most of the developed countries. With the end of the Bretton Woods agreements, exchange rates were then allowed to float causing volatility in interest rates. From the late 1970s, many economic studies were undertaken giving rise to what has been called since, financial theory. On the practitioners' side, many forms of contracts were proposed to the investors to mitigate the increasing volatility on the market, with special clauses allowing them to be optionally protected against changes in the term structure. This produced contracts that not only were sensitive to changes in market factors but also showed discontinuities in them. Therefore, the classical present value of coupon payments and the simple calculation of durations and convexities appeared to be insufficient to monitor and manage those risks.

The interest of academicians in developing new theories to modelize the uncertainty of market risk phenomena has led to a sophisticated set of financial tools inspired from mathematics and physics. The evolution happened on two grounds: financial theory, mostly driven from economics theory at that point, and the inclusion of sophisticated mathematics. On the financial theory side, most of the research attempted to give a value to the market price of risk or *market risk premia*. "Market" because the risk comes from market variables and also because, in order to find a unique market risk premia for each factor, the general hypothesis being made is that only systematic risk (the undiversifiable one) is priced. Why a risk premia? Because of the uncertainty broadly measured through the volatility of the underlying variable. Suppose that you can choose between receiving tomorrow $5 for certain or, accept the uncertainty to have $10 or $0 each with a probability of 50%. Rationally speaking, even if the average value of the second choice is the same as the riskfree value proposed first, the investor will prefer to obtain $5 for certain. Then, the question arises about how much additional expected value should we give him so that he will be indifferent between the two choices? As previously pointed out, we suppose that this investor is representative of the overall market so that the prime he will ask for is the market prime and it is unique.

On the mathematical side, much of today's inheritance comes from the early introduction of stochastic calculus (well known in physics for its application to problems such as health propagation) into modern finance. The contribution of stochastic calculus is firstly its capacity to produce a deterministic solution out of an uncertainty which is modelled as a random process. The dynamics of the unexpected part of the uncertainty is not deterministically specified from the beginning as is the case with chaos theory. Moreover, stochastic calculus allows the refining of the time space into infinitesimal points as a limit of the discrete-time approach. Let us take an example. Suppose that we want to draw the evolution of the stock price and the terminal values that it can take in one month. In discrete-time, we have to choose the number of time steps up to the maturity of one month, while in continuous-time there is an infinity of time steps guiding the stock price to its terminal value. In the latter case, there are no discontinuities at all in the evolution of the stock price. In continuous-time,

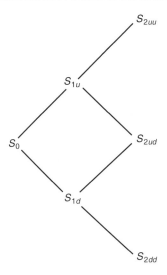

Figure 2.1 This figure shows a typical binomial lattice for the evolution of the stock price (S). The subscript u stands for an up movement while d is for a downside. The number in subscript means corresponds to the period number

the process does not execute jumps to two adjacent values but rather change in a very small period of time to very small different values[1]. Figure 2.1 shows a binomial tree where the stock price can take on two different values at each step. The more steps there are for the same time horizon, the more the model will converge to the continuous case (see Figure 2.2)[2].

The continuous-time framework is very useful because it enables much more easily closed-form solutions to specific financial problems to be obtained, while the discrete approach is still of great help to visualize the choices to make through time. But these choices are made on specific dates while they are made continuously in continuous-time. As noted in Merton's articles, two basic assumptions have to be made to justify the use of continuous-time approaches in the portfolio selection problems of modern finance:

Assumption 1 Capital markets are open at all times meaning that agents can trade continuously, and

Assumption 2 The stochastic processes generating the state variables can be described by diffusion processes with continuous sample paths.

The contribution of Merton resides in his capacity, at that time, to relate financial theory and the continuous-time approach introducing the well-known *continuous-time finance*. Before its emergence, financial theory was limited to static theories. Continuous-time finance allowed the restatement of previous problems dynamically, showing how theories such as the CAPM are influenced if the investor is now allowed to

---

[1] Mathematically, a stochastic process has the property of infinite elasticity at any infinitesimal point in time.
[2] However, with additional conditions.

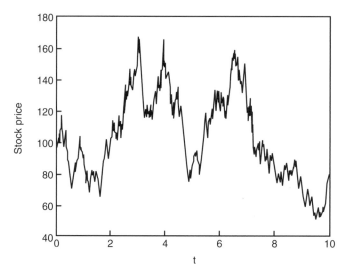

Figure 2.2 This figure shows a typical stochastic trajectory of the stock price given some parameters. In the present case, we assumed a starting value of 100, a volatility of 30%, and a riskfree interest rate of 5%

behave dynamically. The investor is now allowed to react *continuously* to changes in the environment rebalancing and hedging his positions through time. This ability should be taken into account along with transaction costs to show how strategies can be optimized from the beginning. Moreover, having this possibility means that the investor has a nonexecuted option on future allocation which has a price therefore at time 0.

In 1973, Black and Scholes were able to price such complex products as standard call and put options. The contribution of Merton is substantial and visionary, giving rise in the 1980s and 1990s to a rush into the design of derivatives products of increasing complexity. All these tools enable us today to price securities subject to these risks and to design sophisticated contingent claims on the same securities.

Now that market risks seems to be well encompassed, research has turned to credit risk. This interest also fills a need. The wave of developments for markets risks has engendered a sudden awareness in other fields, precisely about credit risk, for several reasons. One of them which is very relevant is the fact that differences between European currencies are vanishing with the appearance and global use of the Euro in financial markets. For European currencies' denominated bonds, credit risk then becomes the main determinant of the spread of a corporate bond yield over the riskfree rate. Here, since a linkage is directly being made between the interest rate risk and the credit risk, we cannot stand on traditional actuarial approaches for the credit risk part to price those bonds. Another reason is the huge movements in credit standing characterizing the end of 1998. From 1996, we observe a continuously growing number of defaults occurring. With the globalization wave, falling economies' effects propagate strongly and quickly to high-grade economies. Investors are thus far aware that credit risk is a real problem and that it cannot be measured and monitored on a stand-alone basis. On September 8, 1997, as Moody's rating agency noted, Yaohan Inc.'s default represented the first public bond default by a Japanese firm since the Second World

War with an unhonored debt of ¥161.3 billion. Moreover, this time, contrary to what has been assured traditionally, banks did not buy back Yaohan's debt from the market. Automated "absorbing means" did not play their role in letting the market absorb these anomalies. Therefore, market efficiency demands that the potentiality of credit losses must be accurately estimated and priced. Even if, in some contracts, mitigating techniques such as guaranties have been used, an equivalent price should be computable[3]. We will finally end up with a pricing scheme which, as with market risks, will allow us to disentangle the systematic risk from the firm or contract-specific risk. But, first, it is important to note that appraisal of credit risk does not allow us to use straightforwardly the same instruments that have been used for market risks. Some of these considerations are discussed in the following paragraph.

One of the problems which will be discussed in Chapter 3 is the survivorship bias. This is one of the particularities of credit risk. It has implications on the theoretical side as well as on the empirical side. For example, one of the statistics we would want to calculate is the percentage of firms defaulting in the course of the year, apart from other considerations like the sector to which the firm belongs or the state of the economy. But it would be naive to use this statistic as the probability for a firm to go bankrupt in general. The sample of firms chosen for the analysis implicitly contains only firms that have not defaulted until then. We are calculating a statistic on firms that have already shown their capability to *survive* so that the estimated probability to default is being minimized. Some of the research is oriented to the integration of a learning process which would mean that we should be following firms grouped by years of experience, sector, and analyze the proportions of default on different time-horizons. This approach would put even more emphasis on the fact that there exists a term structure of credit spreads.

Except for the period comprised between the filing for bankruptcy and the definitive liquidation of the value of the firm with restitution to claimants, bankruptcy truncates the life of the variable under consideration. While for an interest rate dynamic we can analyze the series at any point in time and still can be ensured of the Markov property[4], this is not possible with credit risk. Even if there was a stabilization of interest rates, they will exist, their volatility being low. In the case of credit risk, if we look at the dynamic of the value of the firm, we know that there is a nonnull probability that there will be an endpoint to this value. But, until then, this value is everywhere estimated in continuation terms. Therefore, we need a technique to look at what is the meaning in pricing terms of the potentiality of this discontinuity.

---

[3]The collateral is a large topic in itself. First, because of the market efficiency, markets should be able to estimate the value of this collateral and the remaining credit spread that the contract will still trade for. Secondly, the collateral can itself be a risky asset, such as a real estate asset. Thus, in that case, part of the original credit risk is being swapped against the market risk of the real estate asset. This shows us that market risks and credit risks can really be integrated together, and that the particularities of the contracts subject to credit risk might not straightforwardly be used in mitigation.

[4]The Markov property states that if a process is Markov, then looking at past data is useless, whatever the time period. The best estimator of the future value of our series would be the contemporaneous value of the series. It also implies that the process is time homogeneous, i.e. the characteristics of the dynamic of the process will be preserved in the future whatever the time period examined.

2.1   REFERENCES

Altman, Edward I., R. G. Haldeman and P. Narayana, 1977, "ZETA ANALYSIS: a New Model to Identify Bankruptcy Risk of Corporations", *Journal of Banking and Finance*, June, 29–54.

Altman, Edward and Anthony Saunders, 1996, "Credit Risk Measurement: Developments Over the Last 20 Years", *Working Paper* 96–40, New York University, Salomon Center, September, 38 pp.

Caouette, John B., Edward I. Altman and Paul Narayana, 1998, "Managing Credit Risk: the Next Great Financial Challenge", New York: John Wiley & Sons.

Duffee, Gregory, 1998, "The Relation Between Treasury Yields and Corporate Bond Yield Spreads", *The Journal of Finance*, **53** (6), December, 2225–41.

Duffee, Gregory, 1999, "Estimating the Price of Default Risk", *The Review of Financial Studies*, **12** (1), Spring, 197–226.

Harris, Milton and Arthur Raviv, 1991, "The Theory of Capital Structure", *The Journal of Finance*, **46** (1), March, 297–355.

Tripi, Robert and Efrain Turban, 1996, "Neural Networks in Finance and Investing", see http://www.sigma-research.com/bookshelf/rtbookn2.htm.

3
Merton's Approach: The Intuition Behind Structural Models

A major difficulty of actuarial methods is their complete dependence on historical data. They consist in fitting expectations of default to default data of the past. Their results are thus not coherent with the evolution of fundamentals across time. It is well known, for example, that fitting by taking an average of call values on past data, even calculating call values on expectations of stock values based on historical averages of stock prices, will not give rational call prices. Instead an arbitrage-free theory of option pricing has been developed that relates call prices to current market variables. One can from then on differentiate between the model(s) proposed and the estimates of the variables calculated to look for mistakes and approximation in call prices. Similarly, a rational theory of credit risk based on financial economics was developed as early as 1974 as an application of contingent claim analysis.

Contingent claims analysis (option pricing) can be used to value the component parts of a firm's liability mix. In general, the value of each component will depend upon the stochastic variables which determine the evolution of the firm's asset value, the evolution of the interest rate, the payouts (dividends, coupons, etc.) to the various claimants, and the division of the firm at any point of reorganization (e.g. bankruptcy). Merton (1974) starts with a simplified model that yields useful insights and shows the way to more complete (and more complex) valuation.

Merton has thus provided us with the first optional approach to the structure of the firm. It is called the "structural" approach because it relies entirely upon the sharing rule for the value of the assets of the firm, V, between two main classes of claimholders, the shareholders and the bondholders, in other words, it depends on the actual capital structure of the firm. In short, the idea is to use option pricing to value the default risk spreads of fixed income instruments. Hence the Merton taxonomy of a "risk structure of interest rates" that completes the traditional "term structure of interest rates". The method makes it possible to analyze and measure the impact on credit risk spreads of a change in asset volatility, a change in interest rates volatility, different maturities of debt, etc.

In the liability side of the balance sheet, shareholder's value, denoted S, is opposed to the bondholder's value, D for debt. Because of the limited liability feature of the corporation, the maximum loss of the shareholders is limited to the nominal amount represented by their shares. Therefore, their "downside risk" is limited. On the other hand, the shareholders have a claim on the value of the assets whenever the reimbursement of the debt (F for face value) to the bondholders can be honored. Thus, the profile of the shareholder's value can be well represented by the value of a call, written on the assets of the firm, a point made more precise technically later.

By the same type of analogy, while the shareholder's payoff profile shows up as a call on the assets of the firm, the bondholder's payoff profile results in having a long position in the face value of the debt and selling for free a put on the value of the firm to the shareholders[1]. This will be demonstrated below.

As in other finance fields, Merton (1974) has brought the spark for a whole new perspective. Built on the arbitrage-free pricing methodology, credit risk arises therefore from the potentiality of default, the latter occurring when the value of the assets fall below a certain threshold value, i.e. when the assets value is lower than the face value (F) of the outstanding debt in our case. Stated differently, we could say that in terms of arbitrage-free pricing models, the value of the put option represents the cost of eliminating the credit risk borne by the provider of funds.

Because Merton's framework is straightforward for any researcher versed in option pricing, it allows the formulation of the basis of further research showing what such a simple model implies for credit risk modeling issues. Crouhy and Galai (1997), for example, derive the implicit assumptions of Merton's framework for the default probability and the expected recovery rate, the two essential components of credit risk. The leverage ratio is proved to play a crucial role in the decomposition. Whenever the profile is easily understandable, it assumes that the strategy is replicable and that therefore credit risk is hedgeable which, as the further exposition will show, is controversial. Moreover, using V as the underlying process supposes that V is a traded asset. Discussions on the ways to relax these assumptions are also provided below.

In this limited setting, and simply rearranging terms into Merton's formula, Crouhy and Galai (1997) show that we can decompose the value of the put into the *expected shortfall conditional on the firm being bankrupt at maturity* and the *expected probability of such event*. Moreover, the recovery rate is shown to be endogenously stochastic rather than taken to be some exogenous constant as in many previous (and later!) models. Since this approach relies entirely on an arbitrage relationship between the value of the firm and the two sets of claimants, it allows the expression of credit risk or the propensity to default as a direct function of the value of the stock[2]. This will be helpful for practical reasons since it will enable us to reengineer this framework into a more complete one and infer the parameters from stock market trading data. Under some distributional assumptions for the underlying variables, we will obtain a characterization of credit spreads that highlight the determinants of the time to default and of the recovery rate upon default.

Thus, some of the advantages of the "structural" approach show up already:

- The availability of an economic context underlying the event of default and the clear definition of the latter.
- The possibility to relate this to standard option pricing allowing: (a) an easy pricing framework; (b) a nondeterministic randomness for the event of default since the whole formulation depends on the process for the value of the assets; (c) the use of option relationships to link both claimholders' values and infer the parameters from real market data.

---

[1]At present, we do not make any differentiation between the value of the firm and the value of the assets of the firm. The last one should include the value of tax shields and other side effects. However, the application of the option pricing formula to the corporate case requires the Modigliani–Miller theorem which argues that the "sharing rule" does not have any impact on the value of the firm which is then taken as a purely exogenous process.

[2]This will be analogous to the use of the put–call parity relationship.

In section 3.1, the model of Merton is developed along with its assumptions which have to be clearly stated before getting into more complex derivations. It has to be noted that the present chapter is devoted to the model of Merton without stochastic interest rates. This further sophistication will be introduced in Chapter 4.

3.1   THE ORIGINAL CONTINGENT CLAIM ANALYSIS (CCA) FRAMEWORK: MERTON (1974)

It is important to characterize the assumptions required for the consistency of the application of standard option pricing to corporate credit risk. The Merton (1974) framework, being the original framework, relies on many hypotheses, some of which have been relaxed later. Most of them come straightforwardly from the Black and Scholes option pricing theory.

The objective of this simple methodology is to provide the price of a straight loan granted to a defaultable firm for a given period of time. The following hypothesis set the context in which the value process of this firm evolves through time:

Assumption 1   *Markets are frictionless. There are no transaction costs or taxes. Assets are perfectly divisible and are traded continuously[3]. Nor are there short-selling restrictions. The absence of bid–ask spreads and asymmetry translates into borrowing rates that are equal to lending rates.*

Assumption 2   *We implicitly assume that there are sufficiently many investors with comparable level of wealth such that they can buy or sell as much as they want at a given market price.*

The problem is placed into a partial equilibrium framework that rules out any free-arbitrage opportunity.

Assumption 3   *There is a riskless asset whose rate of return per unit of time is known and constant over time.*

This implies a flat and constant term structure of riskfree interest rates[4]. Thus, the price of a riskless bond paying \$1 at time T will be $B_0(T) = \exp[-rT]$, where r is the instantaneous riskless rate of interest.

Assumption 4   *V_t, the value of the assets of the firm, follows Itô dynamics:*

$$\frac{dV_t}{V_t} = \mu dt + \sigma dZ_t, \tag{3.1}$$

where μ is the instantaneous expected rate of return, σ the variance of the return on the underlying assets, and Z_t a standard Wiener process. Note the special case where C is total cash outflow per unit time (coupons and/or dividends):

$$\frac{dV_t}{V_t} = (\mu - C)dt + \sigma dZ_t. \tag{3.2}$$

---

[3]The fact that the value of the assets of the firm is not represented by a traded asset will be discussed later.

[4]This simplifies the analysis and allows the credit risk problem to be isolated. However, since there is no exact modelization of the term structure of riskless interest rates, it is hard to know which assumption would be neutral. The present simplification also implies that there is no correlation between the level of interest rates and the level of the value of the firm.

Note that the volatility, σ, is assumed constant over time and C is assumed to be zero in the general discussion.

Assumption 5 *On the liability side of the balance sheet of the firm, the total value is financed by equity, E, and one representative zero-coupon noncallable debt contract[5], D, maturing at time T with face value F,*

$$V_t = D_t + E_t. \tag{3.3}$$

Together with assumption 1, this implies that the value of the firm and the value of assets are identical and do not depend on the capital structure itself[6]. This also implies that the drift and the volatility of the returns on assets should not depend upon the level of the value of the firm.

Assumption 6 *Shareholder wealth maximization: management acts to maximize shareholder wealth.*

Assumption 7 *The debt contract is fixed with the initial hypothesis that the firm is not already at default.*

Assumption 8 *There are neither cash flow payouts, nor issues of any type of security during the life of the debt contract, nor bankruptcy costs.*

This implies that default can only happen at maturity, if the firm cannot meet the reimbursement of the face value of the debt, F.

Assumption 9 *The absolute priority rule cannot be violated: shareholders obtain a positive payoff only in the case that debtholders are perfectly reimbursed.*

Thus the firm has two classes of securities: a single homogenous class of zero-coupon discount bonds, with face value F and maturity T, and equity. The indenture ("terms") of the bond issue contains the following simplified event of default covenant: in the event that the face value payment is not met, the bondholders receive the entire value of the firm and the owners of the firm receive nothing. In this framework, the firm is prohibited from issuing any new senior claims on the firm nor can it pay dividends or repurchase shares prior to the maturity of the debt (extensions can be dealt with).

Hence the value of the bond at maturity is

$$D_T(V, T) = \min(V_T, F). \tag{3.4}$$

Proposition 1. *The value of credit risk for this zero-coupon corporate bond, when the only other source of financing is equity, is equal to the value of a put option on the value of the assets of the firm, at a strike price of F, the face value of debt, maturing at time T, the maturity of the bond issue.*

Proof. The different payoffs for the different claims under the alternative states of nature at maturity result in

---

[5]No difference is made here between a private loan and a bond contract since the value of the firm is supposed to be a traded asset.
[6]This is in perfect corresponence with Modigliani–Miller theorem where an invariant value of the firm to its capital structure obtains.

$$V_T \leqslant F \quad V_T > F \qquad (3.5)$$

	$V_T \leqslant F$	$V_T > F$
Equity	0	$V_T - F$
Debt	V_T	F

One way to proceed is to go through the hedging strategy and see that the bondholder should hold a put (P) in order to obtain a riskfree payoff of F[7]. The payoff of this put at maturity would be $\max[F - V_T, 0]$. By the no-arbitrage principle, a riskfree debt position should be equivalent to holding a long position on a debt contract equivalent to D and buying a put on the value of the firm:

$$F e^{-rT} = D_0 + P, \qquad (3.6)$$

where P is straightforwardly computed as a traditional European Black and Scholes put option on V. Alternatively, we could go the other way round and look at the expected loss incurred by the bondholder, given that the reimbursement of the principal, F, is subject to default risk.

$$V_T \leqslant F \quad V_T > F \qquad (3.7)$$

	$V_T \leqslant F$	$V_T > F$
Riskfree debt	F	F
Loss incurred	$F - V_T$	0

We would end up at maturity with $D_T = F - \max[F - V_T, 0]$.   ∎

Thus the terminal payoff to debt is functionally equivalent to owning the assets of the firm and being short a call option on those assets with an exercise price of F.

Alternatively, the debtholders can be considered to have lent money without risk with face value F and gone short a put option on the assets of the firm with an exercise price of F.

Similarly we have for the value of the equity:

$$E_T(V) = \max(0, V_T - F). \qquad (3.8)$$

The payoff structure to the levered corporate equity is isomorphic to the one for a call option on a share of stock where the maturity date of the firm's debt T corresponds to the expiration date of the option, the promised payment on the debt F corresponds to the exercise price of the option, and the firm value V corresponds to the underlying security. We can thus use option pricing to value credit-risky bonds.

As usual in CCA, the value of the equity is given by the following PDE:

$$0 = \frac{1}{2}\sigma_t^2(V)V^2\frac{\partial^2 E_t(V)}{\partial V^2} + rV\frac{\partial E_t(V)}{\partial V} - rE_t(V) + \frac{\partial E_t(V)}{\partial t}, \qquad (3.9)$$

subject to

---

[7] In terms of arbitrage-free pricing models, the value of the put option represents the cost of eliminating the credit risk borne by the provider of funds. Whenever the profile is easily understandable, it assumes that the strategy is replicable and that therefore credit risk is hedgeable which is quite controversial. One of the reasons is that the default event is an absorbing state. Portfolio credit risk management will then rely upon avoiding overconcentrating exposures into the portfolio rather than aiming to counter some credit risks with others. But we could still reconcile credit risk with the hedging argument if we were able to identify a systematic component of credit risk and the way it interacts with market risks.

$$E_t(V)/V \leqslant 1,$$
$$E_t(0) = 0,$$
$$E_T(V) = \max(0, \, V_T - F).$$

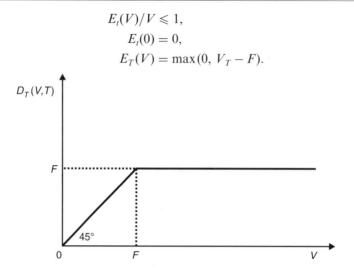

Figure 3.1   Debt value at maturity as a function of the assets value of the firm

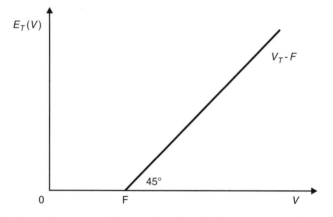

Figure 3.2   Equity value at maturity as a function of the assets value of the firm

In the special case $\sigma = $ constant, we have the classical Black and Scholes results:

$$E_t(V, \, T, \, \sigma, \, r, \, F) = V_t N(d_1) - Fe^{-r(T-t)} N(d_2), \tag{3.10}$$

with

$$d_1 = \frac{\ln\left(\dfrac{V_t}{F}\right) + \left(r + \dfrac{\sigma^2}{2}\right)(T-t)}{\sigma\sqrt{T-t}},$$

$$d_2 = d_1 - \sigma\sqrt{T-t},$$

$$N(y) \text{ or } \Phi(y) = \frac{1}{\sqrt{2\pi}} \int_{-\infty}^{y} e^{-u^2/2} du \text{ (standard normal cumulative density function)}.$$

The value of the debt will also satisfy the same PDE, but with the corresponding boundary conditions:

$$0 = \frac{1}{2}\sigma_t^2(V)V^2\frac{\partial^2 D_t(V,\,T)}{\partial V^2} + rV\frac{\partial D_t(V,\,T)}{\partial V} - rD_t(V,\,T) + \frac{\partial D_t(V,\,T)}{\partial t}, \qquad (3.11)$$

subject to

$$D_t(V,\,T)/V \leqslant 1,$$
$$D_t(0,\,T) = 0,$$
$$D_T(V,\,T) = \min(V_T,\,F).$$

We know that the value of a risky 0-coupon bond is equal to the value of the firm less the value of the equity (the call option) or identically to the value of a riskfree bond less the value of the credit risk put option. Assuming σ constant, we can apply Black and Scholes pricing, and therefore the value of the debt at time 0 under the risk-neutral probability is

$$D_t(V,\,T) = V_t - E_t \text{ (as a European call)}$$
$$= V_t - V_t N(d_1) - Fe^{-r(T-t)}N(d_2)$$
$$= V_t N(-d_1) + Fe^{-r(T-t)}N(d_2)$$

or alternatively:

$$D_0(V,\,T) = Fe^{-rT} - \text{European put} \qquad (3.12)$$
$$= Fe^{-rT} - [-N(-d_1)V_0 + Fe^{-rT}N(-d_2)]$$
$$= V_0 N(-d_1) + Fe^{-rT}N(d_2),$$

where d_1, d_2, and $N(\cdot)$ are defined above.

3.2 THE RISK STRUCTURE OF INTEREST RATES

In this context, we are thus able to obtain analytical expressions for the yield to maturity, the default spread, the default probability, and the discounted expected recovery value.

It is common in dealing with bonds to discuss them in terms of yields rather than prices. The yield-to-maturity, y, of a discount bond in a continuous time framework is the solution to

$$D_t(V,\,T) = Fe^{-y(T-t)}. \qquad (3.13)$$

The yield to maturity at t for the corporate debt maturing at T, $y_t(T)$, is simply

$$y_t(T) = -\frac{\ln(D_t/F)}{T}. \qquad (3.14)$$

Straight substitution of equation (3.10) and knowing that the default spread, $cs_t(T)$, is also $y_t(T) - r$,

$$cs_t(T) = -\frac{1}{T} \ln \left[N(d_2) + \frac{V_t}{Fe^{-rT}} N(-d_1) \right], \qquad (3.15)$$

where it can be seen that the credit spread is a direct function of the quasi-debt ratio $\varrho = Fe^{-r(T-t)}/V_t$ or inversely of the expected relative distance to loss $X = V_t/Fe^{-r(T-t)}$.

The expression for the credit spread shows that the frequently used credit risk premium of a bond of a given maturity is a function of two and only two major variables (under the assumption of a known term structure): the volatility of the firm value ($\sigma\sqrt{T-1}$) and a form of leverage ratio ($Fe^{-r(T-t)}/V_t$) that is the promised payment ratio to the value of the firm. It can be shown that the risk premium is an increasing function of the quasi-debt ratio, as one would intuitively expect, and of the volatility of the firm. As usual in option pricing, but seemingly paradoxical for first users, the rate of return on the underlying security (here the growth rate in the value of the firm) has no impact on the credit spread.

While the *default spread* is the promised risk premium over the remaining life of the bond, the expressions of the standard deviation of the bond is also valuable since it corresponds to the *default risk over the next instant*. From Itô's lemma, we find that

$$\sigma_D = \frac{V_t}{D} \frac{\partial D}{\partial V} \sigma = \eta(\varrho, \sigma^2(T - t))\sigma, \qquad (3.16)$$

where η is the elasticity of the bond price relative to the firm as a whole, and, given previous equations, expression (3.16) can be rewritten as

$$\sigma_D = \eta(\varrho, \sigma^2(T - t)) \sigma = \frac{N(-d_1)}{N(-d_1) + \varrho N(d_2)} \sigma. \qquad (3.17)$$

The standard deviation of the return on the bond as defined above represents the risk of the rate of return over the next trading interval. It is thus a different measure of risk from the spread as defined above. The bond's standard deviation measures the risk over the next instant. The yield spread, on the other hand, is the promised risk premium over the remaining life of the bond. Nonetheless, the standard deviation of the return on the bond depends on the same variables as the spread, notably maturity, quasi-debt ratio, and volatility of the firm. It is interesting to understand which of these two measures of risk is more valid in which environment, especially as practitioners tend to use spreads to compare riskiness of the bonds.

3.3 THE PROBABILITY OF DEFAULT AND THE IMPLICIT RECOVERY IN MERTON'S MODEL

Crouhy and Galai (1997) show that the risk-neutral default probability corresponds to $N(-d_2)$, and rearranging terms, it is easy to verify that, at time $t = 0$,

$$D_0(V, T) = Fe^{-rT} - \text{European put} = Fe^{-rT} - N(-d_2) \left[Fe^{-rT} - \frac{N(-d_1)}{N(-d_2)} V_0 \right], \qquad (3.18)$$

where the fraction $N(-d_1)/N(-d_2)$ in brackets is the expected discounted recovery rate. It must be remembered that this definition supposes that the rule of strict priority at default is respected and that therefore no additional loss is incurred depending on the ending scenario. Then

$$\left[F e^{-rT} - \frac{N(-d_1)}{N(-d_2)} V_0 \right]$$

is the expected discounted shortfall[8] so that equation (3.18) could be simply reinterpreted as

$$D_t(V, T) = F e^{-r(T-t)} - DP \times EDLGD, \qquad (3.19)$$

where DP and $EDLGD$ stand for the default probability and the expected discounted loss given default respectively, this is akin to the KMV[9] nomenclature (see section 20.3) or analogous to the specification of the expected loss due to credit risk in the reduced-form class of models.

Crouhy and Galai (1997) also present the overall expected cost of default at the maturity date (ECD_T), i.e. the default probability (DP) times the loss given default (LGD) which is simply the expectation at T of the future value of the put:

$$ECD_T = DP \times LGD \qquad (3.20)$$
$$= F N(-d_2) - V_0 e^{-rT} N(-d_1)$$

that is similar to that being derived in Jarrow and Turnbull (1995) and that can lead us back to the yield spread through:

$$\pi_T = -\frac{1}{T} \ln \left[\frac{F}{F - ECD_T} \right]. \qquad (3.21)$$

Within this simple model, we can already stress two main conclusions:

1. The expected discounted recovery rate is not constant through time but depends on the same determinants than the expected risk-neutral probability of default, and therefore
2. The DP and the $EDLGD$ components must be correlated (see also Wei and Guo, 1997). This is a source of calibration problems if these two components were to be fitted econometrically on financial time series as it is the case with reduced-form approaches. As an example, in the reduced-form model of Jarrow and Turnbull (1995), by assuming that the recovery factor is given and exogenous to the model, they can directly deduce the forward probability of default from the forward

---

[8]Which is the premium of the insurance policy that the bank buys when buying the default put. This expected shortfall is simply the exchange of a riskless bond promising F at time T against a risk-neutral payment related to the expected value of assets at default.
[9]KMV Corporation is active in the design and implementation of its own credit risk management framework.

spreads obtained through market data[10]. In the present model, however, the probability of default and the recovery rate are simultaneously obtained from equilibrium conditions.

Therefore, in our structural setting, the credit spread has to be directly estimated from the underlying variables which govern the credit standing of the firm by construction, i.e. in Merton's setting, V_0/F and σ_v. Implementing structural models, such as Merton's standard or that presented here below, will be discussed in detail in section 3.7.

3.3.1   A Practical Example

Suppose a firm with a current asset value of 100, with an asset volatility of 40% (very high), a quasi-debt leverage ratio $(1/X)$ of 60%, with a debt maturity at a one-year horizon in an economic environment, where the constant discretely compounded short-term interest rate is 5%. Following Merton's methodology, we can make the following deductions:

1. Knowing that

$$\frac{Fe^{-rT}}{V_0} = 0.6,$$

it follows that $F = 100.(60\%).(1 + 5\%) = 63$. The instantaneous interest rate is $i = \ln(1 + r) = 4.88\%$.
2. The discounted expected recovery value is

$$\frac{N(-d_1)}{N(-d_2)} V_0 = \frac{0.069829}{0.140726} 100 = 49.62,$$

the value of the riskless bond being $63 \exp(-0.0488) = 60$.
3. The expected discounted shortfall amounts, therefore, to

$$63 - 49.62 = 10.3792.$$

4. Knowing that the probability of default $(N(-d_2))$ is 14.0726% the cost of default (or the value of the default put) is worth

$$14.0726\% . 10.3792 = 1.4606.$$

5. The value of the credit-risky bond is thus $60 - 1.4606 = 58.5394$.

Remember that these results are derived under the risk-neutral probability measure (for pricing purposes). For monitoring purposes, one may want to use one's expectation about the return on the asset value of the firm and work through the actual probability of default by replacing r by the drift μ.

---

[10]Indeed, many closed-form formulae suppose the expected recovered value to be some exogenous constant (see Longstaff and Schwartz (1995b), for example).

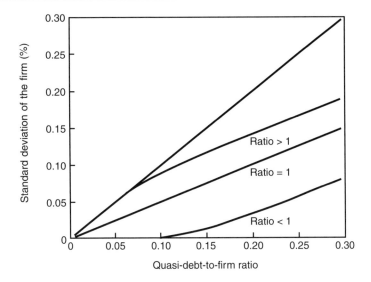

Figure 3.3 Default risk over the next instant versus the "quasi"-debt-to-firm leverage ratio, implied by Merton's model on corporate debt (1974)

3.4 COMPARATIVE STATICS

These analytical formulae give us the ability to study the impact of changes in debt ratio, changes in volatility of the firm, and changes in the maturity of the debt on the credit spreads or on the instantaneous standard deviation of the debt returns, which are two measures of risk of the debt that are not equivalent (see Merton, 1974). One of the most interesting theoretical results of Merton (1974) consists in the impact of a longer maturity on the two measures of risk (see Figures 3.3–3.6). The effect of a longer maturity is indeed not clear: the yield spread can either rise or fall. The spread decreases in maturity if $\varrho \geqslant 1$ (with ρ the quasi-debt ratio). If $\varrho < 1$, the spread first rises and then falls while the risk is rising. Hence the classical hump shape of the term structure of credit spreads that is obtained from the Merton model, a result that is a nonintuitive consequence of the structural model and that is found again and again in many structural models, even when including stochastic term structures or other refinements. Interestingly, it is also a fact that has been found in actual data. This reveals how a full structural model can lead to intuitions that would not be easily obtained from directly modeling the default process. How can we explain this hump shape?

If $\varrho > 1$, the firm is technically insolvent. To avoid bankruptcy, it will need to have increasing earnings. As $(T - t) \to \infty$, the instantaneous risk approaches the limit $\sigma/2$ and the yield spread vanishes, as there is more time for the increasing earnings to occur.

If $\varrho < 1$ and the bond has only a short time to go before maturity, it is unlikely there will be a default of the bond. As maturity increases, the likelihood of default increases and the yield spread widens. For continued increases in maturity, the instantaneous risk continues to rise to its limit, but yield spread begins to fall (as there can never be a default on a perpetual bond). Hence the special case of high leverage firms. Longer maturity need not make debt riskier.

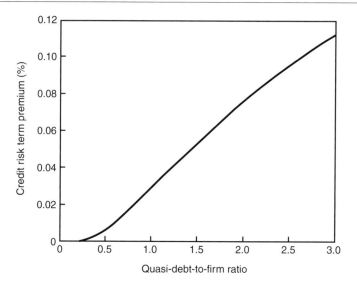

Figure 3.4 Default spread versus the "quasi"-debt-to-firm leverage ratio, implied by Merton's model on corporate debt (1974)

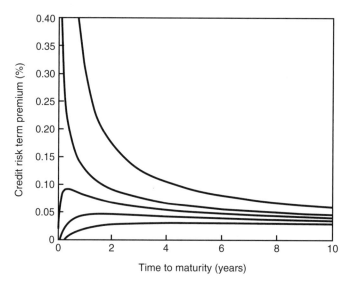

Figure. 3.5 Default spread versus the time remaining until maturity, implied by Merton's model on corporate debt (1974)

This result shows that the yield spread does not necessarily reflect accurately the relative default risks of two bonds of different maturities. The two measures of risk will not agree on which bonds are riskier.

Figures 3.7 and 3.8 show the shapes obtained in this setting for the credit spread and the recovery value depending on the volatility of the value of assets and the time to maturity.

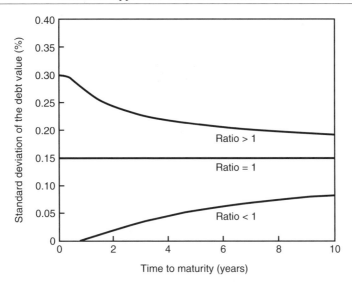

Figure 3.6 Default risk over the next instant versus the time remaining until maturity, implied by Merton's model on corporate debt (1974)

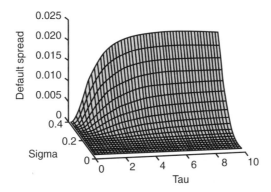

Figure 3.7 Default spread distribution for different values of σ and τ, leaving V, D and r fixed to 100, 50 and 5% respectively

The recovery rate is shown to be variable through time, while many simpler models (and some more complex ones as well) suppose this to be some exogenous constant. Since this approach relies entirely on an arbitrage relationship between the value of the firm and the two sets of claimants, it allows credit risk to be expressed or the propensity to default as a direct function of the value of the underlying assets. This will be helpful for practical reasons since it will enable us to reengineer this framework into a more complete one and then infer the parameters from trading data. Under some distributional assumptions for the underlying variables, we will obtain a characterization of credit spreads that highlight the determinants of the time to default and of the recovery rate upon default.

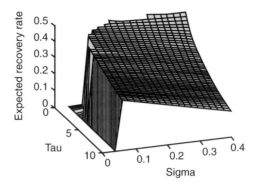

Figure 3.8   Recovery rate distribution for different values of σ and τ, leaving V, D, and r fixed to 100, 50 and 5% respectively

3.5   SOME EARLY EMPIRICAL INVESTIGATIONS OF THE MERTON MODEL

Jones et al. (1984) attempted a true test of the Merton technology. Such a test faces great difficulties: most firms' capital structures consist of many classes of equity and fixed income products (preferreds, callable convertibles, callable nonconvertibles, bonds with sinking fund requirements, etc.). The multiplicity of the issues itself can create major difficulties when looking at the interaction not only of default rules but of call policies that will both affect the pricing. The authors thus use a sample of companies with relatively simple capital structures. They make simplifying assumptions (and notably use a deterministic term structure). They find results that show the superiority of the CCA model over a naive (riskless) model for non-investment grade bonds, but not for investment grade bonds. The authors find low theoretical spreads compared to actual spreads. They do not compare the model to its true competitors, the actuarial models. They also lack some of the modern refinements that would make the CCA model more realistic (stochastic interest rates notably). They nonetheless show how to fully implement the CCA methodology in order to apply it to credit risk measurement.

Although not a true test of the Merton model, the Sarig and Warga (1989) paper presents empirical results that seem to confirm the comparative statics obtained by Merton. The authors analyze 137 corporate issues of zero-coupon bonds representing 42 different companies. They measure the spread of corporate bonds of the yields above the yield on Treasury strips of the same maturity, a traditional credit risk measure, and, as seen above, one for which Merton derived theoretical comparative statics; 15 years after Merton's paper, the authors find an empirical hump shape that corresponds very clearly to the theoretical predictions of the model.

Interestingly, the behavior of comparative statics remain very similar to those in the simple Merton model when the models are made more complex and integrate stochastic interest rate structures (see Shimko et al., 1993 and Longstaff and Schwartz, 1995). The basic intuition of the Merton model seems thus to be useful for pricing risky debt.

3.6 COMPUTING THE NECESSARY INPUTS: PRELIMINARY REMARKS

3.6.1 Estimating the Value of the Firm

• If all claims are publicly traded, then the value of the firm can be observed and prices for all claims, relative to the observed firm value, can be predicted. When all claims are not publicly traded, an alternative approach has to be taken. For example, the total value of all traded claims can be used to infer firm value. The analysis brings out the firm value that is consistent with the observed value of all traded claims. This implied firm value is then used to predict bond prices (iteration may well be necessary). (See Ronn and Verma, 1986, for a methodology that extracts firm value dynamics from traded equity dynamics, Pirotte (1999a), Part Four and section 23.3[11]).

3.6.2 Estimating the Standard Deviation for each Firm

• Two procedures can be used to estimate the standard deviation for each firm:

Method I.   The first procedure is based on forming a monthly time series for the value of the firm using, for example, 24 trailing months of data. The value of the firm is estimated as the sum of the market value of equity, the market value of traded debt, and the estimated market value of nontraded debt. The market value of the nontraded debt is estimated by assuming that the ratio of book to market was the same for traded and nontraded debt. The logarithmic total return on the value of the firm, including any cash payouts/payins is calculated and the standard deviation of these returns determined.

Method II.   The second procedure is a maximum likelihood procedure based on the relationship between the standard deviation of the return to the firm and the equity. Given the assumptions of CCA, it follows from Itô's lemma that the instantaneous standard deviation of equity is given by[12]

$$\sigma_E = \sigma_V \frac{\partial E}{\partial V} \frac{V}{E},\tag{3.22}$$

where σ_V is the standard deviation of the return to the firm and $\partial E/\partial V$ is the partial derivative of the value of equity with respect to the value of the firm. The method II procedure is as follows:

• To run the model using the method I estimate of standard deviation as a seed. The value of the firm, V, the value of the equity, E, and the partial derivative of equity $\partial E/\partial V$, with respect to the value of the firm which are implied by the observed total value of marketable claims are read from this first pass of the model.

• Then the standard deviation of return to the equity is calculated, using market data, over a period immediately preceding the test date. Given equation (3.22), a new

---

[11] In his model (presented in Part Four), Pirotte (1999a) provides an extended version of the one proposed by Ronn and Verma (1986). KMV's model uses an iterative method that allows the joint estimation of the value of the firm and its standard deviation.

[12] Same methodology as that described above for the volatility of the debt value.

estimate of σ_V using σ_E, E, V, and $\partial E/\partial V$. The model is then rerun using the new estimates of σ_V.

The extraction of V and σ from stock market data is the main advantage of the framework developed by Merton since it allows the extraction of market information from stock market data, the stock market being much more liquid than the bond market.

In a recent study, Lardic and Rouzeau (1999) simply use an iterative procedure for each time interval of the sample for a given firm in the spirit described above with the two series of $(\tilde{V}_t)$ and $(\tilde{\sigma}_t)$ stemming from the following system, where S_t and σ_t^S can be observed in the market:

$$
\begin{cases}
S_t = \dfrac{1}{N} E(V_t, F_t, T, r_t(T), \delta_t, \sigma_t) \\[2mm]
\sigma_t^S = \sigma \dfrac{V_t}{N S_t} \dfrac{\partial E}{\partial V}(V_t, F_t, T, r_t(T), \delta_t, \sigma_t), \\[2mm]
\qquad \text{subject to the estimation of } \delta_t(V, E) \text{ aside,}
\end{cases}
\tag{3.23}
$$

where N is the total outstanding number of shares. In the absence of unit-root for the series of $(\tilde{\sigma}_t)$, Lardic and Rouzeau assume that it can be written that

$$
\tilde{\sigma}_t = \hat{\sigma} + \epsilon_t,
$$

where ϵ_t is a white noise. This means that we get back to Merton's hypothesis of a constant volatility parameter if we can assume that the expectation on $\tilde{\sigma}_t$ is a constant. Thanks to this, and since we allow the volatility to vary over time, we can refine the estimation of the system above (see expression 3.24) reestimating the asset market values series $(\tilde{V}_t)$ by solving for V_t in

$$
\begin{cases}
\hat{S}_t = \dfrac{1}{N} \hat{E}(V_t, F_t, T, r_t(T), \delta_t, \hat{\sigma}) \\[2mm]
\qquad \text{subject to the estimation of } \delta_t(V, \hat{E}) \text{ aside,}
\end{cases}
\tag{3.24}
$$

which will produce a series $(\hat{V}_t)$ of the asset market values.

3.6.3   Estimating the Face Value of the Debt (Exercise Price)

The face value (F) of debt commitments is usually estimated starting from accounting data. Several procedures can then be followed and are somewhat *ad hoc* to try and fit somewhat complex balance sheets in the simplified context of the Merton model. For example, in Lardic and Rouzeau (1999), three purely informational accounting aggregates are calculated:

- The required working capital as the difference between current operating assets and current operating liabilities.
- The net cash, mainly as the difference between the available cash and the short-term bank debt.

- The long-term debt (*LTD*), the sum of actual long-term debt and long-term provisions.

The *F* value retained is one combining *LTD*, and *WC* and *NC* should these two latter be negative only. The face value at any intermediate date t, let us say $0 \leqslant t \leqslant 1$, is obtained as an interpolation between the current F_0 value and its anticipated version for the next closing date, $E[F_1]$.

3.6.4 Estimating the Maturity of the Debt

In order to use Merton's formula, we need a unique maturity number. But a classical Merton assumption is that firm's debt is constituted by a unique debt issue. Therefore, a natural way to encompass this problem is to compute a weighted average duration of all long-term liabilities. Because Merton's setting is static until maturity, the liability structure is assumed to remain constant over time. It is also assumed that no default can happen before maturity (as the Merton framework focuses on a zero-coupon unique debt issue). In the study of Lardic and Rouzeau (1999), this amounts to saying that if *WC* and *NC* are negative, their sum has to be considered to be like a structural liability rolled over as long as the working capital is not modified. Lardic and Rouzeau, therefore, focus on stock-based insolvency and assume that the duration of *WC* and *NC* corresponds to that of *LTD*.

3.7 A BOND PRICING IMPLEMENTATION ON THE FRENCH STOCK MARKET

Lardic and Rouzeau (1999) follow Merton's classical pricing model for the pricing of debt and equity and propose a methodology for its implementation to bond market pricing issues. The methodology is close to that being used by KMV and mainly consists in adapting the requirements such that Merton's model can be used without many changes. They refine the framework to allow for a continuous dividend outflow δV_t from time t_0 to the maturity T. Standard pricing formulations for equity and the debt follow then, based on Black–Scholes formula while integrating the dividend flow. Typically:

$$E(V, F, T, r, \delta, \sigma) = BS(V, F, T, r, \delta, \sigma) + \text{dividend stream}$$
$$D(V, F, T, r, \delta, \sigma) = V - E(V, F, T, r, \delta, \sigma),$$

where *F* is again the face value of debt commitments, δ the continuous dividend payout rate, and σ the standard asset volatility.

- The estimation of the dividend payout rate (δ) is based on the future dividend yields for the next five years and on the market equity ratio E_t/V_t. For *rVF* and σ the procedure proposed here let the variables vary through time while Merton's model is a static one. Therefore, it will be of course restrictive, but useful to use Merton's model in a myopic way. A first reconciliation can happen already with the fixing of $\hat{\sigma}$ mentioned earlier.

3.7.1 The Data and the Results

The study was run on 21 bond issues written by 15 different firms, excluding financial institutions, public utilities, or private firms still largely owned by the government. The sample period is November 1997 to June 1998. This short time interval is chosen so that the firm's operating risk (σ) can be considered as constant during this period.

Looking briefly at the displayed market spreads, it appears that a higher mean spread is often related to a higher spread variance. Interestingly, various issues of the same firm do not show the same behavior even when of the same seniority.

At first glance, theoretical spreads poorly reflect the empirical ones. Moreover, during the period concerned, a significant rise in the market value of equity induces a decreasing trend in the theoretical spreads. But, studying more precisely the series of theoretical and empirical spreads, Lardic and Rouzeau obtain the following further conclusions:

- Merton's model provides interesting spreads that reflect the long-term evolution of the empirical ones. As in other empirical studies provided in the following chapters, the model seems to provide valuable and informative results about the fundamental credit quality of the firm which is consistent with the use of these spreads as an alternative to the standard ratings proposed by Moody's or Standard & Poors similarly to the developments of KMV. The study confirms that this class of models seems to be efficient for monitoring purposes although quite inaccurate for trading and pricing needs.
- Pricing results are, however, encouraging when estimating the average spread of a whole bond portfolio. The model can therefore be a first good proxy for the overall behavior of a portfolio of bonds. On the other side, the overall conclusion is that Merton's firm-specific spread does not explain all of the market spread. More precise engineering would have to be applied here, as described in later chapters, to fit more precisely the data.

In general, CCA can be used to price credit risk on any instrument, thanks to the intense engineering that has been going on in the 1980s. Obviously though, analysis can become very complex when the capital structure of the firm becomes complex. Also, two problems that were major impediments to real life applications have been solved only recently: stochastic interest rates and complex bankruptcy rules. General financial engineering methodologies that help deal with more complex situations than the Merton situation are described in Chapter 4.

3.8 REFERENCES

Black, F. and J. C. Cox, 1976, "Valuing Corporate Securities: Some Effects of Bond Indenture Provisions", *Journal of Finance*, **31**, 351–67.

Cossin, D. and H. Pirotte, 1998, "How Well Do Classical Credit Risk Models Fit Swap Transaction Data?", *European Financial Management Journal*, **4** (1), March, 65–78.

Crouhy, Michel and Dan Galai, 1997, "Credit Risk Revisited: An Option Pricing Approach", May 1997, *Working Paper* 97-2, Canadian Imperial Bank of Commerce/Market Risk Management/Global Analytics, 18 pp.

Jarrow, R. and Stuart Turnbull, 1995, "Pricing Derivatives on Financial Securities Subject to Credit Risk", *Journal of Finance*, **50** (1), March, 53–85.

Jones, E. Philip, Scott P. Mason and Eric Rosenfeld, 1984, "Contingent Claims Analysis of Corporate Capital Structures: An Empirical Investigation", *The Journal of Finance*, **39** (3), July, 611–27.

Lardic, S. and E. Rouzeau, 1999, "Implementing Merton's model on the French corporate bond market", *Working Paper*, Crédit Commercial de France, Direction de la Recherche et de l'Innovation, May, 32 pp.

Longstaff, Francis and Eduardo Schwartz, 1995, "A Simple Approach to Valuing Risky Fixed and Floating Rate Debt and Determining Swap Spreads", *Journal of Finance*, **50** (3), July, 789–819.

Merton, Robert C., 1973, "Theory of Rational Option Pricing", *Bell Journal of Economics and Management Science*, **4**, 1973, 141–83.

Merton, Robert C., 1974, "On the Pricing of Corporate Debt: The Risk Structure of Interest Rates", *The Journal of Finance*, **29**, May, 449–70.

Merton, Robert C., 1977, "On the Pricing of Contingent Claims and the Modigliani–Miller Theorem", *Journal of Financial Economics*, **5**, 241–9.

Pirotte, H., 1999a, "Implementing a Structural Valuation Model of Swap Credit-Sensitive Rates", *Working Paper*, Institute of Banking and Finance, Ecole des HEC, University of Lausanne, December, 32 pp.

Pirotte, H., 1999b, "A Structural Model of the Term Structure of Credit Spreads with Stochastic Recovery and Contractual Design", *Working Paper*, Institute of Banking and Finance, Ecole des HEC, University of Lausanne, December, 85 pp.

Ronn, Ehud and Avinash Verma, 1986, "Pricing Risk-Adjusted Deposit Insurance: An Option-Based Model", *The Journal of Finance*, **41** (4), September, 871–95.

Sarig, Oded and Arthur Warga, 1989, "Some Empirical Estimates of the Risk Structure of Interest Rates", *Journal of Finance*, **44** (5), December, 1351–60.

Shimko, David, Naohiko Tejima and Donald Van Deventer, 1993, "The Pricing of Risky Debt When Interest Rates are Stochastic", *The Journal of Fixed Income*, September, 58–65.

Wei, D. G. and D. Guo, 1997, "Pricing Risky Debt: An Empirical Comparison of the Longstaff and Schwartz and Merton Models", *The Journal of Fixed Income*, September, 9–28.

4
Subsequent Financial Engineering

Merton's paper presents an extreme simplification of the real world: a firm with a unique zero-coupon debt issue. Merton himself proposed extensions of his analysis notably to the pricing of a perpetual risky bond with continuous coupon payment (possibly a good approximation for preferred stocks). He shows this is similar to valuing an option on a stock that pays continuous dividends at a constant rate. Many authors have worked on extending Merton's framework further. We propose here a synthesis of the different proposals that have appeared in the literature since the groundbreaking work of Merton in 1974. Ingersoll (1987), notably, shows that the model can be extended to many other cases (sections a to d borrow heavily from this work and complete it as well). These extensions are mostly engineering of more realistic financial structures than a single zero-coupon issue. Greater difficulties (stochastic interest rates, different bankruptcy rules) are approached later.

4.1 COUPON BONDS

Risky coupon bonds cannot be priced as if they were a portfolio of risky pure discount bonds. It would be tempting to look at each coupon payment and price it as if it were a default-risky zero-coupon bond and to combine the different risky coupons thus valued to obtain the price of a risky coupon bond. Unfortunately, this methodology is not valid. Indeed, default at a later time is dependent on no default earlier. Once a firm defaults on a coupon payment all the following coupons and principal payments are also defaulted on. The pricing should rather follow the analogy of the pricing of options with continuous dividend payments. Take the same framework as before with the modification that coupon payments occur continuously at a rate per unit of time C. The coupon bond will satisfy the PDE:

$$0 = \frac{1}{2}\sigma_t^2(V)V^2\frac{\partial^2 D_t(V, T)}{\partial V^2} + (rV - C)\frac{\partial D_t(V, T)}{\partial V} - rD_t(V, T) + \frac{\partial D_t(V, T)}{\partial t} + C,$$

when V follows the process:

$$dV = (\alpha V - C)dt + \sigma V dz$$

and subject to the same boundary conditions as before. The well-known closed-form formula obtained in the perpetual case gives the pricing of preferred stocks with no maturity date (see Merton, 1973). Numerical analysis will be necessary for other cases.

The fact that coupon payments are made as lump sums rather than as a continuous flow can be accounted for in the equation by replacing C by

$$\sum_i C_i \delta(t - t_i)$$

with $\delta(\cdot)$ the Dirac delta function and t_i the time of the payment of coupon number i.

Geske (1977) refines the analysis of risky coupon bonds by specifically considering the option that stockholders have at each coupon payment of buying the next option (coming with the next coupon payment decision) or not (and thus abandoning the firm to the bondholders). The common stock of a firm that has coupon bonds outstanding can thus be seen as a compound option.

Suppose that the coupon bond we consider has n interest payments of X dollars each with $n-1$ of them due at equal times (say annually or biannually) before maturity T. Consider the last coupon payment paid independently of the principal reimbursement. This coupon payment occurs at t_{n-1}. After t_{n-1} the stock can be considered to be the usual Black and Scholes option with exercise price the principal payment plus the interest left at the time or $M = F + X$ following our notations. Let us call $S_{t_{n-1}}$ the value of the stock thus obtained. The value of the debt is as usual the value of the assets of the firm minus the value of the stock or the Black and Scholes call option valued above as $S_{t_{n-1}}$.

At all dates before the final coupon payment the stock can be considered to be a compound option rather than the simple Black and Scholes option. Assume that priority rules are respected (and that there are no dividends). At t_{n-1} the boundary condition for the stock price is $\max(S_{t_{n-1}}, 0)$, where $S_{t_{n-1}}$ is the stock value if the coupon is paid, hence when $V_{t_{n-1}} > \bar{V}_{t_{n-1}}$ if one defines $\bar{V}_{t_{n-1}}$ the integral solution to $S_{t_{n-1}} - X = 0$. At t_{n-1} the value of the coupon bond is $\min(V_{t_{n-1}}, X + V_{t_{n-1}} - S_{t_{n-1}})$ as the bondholders receive the assets of the firm if the stockholders take the firm to bankruptcy and receive the coupon payment plus the optional value of the bond $(V_{t_{n-1}} - S_{t_{n-1}})$ if the stockholders accept to pay the coupon. The compounding of the options becomes clear from this setup. The same form applies at earlier coupons, but the stock price incorporates compound options of increasing degrees of compounding. Geske (1977) thus obtains the value of a risky coupon bond by recursively solving for the values at each coupon as a function of the value of the stock at the next coupon payment. The value of the corresponding risky coupon bond at time 0 is

$$D = V[1 - N_n(h_i + \sigma\sqrt{i}; \{\rho_{ij}\})]$$
$$+ \sum_{i=1}^{n-1} X_i r_f^{-T(i/n)} N_i(h_i; \{\rho_{ij}\}) + M r_f^{-T} N_n(h_i; \{\rho_{ij}\}),$$

where

$\bar{V}_i \equiv$ value of V which solves the integral equation $S_i(V) - X_i = 0$

$$h_i \equiv \frac{\ln(V/\bar{V}_i) + (\ln r_f - \tfrac{1}{2}\sigma^2)T(i/n)}{\sigma\sqrt{T(i/n)}}$$

$$h_n = \frac{\ln(V/M) + (\ln r_f - \tfrac{1}{2}\sigma^2)T}{\sigma\sqrt{T}}$$

$\rho_{ij} \equiv \sqrt{i/j}$ for all i, j pairs, $i < j$

and

$$N_n(h_i; \{\rho_{ij}\}) \equiv \int_{-\infty}^{h_2} N_1(h_1')N_{n-2}(h_i'; \{\rho_{ij\cdot2}\})f(w_2)\,\mathrm{d}w_2,$$

where

$$h_i' \equiv (h_i - \rho_{i2} w_2)/(1 - \rho_{i2}^2)^{1/2}$$
$$\rho_{ij\cdot 2} \equiv (\rho_{ij} - \rho_{i2}\rho_{j2})/[(1 - \rho_{i2}^2)^{1/2}(1 - \rho_{j2}^2)^{1/2}]$$

and

$$N_{n-2}(h_i'; \{\rho_{ij\cdot 2}\}) \equiv \int_{-\infty}^{h_4'} N_1(h_3'') N_{n-4}(h_i''; \{\rho_{ij\cdot 2\cdot 4}\}) f(w_4) dw_4,$$

where

$$h_i'' \equiv (h_i' - \rho_{i4\cdot 2} w_4)/[(1 - \rho_{i4\cdot 2}^2)^{1/2}(1 - \rho_{j4\cdot 2}^2)^{1/2}]$$
$$\rho_{ij\cdot 2\cdot 4} \equiv (\rho_{ij\cdot 2} - \rho_{i4\cdot 2}\rho_{j4\cdot 2})/[(1 - \rho_{i4\cdot 2}^2)^{1/2}(1 - \rho_{j4\cdot 2}^2)^{1/2}]$$

and

$$N(\cdot) \equiv n\text{-dimensional multivariate normal distribution function.}$$

Note that this formula can also accommodate risky coupon bond pricing when there is a sinking fund requirement, as long as sinking fund payments are of equal amounts and occur at the time of coupon payments. In this case, X will represent the coupon plus sinking fund requirement (with the corresponding adjustment to be made to the principal reimbursement at maturity). The pricing of bonds with sinking fund requirements is of fundamental use in practice, of course, and thus the methodology described above should be of particular interest for these applications. Obviously, because sinking fund requirements reduce the risk of the bond, the value of the bond with sinking fund requirements is going to be higher than the value of the bond without.

4.2 DEBT ISSUES OF DIFFERENT SENIORITY LEVEL

Firms rarely have a single issue of debt. It is clear that priority rights to the assets in case of default affect the pricing of the debt. For example, we would expect senior debt to be reimbursed in full priority to junior debt or subordinated debt. In reality, these priority rights are more or less well respected (notably the lower seniority of stock over debt). Although absolute priority rules are not fully effective, recovery rates appear to be in the expected order, with higher seniority obtaining higher recoveries (see Altman and Kishore, 1996, and Izvorski, 1997). We propose here a pricing of debt issues of different seniorities that assumes that priority rules are enforced. We will approach models that leave room for negotiation away from original contracted agreement in Chapter 6.

For example, here is an analysis proposed by Ingersoll (1987). Suppose a firm has two outstanding 0-coupon bonds maturing at the same time T: F dollars are promised on the senior debt, f dollars are promised on the junior or subordinated debt. The senior debt has absolute priority to all the assets of the firm. The value of the junior bond and the senior bond together is equal to that of a single senior bond with a face value of $F + f$. So that:

$$J_t(V, T, F, f) = D_t(V, T, F + f) - D_t(V, T, F).$$

The comparative statics of the junior debt can be determined from these. It could be shown, for example, that when the value of the firm is low, the junior debt tends to behave like equity, while when the value of the firm is high, it has more pronounced debt characteristics.

Madan (1998) shows that the analysis can be developed further into the pricing of any number of debt issues of any seniority level as long as absolute priority rules are enforced and as long as we consider debt of the same maturity. Call F_s the face value of debt of seniority s, with S different classes of seniority (s is between 1 and S) ordered from high to low seniority, so that a large s represents low seniority, a small s represents high seniority. At maturity, in case of default, debt of seniority s obtains

$$\max\left(0, V - \sum_{i<s} F_s\right).$$

Thus debt of seniority s obtains at maturity:

$$\min\left(\max\left(0, V - \sum_{i<s} F_s\right), F_s\right)$$

As shown in Figure 4.1, this is the payoff of a long bull call spread (a low strike long call combined with a high strike short call) with a lower strike of $\sum_{i<s} F_s$ and a higher strike of $\sum_{i\leqslant s} F_s$ (thus a difference of F_s between the two strikes).

- For example, consider the following liability structure: (a) a senior debt issue of face value 100 (seniority class 1); (b) subordinated debt of face value 120 (seniority class 2); (c) a junior debt issue of face value 80 (seniority class 3).

The application of the preceding figure to this case, combining the three payoffs in the same graph, is shown in Figure 4.2.

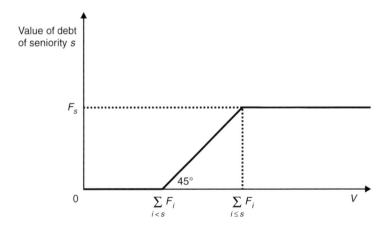

Figure 4.1 Payoff for a debt contract of seniority s

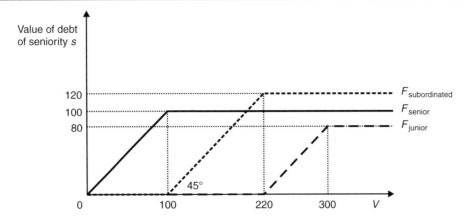

Figure 4.2 Payoff profiles for debt contracts of different seniorities

The value of debt of seniority s can thus be written as the difference between the two calls or

$$D_s(V, F_{i,i=1...S}, S, \tau) = VN(d_{1,s-1}) - \mathrm{e}^{-r\tau}N(d_{2,s-1})\sum_{i<s} F_s$$
$$- VN(d_{1,s}) + \mathrm{e}^{-r\tau}N(d_{2,s})\sum_{i\leqslant s} F_s,$$

where

$$d_{1,s} = \frac{\ln\left(\dfrac{V}{\sum_{i\leqslant s} F_s}\right) + \left(r + \dfrac{\sigma^2}{2}\right)\tau}{\sigma\sqrt{\tau}}$$

and

$$d_{2,s} = d_{1,s} - \sigma\sqrt{\tau}.$$

4.2.1 Different Maturities and Cross Default Condition

When debt of different seniorities also have different maturities, the problem becomes more complex to handle and will depend on the actual contractualization of the debt. When the junior debt matures first and no provisions have been made, the junior debt can effectively be senior. One common way to maintain some priority to senior debt is a cross default indenture. Such a protection is only partial and specific valuation needs to be made (see for example the treatment by Ingersoll, 1987, pp. 426–9). See also the treatment of secured junior debt as approached in Ingersoll (1987), p. 429. The analysis of the different types of debt can be made in a traditional way, starting from the payoff functions at maturity of the different debt components, as shown in the example above. Geske (1977) also shows that the compound option thinking that was developed above for coupon bonds can be applied to the pricing of zero-coupon junior debt when there is zero-coupon junior debt outstanding in the capital structure of longer maturity than the senior debt. The problem again reveals itself to be a compound option pricing problem. The stock can be seen as a compound option, as stockholders will consider at the time of paying the senior debt the value of the option to default on the outstanding junior debt.

4.3 BONDS WITH SAFETY COVENANTS

Black and Cox (1976) analyze the effect of the safety covenant on the pricing of risky zero-coupon bonds (and consequently of the stock). Safety covenants in general are contractual provisions that give bondholders the right to force bankruptcy or reorganization in the considered company. Safety covenants can take many different forms (positive and negative covenants). Some will bear on interest payments (interest coverage). Black and Cox actually consider safety covenants bearing on the overall value of the firm (these can be interpreted as debt ratio covenants). The specific form of the covenant they consider is that if the firm value drops under a prespecified level during the lifetime of the bond, bondholders are entitled to force the firm into bankruptcy and to obtain the assets of the firm. Pricing is done on zero-coupon bonds on a company that pays a continuous dividend at a payout ratio of a (so that continuous payments are aV) and with a safety covenant on the level of the firm that evolves deterministically as $C(t) = Ce^{-\gamma(T-t)}$.

The PDE that D follows, with our usual notations is

$$0 = \frac{1}{2}\sigma^2 V^2 \frac{\partial D_t(V)}{\partial V^2} + (rV - aV)\frac{\partial D_t(V)}{\partial V} - rD_t(V) + \frac{\partial D_t(V)}{\partial t}$$

with the boundary conditions

$$D(V, T) = \min(V, F)$$
$$D(Ce^{-\gamma(T-t)}, t) = Ce^{-\gamma(T-t)}$$

The pricing corresponds to the pricing with an absorbing barrier at $Ce^{-\gamma(T-t)}$. The risk-neutral probability that the firm has not been reorganized before τ is given by

$$N\left(\frac{\ln V - \ln C(\tau) + (r - a - 1/2\sigma^2)(\tau - t)}{\sqrt{\sigma^2(\tau - t)}}\right) - \left(\frac{V}{Ce^{-\gamma(T-t)}}\right)^{1-(2(r-a-\gamma)/\sigma^2)}$$
$$\times N\left(\frac{2\ln Ce^{-\gamma(T-t)} - \ln V - \ln F + (r - a - 1/2\sigma^2)(\tau - t)}{\sqrt{\sigma^2(\tau - t)}}\right)$$

The pricing of the bond with safety covenant $C(t)$ follows, as shown in Black and Cox (1976):

$$D(V, t) = Fe^{-r(t-t)}[N(z_1) - y^{2\theta-2}N(z_2)] + Ve^{-a(t-t)}[N(z_3) + y^{2\theta}N(z_4)]$$
$$+ y^{\theta+\zeta}e^{a(T-t)}N(z_5) + y^{\theta-\zeta}e^{a(T-t)}N(z_6) - y^{\theta-\eta}N(z_7) - y^{\theta-\eta}N(z_8)]$$

with

$$y = Ce^{-\gamma(T-t)}/V$$

$$\theta = (r - a - \gamma + 1/2\sigma^2)/\sigma^2$$

$$\delta = (r - a - \gamma - 1/2\sigma^2)^2 + 2\sigma^2(r - \gamma)$$

$$\zeta = \sqrt{\delta}/\sigma^2$$

$$\eta = \sqrt{\delta - 2\sigma^2 a}/\sigma^2$$

$$z_1 = [\ln V - \ln F + (r - a - 1/2\sigma^2)(T - t)]/\sqrt{\sigma^2(T - t)}$$

$$z_2 = [\ln V - \ln F + 2\ln y + (r - a - 1/2\sigma^2)(T - t)]/\sqrt{\sigma^2(T - t)}$$

$$z_3 = [\ln F - \ln V - (r - a - 1/2\sigma^2)(T - t)]/\sqrt{\sigma^2(T - t)}$$

$$z_4 = [\ln V - \ln F + 2\ln y + (r - a + 1/2\sigma^2)(T - t)]/\sqrt{\sigma^2(T - t)}$$

$$z_5 = [\ln y + \zeta\sigma^2)(T - t)]/\sqrt{\sigma^2(T - t)}$$

$$z_6 = [\ln y - \zeta\sigma^2)(T - t)]/\sqrt{\sigma^2(T - t)}$$

$$z_7 = [\ln y + \eta\sigma^2)(T - t)]/\sqrt{\sigma^2(T - t)}$$

$$z_8 = [\ln y - \eta\sigma^2)(T - t)]/\sqrt{\sigma^2(T - t)}.$$

The presence of safety covenants bearing on the value of the firm thus affect the pricing of credit-risky debt in a complex way that can be explored with the previous formula. Note that the terms in z_1 and z_3 correspond to the Merton valuation while the others give the impact of the safety covenant on the value of the risky bond.

Mason and Bhattacharya (1981) extend the previous analysis (as well as the general pricing of risky debt) to underlying processes that incorporate a Poisson-like jump process. It should be clear that the previous analysis is not valid for jump processes as it is possible that the discontinuous process will jump under the value of the safety covenant, the barrier, without having ever been exactly at that value. Suppose, alternatively, to our usual assumption of a continuous Geometric Brownian process that changes in the value of the firm can be described by a jump process:

$$dV/V = (\alpha - \lambda k)dt + d\pi,$$

where α is the instantaneous expected rate of return on the firm per unit time and $d\pi$ the Poisson process of intensity λ. Mason and Bhattacharya (1981) notably investigate the extent of the pricing error if one uses pricing with a continuous process of the Wiener type to drive the changes in the value of the firm when the true process is actually a Poisson. While the impact on the pricing of the risky debt, without considering the safety covenant, remained limited in their trials (with a maximum of around 5%), the valuation of the safety covenant is truly affected by the use of a Wiener process instead of a Poisson process. Valuation errors of the safety covenant of more than 25% were not rare in their trials. The underlying process shape may thus affect the pricing of the safety covenant in major ways, a concern not extended to the general pricing of risky debt in this study, but that may actually matter there as well.

4.4 CONVERTIBLE SECURITIES

The issue of pricing convertibles has been examined notably by Ingersoll (1977 and 1987).

A common type of security issued by corporations is a convertible bond. A convertible bond has one or more fixed payments like a regular bond, but can also be converted in a certain number of shares of common stocks of the company.

Suppose the firm has a capital structure with a single convertible bond issue and common equity. If the bondholders choose not to convert, they will receive $\min(V(T), F)$. If they convert, they will receive n new shares of common stock that are worth

$$\frac{n}{N+n} V(T),$$

where N is the current number of shares outstanding. Define

$$\gamma \equiv \frac{n}{N+n}.$$

We have the payoffs at maturity, with $C(V, t, T, F, \gamma)$ the value of a convertible bond at time t when the bond has maturity T, the firm value is V, the face value is F, and the conversion ratio is γ:

$$C(V, T, T, F, \gamma) = \begin{cases} \gamma V(T) & \text{if } F \leqslant \gamma V(T) \\ F & \text{if } F \leqslant V(T) < F/\gamma \\ V(T) & \text{if } V(T) < F \end{cases}$$

Indeed, if the value of the firm is low enough at maturity (lower than the face value of the debt), the firm goes bankrupt and the bondholders own the assets of the firm. If it is high enough at maturity (higher than the face value of the debt divided by the conversion factor), the bondholders will convert and the value of the bond will be its conversion value, while in between these two values for the value of the firm, the bond behaves like a nondefaulted normal bond and receives the face value.

Hence

$$C(V, T) = \min(V(T), F) + \max(\gamma V(T) - F, 0)$$

which is the sum of a bond payoff and a call payoff on γV.

In the case of a nondividend-paying stock, it can be shown that no conversion happens before maturity and, in the case of the risk of the firm being constant:

$$C(V, t) = D(V, t) + BS(\gamma V, t),$$

where $BS(\gamma V, t; T, B)$ is the Black–Scholes value of a call on γV with maturity T and exercise price B.

Other convertible securities such as convertible preferred stocks can be analyzed in a similar manner. Similarly, closed form solutions are often easily attainable for non-dividend paying stocks, as the conversion policy is simpler (do not exercise before maturity, just as with any other call option). In the case of dividend paying stocks, the results will be obtained through numerical analysis in most cases and will depend on the cash payments of the stocks (the dividends) as well as on the cash payments from the convertible securities (the coupons in the case of a bond).

4.5   CALLABLE BONDS

Most bonds that are issued are callable. A typical coupon bond issued by a corporation may not be callable for the first six months to five years (call protection period), and then be callable at a price which declines over time until it reaches the face value at maturity. The call option on a bond is just the same as any other call option. A call provision on a convertible bond is slightly different because it may force conversion, hence shortening the maturity of the conversion option that convertible bondholders have. For a zero coupon convertible with a constant call price equal or greater than its face value, the proper call policy for the firm is to force conversion as soon as possible. On the other hand, the bond should never be called when bondholders will take the cash payment.

Contingent claim analysis will allow the establishment of the optimal call policy and then to value the instrument, by solving the usual PDE with boundary and terminal conditions well defined. When closed-form solutions are not known, numerical solutions can easily be obtained.

The empirical literature has recently analyzed whether callable bonds are actually called optimally by firms. Of course, the actual call policy should affect the pricing rather than the theoretical one. Ingersoll (1977) suggested that the actual call policy may not conform to theoretical expectations or, in other words, corporates do not call optimally. He indeed found that firms wait until the conversion price exceeds the call price by 43.9% on average. Recent results tend to suggest that actual and theoretical call policies may actually be closer than that previously believed. Asquith (1995) studies the time period waited after the conversion price exceeds call price (rather than looking at premiums as Ingersoll did). He found that notwithstanding the need to maintain a safety margin as well as the existence of call protection and of different cash flow advantages, firms seem to be calling for conversion efficiently. Theoretical pricing done on this basis should thus prove to be reliable.

4.6   SWAPS

Cooper and Mello (1991) focus on pricing credit risk in swaps. The added complication to modeling credit risk in swaps compared to classical models of credit risk is that the defaulting counterparty may not be due to make any payment (even if it was nondefaulting) given the evolution of the underlying market. In particular, if exchange or interest rates move in a way that the net value of the swap is positive for the defaulting counterparty, there may not be any cost on being defaulted upon.

Throughout their paper, Cooper and Mello (1991) make the following assumptions: swaps are subordinate to debt in bankruptcy; in the event of a default on its debt by a counterparty that is owed value in a swap, the value of the swap will be paid to the bankrupt firm; there is only one risky counterparty. Cooper and Mello derive the relationship between swap market default spreads and debt market default spreads where default spreads for the fixed rate and variable rate debt markets are defined analogously to Merton (1974). The authors then analyze three possible treatments in default and their wealth-transfer impacts (a work extended by Baz, 1995). The authors make assumptions on the stochastic processes followed by the value of the firm, and the variable swap payment. They thus obtain equilibrium swap spreads.

The major flaw of the model for actual swap credit risk pricing is that it remains a one-sided default risk model. Stochastic interest rates should also be introduced, as shown later. More details on swap pricing are introduced in the chapter that is specific to this topic.

4.7   FURTHER ENGINEERING: A JUMP-DIFFUSION APPROACH (ZHOU, 1997)

Based on the fact that earlier empirical studies like that of Jones et al. (1984) show that the diffusion model of Merton systematically produces too low credit spreads, Zhou (1997) proposes a framework with a jump diffusion where the firm can suddenly default because of a downward drop in its value. This approach can also answer the problem that, in the traditional diffusion approach a perfectly healthy firm will have a null default probability and a corresponding credit spread of 0, while there is evidence for a systematic strictly positive credit spread. The advantage of the jump-diffusion process is that it allows us to have an additional degree of freedom such that we can fit a wide diversity of shapes: flat, upward and downward sloping and hump-shaped structures. The variability of the recovery comes out directly from the model since it is related to the uncertain magnitude of the jump when default happens because of the jump.

The value process of the firm is assumed to follow a jump diffusion of the form

$$\frac{dV}{V} = (\mu - \lambda v)\, dt + \sigma\, dZ_1 + (\Pi - 1)\, dY, \tag{4.1}$$

where μ, λ, v and σ are constants, Z_1 a standard Brownian motion, and dY is a Poisson process with intensity parameter λ; $\Pi > 0$ is the jump amplitude with expected value equal to $v + 1$. Z_1, Y, and Π are independent. Π is an i.i.d. log-normal random variable such that $\ln(\Pi) \sim N(\mu_\pi, \sigma_\pi^2)$. Thus,

$$v \equiv E[\Pi - 1] = \exp(\mu_\pi + \sigma_\pi^2/2) - 1.$$

Given that the threshold level is a constant K, and $X = V/K$ as in Longstaff and Schwartz (1995), the process of dX/X has the same dynamics than those of expression (4.1).

Zhou (1997) provides an analytical solution for the case of no early default, i.e. default can only happen at maturity as in Merton's case. The solution for the defaultable zero-coupon bond price $B(X, T)$, has a form similar to that of Merton (1974) for European option prices when the underlying asset follows a jump-diffusion model:

$$B(X, T) = \exp(-rT) \left\{ 1 - F_T^Q(1|X) + (1 - \omega_0) \left[F_T^Q(1|X) - F_T^Q \left(\frac{\omega_0 - 1}{\omega_1} \Big| X \right) \right] \right.$$

$$+ \omega_1 X \sum_{i=0}^{\infty} \frac{\exp(-\lambda T)(\lambda T)^i}{i!} \exp[\mu_i + \sigma_i^2/2]$$

$$\times \left[N \left(\frac{\ln(X) + \mu_i + \sigma_i^2 - \ln((\omega_0 - 1)/\omega_1)}{\sigma_i} \right) - N \left(\frac{\ln(X) + \mu_i + \sigma_i^2}{\sigma_i} \right) \right] \Bigg\},$$

where $F_T^Q(\xi|X)$ is the probability of default such that

$$F_T^Q(\xi|X) = \sum_{i=0}^{\infty} \frac{\exp(-\lambda T)(\lambda T)^i}{i!} N \left(\frac{\ln(\xi) - \ln(X) - \mu_i}{\sigma_i} \right)$$

with

$$\mu_i = (r - \sigma^2/2 - \lambda v)T + i\mu_\pi$$

$$\sigma_i = \sqrt{\sigma^2 T + i\sigma_\pi^2}$$

and the writedown being a function of X assumed to have the general form: $\omega(X) = \omega_0 - \omega_1 X$.

The general model that allows default to happen prior to maturity can also be solved numerically. A Monte Carlo approach is thereby proposed by Zhou.

Two important extensions are still made in Zhou (1997): the application to the pricing of credit default swaps and the introduction of stochastic interest rates with the assumption of a Vasicek model for the default-free bond price.

4.8   REFERENCES

Artzner, Philippe and Freddy Delbaen, 1995, "Default Risk Insurance and Incomplete Markets", *Mathematical Finance*, **5** (3), July, 187–95.

Asquith, P., 1995, "Convertible Bonds are not Called Late", *The Journal of Finance*, **4**, 1275–89.

Baz, Jamil, 1995, "Three Essays on Contingent Claims", Harvard PhD Thesis, August 1995.

Black, Fisher and John Cox, 1976, "Valuing Corporate Securities: Some Effects of Bond Indenture Provisions", *The Journal of Finance*, **31** (2), 351–67.

Claessens, Stij and George Pennacchi, 1996, "Estimating the Likelihood of Mexican Default from the Market Prices of Brady Bonds", *Journal of Financial and Quantitative Analysis*, March, **31** (1), 109–26.

Cooper, Ian A. and Antonio S. Mello, 1991, "The Default Risk of Swaps", *Journal of Finance*, **46**, 597–620.

Ericsson, Jan and Joel Reneby, 1995, "A Framework for Valuing Corporate Securities", *Working Paper*, Stockholm School of Economics, November, 35 pp.

Ericsson, Jan and Joel Reneby, 1996, "Stock Options as Barrier Contingent Claims", *Working Paper*, Stockholm School of Economics, November, 38 pp.

Geske, Robert, 1977, "The Valuation of Corporate Liabilities as Compound Options", *Journal of Financial and Quantitative Analysis*, pp. 541–52.

Iben, Th. and R. Litterman, 1991, "Corporate Bond Valuation and the Term Structure of Credit Spreads", *Journal of Portfolio Management*, Spring, 52–64.

Ingersoll, Jonathan E, Jr., 1987, *Theory of Financial Decision Making*. Rowman and Littlefield Studies in Financial Economics, Totowa, N.J.: Littlefield, Adams; Rowman and Littlefield, p. xix, 474.

Ingersoll, Jonathan, 1977, "A Contingent Claims Valuation of Convertible Securities", *Journal of Financial Economics*, **4**, 289–322.

Longstaff, Francis, 1990, "Pricing Options with Extendible Maturities: Analysis and Applications", *Journal of Finance*, **45** (3), July, 935–56.

Madan, Dilip, 1998, "Default Risk", in *Statistics in Finance*, ed. by D. Hand, Ch. 12.

Mason, Scott and Sudipto Bhattacharya, 1981, "Risky Debt, Jump Processes and Safety Covenants", *Journal of Financial Economics*, **9**, 281–307.

Merton, Robert C., 1974, "On the Pricing of Corporate Debt: The Risk Structure of Interest Rates", *The Journal of Finance*, **29**, May, 449–70.

5
Stochastic Interest Rates and Credit Risk

5.1 INTRODUCTION

The work of Merton spurred enthusiasm in the academic community since it was shown that credit risk could be related to the financial economics of the firm and, moreover, that it was then possible to appraise it with the same kind of technology already developed for market risks. But, from the same reasoning, it also became clear that it could no longer be priced independently from market risks, from interest rate risk in particular. Credit risk exists because of the punctual commitment represented by the principal and interest payment owed to a particular class of claimholders, the debtholders. The creditworthiness of the firm would then be inherently linked to the strictness of this commitment.

Taking into account the term structure of interest rates is important for the specification of the credit risk itself in the pricing of credit-sensitive interest rate instruments. In the case of fixed or floating rate corporate bonds, loans, credit limits, mortgage-backed securities, and even more in interest rate swaps, credit risk is inherently linked to the evolution of the term structure of interest rates through time. In the extreme case of a plain vanilla interest rate swap, even if the event of default occurs, the current payment can be owed by the nondefaulted counterparty instead. Therefore, the amount subject to direct loss can be null depending on the evolution of interest rates.

Even when we are not dealing with instruments whose payoffs depend directly on the term structure of interest rates, the activity of the underlying firm and its capital structure policy can be sensitive to interest rates and that is a sufficient reason to include some correlation between our credit risk process and the process driving the term structure of interest rates; the latter representing the market risk.

It is therefore no longer possible to treat the credit risk problem isolated from the risk of the term structure of interest rates, especially when trying to relate it to a structural framework. One of the first studies that tries to state the problem of risky debt in a context of stochastic interest rates was provided by Shimko et al. in 1993. Other refinements then came afterwards and are given in the following sections.

Before discussing them, a clarification can be made. The kind of reasoning mentioned above obeys the principles of the structure of the capital of the firm, the agency costs of debt, and the principle of no arbitrage: a risky payment should be ex-ante worth less than a nonrisky one. From this point of view, we mainly look at the influence of the term structure of interest rates on the credit riskiness, while in an equilibrium approach, we could also think about the reciprocal. Since there is a demand and an offer of risky capital, and that the strictness imposed by the interest payments can lead to more default, we could also think about a credit risk effect on the level of interest rates. This idea is the one recently developed by Chang and Sundaresan. All the studies below introduce the cross-effect of the variability of interest rates on the value of the firm with a correlation parameter. The idea of Chang and Sundaresan is that, should the model be well stated, this correlation would come out from an equilibrium and not from just another exogenous parameter in the equation.

This discussion is analogous to some ethical thoughts that can arise around credit risk. We are moving towards a system where any credit position is being priced individually while the whole credit portfolio was previously treated like an insurance portfolio: everyone pays a premium related to the overall historical level of defaulted payments. We therefore require a higher spread from a lower rated counterparty. How strict and constraining is this spread? How far do we know how it would affect by itself the future creditworthiness of the firm? None of the models below treats this pervasive effect. The spread results purely from a probabilistic model as if there were a sole debt issue in the liability side of the firm and as if the computed spread would not restrict the liquidities of the firm. That is also why the attained equilibrium in terms of offer and demand has an important role to play. In practice, the spread does not result purely from a one-sided calculation but is confronted by the ratio of available capital at risk to the required investment at risk in the market.

Beyond the integration of stochastic interest rates, the models presented below also focus on the refinement of the oversimplified bankruptcy rule in the original Merton model and on the way to integrate violations of the absolute priority rule that, unfortunately, seem to be commonplace in bankruptcy and will be the topic of Chapter 6.

5.2   SHIMKO ET AL. (1993)

Shimko et al. (1993) observe that, while the determination of the cost of debt is important for the management of the financing sources by the firm, little concern has yet been expressed toward the credit component of this cost. They implement a generalization of Merton (1974) to include stochastic interest rates and use it for pricing as well as management considerations. Their choice of term structure model is Vasicek (1977). We will show below that more sophisticated models and the one finally proposed in Part Four are a generalization of the present approach and much of the technique in deriving those more complicated models is already included here. The Vasicek term structure is used in most of these models. Here, we are focusing on a straight extension of Merton's risky debt with stochastic interest rates. That means that default is supposed to be a possibility only at maturity. In other words, the solvency situation of the firm is analyzed by the debtholders only at the conditions prevailing at maturity. (For the sake of completeness, it has to be said that Merton, 1973, had already presented a valuation of options under stochastic interest rates and time-varying volatility.)

Typical issues that such a model can tackle are:

- the pricing of credit risk with interest rate risk;
- the correlation impact on the overall borrowing cost;
- the "optimal" maturity of face value a treasurer should choose in order to minimize the fluctuations in the price of the stock of the firm;
- the allocation of capital in the bank depending on the degree of credit risk and sensitivity to interest rates, i.e. the capital that should be allocated to finance assets of

different riskiness so that the cost of debt financing for each asset class would be equal.

5.2.1 The Derivation

Shimko et al. (1993) present the framework in the context of a bank and a classical corporation. As in Merton (1974) the value of assets is supposed to be uncertain and have a behavior that follows:

$$\frac{dV_t}{V_t} = \mu dt + \sigma_v dZ_t^1,$$

where μ and σ are the constant drift and volatility parameters. (In the case of banks it should be noted that the uncertainty in the asset value can be somewhat mitigated by the existence of a public or private deposit insurance. This possibility is ignored here. Furthermore, this process is an approximation in the case of a bank's assets since they are constituted in part of fixed-income assets that will not follow geometric Brownian motion (GBM) processes.)

The assumptions that apply are again mainly: perfect markets free of transaction costs, taxes, and homogeneous information in the market. Furthermore, there is no payment to equity until the maturity of the debt contract. Overall, this corresponds to a Modigliani–Miller environment where the value of the firm is independent of its capital structure[1].

Again, as in Merton's setting, the equity value is simply a call on the assets value such that

$$E_T = \max[V_T - F, 0],$$

where F is the principal value of the zero-coupon debt. Moreover, at any time the relationship $V_t = E_t + D_t$ is verified.

Then, in order to use Merton's (1973) model, we must rely on the assumption that the instantaneous variance of the return on a riskfree zero-coupon bond depends at most solely on the time parameter, i.e. that it has the same value whatever the level of interest rates or the level of the bond price. This requirement is typically not verified in the case of a square-root process for the interest rate such that Cox, Ingersoll, and Ross (1985) (CIR), but it is consistent with the choice of a Vasicek model. Therefore it is assumed that the short-term riskless interest rate follows an Ornstein–Uhlenbeck process of the form

$$dr = a(b - r)dt + \sigma_r dZ_t^2,$$

where b is the long-run mean which the short-term rate is reverting to, at a speed a, with a variability σ_r. This choice is made by many of the models that will be presented here. The main drawback of the Vasicek model is that it allows negative interest rates although with a small probability for realistic parameter values. Second, the limit of the spot-rate for a maturity that goes to infinity, namely when $\lim_{\tau \to \infty} R(\tau) = b - \sigma_r^2/2a^2$ has a constant asymptotic value. However, this particular model can be used to fit many

---

[1]The assets value of the firm is therefore equal to its total value, debt plus equity.

types of term structures as shown by Hull and White (1990) with the modified Vasicek model (while the CIR model cannot). Stating $P(\tau)$ as the price at time 0 of a riskfree bond with a remaining maturity of τ, we have that

$$P(\tau) = \exp[A(\tau) - B(\tau)r],$$

$$B(\tau) = \frac{1}{a}[1 - e^{(-a\tau)}],$$

$$A(\tau) = B(\tau)R(\infty) - \tau R(\infty) - B(\tau)^2 \frac{\sigma_r^2}{4a},$$

where

$$R(\infty) = b - \frac{\lambda\sigma}{a} - \frac{\sigma_r^2}{2a^2},$$

λ being identified as the market price of risk, which for the solution and because of the no-arbitrage assumption, is assumed not to depend on the maturity.

Additionally, the two stochastic factors, Z^1 and Z^2, are assumed to be correlated such that $dZ_t^1 \times dZ_t^2 = \rho\,dt$.

Shimko et al. (1993) show that the solution for the defaultable debt price D must satisfy the following PDE, using Itô's lemma and the standard no-arbitrage argument:

$$0 = \frac{\partial D}{\partial t} + \frac{1}{2}\frac{\partial^2 D}{\partial V^2}V^2\sigma_v^2 + \frac{1}{2}\frac{\partial^2 D}{\partial r^2}\sigma_r^2$$
$$+ \frac{\partial^2 D}{\partial V\partial r}\rho\sigma_v\sigma_r + \frac{\partial D}{\partial r}[a(b-r) - \lambda] - rD + rV\frac{\partial D}{\partial V},$$

with the following boundary condition:

$$D(V, r, \tau = 0) = \min(F, V_T).$$

Using the methodology introduced by Merton (1974), we can solve this problem for the price of a defaultable bond as

$$D_0(V, r, \tau) = V_0 - V_0 N(d_1) + F P(\tau) N(d_2)$$

with the instantaneous volatility of the return on the riskfree zero-coupon bond with maturity s $\sigma_p(s)$ and the instantaneous volatility of the risky debt return $\nu(s)$ derived as

$$\sigma_p(s) = -\frac{1 - e^{-as}}{a}\sigma_r,$$

$$\nu^2(s) = \sigma_v^2 + \sigma_p^2(s) - 2\rho\sigma_v\sigma_p(s).$$

And making a change of the time variable, we can redefine the time associated to the volatility in d_1 and d_2 such that it becomes a unit-volatility parameter times a new time variable T^* given by

$$T^* = \int_0^\tau \nu^2(s)\,ds,$$

i.e. it is the integrated instantaneous variance of the risky debt function $D(V, r, \tau)$ over the life of the risky debt contract.

The computation of this integral gives

$$T^* = \tau \left(\sigma_v^2 + \frac{\sigma_r^2}{a^2} + \frac{2\rho\sigma_v\sigma_r}{a} \right)$$

$$- B(\tau) \left(\frac{2\sigma_r^2}{a^2} + \frac{2\rho\sigma_v\sigma_r}{a} \right)$$

$$- \frac{\sigma_r^2}{2a^3} (e^{-2a\tau} - 1).$$

Therefore,

$$d_1 = \frac{\ln\left(\dfrac{V_0}{P(\tau)F}\right) + \frac{1}{2}T^*}{\sqrt{T^*}} = d_2 + \sqrt{T^*}.$$

$N(\cdot)$ is the cumulative standard normal distribution.

5.2.2   Static Comparatives

The credit spread is derived analogously to Merton's case:

$$cs = y(\tau) - R(\tau) \tag{5.1}$$

$$= -\frac{1}{\tau} \ln(D(V, r, \tau)/F) + \frac{1}{\tau} \ln(P(\tau))$$

$$= \frac{1}{\tau} \ln(P(\tau)F/D(V, r, \tau)).$$

The credit spread is, in general, a monotically upward-sloping function with maturity (except when the leverage or the volatility are high enough) and with the leverage. And it always increases with the face value or with σ_v. At high leverages, the credit spread experience increases when σ_r is raised. But the opposite is also possible given the impact that σ_r may have through the slope of the interest rate term structure and through the correlation of asset returns and interest rate changes.

The impact of correlation is also interesting. As correlation increases, so does the credit spread, even more strongly when the leverage is high. It is also important to notice that the credit spread may not increase when the correlation is negative.

5.2.3   Implications for Asset-liability Management

The main motivation of asset-liability managers and of fund providers in general is to be able to match the maturities of inflows (funding receivables) and outflows (funding commitments) of their assets and liabilities, or the durations of assets and liabilities for a borrowing and lending activity.

Shimko et al. (1993) show a strategy that allows the removal of the dependence of equity returns on the interest rate, which is actually our external funding cost. The remaining diffusion element in the equity return would be only the part that is correlated to the asset volatility. Using Itô's lemma and making the asset and debt sensitivities binding in dollar terms, we find that the minimum-risk point is achieved when the following relationship is satisfied:

$$F = \frac{[1 - N(d_1)]\sigma_v \rho a V}{P(\tau)\sigma_r N(d_2)(1 - e^{-a\tau})}. \tag{5.2}$$

This means that there will be combinations of the maturity and the face value that will be optimal for interest rate hedging for shareholders. Although this means that the firm can unilaterally choose the terms of the contract[2], it is interesting to see that the pricing model is not only a pricing tool but can also help the deciders into their decision-making process. Even if the definition of the contract is negotiated, the model can result in a useful instrument for the firm to assess the impact of the debt issue on some fundamentals of the firm and its claimholders.

Given the previous comments, there is only one step to find analogies between the objective pursued when eliminating sensitivities to some variables and defining the required amount of capital and its subsequent allocation. It is in this spirit that the RAROC (risk-adjusted return on capital) measure has been created. Each profit unit in a firm generates a series of cash flows for which we can compute a historical average as well as a standard deviation. In this context the capital adequacy objective is to determine the amount of capital necessary to the unit such that it remains solvent on a stand-alone basis and for some percentage confidence level. Returns of this unit can then be computed with respect to their capital requirement. With the structural approaches, the total financing requirement for this unit would consist in estimating the amount of assets V implicitly, having chosen the time horizon, the face amount of the zero-coupon debt, having estimated the volatility of interest rates and that of the underlying asset class of the activity of the unit along with the correlation between the two sources of risk. Also having defined D such that the continuous yield on this debt corresponds to the marginal external financing cost of the bank or any other type of firm[3]. Once identified the amount of assets in reverse, the sole application of the ratio $(V - F)/V$ to this amount provides us with the "domestic" capital that must be allocated to the unit.

In conclusion, the contribution of Shimko et al. (1993) is not only that of a more sophisticated model but it is also an extended reasoning that shows us how far a structural model can allow us to think beyond the pricing issue for the monitoring and the management of the financial funding activity. More precisely, this methodology, independently of the underlying structural model chosen, could be analogously applied to the instrument classes of a client's portfolio to estimate its borrowing limit that can be allowed to the client on the basis of these different instruments. In this sense, her/his portfolio is acting as a collateral asset. Furthermore, we could also imagine calculating the trading limit of each trading desk, trader's portfolio, or management portfolio, after some tailored rearrangements, to fit the valuation system to the nature of the activity of the portfolio unit. When a portfolio manager is shorting an asset to buy another, for

---

[2]This is in contradiction with all recent theories that are trying to stress the bargaining behavior of equityholders and debtholders into the definition of the contract parameters.

[3]This could be straightforwardly applied to an industrial firm if it is somewhere possible to correctly attribute the risk-return performance to every unit. Of course, tangible nonfinancial assets are cumbersome to evaluate and attribute compared to financial traded assets.

example, s/he is implicitly borrowing an asset instead of using internal capital. Of course, refinements would have to be made to differentiate between a simply shorted asset and a shorted asset on behalf of the asset reserves of the institution. But, overall, what is important to notice is that structural models tell us a story about the firm. That is why the assumptions presented are financially fundamental, because they inform us about the limits of our argument from a financial point of view and not only from a mathematical one.

5.3 LONGSTAFF AND SCHWARTZ (1995b)

The clear drawback of Merton's model and of Shimko et al. (1993) is that the firm can only default at the debt maturity and the default is assumed to occur only when the firm exhausts its assets. Longstaff and Schwartz (1995b) recall that Jones et al. (1984) and Franks and Torous (1989) have shown that this kind of model produces credit spreads that are systematically lower than the actual credit spreads in the market. That is why Longstaff and Schwartz (1995b) were tempted by the approach of Black and Cox (1976) where a down-and-out barrier is added to the classical Black–Scholes–Merton framework such that default can be triggered earlier should this barrier be breached before maturity of the debt contract. This has the enormous advantage of allowing asset insolvency but also cash-flow insolvency. The firm can default just because the value of the assets has not been able to cope with a "bottleneck" during the life of the debt contract[4].

Introducing stochastic interest rates is therefore seen as the main new ingredient, not to a classical Black–Scholes–Merton framework as with Shimko et al. (1993), but to an extended one.

Furthermore, and contrary to Black and Cox (1976), Longstaff and Schwartz (1995b) also suppose that deviations from the strict priority rule (APR) are possible since they are widely evident in the credit practice.

5.3.1 The Framework and its Assumptions

The theory of Longstaff and Schwartz (1995b) is to evaluate a risky corporate zero-coupon bond as a riskfree bond minus a value resulting from the loss that can be incurred, times the probability of defaulting, either during the life of the bond or at maturity when the assets value process reaches the barrier. The solution for a floating rate debt is also provided. Interestingly, the loss at default is a proportion — which is exogenous so that violations of the APR can/have to be assumed — of an otherwise riskfree bond. Briefly, without any other detail for the moment, Longstaff and Schwartz (1995b) would want to price the zero-coupon bond, for example, as

$$D_0(V, r, T) = P_0(r, T) - \omega P_0(r, T) P[V_t < K, \forall t \in [0, T]], \qquad (5.3)$$

where $P_0(r, T)$ is the value of a riskfree zero-coupon bond, ω the exogenous loss rate that can be assumed at default, and K the threshold value or barrier. No reference is being made on the face value of the debt contract as in Shimko et al. (1993). At T or

---

[4]Again, assuming that all the external financing of the firm is represented by a sole debt issue.

between $t = 0$ and T default is triggered by the same value K. As we will show in other chapters, not considering a face value as in the classical Black–Scholes–Merton framework can be a disadvantage: the value at default here can never be less than K, even at default. That is why we need an exogenous ω. In the Black–Scholes–Merton framework, V_T can end up smaller than F since F is not a barrier and therefore the loss at default will be related to the final distance $F - V_T$, which is stochastic but predictable. Here, there is nothing to relate ω to. Thus, the present approach relaxes the hypothesis of constant interest rates and default only at T, but it does not accommodate the Black–Scholes–Merton framework.

For the sake of the final valuation, the following additional assumptions are made:

- The total assets value of the firm is equivalent to the assets value of the firm, since it is considered as being independent of the capital structure. Coupons and other payments are assumed to be paid by issuing new debt. The total assets value of the firm has the following dynamics:

$$dV_t = \mu V_t \, dt + \sigma_v V \, dZ_t^1.$$

- The term structure of interest rates is assumed to be consistent with Vasicek's model (1977). Therefore, the dynamics of the short-term interest rate are of the form

$$dr = (\zeta - \beta r) \, dt + \sigma_r \, dZ_t^2.$$

Longstaff and Schwartz (1995b) use the alternative formulation of the Ornstein–Uhlenbeck process. A more usual formulation is $dr = a(b - r) \, dt + \sigma_r \, dZ_t^2$. Therefore the correspondence is given by $\zeta = ab$ and $\beta = a$. Moreover, the process dV/V is assumed to be correlated to dr by a factor ρ.

- Longstaff and Schwartz (1995b) do not intend to model the bargaining process or the mechanisms that define the value that will be recovered at default. Therefore, they simply assume that in the case of a reorganization, the debtholder would receive a fraction $1 - \omega$ of the face value of the issued security.

- In addition, Longstaff and Schwartz (1995b) stress that V is a difficult variable to estimate consistently since there is no traded data directly available for it[5]. Therefore, they propose to derive their solution as a solution of the ratio of V and K, $X = V/K$. X is merely the relative distance of V to default. By providing the barrier not as an exogenous absolute value but as an exogenous relative value, we only need to have an estimate for one variable instead of two. Note that while V was studied with respect to K, the behavior of X will be studied with respect to 1, and more precisely, the behavior of $\ln(X)$ will be examined with respect to 0.

- Other assumptions include the fact that the framework is placed into a continuous context where trading takes place continuously and without any friction.

5.3.2 The Basis of Valuation

The value of the zero-coupon bond under this framework is derived by Longstaff and Schwartz (1995b) as

---

[5] Of course, one could rely on the market values of equity and debt to implicitly compute a proxy of V.

$$D_0(X, r, T) = P_0(r, T) - \omega P_0(r, T)Q[X, r, T], \tag{5.4}$$

where

$$Q[X, r, T] = \boldsymbol{P}[V_t < K, \forall t \in [0, T]].$$

$P_0(r, T)$ is the value of a bond under Vasicek's model (see section 5.2).

Since the derivation of this probability, through the way chosen by Longstaff and Schwartz (1995b) requires the resolution of an integral, an approximation of $Q[X, r, T]$ is provided by $Q[X, r, T, n]$ where

$$Q[X, r, T, n] = \sum_{i=1}^{n} q_i,$$

$$q_1 = N(a_1),$$

$$q_i = N(a_i) - \sum_{j=1}^{i-1} q_j N(b_{ij}), \text{ for } i = 2, 3, \ldots, n,$$

$$a_i = \frac{-\ln X - M(iT/n, T)}{\sqrt{S(iT/n)}},$$

$$b_{ij} = \frac{M(jT/n, T) - M(iT/n, T)}{\sqrt{S(iT/n) - S(jT/n)}},$$

with

$$M(t, T) = \left(\frac{\alpha - \rho\sigma_v\sigma_r}{\beta} - \frac{\sigma_r^2}{\beta^2} - \frac{\sigma_v^2}{2} \right) t$$

$$+ \left(\frac{\rho\sigma_v\sigma_r}{\beta^2} + \frac{\sigma_r^2}{2\beta^3} \right) \exp(-\beta T)(\exp(\beta t) - 1)$$

$$+ \left(\frac{r}{\beta} - \frac{\alpha}{\beta^2} + \frac{\sigma_r^2}{\beta^3} \right) (1 - \exp(-\beta t))$$

$$- \left(\frac{\sigma_r^2}{2\beta^3} \right) \exp(-\beta T)(1 - \exp(-\beta t)),$$

and

$$S(T) = \left(\frac{\rho\sigma_v\sigma_r}{\beta} + \frac{\sigma_r^2}{\beta^2} + \sigma_v^2 \right) t$$

$$- \left(\frac{\rho\sigma_v\sigma_r}{\beta^2} + \frac{2\sigma_r^2}{2\beta^3} \right) (1 - \exp(-\beta t))$$

$$+ \left(\frac{\sigma_r^2}{2\beta^3} \right) (1 - \exp(-2\beta t)).$$

where α is simply the sum of ζ and some market price of risk. Longstaff and Schwartz (1995b) do not provide any further explanation or assumption on its form.

5.3.3 A Caveat

There are some technical ambiguities about this well-known and important model that should be stressed. First, there seems to be a mistake in their transcription of Vasicek's bond formula and this may have also an impact in the formulation of Q (this seems to have a second-order effect on the overall result that remains a good approximation). Second, it seems that the derivation of Q is not fully exact mathematically. It can be argued that the fact that the V process has a drift equal to r in a risk-neutral world, along with the assumption of correlation between the two processes, is not correctly taken into account in the derivation. The fact that V is inherently linked to r by its drift and by its correlation to r will certainly have an impact on the expected time of default, i.e. on the propensity of V to get closer to or away from K. Therefore the derivation above should be taken carefully until a correction note has been issued. It is, however, transcribed here because Longstaff and Schwartz's model has been widely used since by practitioners and for practical reasons it still appears to be a good approximation (and presents some interesting conceptual challenges).

5.3.4 Floating Rate Debt Valuation

Longstaff and Schwartz (1995b) provide then the solution also for a floating rate debt. Let us suppose a function $D^{FR}(X, r, \tau, T)$ that pays a coupon at T that has been determined at time τ, $\tau \leqslant T$. Moreover, this coupon payment is equal to r if there has been no default until T, or $(1 - \omega)r$ in the opposite case. They obtain

$$D_0^{FR}(X, r, \tau, T) = D_0(X, r, T) R^*(r, \tau, T) + \omega P_0(r, T) G(X, r, \tau, T), \qquad (5.5)$$

where

$$R^*(r, \tau, T) = r \exp(-\beta\tau)$$

$$+ \left(\frac{\alpha}{\beta} - \frac{\sigma_r}{\beta^2} \right)(1 - \exp(-\beta\tau))$$

$$+ \left(\frac{\sigma_r^2}{2\beta^2} \right) \exp(-\beta T)(\exp(\beta\tau) - \exp(-\beta\tau))$$

and $G(X, r, \tau, T)$ being the limit as $n \to \infty$ of $G(X, r, \tau, T, n)$

$$G(X, r, \tau, T, n) = \sum_{i=1}^{n} q_i \frac{C(\tau, iT/n)}{S(iT/n)} M(iT/n, T),$$

with

$$C(\tau, iT/n) = \left(\frac{\rho\sigma_v\sigma_r}{\beta^2} + \frac{\sigma_r^2}{\beta^2} \right) \exp(-\beta\tau)(\exp(\beta \min(\tau, t)) - 1)$$

$$- \frac{\sigma_r^2}{2\beta^2} \exp(-\beta\tau) \exp(-\beta t)(\exp(2\beta \min(\tau, t)) - 1).$$

The notation R^* is to differentiate this function from the classical R calculated under the standard model of Vasicek as presented previously in section 5.2. The first term of equation (5.5) is simply the price of a risky zero-coupon bond times the expectation of the value of the payment r determined at time τ but paid at time T under the risk-neutral probability measure. $C(\tau, t)$ in the second term, is assumed to adjust for the correlation between X and r. $C(\tau, t)$ represents "the covariance of the value of r at time τ with the value of $\ln(X)$ at the time t of its first passage to *zero*". As mentioned by Longstaff and Schwartz (1995b), this correlation will not be null even if ρ is set at 0 simply because the drift of the risk-neutral process of X is a function of r.

Straight interpretations about the floating-rate debt are as follows:

- Its value can also increase with T while D_0 was always a monotically decreasing function of T. This comes from the fact that r is mean reverting and, depending on its current location with respect to its long-term target, the expected payment of r at T, if no prior default, can increase with T (if below the target).
- This effect will be added to or compensate the effect of the risky discount factor in equation (5.5). This will depend on the values of r and T. As mentioned by Longstaff and Schwartz (1995b) as $T \to \infty$ the present value of the floating-rate payment will approach 0. The intuition is as follows: under Vasicek's model, the long-term value of r, $R(\infty)$, is equal to $\alpha/\beta - \frac{1}{2}\sigma_r^2/\beta^2$, i.e. $R(\infty)$ is a known constant[6] while the value of the risky discount factor will vanish.
- The same remark on the maturity can be made with respect to the value of r, i.e. $D_0^{FR}(X, r, \tau, T)$ can also be an increasing function of r. The payment if no prior default is r, but the risky discount factor is a decreasing function of r. And finally, the effect of the correlation factor must be again added to these considerations. Typically, when $\rho > 0$, an increase in r makes an increase in X more likely, i.e. an increase of the distance to default and therefore a higher expected floating-rate payment.

Furthermore, the ratio of the value of risky floating-rate debt to its riskless version makes appear a high dependence on the value of X. The lower is X, the higher is the (negative) sensitivity of this ratio to the maturity.

5.4 SAÁ-REQUEJO AND SANTA CLARA (1997)

Saá-Requejo and Santa Clara (1997) base their proposal on two main previous developments:

- They advocate for the "economic-meaning" advantage of structural models and the assumption of Black and Cox (1976) and Longstaff and Schwartz (1995b) models that allow for a continuous boundary such that default can occur at any point in time between the contract origination and its maturity T. They point out a weakness of reduced-form models (see the chapter on reduced-form approaches). In the modelizations being proposed by these models, the future probability of default, conditional on no prior default, does not go to zero with the length of the time horizon. There is no resolution of the uncertainty about the arrival of the event of default in that class of models.
- They recall the fact that we can avoid a direct parametrization in terms of V, the value of the firm and K, the default triggering point, by directly examining their ratio X as Longstaff and Schwartz (1995b) did.

---

[6]The definition of $R(\infty)$ is here the same as the one provided previously in section 5.2.

But they have a criticism. If V is some asset that the agents are willing to hold, then its risk-adjusted drift is r, the instantaneous interest rate minus eventually some payout rate. Since K is a constant in Black and Cox (1976) and Longstaff and Schwartz (1995b) settings, by Itô's lemma the drift of the natural logarithm of X is then also r. They argue that this dependency is inconsistent with an event of default being interpreted as being caused by insolvency unless the payout rate of the liabilities corresponds to r itself.

In Saá-Requejo and Santa Clara (1997) the default barrier K is specifically assimilated to the value of the liabilities of the firm.

Saá-Requejo and Santa Clara (1997) therefore introduce two diffusion processes, one for dV/V and one for dK/K, which risk-adjusted dynamics are defined as

$$\frac{dV}{V} = (r(t) - \delta_v)dt + \sigma_v dZ_v,$$

$$\frac{dK}{K} = (r(t) - \delta_k)dt + \sigma_{kr} dZ_r + \sigma_{kv} dZ_v,$$

where σ_v, σ_{kr}, σ_{kv} are constant parameters for the volatility of the returns on V and the volatilities of the changes in K due to interest rate changes and to V changes respectively; δ_v and δ_k are constant payout rates to the general claimholders and particular debtholders of the firm respectively; Z_r and Z_v are Brownian motions and Z_v is itself correlated to Z_r.

In this way, Saá-Requejo and Santa Clara are able to argue that their default boundary is stochastic and therefore more general than that previously proposed. Moreover, the payout rates to each category of investors and the link with interest rates is well established.

Furthermore, the particular definition of both processes allows them easily to derive through Itô's lemma the following expression for the changes in the solvency ratio X:

$$dX = \mu \, dt + \sigma \, dZ_x,$$

where

$$\mu = \delta_k - \delta_v - \tfrac{1}{2}(\sigma_v^2 - (\sigma_{kv}^2 + \sigma_{kr}^2 + 2\rho_{rv}\sigma_{kv}\sigma_{kr})), \tag{5.6}$$

and

$$\sigma^2 = (\sigma_v - \sigma_{kv})^2 + \sigma_{kr}^2 - 2\rho_{rv}(\sigma_v - \sigma_{kv})\sigma_{kr}, \tag{5.7}$$

where ρ_{rv} is the correlation parameter between the interest rate process and the value process of the firm. Z_x is simply a new Brownian motion defined such that

$$\sigma Z_x = (\sigma_v - \sigma_{kv})Z_v - \sigma_{kr}Z_r.$$

This definition allows for an elegant derivation thereafter. On the other hand, while many models agree on the form of the diffusion process for dV/V since the dynamics of V are far or nearly assimilated with those of the share price, such a definition for dK/K may seem *ad hoc* (but useful mathematically!). The meaning of a stochastic K given the notion stated for K is also unclear. The payout rate δ_k could be easily explained by the coupons being paid to the debtholders, even more in the case of constant annuity payments where part of the coupon corresponds to some amortization of the owed face value. It is understandable to relate the diffusion component to that of the interest rate process. It may be less obvious to have a part of the variability of K that comes out from V. Any model aims to provide a nonexplicit output given some acceptable starting hypothesis. For consistency the model, interesting for the extensions it proposes, also has an ambiguous relationship as the input may be somewhat related to the desired output. Saá-Requejo and Santa Clara (1997) assess that K "can be the (market) value of the total debt . . . or . . . the present value, discounting at the default riskless rate of the face value of the liabilities". Let us take K as the market value of the total debt. The credit-risky market value is the desired output. So, let us assume, as in the second part of the citation, that we are talking about the market value in terms of the interest rate risk, but riskless in credit-risk terms. Even though we could do so, there is a diffusion argument that links the evolution of K to V. Doing so means that we already force the model to include an explicit starting relationship between the value of the firm and the way it will impact the value of the debt. And that is precisely what we would want the model to reveal. But Saá-Requejo and Santa Clara (1997) are forced to do so because they need to rely on only two main sources of risk, where the credit risk is related entirely to one of them. Therefore, the definition of dK/K is mathematically desirable, but presents some economic difficulties, notably because it implicitly assumes that the user of the model already knows the cross-effect of the value of the firm on the value of the debt.

Given these remarks, the model presents a rigorous treatment of a stochastic barrier setup that brings many insights and drives to an interesting empirical implementation. As in the models studied earlier, Saá-Requejo and Santa Clara (1997) want to divulge the price of a default-risky zero-coupon bond with a T maturity that would be commonly valued as

$$D(t, T) = P(t, T) - E_t\left[W(T)\mathbf{I}_{\{\tau<T\}}e^{-\int_t^T r(u)\,du}\right], \tag{5.8}$$

where $D(t, T)$ is the value of the credit-risky debt, $P(t, T)$ the value of the debt free from credit risk, E_t the expectation operator, $W(T)$ the explicit write-down for a given contract maturity, and τ the first time that the V process reaches from above the K value. It can be seen that this expression is close to that of Longstaff and Schwartz (1995b). In fact, deriving further, equation (5.8) gives

$$D(t, T) = P(t, T) - W E_t\left[\mathbf{I}_{\{\tau<T\}}e^{-\int_t^T r(u)\,du}\right] \tag{5.9}$$

$$= P(t, T) - W P(t, T) E_t[\mathbf{I}_{\{\tau<T\}}]$$

$$= P(t, T) - W P(t, T) Q_t^T(\{\tau < T\}),$$

where $Q_t^T(\{\tau < T\})$ is the forward risk-adjusted probability of default before T given no prior default to t, i.e. the probability under which "asset prices normalized by the price of the T-maturity default riskless bond are martingales". Under the spot risk-adjusted probability measure, the last result should be written as

$$D(t, T) = P(t, T) - W P(t, T) Q_t(\{\tau < T\}) \tag{5.10}$$

$$- W \operatorname{Cov}_t\left[\mathbf{I}_{\{\tau<T\}}, e^{-\int_t^T r(u)\,du}\right],$$

where $Cov_t[\cdot]$ is the covariance stemming from the inclusion of ρ_{rv}. It is only the normalization of the asset price by the bond price (and therefore the forward probability measure), or a null correlation parameter that allows us to avoid this third term.

Let us return to equation (5.9). From the previous section, we remember that it is being argued that the Longstaff and Schwartz model is incorrect in that they cannot really write their expression as in equation (5.9) above. But, Saá-Requejo and Santa Clara can. The reason lies in the fact that they really make the change of variable that is necessary, i.e. they replace the underlying X by an X which is normalized by the price of the zero-coupon riskfree bond.

Moreover, the drift of their solvency ratio X, once applied Itô's lemma no longer depends on r. So, X is solely influenced by r on its diffusion argument. With the change of probability measure to the forward probability measure, X has the following new dynamics:

$$dX = (\mu - \rho_{rv}\sigma s(t, T))dt + \sigma dW_x. \tag{5.11}$$

We see that the Brownian Z_x has been substituted by a new Brownian W_x with a new add-in to the drift of $-\rho_{rv}\sigma s(t, T)$, where $s(t, T)$ is the volatility of the bond price for the T maturity. It has to be the volatility of the bond price and not of the interest rate since $E_t\left[\mathbf{I}_{\{\tau<T\}} e^{-\int_t^T r(u)du}\right]$ is an expectation on the combination of an indicator function and a discount function that depends on the whole term structure until T. If the drift of the original X was dependent on r, we should also modify the new drift of X by adding $s^2(t, T)$ to it as it will be shown in a standard setting by Briys and De Varenne (1997) in the next section. That is why it is sufficient here to take into account the covariance term (the third term in equation (5.10)) to be able still to separate $P(t, T)$ and $Q_t(\{\tau < T\})$ without changing the probability measure.

5.4.1 When Risks are Independent

When $\rho_{rv} = 0$, equation (5.10) simplifies to

$$D(t, T) = P(t, T) - W P(t, T)Q_t(\{\tau < T\}), \tag{5.12}$$

where the probability $Q_t(\{\tau < T\})$ is the probability that the arithmetical Brownian motion X hits one before the maturity. Following Karatzas and Schreve (1991) or Don Rich (1994), $Q_t(\{\tau < T\})$ has the following closed-form solution:

$$Q_t(\{\tau < T\}) = 1 - N\left(\frac{X(t) - \mu(T - t)}{\sigma\sqrt{T - t}}\right) + e^{(2\mu/\sigma^2)X(t)}N\left(\frac{-X(t) - \mu(T - t)}{\sigma\sqrt{T - t}}\right),$$

where $N(\cdot)$ is the standard normal cumulative density function.

Thanks to a drift of X that is independent of r and a null correlation between the two sources of risk, the two factors, each one related to one of the two sources of risk, can be priced separately through their analytical expressions.

5.4.2 When Risks are Dependent

When it can be assumed that the relative volatility of bond prices, $s(t, T)$ is a deterministic function of time, then we can still compute the first hitting time probability of X. Saá-Requejo and Santa Clara propose to restate the problem as the computation of the first hitting time probability of a standard Brownian motion through a new boundary directly issued from the X form that is thus also a deterministic function of time. From equation (5.11) and for $y \in [t, T]$ this boundary is given by

$$G(y) = -\frac{X(t) + \mu(y - t)}{\sigma} - \rho_{rv} \int_t^y s(u, T)\, du.$$

Since the bond volatility is not a constant parameter, Saá-Requejo and Santa Clara propose from Durbin (1992), the following approximation:

$$Q_t^T(\{\tau < T\}) \approx \int_t^T \left(\frac{G(s)}{u} - G'(s) \right) \varphi(s)\, ds$$

$$- \int_t^T \int_t^s \left(\frac{G(s)}{s} - G'(s) \right) \left(\frac{G(s) - G(u)}{s - u} - G'(u) \right) \varphi(s, u)\, du\, ds,$$

where $G'(s)$ denotes the slope of the boundary at s, $\varphi(s)$ is the density of the Brownian at time s, and $\varphi(s, u)$ the analog bivariate density:

$$\varphi(s) = (2\pi(s - t))^{-1/2} \exp\left[\frac{-(G(s) - G(t))^2}{2(s - t)} \right],$$

$$\varphi(s, u) = f(s)(2\pi(u - s))^{-1/2} \exp\left[\frac{-(G(u) - G(s))^2}{2(u - s)} \right].$$

Thus, numerical solutions are easy to compute for term structure models where a closed form for the percentage volatility of the bond price obtains. This is true for any model of the HJM class where the volatility is a deterministic function of time. Otherwise, in the case of CIR (1985) for example, the final price of the defaultable bond must be computed through a simulation.

5.4.3 Credit Risk Measures

To have comparative statics between the models that are being presented in this chapter, it is always useful to look at the expression and thus the behavior of the yield spread. In the present case, we can derive it as

$$y_c(t, T) = -\frac{\ln D(t, T)}{T - t}$$

$$= -\frac{\ln P(t, T)}{T - t} - \frac{\ln(1 - W Q_t^T(\{\tau < T\}))}{T - t}$$

$$\approx y_p(t, T) + \frac{W Q_t^T(\{\tau < T\})}{T - t},$$

where $y_c(t, T)$ and $y_p(t, T)$ are the corporate yield and the riskfree yield, respectively.

Then, we can also compute the forward corporate yield. Assume that we have the suite of instantaneous forward risky rates, then

$$D(t, T) = \exp\left(-\int_t^T f_c(t, u)\,du\right).$$

We can compute $f_c(t, T)$ values by

$$f_c(t, T) = -\frac{\partial \ln D(t, T)}{\partial T}.$$

Then deriving this expression further and assuming a constant W we have

$$f_c(t, T) = -\frac{\partial \ln P(t, T)}{\partial T} - \frac{\partial \ln(1 - W Q_t^T(\{\tau < T\}))}{\partial T}$$

$$= f_p(t, T) + \frac{W}{1 - W Q_t^T(\{\tau < T\})} \frac{\partial Q_t^T(\{\tau < T\})}{\partial T}$$

$$= f_p(t, T) + \frac{W(1 - Q_t^T(\{\tau < T\}))}{1 - W Q_t^T(\{\tau < T\})} \frac{\partial Q_t^T(\{\tau < T\})/\partial T}{1 - Q_t^T(\{\tau < T\})}$$

$$= f_p(t, T) + l(t, T)h(t, T),$$

where we obtain l as the percentage write-down, given default and h as the density of default evaluated at T given no prior default, which is the hazard rate in the common terminology of reduced-form models. This confirms the fact that any model, either structural or reduced-form, leads to a simple probabilistic answer of the form

Conditional probability of default × loss given default.

Looking then at the form of $l(t, T)$ and $h(t, T)$, Saá-Requejo and Santa Clara point out that in such a setting the expected loss can converge to zero when the maturity goes to infinity. The fact that the firm survives for a long period of time would affect the expected loss at default, contrary to some implementations of Duffie and Singleton (1999) where the expected loss is modeled as a variable whose dynamics follow some square root process that converges to a positive constant when $T \to \infty$.

5.4.4   An Empirical Implementation

The contribution of Saá-Requejo and Santa Clara does not stop here. They also provide the implementation of their model through a general method of moments (GMM) procedure that allows the simultaneous extraction of the write-down parameter and the term structure of default spreads.

Two cases were examined, with and without the assumption of independent risks. In both cases, the solvency ratio X is considered as the state variable that can be directly extracted from the data.

Saá-Requejo and Santa Clara retained 42 monthly prices for five straight corporate coupon bonds issued by RJR Nabisco for maturities ranging from 2 to 8.5 years. The riskfree zero-coupon rates were obtained by combining LIBOR and swap rates and fitting them with piecewise constant forward rates until the maturity[7]. It is

---

[7] This method has been proposed by Coleman et al. (1992).

interesting to note that the diffusion term of the T-maturity bond $P(t, T)s(t, T)$ can be deduced from the volatility of forward rates through $P(t, T) \int_t^T \sigma(t, y)dy$, where $\sigma(t, y)$ is the diffusion component of the forward rate with maturity y. Finally, for the model with dependent risks, however, a different term structure must be estimated at each sample date.

Following the model previously described, the price of a corporate coupon bond j with a coupon rate of c_j could be determined by

$$\hat{M}_{jt} = \sum_{n=1}^{N_j} D(t, t_n; \theta, X(t))c_j + D(t, t_{N_j}; \theta, X(t)),$$

where $D(t, t_n; \theta, X(t))$ is the same zero-coupon bond pricing formula shown earlier, but for a maturity t_n and stressing the fact that it depends on the parameter vector $\theta = \{\mu, \sigma, \rho, W\}$ and the state variable X.

The estimator $\hat{M}_t$ is related to the true observed value through

$$M_t = \hat{M}_t + \epsilon_{jt},$$

where ϵ_{jt} is a white noise, i.e. the norm of the error term is minimized at the true parameter values and at the realized value of the state variable. The econometric method would consist in estimating jointly the set of parameter values θ and X by minimizing jointly the norm of each of the vectors ϵ_j for the 42 sample dates $(t = t_1, \ldots, t_{42})$, knowing that we have a set of five bonds for five unknown parameters.

At each sample date and for each bond, C_{jt} values are produced using equation (5.12) when risks are independent (Model I), and by simulation, for the case of dependent risks still with a deterministic structure of bond volatilities (Model II).

The simulation consists in producing i simulated paths of the standard Brownian motion W_x for each date t and for each cash flow of each bond (for each coupon payment). These paths allow us to obtain the forward risk-adjusted and discretized process $\hat{X}$ starting at $X(t)$ from

$$\hat{X}(t + (n + 1)h) = \hat{X}(t + nh) + [\mu - \rho\sigma s(t + nh, T)]h$$
$$+ \sigma[W_x(t + (n + 1)h) - W_x(t + mh)],$$

where $n = 1, \ldots, N$, h is a daily interval expressed in years, and N the number of days between the sample date and the cash-flow date.

The necessary $Q_t^T(\{\tau < T\})$ is approximated by the number of $\hat{X}$ paths that fall below zero (see equation (5.9)). Following the GMM methodology[8], the problem is stated as the minimization of the distance function of the form

$$J(\theta, X) = \sum_{t=1}^{42} (\hat{V}_t(\theta, X(t)) - V_t)'S^{-1}(\hat{V}_t(\theta, X(t)) - V_t),$$

where V_t and $\hat{V}_t$ are the vectors of observed and computed prices for the five bonds at date t. S is a 5×5 weighting matrix. It is important to note that X is determined, as it would be an additional vector of parameters without taking into account the

---

[8]A very well explained and detailed GMM implementation is provided by Chan et al. (1992) for the case of one-factor models of the term structure of interest rates.

particularities of its dynamics. Saá-Requejo and Santa Clara argue that even if not efficient, the method remains consistent.

As for any GMM estimation an important ingredient is the form of the weighting matrix **S**. Saá-Requejo and Santa Clara decided to choose as an alternative a two-step procedure. First **S** is simply an identity matrix. Then once the errors from the first set of estimators are retrieved the minimization is run again but taking the variance–covariance matrix of these errors as the new **S** matrix. The underlying assumption is that of no serial correlation in the errors.

The main results are as follows:

- The parameter estimates in the case of independent risks (Model I) do not provide the expected value order for σ, nor the expected sign for μ, which negativeness is a necessary condition for the absence of arbitrage opportunities[9]. The rest of the results concern only Model II.
- Thanks to a pseudo-likelihood test based on the difference in $J(\theta, \mathbf{X})$ values with and without $\rho = 0$ which is χ^2-distributed, it has been established that the correlation between the interest rates and the assets value of the firm is highly significantly different from zero and negative. That directly means that interest rates are significantly and positively correlated to the default risk.
- The write-down (W) is estimated at 45.5% which means a recovery of 55% of an otherwise riskfree coupon bond[10].
- The comparison between the pricing errors and the noise in the data let the authors conclude that this estimation procedure provides a quite accurate pricing scheme. A typical alternative to this method would be that consisting in inferring recovery and default probabilities from historical data as presented throughout the review in Chapter 13.

5.5 BRIYS AND DE VARENNE (1997)

As in the two previous modeling approaches Briys and de Varenne (1997) combine the advantages of a model including the effect of interest rates and the early default problem. But, Briys and de Varenne (1997) focus on two main drawbacks of previous models. First, when looking at equations (5.3) and (5.8), we notice that the fraction ω or W respectively means that some exogenous fraction of an otherwise riskfree bond is lost at default. This fraction is not related at all to the level of assets reached at the time of default, upon either early bankruptcy or bankruptcy at maturity. In both cases only the probability of default is related to the level of assets. Nothing ensures that the value that is recovered at default is not actually higher than the value of assets reached at default. Second, when the corporate bond reaches the maturity nothing prevents the model to allow a firm to be solvent, but without sufficient assets to cover the face value of debt. In conclusion these models use the structural approach for the modelization of the probability of default, but the payoff at default may not be consistent with this approach.

---

[9] Moreover, the J value is considerably lower in the case of Model II.

[10] And not of the face value of the securities as Saá-Requejo and Santa Clara say in their article. This is visible in the formulation of equation (5.8).

5.5.1 The Framework

As in the previous models, the total assets value of the firm is assumed to follow a stochastic process, which in a risk-neutral world, is of the form

$$\frac{dV_t}{V_t} = r_t\,dt + \sigma_v(\sqrt{1-\rho^2}\,dZ_t^1 + \rho dZ_t^2), \qquad (5.13)$$

where, as is usual now, σ_v is the volatility of assets returns, ρ the correlation factor of the unexpected movements in the assets returns with those of the interest rate, the second source of risk in this class of models, Z_t^1 and Z_t^2 two Brownian motions where Z_t^1 is specific to the assets process, and Z_t^2 the risk source related to the interest rate movements in the following stochastic differential equation:

$$dr_t = a(t)(b(t) - r_t)\,dt + \sigma_r(t)\,dZ_t^2, \qquad (5.14)$$

i.e. the short-term interest rate is assumed to follow a general Gaussian diffusion where $a(t)$, $b(t)$, and $\sigma_r(t)$ are some deterministic functions[11]. In this setting, the dynamics of the credit riskfree bond are well known and given by

$$\frac{dP(t, T)}{P(t, T)} = r_t\,dt - \sigma_p(t, T)\,dZ_t^2, \qquad (5.15)$$

where σ_p is a deterministic function of time thanks to the particular specification of dr_t. More precisely, it can be shown that[12]

$$\sigma_p(t, T) = \sigma_r(t) \int_t^T \exp\left(-\int_t^u a(s)\,ds\right) du. \qquad (5.16)$$

Other assumptions include the fact that the total value of the firm is assumed to be independent of its capital structure, i.e. that the values of assets and the value of the firm are identical in the sense of the first proposition of Modigliani–Miller. As in the sense of Black and Cox (1976) debtholders have the right to trigger bankruptcy should the value of assets fall below a threshold which is typically a safety covenant in this case. Let us define here this threshold as $K(t)$ and assume that it is exogenously specified as

---

[11]Similar to the Hull and White model, a generalization of the standard Ornstein–Uhlenbeck process.

[12]Taking a classical Vasicek model for the price of the bond, i.e. with constant parameters a, b, and σ_r, it is easy to show that equation (5.16) will lead to the same result for σ_p as the one obtained, knowing that the volatility of the bond price return can be expressed as a function of the elasticity of the bond price to the underlying interest rate. More precisely, we know that

$$\sigma_p = \sigma_r \frac{1}{P(t, T)} \frac{\partial P(t, T)}{\partial r}.$$

From the analytical solution of Vasicek for the bond price it is easy to show that

$$\sigma_p = \sigma_r \frac{1 - \exp(-a(T - t))}{a},$$

i.e. exactly the same solution as the one resulting from the computation of the integrals in equation (5.16).

$$K(t) = \alpha F P(t, T),$$

where F is the face value of debt and α some exogenous parameter between 1 and 0. It is suggested by Briys and de Varenne (1997) that the reliance of $K(t)$ on the price of a zero-coupon debt price $P(t, T)$ makes it stochastic. This may not be fully the case. Of course, it makes it more general. But, we have to remember that $P(t, T)$ is a well-known expectation value, even though it relies on a stochastic term structure of interest rates. Typically, we know that $0 \leqslant P(t, T) \leqslant 1$ with $P(T, T) = 1$. Therefore, even if the price $P(t, T)$ will evolve through time we know that its ending value will surely be 1. Moreover, Briys and de Varenne (1997) do not discuss in detail what is the effect of this assumption on the default behavior of the firm. And this is important; $P(t, T)$ is an increasing function as time $t \to T$. It means that a corporate bond with a smaller maturity will be priced respectively to a higher threshold than for a longer bond (see Figure 5.1)[13]. Overall, they justify their choice by taking back the evidence given by Franks and Torous (1994) that shows that, irrespective of the form of reorganization, the creditor receives some securities for the claim on the firm. Taking a fraction of some zero-coupon riskless bond as a proxy for this payoff, they argue that a typical safety covenant would be the one where the value of the firm would fall below this payoff, i.e. the payoff they would otherwise receive at default. And finally this assumption also has the advantage of ensuring that, by construction, the recovered value at default will not be higher than the assets value reached at default.

In conclusion, this choice of threshold is accommodating technically, while it is still not sure that the behavior of this barrier through time or for bonds with different maturities is fully desirable. In other words it must be understood that this assumption is not really a generalization alone because it has an undeniable *ad hoc* impact on the way default is triggered and therefore on the term structure of credit spreads stemming from the model. Nonetheless, they provide a significant development that can promote further thinking. Another proposition inspired notably from their work will be presented in later chapters.

We can deduce the impact of the different values that α can take; $\alpha = 0$ would make the present model revert to Merton's framework, although in a stochastic interest rates environment. In the absence of violations of the strict priority rule, $\alpha = 1$ would mean a riskless debt. It would mean that the value process would cease precisely at the discounted face value of debt at that time[14]; $F P(\tau_b, T)$ which is a nice property *a priori* since this is the value that is really owed at that time to debtholders, accounting for the time value of money[15]. This time value of money is given by the multiplication of F by $P(t, T)$, i.e. a credit-riskless discounting function which is coherent in this case with $\alpha = 1$.

To extend their model somewhat, Briys and de Varenne (1997) assume the possibility of some additional write-down (f) that may occur if the absolute priority rule (APR)

---

[13]It is sustainable to admit that, everything else being equal, the default of a shorter corporate bond is a less rare event than for an otherwise identical longer one, if issued at the same time.

[14]Let us denote that time as τ_b.

[15]There is no given reason, however, why this desired payoff should be included directly in the threshold itself and not in the payoff that would be obtained after an exogenous threshold would have been reached.

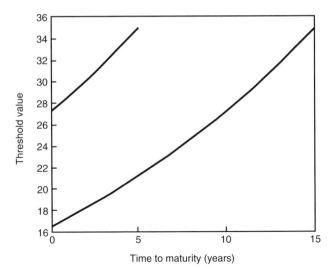

Figure 5.1 Behavior of the threshold values ($\alpha F\, P(t,\, T)$) for two different bonds issued by the same firm, one with a maturity of 5 years and the other with a maturity of 15 years. It is assumed a face value of 70, an α of 0.5, and a constant interest rate for the sake of simplicity of 5%

cannot be perfectly enforced[16]. To be complete there is no reference in Briys and de Varenne (1997) about the impact of this additional write-down on the value of the firm versus the value of assets. Moreover, they assume that we could have different f values depending on whether default happens prior to T because of the execution of the safety covenant, or whether default happens at T because of a final value of assets lower than F.

Thus, the different scenarios are as follows:

- No default prior to maturity. As earlier, if we denote τ_b as the first passage time of V_t under $K(t)$ the present scenario means that this threshold has not been reached. However, there is still the remaining possibility of an ending value V_T lower than F, the value owed to debtholders at maturity. Additionally, let us consider the APR write-down f_2. Thus, the payoff equation at T can look like

$$F\mathbf{I}_{\{\tau_b>T,\,V_T\geqslant F\}} + f_2\, V_T\mathbf{I}_{\{\tau_b\geqslant T,\,V_T<F\}}. \tag{5.17}$$

- Default prior to maturity. In this case V_t has reached $K(t)$ at $t=\tau_b$. With some specific APR write-down f_1, this gives

$$D_{\tau_b} = f_1 . V_{\tau_b} \tag{5.18}$$
$$= f_1\,\alpha\, F\, P(\tau_b,\, T).$$

It should be noted that it can be seen as somewhat inconsistent to assume two different values f_1 and f_2, because it conveys a problem of continuity. Imagine that the

---

[16]As noticed by Briys and de Varenne (1997), the bargaining process itself occurring at default when a firm tries to survive through some reorganization, causes the bondholders to incur some additional losses.

asset value of a firm ends up at T at a level $V_T = K(t) + \epsilon < F$, where ϵ is an infinitesimal step. Therefore, there is a default not because of the threshold but because of $V_T < F$. In that case, a ratio f_2 is applied. Suppose now the case $V_T = K(t) - \epsilon$. There is a default at T because of the threshold that has been reached. In that case, a ratio f_1 is considered. Because of an infinitesimal difference you could be better off in one scenario relative to the other, since $f_1 \neq f_2$. The economic sense of this problem may be difficult to grasp even though the generalization to several values is interesting in principle. Notice, though, that the above-mentioned problem would certainly induce gaming of the participants. Both default cases, because of their possible proximity, should give the same final payoff at T.

Looking at the overall value of the debt from the maturity point taking equations (5.17) and (5.18) together, we can write the following expression:

$$D_T = F\mathbf{I}_{\{\tau_b \geqslant T, V_T \geqslant F\}} + f_2 V_T \mathbf{I}_{\{\tau_b \geqslant T, V_T < F\}}$$
$$+ \exp\left(\int_{\tau_b}^{T} r_s\, ds\right) f_1 \alpha\, F\, P(\tau_b, T)\mathbf{I}_{\{\tau < T\}} \tag{5.19}$$

It can be seen in equation (5.19) that, thanks to the inclusion in the threshold of $P(t, T)$, we have the term $P(\tau_b, T)$ that is exactly the inverse of $\exp\left(\int_{\tau_b}^{T} r(s)\, ds\right)$ since the realized spot rates are known at T. These two terms will vanish allowing us to avoid the problem of knowing when the early default has been precisely triggered. Thus, we will recover the typical barrier option pricing problem, that is "some payoff at maturity if no prior touch of the barrier, no matter when it has exactly arrived".

Equation (5.19) from time t would then be

$$D_t = E_t\left[\exp\left(-\int_{t}^{T} r_s\, ds\right)(F\mathbf{I}_{\{\tau_b \geqslant T, V_T \geqslant F\}}\right.$$
$$\left. + f_2 V_T \mathbf{I}_{\{\tau_b \geqslant T, V_T < F\}} + f_1 \alpha\, F\mathbf{I}_{\{\tau_b < T\}})\right] \tag{5.20}$$

Thanks to some technical derivations, namely the change of numeraire, the time change, and the application of the reflection principle, Briys and de Varenne (1997) obtain the following closed-form solution[17]:

$$D_t = F\, P(t, T)\left[1 - P_E(l_t) + \frac{q_t}{l_t}P_E\left(\frac{q_t^2}{l_t}\right) - (1 - f_1)\frac{1}{l_t}(N(-d_3) + q_t N(-d_4))\right.$$
$$\left. - (1 - f_2)\frac{1}{l_t}(N(d_3) - N(d_1) + q_t(N(d_4) - N(d_6)))\right], \tag{5.21}$$

where

$$l_t = \frac{F\, P(t, T)}{V_t},$$

$$q_t = \frac{K(t)}{V_t} = \frac{\alpha\, F\, P(t, T)}{V_t},$$

---

[17]See Briys et al. (1998) for a more detailed presentation of this model.

with

$$d_1 = -\frac{\ln(l_t)}{\Sigma(t, T)} + \frac{1}{2}\Sigma(t, T) = d_2 + \Sigma(t, T),$$

$$d_3 = -\frac{\ln(q_t)}{\Sigma(t, T)} + \frac{1}{2}\Sigma(t, T) = d_4 + \Sigma(t, T),$$

$$d_5 = -\frac{\ln(q_t^2/l_t)}{\Sigma(t, T)} + \frac{1}{2}\Sigma(t, T) = d_6 + \Sigma(t, T),$$

and

$$\Sigma(t, T)^2 = \int_t^T [\sigma_v^2 + 2\rho\sigma_v\sigma_p(u, T) + \sigma_p(u, T)^2]\, du$$

$P_E(l_t)$ and $P_E(q_t^2/l_t)$ are two particular European put options with a maturity T such that

$$P_E(l_t) = -\frac{1}{l_t}N(-d_1) + N(-d_2),$$

$$P_E\left(\frac{q_t^2}{l_t}\right) = -\frac{l_t}{q_t^2}N(-d_5) + N(-d_6).$$

A development of the technicalities underlying the derivation of such a problem in another setting is provided in Chapter 19. For the current setting an extensive presentation is being made in Briys et al. (1998).

5.5.2 Credit Risk Measures

Analogously to what has been derived for the Saá-Requejo and Santa Clara case, the yield on this corporate bond, assuming a generic face value $F = 1$ can be computed as

$$y_c(t, T) = -\frac{\ln D(t, T)}{T - t}$$

$$= -\frac{1}{T-t}\ln\left(P(t, T)\left(1 - P_E(l_t) + \frac{q_t}{l_t}P_E\left(\frac{q_t^2}{l_t}\right) - (1-f_1)\frac{1}{l_t}(N(-d_3) + q_tN(-d_4))\right.\right.$$

$$\left.\left. - (1-f_2)\frac{1}{l_t}(N(d_3) - N(d_1) + q_t(N(d_4) - N(d_6)))\right)\right)$$

$$= -\frac{1}{T-t}\ln(P(t, T)) + \left[-\frac{1}{T-t}\ln\left(1 - P_E(l_t) + \left(\frac{q_t}{l_t}\right)P_E\left(\frac{q_t^2}{l_t}\right)\right.\right.$$

$$\left.\left. - (1-f_1)\frac{1}{l_t}(N(-d_3) + q_tN(-d_4)) - (1-f_2)\frac{1}{l_t}(N(d_3) - N(d_1) + q_t(N(d_4) - N(d_6)))\right)\right]$$

where the second term of this equation is the corporate credit spread.

As with Merton's model, the advantage of such an elegant final solution is that it is easy to decompose into well-known components. In the present case l_t corresponds to the so-called quasi-debt ratio of Merton, i.e. a debt ratio where the forward price of the asset value is considered instead of the current one. Analogously, q_t is simply an early default ratio. Moreover, equation (5.21) can be decomposed into four components:

1. A zero-coupon bond, plus
2. The traditional put-to-default at maturity of Merton, plus
3. A long position in a European put because of the possibility of early default triggered by the default covenant, plus
4. Two last terms accounting for the additional cost driven by the potential violations of the APR.

Graphically it is interesting to see that this framework produces the same kind of hump-shaped credit spread structures with respect to the maturity than in Merton's case for similar parameter values. Additional effects are evident because of the effect of the barrier level and the f values.

To conclude on stochastic interest models, note that Wang (1999) proposes a CIR extension of Merton (1974) that has the advantage of not being exposed to the Vasicek limitations of most of the models presented here, a line of research that will surely be extended in the future.

5.6 REFERENCES

Artzner, Philippe and Freddy Delbaen, 1992, "Credit Risk and Prepayment Option", *Astin Bulletin*, **22** (1), 81–96.

Black, F. and J. C. Cox, 1976, "Valuing Corporate Securities: Some Effects of Bond Indenture Provisions", *Journal of Finance*, **31** (2), 351–67.

Brennan, M. J. and E. S. Schwartz, 1979, "A Continuous Time Approach to the Pricing of Bonds", *Journal of Banking and Finance*, **3**, 133–55.

Briys, Eric and François de Varenne, 1997, "Valuing Risky Fixed Rate Debt: An Extension", *Journal of Financial and Quantitative Analysis*, **32** (2), June, 239–49.

Briys E., M. Bellalah, H. M. Mai and F. de Varenne, 1998, *Options, Futures and Exotic Derivatives: Theory, Application and Practice*, John Wiley, 1st edn, 459 pp.

Chan, K. C., Andrew Karolyi, Francis Longstaff and Anthony Sanders, 1992, "An Empirical Comparison of Alternative Models of the Short-Term Interest Rate", *Journal of Finance*, **47** (3), July, 1209–27.

Coleman, Thomas S., Lawrence Fisher and Roger G. Ibbotson, 1992, "Estimating the Term Structure of Interest Rates from Data that Include the Prices of Coupon Bonds", July, Yale. *Working Paper*.

Cossin, D. and H. Pirotte, 1997, "How Well do Classical Credit Risk Models Fit Swap Transaction Data", *European Financial Management*, **4** (1), March, 65–78.

Cox, J. C., J. E. Ingersoll and S. A. Ross, 1985, "A Theory of the Term Structure of Interest Rates", *Econometrica*, **53**, 385.

Das, Sanjiv and Peter Tufano, 1996, "Pricing Credit Sensitive Debt when Interest Rates, Credit Ratings and Credit Spreads are Stochastic", *Journal of Financial Engineering*, **5** (2), June.

Duffie, Darrell and Ken Singleton, 1999, "Modeling Term Structures of Defaultable Bonds", *Review of Financial Studies*. Special 1999, **12**(4), 687–720.

Fama, Eugene F., 1984, "Term Premiums in Bond Returns", *Journal of Financial Economics*, **13**, 529–46.

Franks, J. R. and W. Torous, 1989, "An Empirical Investigation of US Firms in Reorganization", *The Journal of Finance*, **44**, 747–69.

Franks, Julian R. and Torous, Walter N., 1994, "A Comparison of Financial Recontracting in Distressed Exchanges and Chapter 11 Reorganizations", *Journal of Financial Economics*, **35** (3), June, 349–70.

Hübner, Georges, 1997, "A Two-Factor Gaussian Model of Default Risk", *Working Paper*, INSEAD, January, 97/23, 84 pp.

Hull, John and A. White, 1990, "Pricing Interest Rate Derivative Securities", *Review of Financial Studies*, **3**, pp. 573–92.

Iben, Th. and R. Litterman, 1991, "Corporate Bond Valuation and the Term Structure of Credit Spreads", Spring.

Ikeda, Masayuki, 1995, "Default Premiums and Quality Spread Differentials in a Stochastic Interest Rate Economy", *Advances in Futures and Options Research*, **8**, 175–202.

Jones, E. Philip, Scott P. Mason and Eric Rosenfeld, 1984, "Contingent Claims Analysis of Corporate Capital Structures: An Empirical Investigation", *The Journal of Finance*, **39** (3), July, 611–27.

Karatzas, I. and S. Shreve, 1988, *Brownian Motion and Stochastic Calculus*, Springer, Berlin, Heidelberg, New York.

Litzenberger, R. H., 1992, "Swaps: Plain and Fanciful", *The Journal of Finance*, **47**, 831–50.

Longstaff, F. and E. Schwartz, 1994, "A Simple Approach to Valuing Risky Fixed and Floating Rate Debt and Determining Swap Spreads", *Working Paper* (#22–93), Anderson Graduate School of Management, University of California, April 1994.

Longstaff, F. and E. Schwartz, 1995b, "A Simple Approach to Valuing Risky Fixed and Floating Rate Debt", *Journal of Finance*, **50** (3), July, 789–819.

Merton, R. C., 1974, "On the Pricing of Corporate Debt: The Risk Structure of Interest Rates", *Journal of Finance*, **29**, May.

Pirotte, H., 1999a, "Implementing a Structural Valuation Model of Swap Credit-Sensitive Rates", *Working Paper*, Institute of Banking and Finance, Ecole des HEC, University of Lausanne, December, 32 pp.

Ramaswamy, K. and S. Sundaresan, 1986, "The Valuation of Floating-Rate Instruments", *Journal of Finance*, **17**, February, 251–72.

Rich, Don, 1994, "The Mathematical Foundations of Barrier Option-Pricing Theory", *Advances in Futures and Options Research*, **7**, 267–311.

Saá-Requejo, Jesús and Pedro Santa Clara, 1997, "Bond Pricing with Default Risk", *Working Paper*, John E. Anderson Graduate School of Management, UCLA, Los Angeles, 23 pp.

Shimko, David, Naohiko Tejima and Donald Van Deventer, 1993, "The Pricing of Risky Debt When Interest Rates are Stochastic", *Journal of Fixed Income*, September, 58–65.

Titman, Sheridan and Torous, Walter N., 1989, "Valuing Commercial Mortgages: An Empirical Investigation of the Contingent-Claims Approach to Pricing Risky Debt", *Journal of Finance*, **44**(2), 345–73, June.

Vasicek, O., 1977, "An Equilibrium Characterization of the Term Structure", *Journal of Financial Economics*, **5**, 177–88.

Wei, D. G. and D. Guo, 1997, "Pricing Risky Debt: An Empirical Comparison of the Longstaff and Schwartz and Merton Models", *The Journal of Fixed Income*, September, 9–28.

6
Advanced Considerations on Bankruptcy Endogeneity

6.1 THE CORPORATE OPTIMAL DEBT POLICY AND CREDIT SPREADS WITH ENDOGENOUS BANKRUPTCY DECISIONS: LELAND AND TOFT (1996)

Determining the optimal debt policy for a firm or the optimal leverage on a specific contract has long been a challenge of financial theory. The determination of the optimal leverage level for a firm corresponds to the endogenous choice of its bankruptcy level or credit risk. Merton Miller and Franco Modigliani have produced in the 1950s and 1960s the basis of modern capital structure theory by showing, through an arbitrage argument that transformed financial theory, that under a set of assumptions, capital structure does not matter, i.e. the value of the firm is not affected by the level of debt in the firm. In other words, they have found that there is no optimal debt policy. Later refinements (tax considerations, bankruptcy cost considerations, agency or conflict of interest issues, Jensen and Meckling, 1976, and information issues, Myers and Majluf, 1984) have identified clearly why and how a certain debt policy can be better than another. Nonetheless, these refinements have had a major drawback: because their basis is conceptual but not mathematical, they have not been operational. Indeed, the intuitions they provide are interesting. But they do not give any quantifiable result, no numerical impact that would allow practitioners to actually determine whether such a debt policy is better than another. Or to determine the actual debt policy overall. More recent models based on the structural analysis seen previously are getting closer to an answer.

It is clear that the value of corporate debt and capital structure are linked. In structural models, credit-risky debt cannot be priced without knowing the capital structure of the corresponding firm. But, correspondingly, capital structure cannot be optimized without knowing the effect of leverage on debt prices. Credit-risky debt valuation models, at least the structural models, should thus provide us a first step toward a meaningful theory of optimal capital structure, by making the link between cost of debt and capital structure finally explicit mathematically.

Ignoring the asset substitution problem, where shareholders of high debt firms may choose too risky activities in order to transfer some value from the bondholders to themselves, and assuming a static debt structure, one can then use the structural models to capture the effects of taxes, bankruptcy costs and bond covenants on the optimal bankruptcy decision of the firm and thus on its optimal capital structure. This is what Leland obtains in his 1994 *Journal of Finance* paper. Brennan and Schwartz had worked out a related but much less detailed analysis in 1979. Note that these models can be a good base to examine the transfer of wealth from bondholders to shareholders via risk shifting under a number of environments (secured debt, covenants presence, etc.).

Leland and Toft (1996) relax the assumption of infinite life debt of Leland (1994) in order to study both the impact of the choice of debt amount on the capital structure and thus on credit spread, but the impact of the maturity of the debt chosen as well. This leads to interesting considerations, not only on firm leverage but also on true bond duration as well as on the convexity of bond prices, elements of interest to practitioners in the field.

As in other structural models, debt and equity are contingent claims on the value of the assets of the company. In particular, equity is assimilated to a call option with a strike price that arises from an endogenously determined bankruptcy decision. This decision depends notably on the amount of debt outstanding and its maturity.

As usual, assume that the value of the assets follows the process:

$$dV = (\mu V - \delta)dt + \sigma V dz \qquad (6.1)$$

with δ the constant fraction of value paid out to security holders.

Assume also a constant interest rate of r, and with the usual notations, we have, using risk-neutral valuation and denoting $f(s, V, B)$ the density (F the cumulative density) of the first passage time s to B (bankruptcy barrier) from V when the drift is $(r - \delta)$ that:

$$D(0, T) = \int_0^T e^{-rs} c(T)[1 - F(s, V, B)]ds + e^{-rT} p(T)[1 - F(T, V, B)]$$

$$+ \int_0^T e^{-rs} \varphi(T)Bf(s, V, B)ds \qquad (6.2)$$

with $c(T)$ the continuous coupon rate, $p(T)$ the principal repayment for debt of maturity T, and $\varphi(T)$ the fraction of the assets accruing to the debt in case of default (recovery rate). The first term of the equation represents the expected discounted value of the coupon flow, the second the expected discounted value of the principal repayment, the third the expected discounted value of the fraction of the assets accruing to debt of maturity T in the event of bankruptcy.

Using results from Harrison (1985) and Rubinstein and Reiner (1991) yields a closed-form solution for risky debt value when B, the bankruptcy barrier, is constant:

$$D(0, T) = \frac{c(T)}{r} + e^{-rT}\left[p(T) - \frac{c(T)}{r}\right][1 - F(T, V, B)] + \left[\varphi(T)B - \frac{c(T)}{r}\right]G(T) \quad (6.3)$$

with

$$F(T) = N(h_1(T)) + \left[\left(\frac{V}{V_B}\right)^{-2a} N(h_2(T))\right] \qquad (6.4)$$

$$G(T) = \left(\frac{V}{V_B}\right)^{-a+z} N(q_1(T)) + \left(\frac{V}{V_B}\right)^{-a-z} N(q_2(T)),$$

where

$$q_1(T) = \frac{-b - z\sigma^2 T}{\sigma\sqrt{T}},$$

$$q_2(T) = \frac{-b + z\sigma^2 T}{\sigma\sqrt{T}},$$

$$h_1(T) = \frac{-b - a\sigma^2 T}{\sigma\sqrt{T}},$$

$$h_2(T) = \frac{-b + a\sigma^2 T}{\sigma\sqrt{T}},$$

$$a = \frac{r - \delta - (\sigma^2/2)}{\sigma^2},$$

$$b = \ln(V/B),$$

$$z = \frac{[(a\sigma^2)^2 + 2r\sigma^2]^{1/2}}{\sigma^2}.$$

A debt structure that has time-independent service payments is consistent with a constant endogenously determined bankruptcy level B. Assume, for example, that the firm continuously issues a constant principal amount of new debt of maturity T. New bond principal is issued at a rate of $p = P/T$, where P is the total principal value of all outstanding bonds that also pay a constant coupon rate $c = C/T$, where C is the total coupon payments for all outstanding bonds per year. Yearly debt service payments are then time independent (of value $C + P/T$). The hypothesis of a constant endogenously determined bankruptcy level then holds.

Using these assumptions, one can then calculate total debt value at any point in time from the above formula:

$$\text{Total debt value} = \int_0^T D(s, T)\, ds. \tag{6.5}$$

Total firm value is then given by

$$\text{Total firm value} = V + \tau C/r \left[1 - \left(\frac{V}{B}\right)^{-x} \right] - \alpha B \left(\frac{V}{B}\right)^{-x}, \tag{6.6}$$

where $x = a + z$, α is the fraction of firm asset value lost in bankruptcy, and τ is the tax rate. (Note that a separate barrier can be built for tax benefits, so that the model can allow for tax benefits to be lost before bankruptcy.)

We have that

$$\text{Total equity value} = \text{total firm value} - \text{total debt value.} \tag{6.7}$$

We can now determine the endogenous bankruptcy level B as the minimum level at which equityholders are ready to continue injecting capital into the firm. At this level, the future expected risk-neutral appreciation of the value of their equity E just equals the cash paid in. Below this level, equity appreciation from future cash flows insufficiently compensates equityholders and they would rather relinquish control than receive nothing (under the absolute priority rule the model can be extended to violations of priority rules where shareholders still obtain some value in bankruptcy). Mathematically, it means that B is determined by the smooth pasting condition:

$$\left(\frac{\partial E(V, B, T)}{\partial V} \right)_{V=B} = 0. \tag{6.8}$$

The solution for the bankruptcy level (which will affect debt prices and thus credit spreads) is

$$B = \frac{(C/r)(A/(rT) - B) - AP/(rT) - \tau Cx/r}{1 + \alpha x - (1 - \alpha)B}, \tag{6.9}$$

where

$$A = 2a\,e^{-rT}N(a\sigma\sqrt{T}) - 2zN(z\sigma\sqrt{T}) - \frac{2}{\sigma\sqrt{T}}\,n(z\sigma\sqrt{T}) + \frac{2\,e^{-rT}}{\sigma\sqrt{T}}\,n(a\sigma\sqrt{T}) + z - a,$$

$$B = -\left(2z + \frac{2}{z\sigma^2 T} \right)N(z\sigma\sqrt{T}) - \frac{2}{\sigma\sqrt{T}}\,n(z\sigma\sqrt{T}) + z - a + \frac{1}{z\sigma^2 T},$$

where $n(\cdot)$ is the standard normal density function.

It is interesting to check that B is not time dependent (because of the debt payment chosen, which reflects a static debt structure). On the other hand, it depends on the maturity of the debt, a fact not accounted for in the exogenous bankruptcy barrier models seen previously (such as that of Longstaff and Schwartz, 1995).

We can now substitute for B in the previous equations and obtain the value of debt, of equity, and of credit spreads with an endogenous bankruptcy barrier. One interesting consequence of the model is that debt maturity will impact the capital structure choice and thus the value of the debt.

The model thus allows for pricing of debt with endogenous bankruptcy. It also gives the value of the overall firm depending on its capital structure. The model can thus be used as a basis for optimal capital structure determination, as well as for credit spread determination. Obviously some refinements seen in previous models can be added to this framework (notably stochastic interest rates, stochastic recovery rates, etc.), but numerical analysis will then be necessary (rather than obtaining closed-form solutions).

Note that many of the results obtained by previously described structural models hold. Highly levered firms have bonds that obtain a hump-shaped term structure of credit spreads. Low leverage firms, on the other hand, have monotonously increasing credit spreads as a function of maturity. This classical result, first described in Merton (1974), confirms that credit spreads may not increase with maturity of the bond, when the bonds are of low quality. Another classical result is that credit spreads fall when the default-free interest rate rises.

Another interesting analysis of the model bears on the *duration of bonds*. Duration measures the percentage change of a bond price in response to a parallel shift to the yield curve increasing all interest rates by a set amount (e.g. 1%). The concept of duration is based on default-free bonds but is often used for corporate, default-risky bonds too. It is thus important to check its validity in the use of corporate bonds. In other words, we are concerned whether duration captures somewhat closely the change in bond value in response to a change in the default-free interest rate.

The model can be used to calculate the change in value of a bond when interest rates change by 1% and compare it to the Macaulay duration formula:

$$Dur = \frac{\int_0^T s e^{-Rs} c\, ds + T e^{-rT} p}{\int_0^T e^{-Rs} c\, ds + e^{-rT} p} = \frac{1 - e^{-RT}}{R} \tag{6.10}$$

with R the yield ($= c/p$).

The percentage change in bond prices obtained from the model is very close to the numbers obtained from the above duration formula when credit spreads are small (less than 10 bp). When leverage increases, though, differences become important. For spreads of 200 bps, under realistic environmental assumptions, duration can be reduced by two-thirds. With large credit spreads (e.g. 400 bps under the same environment), bond prices increase with the riskfree rate, thus obtaining negative duration (that cannot be accounted for in the above duration formula).

Fixed-income traders should certainly amend duration hedging, duration matching, and all other duration-based risk management or security selection techniques with models of the type proposed here when they deal with default-risky (high credit spreads) bonds.

Most fixed-income traders go beyond duration-based techniques though, as it is well known that convexity also affects hedging and selection techniques. Convexity is a measure of the curvature of the relationship between changes in interest rates and changes in prices (it is the second derivative impact, or the gamma impact referred to by options traders). Portfolios of the same duration may have different convexities and thus behave quite differently for medium or large interest rate changes. In general though, riskless debt is a convex function of the default-free interest rate. In other words, duration falls when the interest rate increases (and vice versa). Using the previous model of risky debt shows that riskiness of debt affects convexity. Changes in convexity when credit spreads increase are important, particularly for long-term debt. When credit spreads become large (i.e. when debt becomes riskier), convexity is reduced and may even become negative, with the relationship between interest rate changes and relative bond price changes actually becoming concave. Convexity can become concavity with risky debt. It is clear then that dynamic strategies using convexity of riskfree bonds cannot be used straightforwardly for credit-risky, fixed-income instruments. Models such as the one proposed here or the others presented previously give the information necessary for trading, hedging, and selecting fixed-income instruments facing credit risk.

Harbonn and Keller (1999) attempt an implementation of the Leland and Toft model on the multinational Nestlé's capital structure. They obtain results that are satisfying, knowing they take as given a short maturity of debt (one year) as Nestlé is mainly short-term debt levered. As shown in Figure 6.1, they find a somewhat underlevered structure that corresponds to intuition, but proves it in a way that was not available before the existence of this model.

The model shows that after the acquisition of Rowntree in 1988, Nestlé has been underlevered by an average of 6.24%, leading to a loss in value of close to 1% of levered firm value.

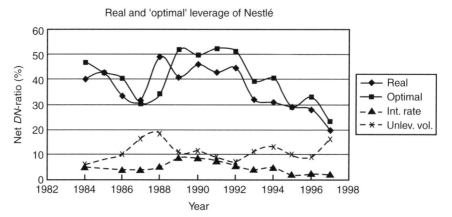

Figure 6.1 Comparison between the real and "optimal" net leverage of Nestlé, and evolution of the underlying parameters, riskfree interest rate and estimated volatility of the unlevered assets using the Ronn and Verma (1986) procedure. Reprinted with authorization from Harbonn and Keller (1999)

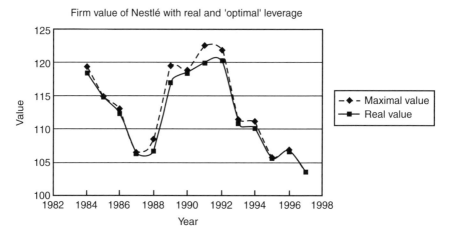

Figure 6.2 Comparison of the firm value between the real and "optimal" net leverage of Nestlé. Reprinted with authorization from Harbonn and Keller (1999)

The impact on the value of the firm of not using the model optimal capital structure can indeed be obtained, as shown in Figure 6.2.

6.2 STRATEGIC DEFAULT AND DEBT DESIGN: ANDERSON AND SUNDARESAN (1996)

The understanding of the bankruptcy decision and its impact on debt prices can be pushed further than the smooth pasting condition of Leland and Toft. Several models have recently addressed this issue, incorporating some of the empirical and theoretical advances of modern corporate finance. Some empirical facts are not necessarily well accounted for by previously presented models:

1. Bankruptcies are costly (both in terms of direct costs, such as lawyers' fees and in terms of indirect costs such as disrupted relationships to suppliers).
2. Bankruptcy procedures leave considerable scope for strategic (opportunistic) behaviors from the different claimants.
3. Deviations from absolute priority of claims are common. For example, common stockholders tend to obtain nonnull outcomes even when senior claims are not fully paid off.

These results appear for example in the recent financial economics empirical literature in Weiss (1990) and in Franks and Torous (1994). Game-theoretical models have also approached the problem, and several papers have modelled default and renegotiation around bankruptcy as a game (see for example Aghion and Bolton, 1992). Models of this kind provide for a better analysis of the bankruptcy decision itself, but do not usually rely on explicit pricing methodologies and realistic assumptions that would allow them to obtain directly usable results. Anderson and Sundaresan (1996) attempt to combine the contingent claim approach and its powerful pricing methodology with the better design of the bankruptcy decision via a game framework. Mella-Barral and Perraudin (1997) offer a different model on a closely related problematic. They build on the real option analogy and use as an underlying process the output price of the firm (assumed to follow a geometric Brownian motion (GBM)). They further assume some constant costs to the firm. After bankruptcy there is a loss of efficiency, and new owners can generate output with proportionately lower prices and higher costs. Alternatively, the firm can be liquidated for a set amount. The authors find closed-form solutions in the specific case of perpetual bond contracts paying a constant coupon. The solution is described by several threshold values for the output price. Above a critical level, the debtholder is paid the coupon specified in the original contract. Under a lower critical level, the firm is liquidated and the bondholder obtains the collateral value. In between the two critical levels of output prices, there is a strategic default in which equityholders make bondholders take-it-or-leave-it offers of coupon payments and debt values approximate to the firm's liquidation value. If bankruptcy is imminent, this strategic bankruptcy can happen even when the firm is making significant profits. The methodology has the advantage of yielding closed-form solutions, but does not fit naturally with the framework of the structural models (notably by using output prices rather than firm values) and is restricted to unrealistic debt structures (perpetual bonds, while we have seen above the impact of maturity choices; no sinking funds, no calls or convertibles, etc.). The bankruptcy process is also somewhat implicit in the model and cannot be made more realistic, more fitting to actual situations, without an overhaul of the model that would require important financial engineering.

We focus here on the Anderson and Sundaresan approach as it is more in line with the other models we have seen up until now. This model is explicit in the bankruptcy game described and uses a binomial approach that can be easily extended to many different forms of debt. It has the disadvantage of not yielding closed-form solutions (but an extension of the model provides for a parallel continuous-time approach to the same problem).

6.2.1   The Framework

The model assumes that an owner–manager–equityholder has a project of stochastic value V_t (with the usual binomial representation, where V_{t+1} can take either the value uV_t or dV_t with $d = 1/u$). The project requires a financing of D (the best way to finance it is assumed to be with a debt contract). The debt contract calls for payments CS_t made in period t with a maturity of T. Cash flows f_t are assumed to be proportional to the project value at the same time ($f_t = \beta V_t$).

There is a cost K to transfer ownership of the project from the equityholder to the bondholders so that the collateral value for bondholders at any point in time t is truly of $V_t - K$. Then:

- When the project is going on, there is a realization of the cash flow f_t. At any time t, the owner–manager chooses a debt servicing level S_t where $S_t \in [0, f_t]$. In other words, the manager proposes a payment to debtholders that is less than the cash flows of the firm. Clearly, if the payment proposed is larger than the debt service contracted ($S_t \geqslant CS_t$), the game continues to the next period. If it is less than the debt service contracted ($S_t < CS_t$), there are two possibilities. Either the bondholders accept the debt service proposed and the game continues. Or they reject the debt service and force the liquidation that occurs with a cost K, so that they obtain $V_t - K$. The subgame perfect equilibria of the game will be determined by the best responses of the owner and the creditor. The equilibrium is analyzed recursively starting at T.

- At maturity T, the firm value is V_T and the owner selects a debt service payment S_T. (a) If $S_T \geqslant CS_T$ the game ends there with the debt fully paid. (b) If $S_T < CS_T$, and if the creditor accepts payment, the respective payoffs to the debtholders and to the owner are

$$(S_T, \ V_T - S_T). \tag{6.11}$$

If the creditor rejects payment, the respective payoffs are:

$$(\max(V_T - K, 0), \ 0). \tag{6.12}$$

Thus the creditor accepts if $S_T \geqslant \max(V_T - K, 0)$ and rejects if otherwise.
The best response of the owner is to set

$$S_T = CS_T \quad \text{if } V_T - K > CS_T, \tag{6.13}$$

and

$$S_T = \max(V_T - K, 0), \text{ otherwise.} \tag{6.14}$$

We thus obtain a debt value of

$$D(V_T) = \min(CS_T, \ \max(V_T - K, 0)), \tag{6.15}$$

and an equity value of

$$E(V_T) = V_T - \min(CS_T, \ \max(V_T - K, 0)). \tag{6.16}$$

There is strategic debt service here as when

$$V_T > CS_T > V_T - K, \tag{6.17}$$

the owner–manager underperforms the debt contract and pays something between CS_T and $V_T - K$. In other words, it underperforms but not by enough to provoke costly legal action.

- At time $t < T$, the reasoning is similar, assuming that the project has not yet been closed.

   If $S_t < CS_t$, there are two possibilities: (a) If the creditor rejects, s/he gets $\max(V_t - K, 0)$. (b) If he or she accepts, s/he gets the payoff:

$$S_t + \frac{pD(u\,V_t) + (1-p)D(d\,V_t)}{r},$$

where r is one plus the riskfree rate and p is the time independent martingale probability mapping the value and cash flow processes $p = [r(1-\beta) - d]/(u-d)$.

S/he can thus compare the payoffs to make the decision. The best response of the owner–manager is determined in this light. For high firm values ($V_T - K > CS_T$), the owner simply matches the contract. For low firm values, the owner–manager pays less than contracted but enough to avoid liquidation. If liquidation does not occur:

$$S(V_t) = \min\left(CS_t,\ \max\left(0,\ \max(V_T - K, 0) - \frac{pD(u\,V_t) + (1-p)D(d\,V_t)}{r}\right)\right). \tag{6.18}$$

The value of debt and equity follows:

$$D(V_t) = S(V_t) + \frac{pD(u\,V_t) + (1-p)D(d\,V_t)}{r}, \tag{6.19}$$

$$E(V_t) = f_t - S(V_t) + \frac{pE(u\,V_t) + (1-p)E(d\,V_t)}{r}.$$

In some states though, cash flows will be insufficient to avoid a forced liquidation. So that if $f_t < S(V_t)$,

$$D(V_t) = \max(0,\ \min(V_t - K,\ CS_t + P_t)), \tag{6.20}$$

$$E(V_t) = V_t - K - D(V_t).$$

The states in which default occurs are determined endogenously here through a clear (and easily modifiable) game. Liquidation may occur before the end of the project. The *ex post* inefficiency of costly forced liquidation implies an *ex ante* inefficiency: since the debt capacity of the project may be lower than its full asset value (due to the costly forced liquidation) the firm may pass up positive NPV projects, as it is not able to raise enough money.

Note that tax shields can be integrated in the model to incorporate the valuable tax dimension of the negotiations and values. Full valuation using the methodology can then be applied to straight debt contracts or easily to more complex contracts.

6.2.2 Applications

Consider the classical coupon bond issue where

$$CS_t = \begin{cases} cP & \text{for } t < T, \\ (c+1)P & \text{for } t = T. \end{cases} \tag{6.21}$$

The Merton (1974) model corresponds to

$$CS_t = \begin{cases} 0 & \text{for } t < T, \\ P & \text{for } t = T. \end{cases} \tag{6.22}$$

Two cases can then be considered:

1. $K = 0$: this is the actual Merton model. No gaming occurs.
2. $K > 0$: yield spreads exceed those found with $K = 0$, for all degrees of leverage. Strategic debt may thus explain a good part of the credit spread observed.

Notice that the model can also be used for security design. For example, the manager can choose the contractual features of the contract so as to minimize the inefficiencies that emerge in the associated equilibrium.

Consider a coupon bond with an amortization schedule with a grace period of g and principal amount amortized in t of A_t. So that the *ex ante* contracted debt service is

$$CS_t = cP_t + A_t, \tag{6.23}$$

with

$$P_t = P_{t-1} - A_{t-1},$$
$$A_t = 0 \text{ for } t \leqslant g,$$
$$A_t = \frac{P}{T-g}.$$

The manager's problem is thus:

$$\max_{c, T, P, g} E(V, \sigma, \beta, r, K, \tau)$$

such that the value of debt $D(V, \sigma, \beta, r, K, \tau)$ is at least equal to the funding requirement.

It is important to consider tax effects for security design, hence the derivation of a similar formula to the previous ones that incorporates the tax rate τ_c.

In this context, equation (6.20) has to be modified in case of no forced liquidation into

$$E(V_t) = (f_t - S(V_t))(1 - \tau_c) + \frac{pE(u V_t) + (1 - p)E(d V_t)}{r}$$

for $t < T$.

At maturity

$$E(V_T) = (1 - \beta)V_T + \left(f_T - S(V_T)\frac{cP}{(1+c)P} \right)(1 - \tau_c) - S(V_T)\frac{P}{(1+c)P}$$

and in case of forced liquidation tax liabilities are deducted before calculating liquidation values.

The solution to this security design problem may be *ex ante* inefficient in the sense that it may well result in forced liquidations in the future and that positive NPV projects may be bypassed. It is nonetheless optimal in the sense that it maximizes shareholder value under some financing constraint.

Some interesting results arise from immediate numerical application of the model. For example, in general, optimal debt contracts typically require partial repayments of principal prior to maturity (bullet loans are not optimal). If the grace period g is too low, amortization starts too early (which reduces tax shields). If the grace period g is too high, the debt service payments toward the end of the life of the bond are relatively heavy, which creates a greater risk of provoking liquidation. The optimal solution obtained from the program described above balances both. Optimal debt design thus arises from a balancing of tax shields and forced liquidations, in a nontrivial way, as strategic debt servicing occurs. The model could easily be extended (in binomial form) to more complex contracts. Anderson et al. (1996) provide a continuous-time interpretation of the exact same framework.

Anderson and Sundaresan (1999) propose a general model of perpetual coupon bond that encompasses as special cases slightly modified versions of Merton (1974), Leland (1994), and Anderson et al. (1996). They use US corporate bond aggregate data to estimate the different models between 1970 and 1996. They find better fitting from the endogenous bankruptcy models (Leland, 1994, and Anderson et al. 1996, with the latter obtaining still better results in their study), but overall good fitting of the structural models on these aggregate data. They can then use the models to derive default probabilities that appear sensible compared to historical Moody's data.

6.3 REFERENCES

Aghion, Philippe and Patrick Bolton, 1992, "An Incomplete Contracts Approach to Financial Contracting", *The Review of Economic Studies*, **59** (3), July, 473–94.

Anderson, R. and S. Sundaresan, 1996, "Design and Valuation of Debt Contracts", *Review of Financial Studies*, **9**, 37–68.

Anderson, R., S. Sundaresan and P. Tychon, 1996, "Strategic Analysis of Contingent Claims", *European Economic Review*, **40** (3–5), April, 871–81.

Beneish, Messod D. and Eric Press, 1995, "Interrelation Among Events of Default", *Contemporary Accounting Research*, Summer.

Franks, Julian R. and Walter N. Torous, 1994, "A Comparison of Financial Recontracting in Distressed Exchanges and Chapter 11 Reorganizations", *Journal of Financial Economics*, **35** (3), June, 349–70.

Harbonn, Claude and Peter Keller, "Optimal Capital Structure, the Case of Nestlé". Masters Thesis, MBF, University of Lausanne.

Harrison, Michael J., 1985, *Brownian Motion and Stochastic Flow Systems*, Wiley Series in Probability and Mathematical Statistics, John Wiley.

Jensen, M. and J. Meckling, 1976, "Theory of the Firm: Managerial Behavior, Agency Cost and Ownership Structure", *Journal of Financial Economics*, **3**, 305.

Leland, Hayne E., 1994, "Corporate Debt Value, Bond Covenants and Optimal Capital Structure", *Journal of Finance*, **49** (4), September, 1213–52.

Leland, H. E. and K. B. Toft, 1996, "Optimal Capital Structure, Endogenous Bankruptcy and the Term Structure of Credit Spreads", *Journal of Finance*, **51** (3), July, 987–1019.

Longstaff, Francis and Eduardo Schwartz, 1995b, "A Simple Approach to Valuing Risky Fixed and Floating Rate Debt and Determining Swap Spreads", *Journal of Finance*, **50** (3), July, 789–819.

Mella-Barral, P. and W. Perraudin, 1997, "Strategic Debt Service", *The Journal of Finance*, **52** (2), June, 531–56.

Merton, Robert C., 1974, "On the Pricing of Corporate Debt: The Risk Structure of Interest Rates", *The Journal of Finance*, **29**, May, 449–70.

Myers, S. and M. Majluf, 1984, "Corporate Financing and Investment Decisions When Firms Have Information that Investors Do Not Have", *Journal of Financial Economics*, **13**, 187–222.

Rubinstein, M. and E. Reiner, 1991, "Breaking down the Barriers", *Risk Magazine*, **4**, 28–35.

Ronn, Ehud and Avinash Verma, 1986, "Pricing Risk-Adjusted Deposit Insurance: An Option-Based Model", *The Journal of Finance*, **41** (4), September, 871–95.

Shalev, Jonathan, 1997, "Loss Aversion Equilibrium", *Working Paper*, CORE, Université Catholique de Louvain-la-Neuve, Belgium, 26 pp.

Weiss, L. A., 1990, "Bankruptcy Resolution: Direct Costs and Violation of Priority of Claims", *Journal of Financial Economics*, **27**.

Yan, Ying, 1997, "Credit Rationing, Bankruptcy Cost, and the Optimal Debt Contract for Small Business", *Working Paper*, Federal Reserve Bank of Cleveland, no. 2, March, 24 pp.

7

Reduced-form/Mixed Approaches

Structural models rely upon the balance sheet of the borrower and the bankruptcy code then to derive endogenously the probability of default and the credit spreads based on no-arbitrage arguments, making some additional assumptions on the recovery and the model for default-free interest rates.

In opposition, *reduced-form models* work directly on the probability of default as an exogenous variable calibrated to some data, their name coming from this reduction of the credit economics behind the probability of default. The calibration of this probability of default is made with respect to ratings agencies' data or to financial markets series acting as state variables. Indeed in the latter case, Duffie and Lando (1997) have proposed a framework that allows the connection of the exogenous probability of default back to the balance sheet information.

To summarize, reduced-form approaches view the credit event as a perfectly unpredictable event. The probability of arrival of this event is in fact a hazard rate, also called intensity rate since it represents the frequency of defaults that can occur in a given time interval, even though we are interested in the first. In this setting, default follows a jump process: the event of default, state 1, is an unpredictable discontinuity in the life of the firm, state 0. This predictability feature will be further discussed in section 7.5.

There is a large literature on this kind of approach[1], going from the most simple hazard rate case up to the most complex model issues where the hazard rate is shown to be linked to the recovery rate at default. Some of these models are in discrete time, others are in continuous time.

The final motivation in this approach is to be able to model the credit spread as a particle that must be added to the riskfree rate term structure. As an example, consider a default-free discount bond. Under the local expectations hypothesis, the bond price should satisfy, at any instant t,

$$E_t\left[\frac{dP}{P}\right] = r\,dt, \tag{7.1}$$

where $E_t[\cdot]$ is the expectations operator. The integration of default risk to this scheme by the authors of reduced-form models has in fact already been introduced by Ramaswamy and Sundaresan (1986) in the context of corporate floating-rate debt[2]. If we denote the credit spread defined at t as π for a given maturity T, then the floating rate is shown to satisfy a modified version of equation (7.1):

---

[1] *Reduced-form* models include the works of Iben and Litterman (1991), Das and Tufano (1996), Jarrow et al. (1997), Lando (1998), Duffie and Singleton (1999), Madan and Unal (1995) and Schönbucher (1997) among others.

[2] In this context, modeling credit uncertainty in the structure is crucial. In effect, the coupon stream associated with the floating-rate note would become known if a deterministic model of the interest rate term structure was used and the floating-rate note would be equivalent to standard fixed rate debt.

$$E_t \left[\frac{dF}{F} \right] = (r_t + \pi) \; dt, \tag{7.2}$$

As will be emphasized through the contribution of Duffie and Singleton (1999) in section 7.3, the main advantage of being able to model the defaultable term structure of interest rates in the terms of equation (7.2), is to allow the use of the standard modeling of the term structure of riskfree interest rates and the techniques of estimation already developed into this new context. Thus, the main objective of "reduced-form" models is to provide sufficient motivation, in a nonarbitrage universe, that justify the formalization of equation (7.2).

Again, the traditional assumptions already introduced in Chapter 3 apply here, mainly:

Assumption 1   Markets are frictionless (no taxes, trading fees, etc.) and trading takes place continuously.

Assumption 2   There are no arbitrage opportunities in the sense that participants are rational and competitive. They prefer more wealth to less, particularly when risk is also greater.

We will start by the discrete approach of Jarrow and Turnbull which is very useful as an initial approach, although restricted to discrete derivations that are less desirable, from an analytic point of view, than the continuous-time one.

7.1   JARROW AND TURNBULL (1995): THE DISCRETE APPROACH

As for any reduced-form model, Jarrow and Turnbull's model is consistent with the existence of a zero-coupon government bond term structure and a zero-coupon corporate bond term structure for a given credit standing class. The main argument of Jarrow and Turnbull for this discrete approach is that many kinds of payoffs can be reproduced and priced while taking advantage of existing calibration techniques of the term structure of interest rates.

First of all, they suppose that a riskfree term structure of interest rates can be easily identified with traded discount bond prices $P_t(T)$. Corporate discount bonds $D_t(T)$ are also traded for a given credit standing category which is identified through a rating class. Let us consider a particular firm of this class, say firm F.

Using the riskfree rate as the numeraire, Jarrow and Turnbull build a discrete lattice for the default-free term structure as well as for the defaultable one and show that, under this numeraire, they can obtain unique "risk-neutral" or martingale probabilities such that the value of the defaultable instrument can be expressed as a discounted expectation under the risk-neutral measure.

Remember now that our objective is to end up with a corporate term structure that has similar properties to the default-free one. Jarrow and Turnbull suppose this and compare it to the problem of an exchange rate. Let us imagine that the firm owes you $1. If the firm is not perfectly riskfree, there is a positive probability that the delivery of this promised dollar would end up to be less than $1. It is like an exchange of $1 with a foreign exchange exposure. And the price for this risk, perfectly correlated with the amount of credit risk, will be the required credit spread

$$D_t(T) = P_t^f(T)e_t^f, \tag{7.3}$$

conditional on no prior default, where

- $D_t(T)$ is the value today, at t, of \$1 promised at T.
- $P_t^f(T \mid s)$ is the time t price of the promised dollar to be received at T, for certain in firm F's "money"[3]. $P_t^f(T)$ can be considered as the time value of money in the foreign currency; s depends on the state of default/no-default of the firm.
- e_t^f is the true spot exchange rate prevailing at time t to convert F's money into "domestic" money.

It should be noted that the foreign currency analogy has a great pedagogical insight. It helps in understanding why we cannot write directly $D_t(T) = P_t(T)e_t^f$. We first work out the analysis in terms of the foreign numeraire and then we will show how martingale probabilities are obtained in order to be able to use the observed riskfree term structure[4].

Let us first present the binomial lattice for the default-free term structure. In this riskfree universe, "risk-neutral" or martingale probabilities q^P apply directly such that the default-free discount bond price can experience up and down movements with a q^P and $(1 - q^P)$ probability, respectively. Using Jarrow and Turnbull's terminology, a *term structure with discount bonds* existing for all maturities in a range $T \in [1, 2]$ could be therefore presented by the following tree:

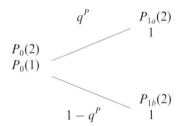

The term structure of *spot* interest rates will follow directly as the inverse of the bond prices for a remaining time to maturity of 1:

$$r_0 = \frac{1}{P_0(1)+} \qquad
\begin{array}{l}
q^P \qquad r_{1a} = \dfrac{1}{P_{1a}(2)} \\[2em]
1 - q^P \qquad r_{1b} = \dfrac{1}{P_{1b}(2)}
\end{array}$$

The martingale probabilities will exist and will be unique as long as the conditions for the AOA are respected, i.e. in particular that at any node the value can be computed as the discounted expectation under the risk-neutral probabilities of the values at the branches going from that node. Also, the price of a bond is bounded by 0 and 1. Therefore

---

[3] In firm F's money, $V_t(T)$ is credit riskfree.
[4] The technology of foreign currency options is a well-developed area so that we can apply some of its results here.

$$0 < P_0(1) < 1, \tag{7.4}$$
$$0 < P_{1b}(2) < P_{1a}(2) < 1,$$

since the investor is rational and prefers more to less wealth, and

$$P_0(2) = \frac{[q^P P_{1a}(2) + (1 - q^P) P_{1b}(2)]}{r_0}.$$

Until here, either the structure of yields or either the structure of discount bond prices can be fitted to one of the classical models of interest rates (see Appendix).

Now, suppose that we refine the previous trees and allow for positive martingale probabilities of default, denoted by q^D and a given delivery payoff given default, δ. First, let us construct the lattice for the so-called "exchange rate", independently from the structure of interest rates:

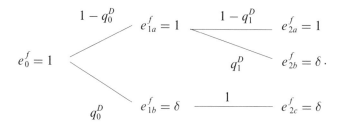

The next step is to join both lattices into a kind of quadrinomial tree with the "foreign" structure of interest rates. The parameter s in $P_t^f(T \mid s)$ takes on the values 1 or δ depending on the state of default/no-default. Therefore we have

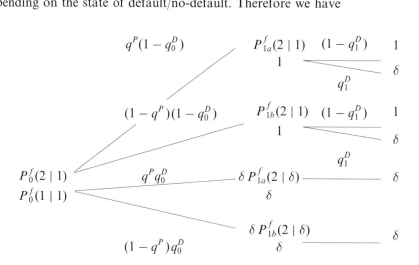

In a way similar to that of equation (7.4), we can provide the no-arbitrage conditions such that the martingale probabilities also exist in our combined tree and are still unique:

$$P^f_{1a}(2 \mid 1) = \frac{[(1 - q^D_1) + q^D_1 \delta]}{r_{1a}},$$

$$P^f_{1b}(2 \mid 1) = \frac{[(1 - q^D_1) + q^D_1 \delta]}{r_{1b}},$$

$$P^f_{1a}(2 \mid \delta) = \frac{1}{r_{1a}},$$

$$P^f_{1b}(2 \mid \delta) = \frac{1}{r_{1b}},$$

and

$$P^f_0(1 \mid 1) = \frac{q^P(1 - q^D_0) + (1 - q^P)(1 - q^D_0) + \delta\, q^P q^D_0 + \delta(1 - q^P) q^D_0}{r_0}$$

$$= \frac{(1 - q^D_0) + \delta\, q^D_0}{r_0},$$

$$P^f_0(2 \mid 1) =$$

$$\frac{q^P(1 - q^D_0) P^f_{1a}(2 \mid 1) + (1 - q^P)(1 - q^D_0) P^f_{1b}(2 \mid 1) + P^f_{1a}(2 \mid \delta)\delta\, q^P q^D_0 + P^f_{1b}(2 \mid \delta)\delta(1 - q^P) q^D_0}{r_0},$$

and

$$P_1(2) > D_{1a}(2),\ D_{1b}(2) > \delta P_1(2),$$
$$P_0(2) > D_0(2) > \delta P_0(2).$$

Returning to expression (7.3), and with the previous derivations, we can show that

$$D_t(T) = P_t(T)\, E^Q_t[e^f_t], \tag{7.5}$$

which means that the value of the promised \$1 (after "delivery") corresponds to the discounted value of the cash flows under the risk-neutral measure, i.e. using the derived martingale probabilities. This allows us to discount at the riskfree time value of money. The credit spread is therefore simply $E^Q_t[e^f_t]$. As Jarrow and Turnbull show, equation (7.5) allows us to estimate recursively the credit risk parameters q^D_0 and q^D_1 (and so forth for longer maturities and more underlying factors) once known as δ, $D_t(T)$, and $P_t(T)$.

The discrete framework introduced by Jarrow and Turnbull is very flexible in the sense that their discrete tree can be used to price the following:

- Coupon-bearing corporate bonds. Whenever the $D_t(T)$s are available for different terms, we can straightforwardly use these $D_t(T)$s as new discounting factors in place of the riskfree $P_t(T)$s. Thus, the complete expression for the price of a coupon-bearing bond will be

$$D^c_t(T) = \sum_{i=1}^{n} D_t\left(i\frac{T}{n}\right) c_s + D_t(T)M, \tag{7.6}$$

for n coupon payments in T years, where M is the reimbursement value or face value of the bond for the F issuer in our case.

Using the lattice presented above and the martingale approach, this result obtains because each $D_t(T)$ in the credit term structure is implicitly derived on the condition of no prior default. Then, it suffices to apply this structure to any cash flow stream to obtain the overall price, as for any other standard market pricing though the NPV approach.

Hence the framework can applied to:

- Futures and options on corporate bonds,
- American options, by backward induction and control at each node of the tree, and
- Vulnerable options by introducing a second stochastic process for the issuer of the option.

7.2   JARROW, LANDO AND TURNBULL (1997)

Their model is a Markov model for the term structure of credit spreads based on the earlier Jarrow and Turnbull (1995) paper, but linking the default process to a discrete state space Markov chain in credit ratings, i.e. the life of a firm is viewed as a journey through the possible rating states where one of them is an absorbing state.

The advantage of this model rests in its great flexibility to calculate the parameters to observable data and to use it for many purposes: pricing and hedging of bonds with embedded options, OTC vulnerable derivatives, pricing and of credit derivatives and credit-risk management.

The main assumption of the present approach is that ratings are an accepted indicator of the creditworthiness. Even if ratings have been shown to be quite unreactive to new information, they are the key variable on which the payoff of certain credit derivatives is dependent.

Again, here the default is an exogenous process that does not require dependence on the underlying assets of the firm. The advantage of such methods against the structural ones is that we can restrict the calibration to the available observables; there is no particular economic requirement.

Additional characteristics with respect to Jarrow and Turnbull (1995) are as follows:

- Different seniorities are examined through different recoveries.
- It is easily implementable in the context of any specification of the term structure of risk-free interest rates.
- Historical transition probabilities between rating categories are used for the estimation of martingale probabilities.

It should be noted that for a matter of feasibility of the implementation, they assume the process for the default risk and for the risk-free term structure to be independent.

7.2.1   The Model

Although Jarrow et al. (1997) provide a discrete and a continuous setting, we will only present hereafter the discrete case because it will help us in showing up the fundamental intuitions.

- There exists a frictionless economy with a finite horizon τ.
- Risk-free zero-coupon bonds (of price $p(t, T)$) and risky zero-coupon bonds as well as a riskfree money market account are continuously traded.

- There exists an equivalent martingale measure Q such that all risk-free and risky bond prices normalized by the money market account are martingales (markets are complete and arbitrage-free).
- Forward rates are defined in discrete time as

$$f(t, T) \equiv - \ln \left(\frac{p(t, T+1)}{p(t, T)} \right). \tag{7.7}$$

Under this construction, the instantaneous interest rate $r(t)$ is equivalent to $f(t, t)$.

- The money market account value is similarly given by

$$B(t) = \exp \left(\sum_{i=0}^{t-1} r(i) \right). \tag{7.8}$$

- Under the assumption of complete and arbitrage-free markets, we have the following relationship:

$$p(t, T) = \tilde{E}_t \left(\frac{B(t)}{B(T)} \right). \tag{7.9}$$

- Let $v(t, T)$ represent the price of a risky zero-coupon bond τ^*, the random time at which bankruptcy takes place, and δ the recovery rate related to the seniority, then

$$v(t, T) = \tilde{E}_t \left(\frac{B(t)}{B(T)} (\delta \, \mathbf{I}_{\{\tau^* \leqslant T\}} + \mathbf{I}_{\{\tau^* > T\}}) \right). \tag{7.10}$$

It must be noticed that since δ is an exogenous constant, the resulting stochastic structure of credit spreads will be independent of the recovery rate (as in Jarrow and Turnbull, 1995).

- If bankruptcy happens prior to t it is assumed that bondholders receive for certain δ at maturity, i.e.

$$v(t, T) = \delta \, \tilde{E}_t \left(\frac{B(t)}{B(T)} \right) = \delta \, p(t, T).$$

This is important since it means that at bankruptcy, the term structure of credit spreads is that of the default-free interest rates.

- Under the assumption mentioned above of independence between the realization of τ^* and the default-free term structure of interest rates, we can write

$$v(t, T) = \tilde{E}_t \left(\frac{B(t)}{B(T)} \right) \tilde{E}_t (\delta \, \mathbf{I}_{\{\tau^* \leqslant T\}} + \mathbf{I}_{\{\tau^* > T\}}) \tag{7.11}$$

$$= p(t, T)(\delta + (1 - \delta) \tilde{Q}_t(\tau^* > T)),$$

where $\tilde{Q}_t(\tau^* > T)$ is the probability under the $\tilde{Q}_t$ measure that the firm will not default before the maturity.

- Now the contribution of Jarrow et al. (1997) articulates around the specification of the bankruptcy process as the first hitting time of a time-homogeneous Markov chain. This Markov chain is modeled on a finite state space S consisting in the credit rating classes $\{1, \ldots, K\}$, where the $K - 1$ class is the lower credit rating class, while class K is the absorbing state representing the bankruptcy state. This Markov chain is specified by a $K \times K$ transition probability matrix:

$$Q = \begin{pmatrix} q_{11} & q_{12} & \cdots & q_{1K} \\ q_{21} & q_{22} & \cdots & q_{2K} \\ \vdots & & & \\ q_{K-1,1} & q_{K-1,2} & \cdots & q_{K-1,K} \\ 0 & 0 & \cdots & 1 \end{pmatrix}, \tag{7.12}$$

where all transition probabilities are positive and $q_{ii} \equiv 1 - \Sigma_{\substack{j=1 \\ i \neq j}}^{K} q_{ij}$ for all i. Each of the q_{ij} probabilities represent the probability of getting from class i to class j in one period of time. The last line represents the probabilities attached to the absorbing state: the probability of leaving this state is always null and the probability of staying in this state is 1. Estimates of these transition probabilities can be found in the reports of Moody's or Standard and Poors. As mentioned by Jarrow et al., nonzero probabilities tend to concentrate on the diagonal for a 1-year transition matrix since a movement of more than one rating class is quite improbable.

- We can then compute the transition matrix under the equivalent martingale measure maintaining the assumptions of complete and arbitrage-free markets. This matrix is written as

$$\tilde{Q}_{t,t+1} = \begin{pmatrix} \tilde{q}_{11}(t, t+1) & \tilde{q}_{12}(t, t+1) & \cdots & \tilde{q}_{1K}(t, t+1) \\ \tilde{q}_{21}(t, t+1) & \tilde{q}_{22}(t, t+1) & \cdots & \tilde{q}_{2K}(t, t+1) \\ \vdots & & & \\ \tilde{q}_{K-1,1}(t, t+1) & \tilde{q}_{K-1,2}(t, t+1) & \cdots & \tilde{Q}_{K-1,K}(t, t+1) \\ 0 & 0 & \cdots & 1 \end{pmatrix}, \tag{7.13}$$

where again

$$\tilde{q}_{ij}(t, t+1) \geqslant 0, \forall i, j, i \neq j \text{ and } \tilde{q}_{ii}(t, t+1) \equiv 1 - \sum_{\substack{j=1 \\ i \neq j}}^{K} \tilde{q}_{ij}(t, t+1).$$

Additionally

$$\tilde{q}_{ij}(t, t+1) > 0, \text{ iff } q_{ij} > 0 \text{ for } 0 \leqslant t \leqslant \tau - 1.$$

- Jarrow et al. assume that the risk premia adjustments must be consistent with the following credit rating process under the martingale probabilities:

$$\tilde{q}_{ij}(t, t+1) = \pi_i(t) q_{ij}, \forall i, j, i \neq j,$$

where $\pi_i(t)$ is a deterministic function of time that ensures that

$$\tilde{q}_{ij}(t, t+1) \geqslant 0, \forall i, j, i \neq j \text{ and } \sum_{\substack{j=1 \\ i \neq j}}^{K} \tilde{q}_{ij}(t, t+1) \leqslant 1$$

for $i = 1, \ldots, K$.

Using the matrix notation, this collapses to

$$\tilde{Q}_{t,t+1} - I = \Pi(t)[Q-1],\tag{7.14}$$

where I is the $K \times K$ identity matrix and $\Pi(t)$ is a $K \times K$ diagonal matrix such that its diagonal consists of $\pi_1(t), \ldots, \pi_{K-1}(t), 1$. The $\pi_i(t)$ represent the risk premiums that, given the conditions just after expression (7.13), should all be positive.

- $\tilde{Q}_t(\tau^* > T)$ can now be computed. Assuming that the notation $\tilde{q}_{ij}(0, n)$ expresses the probability of going from class i to class j in n steps then the n-step transition matrix $\tilde{Q}_{0,n}$ verifies

$$\tilde{Q}_{0,n} = \tilde{Q}_{0,1} \cdot \tilde{Q}_{1,2} \cdots \tilde{Q}_{n-1,n}.\tag{7.15}$$

It follows that

$$\tilde{Q}_t^i(\tau^* > T) = \sum_{j \neq K} \tilde{q}_{ij}(t, T) = 1 - \tilde{q}_{iK}(t, T)\tag{7.16}$$

Now, knowing the i class of the firm whose bond is being priced, we can write

$$v^i(t, T) = p(t, T)(\delta + (1 - \delta)\tilde{Q}_t^i(\tau^* > T)).\tag{7.17}$$

- The forward rate for the risky zero-coupon bond for a firm in the i class is derived then as

$$f^i(t, T) \equiv -\ln\left(\frac{v^i(t, T+1)}{v^i(t, T)}\right),$$

i.e.

$$f^i(t, T) \equiv f(t, T) + I_{\{\tau^* > T\}} \ln\left(\frac{\delta + (1-\delta)\tilde{Q}_t^i(\tau^* > T)}{\delta + (1-\delta)\tilde{Q}_t^i(\tau^* > T+1)}\right).\tag{7.18}$$

- $f^i(t, T) - f(t, T)$ is the forward credit spread and in bankruptcy, given the earlier remark at the beginning of this presentation, $f^K(t, T) = f(t, T)$.
- In spot rate terms, with $T = t$,

$$r^i(t) \equiv r(t) + I_{\{\tau^* > T\}} \ln\left(\frac{1}{1 - (1-\delta)\tilde{q}_{iK}(t, t+1)}\right).\tag{7.19}$$

The same developments are provided in the continuous-time case. Jarrow et al. also provide a whole discussion on how to hedge jumps in risky bonds and vulnerable options on the term structure of credit risk spreads. The ultimate question that is being answered is how to select the risk premiums $\pi_i(t)$ such that the theoretical pricing formula fits an observed term structure of zero-coupon defaultable bonds. This procedure is recursive and makes use of expressions (7.11), (7.14), (7.15), and (7.16).

7.3 THE CONTINUOUS CASE: DUFFIE AND SINGLETON (1999)

Reduced-form models are not easy to encompass since, on one hand they obey to the same general idea, but on the other hand because they do not rely on actual economic behavior of the firms the degrees of freedom for formulations are large. A typical example is the recent reconciliation of the reduced-form methodology with the structural approach, by Duffie and Lando (1997)[5].

Duffie and Singleton (1999) represent the main stream of a line of reduced-form models that were originally inspired by the founding paper of Madan and Unal (1993).

In Duffie and Singleton (1999) default is again treated as an unpredictable event governed by a hazard rate process. The only difference relies on the continuous-time specification of the claim subject to default. The objective is to end up with an expression for the price at time 0 of a risky corporate zero-coupon bond D paying \$1 ($X = 1$) at maturity T, of the form

$$D_0(T) = E_0^Q \left[\exp\left(-\int_0^T R_u \, du \right) X \right],$$ (7.20)

where E_t^Q is the risk-neutral expectation at time t conditional on no prior default, and R is a default-adjusted short-term rate process computed as the sum of a short-term rate process r and a credit risk premia π, i.e. a *risk-neutral mean-loss rate*[6], that can vary through time

$$R = r + \pi.$$ (7.21)

As equation (7.20) proposes, this will enable us to price the claim as if it was riskless. The existence of the risk-neutral expectation assumes that we have complete markets and a no-arbitrage setting in which all securities can be priced in terms of r, the rate of return on a riskfree asset, and the equivalent martingale measure Q[7].

Moreover, under this risk-neutral measure, π_t must still be characterized. In particular, it will be defined such that it is exogenous in the sense that it does not depend on the defaultable claim itself. Subsection 7.3.1 provides motivation for this.

This independence has the advantage of permitting us to use standard term structure modeling of interest rates and substitute R for r. On the other hand, we can think of some cases where dependency of π on D can be desirable as is the case with swap contracts where the legs are of asymmetric counterparty credit quality. Many studies of defaultable swap pricing have focused on the pricing of each leg separately, as with a back-to-back loan which would be consistent with the hypothesis of independency, but not sustainable with respect to the real risk borne by the counterparties. Duffie and Huang (1996) have been the first in proposing a swap valuation scheme that takes into consideration this credit risk asymmetry which is therefore nonlinear in the underlying promised exchange of cash flows (as analyzed in the chapter on swap credit risk pricing).

---

[5] They show how the reduced-form approach can be consistent with the issuer's balance sheet modeling h_t in terms of the dynamics of the asset value of the firm, the volatility of assets and the level of the threshold value.

[6] Following the definition by Duffie and Singleton (1999).

[7] The concept of equivalent martingale measure has been already presented in the discrete-time section. A more detailed presentation of the existence and uniqueness property of equivalent martingale measures in continuous time can be found in Harrison and Kreps (1979) and Harrison and Pliska (1981).

7.3.1   Motivations for $R_t = r_t + \pi_t$

A rigorous demonstration with the specification of π_t, related to equation (7.20), is provided by Duffie and Singleton (1999).

Assumption 1   Suppose we are in presence of a defaultable claim of market value $D(T)$, that promises a payment F_T at the maturity date T. At any time t before this maturity, let us define:

- h_t, as the risk-neutral probability at time t, of a default on a short time interval between t and $t+1$, conditional on no prior default up to t.
- φ_t, as the recovery in dollars, should default occur at t.
- r_t, as the riskfree short-term interest rate at t.

Conditional on no prior default up to t, the market value of this claim at t should be the present value of receiving φ_{t+1} if default occurs, or D_{t+1} in the other case:

$$D_t = \mathrm{e}^{-r_t} h_t E_t^Q(\varphi_{t+1}) + \mathrm{e}^{-r_t}(1 - h_t) E_t^Q(D_{t+1}). \tag{7.22}$$

By recursion, from T back to time t,

$$D_t(T) = E_t^Q \left[\sum_{j=0}^{(T-t)-1} h_{t+j} \mathrm{e}^{-\Sigma_{k=0}^j r_{t+k}} \varphi_{t+j+1} \prod_{l=0}^{j} (1 - h_{t+l-1}) \right]$$

$$+ E_t^Q \left[\mathrm{e}^{-\Sigma_{k=0}^{(T-t)-1} r_{t+k}} F_T \prod_{l=1}^{T-t} (1 - h_{t+l-1}) \right] \tag{7.23}$$

The evaluation of this equation is complex because of the joint "term" behavior of h, φ, r. Duffie and Singleton (1999) propose, therefore, different alternatives for the formulation of φ that will help us back in simplifying its risk-neutral expectation. The first alternative is to assume a so-called "recovery-of-market-value" (RMV).

Assumption 2   Suppose that the recovery is a fraction of the market value of our contract, i.e. 1 minus our loss function L (conditional on the information set available at t):

$$E_t^Q(\varphi_{t+1}) = (1 - L_t) E_t^Q(D_{t+1}). \tag{7.24}$$

Substituting this back into equation (7.23) leads us to a simple transition equation similar to equation (7.22).

$$D_t = \mathrm{e}^{-r_t} h_t (1 - L_t) E_t^Q(D_{t+1}) + \mathrm{e}^{-r_t}(1 - h_t) E_t^Q(D_{t+1})$$

$$= [\mathrm{e}^{-r_t} - \mathrm{e}^{-r_t} h_t L_t] E_t^Q(D_{t+1})$$

$$= E_t^Q(\mathrm{e}^{-\Sigma_{k=0}^{(T-t)-1} R_{t+k}} F_T)$$

where $\mathrm{e}^{-R_t} = \mathrm{e}^{-r_t} - \mathrm{e}^{-r_t} h_t L_t$. For annual rates but short time periods, the approximation of $\mathrm{e}^{-c} = 1 - c$ can be used, leading to

$$R_t \simeq r_t + h_t L_t - r_t h_t L_t$$

which is approximately

$$R_t \simeq r_t + h_t L_t \qquad (7.25)$$

leading to Duffie and Singleton's initial proposition with equation (7.21)[8].
Some observations:

- In continuous time, equation (7.25) is precise under certain technical conditions.
- The RMV formulation can accommodate for correlation between the set (h_t, L_t) and the default-free term structure. Particular evidence about the reasons that should require the specification of such a correlation, is presented in Chapter 12. Broadly, recovery data seem to show a link with the stage of the business cycle. On the other hand, even if we do not allow any correlation between the recovery and the dynamics of the riskfree interest rate, it suffices to let the recovery rate vary over time to induce some correlation between the resulting credit spreads of the model and the interest rate (see Das and Tufano, 1996).

  Even if some studies propose a fitting of this pair to financial markets or macroeconomic data, and firm-specific factors, the original reduced-form approach, such as the present one of Duffie and Singleton (1999), does not constrain the dependence on a theoretical model of default rates as is the case with structural approaches.
- The exogeneity of h and L can misspecify some contractual features in some cases. Typically, the fractional recovery can be thought of as being endogenous if the contract fixes the market value of the recovery at default.
- There can be another type of difficulty with the parametrization of h and L: the expected loss rate can switch from one regime to another in swap contracts depending on the reciprocal "moneyness" and "nonmoneyness" of both counterparties through time. Unfortunately, accounting for this leads to a nonlinear difference equation and it should be solved with numerical methods.
- "Liquidity" effects can arise because the defaulted market security experiences a loss of attractiveness. This adds some carrying cost or "holding risk", l. Duffie and Singleton propose in this case to adapt R to be a "default-and-liquidity" adjusted short-rate process

$$R = r + hL + l.$$

- Since the T-Bill rate is often used in place of the pure riskfree short rate, one could treat it as a spread to the latter, including some effects such as repo specials. Assuming that these effects are absorbed together with carrying costs into a new l^* variable, this would modifiy our earlier equation for R into

$$R^* = r^* + hL + l^*$$

---

[8]Hübner (1997b) gives a simpler intuition of $R = r + hL$. Imagine a discrete binomial tree: in an interval Δt, the firm can default with a risk-adjusted probability $h\Delta t$ with a risk-adjusted recovery of $(1 - L)$ times the market value of the security, called "recovery-of-market-value" (RMV). Then, the proper discount rate R must satisfy

$$\frac{1}{1 + R} = \frac{1}{1 + r}[h\Delta t(1 - L) + (1 - h\Delta t)].$$

Taking the limit as $\Delta t \to 0$, it follows that $R = r + hL$.

7.3.2 Generalization to Continuous Time

Now that we have studied π_t, we must prove that the discounted expectation of a risky security can be priced simply by replacing r_t with R_t as proposed in equation (7.20).

Setup

Consider that all public information up to time t is integrated into current market prices and that any information at a time $t + \epsilon$ will be instantaneously integrated, so that any process at time t governing the evolution of an exogenous variable will be said to be $\mathcal{F}_t$-adapted. There also exists a riskfree asset through which one invested and roll-overed unit from time t will generate a market value at time T of $\int_t^T r_u du$. There is no need, at this point, to make any assumption on the underlying model specifying the structure of rs.

Imagine that a creditor has a general claim U_t at t on an outcome X. Suppose also that this claim can be "stopped" at τ, the first of two different times: either at maturity T, by the contractual settlement, or at a date τ_b between 0 and T if the counterparty reaches default. Assuming that this variable is $\mathcal{F}_t$-measurable, that is X is known and contemporaneous with the information set available at t, and that there exists an equivalent martingale measure Q with respect to r, the ex-dividend price process of U_t, contingent on (X, τ) is defined by

$$\begin{cases} U_t = 0, & \text{for } t \geqslant \tau \\ U_t = E_t^Q \left[\exp\left(-\int_t^\tau r_u du \right) Z \right] & \text{for } t < \tau \end{cases}$$

where $\tau = \min(\tau_b, T)$. Duffie and Singleton separate this defaultable claim into a pair of subcontingent claims $((X, T), (X', \tau_b))$, where X is the payment made at T if no default occurs previously and X' is the payment upon default such that

$$Z = X \mathbf{I}_{\{T < \tau_b\}} + X' \mathbf{I}_{\{T \geqslant \tau_b\}}$$

where X can be thought of as the payoff of a zero-coupon bond maturing at T ($X = 1$) or some other contingent claim based on market prices, an OTC option or credit derivative on an underlying bond where the issuer of the derivative will not be the same as that of the underlying bond.

If therefore τ_b has a risk-neutral default hazard-rate process h, the process of Λ which is 0 before default and 1 afterwards[9], can be written as

$$d\Lambda_t = (1 - \Lambda_t) h_t \, dt + dM_t,$$

where M is a martingale under Q.

To characterize and prove the existence of the unique arbitrage-free price process U_t at time t, we need a specification for the payoff at default, X'. In our first RMV formulation, we suppose that the payoff is equivalent to the value of the security just prior to default, U_{t-}, minus some discount, L_t[10]:

---

[9] Thus, the analogy with a Dirac-delta function.

[10] See subsection 7.6.1 for a more precise exposition of the implications of this assumption.

$$X' = (1 - L_t)U_{t-} \tag{7.26}$$

where L_t is bounded by 1, and by now assumed predictable in the sense that we could estimate h_t and L_t based on the information available up to t.

While U is a function of r_t, the link is made with R_t, supposing that there exists a process D such that

$$U_t = D_t \text{ for } t \leqslant \tau_b.$$

In particular, $D_T = X$. Technical conditions on the existence of the intensity rate under Q can be found in Artzner and Delbaen (1995).

With an Exogenous Expected Credit Spread

It is proposed then to price the claim D as given by equation (7.20) based on

$$R_t = r_t + h_t L_t. \tag{7.27}$$

To verify this, suppose that we are interested in the gain process (price and accrued dividend), after discounting at the riskfree short-rate process $r(t)$. This discounted process, valued at t, should be a martingale under Q, such that

$$G_t = \exp\left(-\int_0^t r_u\,du\right)D_t(1 - \Lambda_t) + \int_0^t \exp\left(-\int_0^t r_u\,du\right)(1 - L_s)D_{s-}\,d\Lambda_s. \tag{7.28}$$

The first term is the discounted value of the security if no default has happened before t, and the second term is the discounted value upon default given the probability distribution of a default arrival at any instant dt between time 0 and t. Arbitrage-free pricing is ensured by the Q-martingale character of G and the boundary condition $V_T = X$ that allows us to relate equations (7.20) and (7.28).

Assumption 3 A major assumption and technical requirement for the following developments is that, although there may be unpredictable jumps in the behavior of the value of the security, they do not occur precisely at default, i.e. at τ_b. This means in particular that the uncertainty is perfectly unfolded once default is triggered. This condition is automatically satisfied in some contexts.

Given this assumption and expression (7.26), an application of Itô's lemma to equation (7.28) allows us to write

$$D_t = \int_0^t R_s D_s\,ds + m_t \tag{7.29}$$

for some Q-martingale[11].

In this setting, where h and L are exogenous processes, we can consider the value of a coupon-bearing bond as the sum of the values of each intermediate payment assuming no prior default for each of them. This, of course, is not the case when h and L are allowed to depend on the security itself.

---

[11]Uniqueness of the defaultable claim, the process U and the solution to equation (7.29) is proved.

Dependence on a Continuous-time Markovian State Variable

For the purpose of being able to relate the presented setting to continuous-time financial variables and to the modeling literature on default-free term structures, suppose that we can make the promised claim X and R depend on some underlying continuous state variable Y such that $X = g(Y_T)$ and $R_t = p(Y_t)$. Equation (7.20) can be then rewritten as

$$F_0(Y_t, T) = E_0^Q \left[\exp \left(-\int_0^T p(Y_u) \, du \right) g(Y_T) \mid Y_t \right]. \tag{7.30}$$

Indeed, suppose an n-dimensional $\mathbf{Y}$ process and that it can be expressed as

$$d\mathbf{Y}_t = \mu(\mathbf{Y}_t) dt + \sigma(\mathbf{Y}_t) dW_t,$$

where W_t is an n-dimensional Wiener process in Q.

Under some technical conditions, the straight application of the Feynman–Kac formula tells us that equation (7.30) implies that F solves the backward Kolmogorov PDE:

$$\mathcal{D}^{\mu,\sigma} F(\mathbf{y}, t) - p(\mathbf{y}) F(\mathbf{y}, t) = 0, \tag{7.31}$$
$$(\mathbf{y}, t) \in \mathcal{R}^n \times [0, T],$$

with the boundary condition that

$$F(\mathbf{y}, T) = g(\mathbf{y}), \, \mathbf{y} \in \mathcal{R}^n, \tag{7.32}$$

and

$$\mathcal{D}^{\mu,\sigma} F(\mathbf{y}, t) = \frac{\partial F(\mathbf{y}, t)}{\partial t} + \frac{\partial F(\mathbf{y}, t)}{\partial \mathbf{y}} \mu(\mathbf{y}) + \frac{1}{2} \text{trace} \left[\frac{\partial^2 F(\mathbf{y}, t)}{\partial \mathbf{y}^2} \sigma(\mathbf{y}, t) \sigma(\mathbf{y}, t)' \right]. \tag{7.33}$$

Dependence on a Jump-diffused State Variable

As Duffie and Singleton (1999) note, the continuous-time diffusion character of some instruments of low credit quality can be controversial. An example could be the Brady bonds. In turn, a hybrid jump-diffusion could be desired for Y. $\mathcal{D}^{\mu,\sigma}$ should then be replaced in equation (7.18) by the operator $\mathcal{D}^{\text{jump}}$:

$$\mathcal{D}^{\text{jump}} F(\mathbf{y}, t) = \mathcal{D}^{\mu,\sigma} F(\mathbf{y}, t) + \lambda(\mathbf{y}) \int_{\mathcal{R}^n} [F(\mathbf{y} + z, t) - F(\mathbf{y}, t)] \, d\nu^y(z), \tag{7.34}$$

where $\lambda: \mathcal{R}^n \to [0, \infty]$ determines the arrival intensity of jumps in $\mathbf{Y}$, under the risk-neutral probability measure, for each y, ν^y is a probability distribution for the jump size of $\mathbf{Y}$, z.

Endogenous Credit Spread

As has been stated earlier, the model would not be linear in the promised cash flows should R_t depend upon the price level of the security, i.e. h_t and L_t could depend on the price of the defaultable claim U_t.[12] This is the case when we allow for a recovery at

---

[12] The price of this claim just after default is $(1 - L_t)U_t$.

default of an exogenously specified fraction of the face value, denoted from now on by recovery of face value (RFV). The new risk-adjusted short-rate process could be rewritten as follows:

$$\hat{R}_t = p(\mathbf{Y}_t, U_t) = \hat{h}(\mathbf{y}, u)\hat{L}(\mathbf{y}, u) + \hat{r}(\mathbf{y}), \tag{7.35}$$

where hats above the parameters are used to differentiate them from previous specifications. Since, in a practical implementation, these parameters will be found by calibration, it is important to make the distinction from now on between the original exogenous definition and the actual one. Therefore, the price of any defaultable claim U_t at any point in time t is given by

$$F_t(\mathbf{Y}_t, T) = E_t^Q \left[\exp \left(-\int_t^T p(\mathbf{Y}_u, F(\mathbf{Y}_u, u)) \, du \right) g(\mathbf{Y}_T) \mid \mathbf{Y}_t \right], \tag{7.36}$$

where time subscripts stand for the timing of the valuation. F can follow a standard diffusion or a jump-diffusion process, following the specifications given in earlier paragraphs.

Under some additional technical conditions, F solves the following quasi-linear PDE:

$$\mathcal{D}F(\mathbf{y}, t) - p(\mathbf{y}, F(\mathbf{y}, t))F(\mathbf{y}, t) = 0, \tag{7.37}$$

$$(\mathbf{y}, t) \in \mathcal{R}^n \times [0, T],$$

where $\mathcal{D}F(\mathbf{y}, t)$ is defined as in equation (7.34) and given that the boundary condition $F(\mathbf{y}, T) = g(\mathbf{y})$ is again required. Duffie and Huang (1996) provide a numerical application of this framework to defaultable swaps. Duffie et al. (1996) provide technical requirements for the existence and uniqueness of pricing when $\mathbf{Y}$ is not necessarily defined over a Markovian state-space.

7.3.3   The Pricing of Corporate Bonds

Given that Duffie and Singleton provide a framework which has the advantage of enabling the use of the standard term structure of interest rates while refining it for an additional credit risk spread, we could be interested analogously in the term structure of discount bond prices by the straight use of expression (7.20). The presentation will be developed around three axes: the definition of the recovery in such an instrument, the valuation procedure *per se*, and the proposition for an updated Heath–Jarrow–Morton (HJM) framework.

The Recovery

Suppose the main alternative bankruptcy proceedings could be summarized into the following "instantaneous" versions of recovery at default:

- The RMV, previously defined.
- The recovery-of-face-value (RFV), where the creditor receives instantaneously at default a fraction $(1 - L_t)$ of the promised \$1 at maturity. This is an assumption frequently used in the previous theoretical literature.
- The recovery-of-treasury (RT), where the creditor receives instantaneously a fraction $(1 - L_t)$ of an identical but default-free bond. This is the approach chosen by Jarrow and Turnbull (1995) and Longstaff and Schwartz (1995b), among others.

The RT definition offers some difficulty when typically computing D_t from equation (7.10) in order to be able to express R_t as a sum of r_t and $h_t L_t$. For the latter to still work, some additional simplifications must be assumed:

- h is independent of $r(t)$ and L is a predefined constant. This is the choice of Jarrow and Turnbull (1995).
- Lando (1998): h is dependent on $r(t)$ and follows a specific process that still allows tractable computation, although of a certain complexity.

Let us examine the advantages of having L_t fixed. One of the major complications of credit pricing models comes from the fact that, since the time of default is not deterministic, any variable dependent on this time will add to the problem of the overall expectation, thereby requiring the conditional joint distribution of h_t, L_t, and r_t to be known or derivable.

Now, the mathematical complexity and the ways to overcome it should be opposed to the empirical evidence on bankruptcy proceedings and the contractual features on which the instrument is based, in order to provide us with a sound model. In that respect, the RMV assumption seems to be quite in line with the structure of a swap contract (see Chapter 8). For corporate bonds, however, a trade-off must be operated. While the RMV assumption provides easier developments, the RFV assumption is more in line with the absolute priority rule and the existence of a cross-default covenant. In that case, bonds of equal seniority from an issuer should be paid equally at default. This requirement is, however, confirmed by the empirical evidence on defaults (see Moody's report, 1998). A useful comparison between RFV and RMV methodologies is provided in Duffie and Singleton (1999) with a numerical example.

The Valuation per se

Duffie and Singleton provide a general affine formulation that offers flexibility in explaining the evidenced term structures of corporate yield spreads allowing for correlation between the processes constituting the **Y** vector. The limitation to the range of possibilities comes, however, from the fact that the positivity of h_t should be verified for the soundness of the implementation.

Away from the particular specification that can be chosen for h_t, L_t, and r_t, and their implicit complexity in terms of the resulting joint conditional distributions, the flexibility of reduced-form models is also one of their weaknesses. While the credit spread expressed as $h_t L_t$ permits the use of the standard modeling of the term structure of default-free interest rates, it poses some critical issues in terms of calibration. The separate estimation of h_t and L_t, out from the product $h_t L_t$, requires expressions that depend differently on h and L to be calibrated to market data (in the RMV setting).

The problem with corporate bonds is that (assuming independence) they are the sum of discount bonds with face values corresponding to the coupons and the principal payment at maturity. In this sense, we do not have expressions behaving differently with respect to the product $h_t L_t$ and the joint effect of the hazard rate and the loss-given default cannot be disentangled. Since one bond would not be enough to learn specifically about each parameter, we will therefore need to combine the information stemming out from bonds of the same borrower but still of a different nature, while being precise on the particular determinants that would allow this separate identification in order to define the required "difference in nature"[13]. Let us consider the example presented by Duffie and Singleton (1999) in their paper. Suppose that we are provided with the market prices of senior (D_t^S) and junior (D_t^J) corporate bonds of a given issuer, and a default-free government bond. Moreover, we can reasonably argue that the corporate securities will be characterized by a different expected fractional loss-given default ($(L_t^S <> L_t^J)^{14}$, but the default event will be triggered by the same process or hazard rate h^{15}. The latter assumption is consistent with the economic intuition that default will be that of the firm and not of a particular bond issue[16]. Given the processes specified for $r(t)$ and $\mathbf{Y}$, it will be possible to identify $h_t L_t^S$ and $h_t L_t^J$. But, as Duffie and Singleton recognize, even if the ratio L_t^S/L_t^J could be computable, h_t would be still impossible to isolate unless one of these parameters could be related to other observable variables[17] or directly observed.

By now, keeping apart this identification problem, let us assume that we have bonds of the same seniority, default intensity and recovery rate, but different in terms of maturity. That would allow us to model/estimate the properties of $r(t)$ and the short spread process $s(t) \equiv h_t L_t$. Let us also assume that the observable vector $\mathbf{Y}$ is constituted of three square-root processes such that $r(t)$ would be modeled by a three-factor polynomial:

$$r_t = \delta_0 + \delta_1 Y_{1t} + \delta_2 Y_{2t} + \delta_3 Y_{3t} = \delta_0 + [\delta_1 \delta_2 \delta_3] \mathbf{Y}_t, \tag{7.38}$$

where the conditional volatility of Y_{it} is proportional to $\sqrt{Y_{it}}$. In the same manner, the credit spread would be given by

$$s_t = \gamma_0 + \gamma_1 Y_{1t} + \gamma_2 Y_{2t} + \gamma_3 Y_{3t} = \gamma_0 + [\gamma_1 \gamma_2 \gamma_3] \mathbf{Y}_t. \tag{7.39}$$

In the literature, different propositions are in fact nested by this framework.

Dai and Singleton (1998)

They showed that the "most flexible" affine terms structure model coherent with the volatility structure defined previously would require $\mathbf{Y}_t$ to follow square-root processes of the general form

$$d\mathbf{Y}_t = \mathcal{K}(\Theta - \mathbf{Y}_t)dt + \sqrt{S_t}d\mathbf{W}_t,$$

where $\mathcal{K}$ is a 3×3 matrix with positive diagonal elements and non-positive diagonal elements, Θ is a vector with three elements, S_t is a 3×3 diagonal matrix with diagonal elements Y_{1t}, Y_{2t}, and Y_{3t}, and $\mathbf{W}_t$ is a standard Wiener process in $\mathbb{R}^3$ under Q.

---

[13] We can remark here that the choice between a structural modeling approach and a reduced-form setting will depend on such trade-offs as this one: the flexibility of the reduced-form approach against the risk of misspecification in the determinants assumed to lead to the identification of both the hazard rate and the loss-given default (both as single variables or time-dependent processes). Reduced-form approaches therefore provide a versatile pricing instrument, but they do not provide the recipe for the calibration.

[14] $L_t^S > L_t^J$ would be consistent with the APR.

[15] However, remember that the RVM setting does not ensure that bonds of the same seniority would have the same recovery.

[16] This is even more the case if the "cross-default" rule applies.

[17] Madan and Unal (1995) use a hybrid structural-reduced-form approach that allows them to infer variables using different seniorities and assuming no violation of the APR.

But they showed that more flexibility in the specification of the correlations among the state variables constituting **Y** could be obtained by letting the conditional variances of the square-root processes be proportional to **Y**:

$$d\mathbf{Y}_t = \mathcal{K}(\Theta - \mathbf{Y}_t)dt + \Sigma\sqrt{\mathcal{S}_t}d\mathbf{W}_t,$$

where Σ is a 3×3 matrix and

$$\mathcal{S}(t) = \begin{bmatrix} Y_1(t) & 0 & 0 \\ 0 & [\beta_2]_2 Y_2(t) & 0 \\ 0 & 0 & \alpha_3 + [\beta_3]_1 Y_1(t) + [\beta_3]_2 Y_2(t) \end{bmatrix},$$

where the $[\beta_i]_j$s are strictly positive.

Then, let us take some simplified versions of equations (7.38) and (7.39)

$$r_t = \delta_0 + \delta_1 Y_{1t} + Y_{2t} + Y_{3t}, \tag{7.40}$$

$$s_t = \gamma_0 + \gamma_1 Y_{1t} + \gamma_2 Y_{2t},$$

with all coefficients being positive. The most flexible admissible affine term structure model is then shown to require the following specification:

$$\mathcal{K} = \begin{bmatrix} \kappa_{11} & \kappa_{12} & 0 \\ \kappa_{21} & \kappa_{22} & 0 \\ 0 & 0 & \kappa_{33} \end{bmatrix}, \quad \Sigma = \begin{bmatrix} 1 & 0 & 0 \\ 0 & 1 & 0 \\ \sigma_{31} & \sigma_{32} & 1 \end{bmatrix}.$$

Given expression (7.40) and the square-root form of $d\mathbf{Y}_t$, the credit spread is strictly positive. Moreover, since σ_{31} and σ_{32} are not constrained to be positive, all scenarios of correlation of the third state variable with the first two are enabled, allowing for the possibility of negative correlation between the changes in r and the changes in s. Because of these interdependencies among the state variables, calibration should be undertaken simultaneously with corporate and default-free bond market data. Separate calibration can, however, be justified with additional assumptions that will make $r(t)$ independent from $s(t)$:

- $\delta_1 = 0$, so that Y_1 and Y_3 are idiosyncratic risks to s and r respectively;
- $\kappa_{21} = 0$, $[\beta_3]_1$, $\sigma_{31} = 0$, that ensure that changes in Y_1 are completely isolated from changes in Y_3.

The parameters of the resulting two-factor affine model of the term structure of default-free interest rates can be estimated without having recourse to corporate data. The above presentation of the reduced-form approach provides an important argument to the requirement of an integrated framework for the monitoring and management of market risks and credit risks. It shows that, should they be related through some underlying state variables, then any inference on the default-free term structure independently from the corporate reality would give a biased estimation.

With these additional restrictions, corporate bond data will only be required for the estimation of Y_1 parameters and γ_0, γ_1, γ_2. Note that, whenever the state variables are constrained to be independent, correlation between the changes in r and the changes in

s still obtain since κ_{12} is still nonnull. Negative correlation will be induced by $\sigma_{32} < 0$, although limited by the fact that it could no longer come from any interdependence between Y_1 and Y_3 since $\sigma_{31} = 0$.

For a matter of exhaustiveness, it should be noted that Duffie and Kan (1996) and Duffie et al. (1999) show the implications of the introduction of jumps into the framework.

Duffee (1997 and 1999)

Duffee's reduced-form proposition can again be nested in the present framework. He considered a setting where the process $r(t)$ depends only on the first two state variables and can take on negative values with $\delta_0 = -1$. Moreover, $\mathcal{K}$ is a diagonal matrix thereby implying that the three state variables are independent square-root diffusions under Q. Also again, this restriction allows him to infer the parameters of $r(t)$ from the sole use of Treasury prices while still permitting correlation between $r(t)$ and $s(t)$ through nonnull γ_is in expression (7.40). More precisely, since the nonnull δs are normalized to unity, negative correlation can be introduced into the system only by considering negative values for the γ_is. The problem is then that this would also suppose negative hazard rates which is technically unsustainable. But he obtained, however, a fairly accurate pricing with a gap of less than 10 basis points.

Duffie and Singleton analyze Duffee's model and state that, in this kind of framework, one cannot simultaneously require nonnegative hazard rates and negatively correlated changes in r and h. This comes directly from Dai and Singleton (1998) who show that well-defined square-root models require that off-diagonal elements of $\mathcal{K}$ must be nonpositive, thereby impeding negative correlation among the state variables. And therefore, the only way to still obtain negative correlation between the changes of r and s is to have one or more δ_is or γ_is that are negative.

A Modified HJM Framework

As mentioned earlier the construction of the risk-neutral mean loss rate as hL allows us to use a wide variety of existing term structure models. Here we will focus on the implementation under the HJM framework and the corresponding drift restriction.

Suppose we can write the price at some time t of a defaultable zero-coupon bond as

$$p_{t,T} = \exp\left(-\int_t^T F(t, u)\,du \right),\tag{7.41}$$

where

$$F(t, T) = F(0, T) + \int_0^t \mu(s, T)\,ds + \int_0^t \sigma(s, T)\,dB_s,\tag{7.42}$$

where B is a standard Brownian motion in $\mathbb{R}^n$ under Q.

The typical drift restriction in HJM is

$$\mu(t, T) = \sigma(t, T) \int_t^T \sigma(t, u)\,du.\tag{7.43}$$

The discounted gain process G (see equation (7.41)) can be written then as

$$G = \exp(1 - \Lambda_t)D_t p_{t,T} + \int_0^t (1 - L_s)D_s p_{s-,T} d\Lambda_s, \tag{7.44}$$

where $D_t = \exp(-\int_0^t r_s ds)$. Since G is a Q-martingale, it has a zero drift, $\alpha_{s,T} = 0 = \int_0^t D_s p_{s,T} \alpha_{s,T} ds$, and after a few computations

$$\alpha_{s,T} = F(t, t) - r_t - \int_t^T \mu(t, u) du \tag{7.45}$$

$$+ \frac{1}{2}\left(\int_t^T \sigma(t, u) du\right) \cdot \left(\int_t^T \sigma(t, u) du\right) - h_t L_t.$$

The latter expression can be shown to be compatible with the HJM drift restriction of equation (7.43). This expression also implies that

$$h(t) = \frac{F(t, t) - r_t}{L_t}.$$

Duffie and Singleton (1999) show that, in the recovery case of Jarrow and Turnbull (1995), i.e. a recovery of a δ_t fraction of a default-free zero-coupon bond, there is a lack of homogeneity that imposes a correction term to expression (7.43) which becomes

$$\mu^*(t, T) = \sigma(t, T) \int_t^T \sigma(t, u) du + h_t \delta_t \frac{q_{t,T}}{p_{t,T}} [F(t, T) - f(t, T)],$$

where $q_{t,s} = \exp(-\int_t^s f(t, u) du)$ is the price of a default-free zero-coupon bond maturing at T as a function of the forward term structure $f(t, T)$.

7.4   CONCLUSION

We have limited our presentation here to the case of the valuation of straight noncallable defaultable bonds. Duffie and Singleton (1999) show that their framework is also suitable for the call feature that can be associated with a corporate bond or to the case of credit derivatives, in particular, a credit-spread put option.

However, in any case, as it is with any model, the final objective is to be able to use it back in a real-world context. The main problem resides then in estimation of its parameters. Since, by nature, reduced-form models do not rely on any background economics, the calibration of the hazard rate[18] has to be done formally. See the chapter on empirical evidence and the paper by Duffee (1999) on the topic.

7.5   TECHNICAL NOTE

The present section provides additional derivation on the basis presented earlier but whose formulation will be helpful for further presentations, in particular, for Chapter 8.

---

[18] The recovery rate is also a problem for structural models, with many different proposals, depending on the adopted formulation of the resolution of default. The opposition of structural and reduced-form models reside firstly on their definition of default.

7.5.1 Hübner (1997a)

The general setup of Hübner relies upon the same methodology as in Duffie and Singleton (1999). In particular it deals with the loss at default being represented as a fraction of the market value of the security just prior to default. This latter is found suitable for the case of swaps where the agreement is immediately unfolded should default occur and will be discussed further in subsection 8.3.2.

First of all, the following assumptions are necessary:

- The short-term riskfree interest rate is assumed to follow a risk-neutral Vasicek process:

$$dr(t) = a_r(b_r - r(t)) dt + \sigma_r dZ_r(t), \tag{7.46}$$

where Z_r is a Wiener process given the set of information available at t. Under the risk-neutral probability measure, and given a constant risk premia per unit of time of λ_r,

$$dr(t) = a_r(b_r' - r(t)) dt + \sigma_r dZ_r^*(t)$$

with

$$b_r' = b_r - \frac{\sigma_r \lambda_r}{a_r},$$

$$Z_r^*(t) = Z_r(t) + \lambda_r t.$$

- The event of default, represented by the possibility of the stopping time τ_b to occur before maturity of the contract T, is assumed to have an exponential distribution under the risk-neutral probability measure of the form

$$P^q[\tau_b \leqslant T] = \int_0^T h e^{-h\tau} d\tau,$$

where h is the hazard rate.

- Hübner assumes that a fraction L of the market value just prior to default of the claim, in the sense of Duffie and Singleton, is instantaneously lost in the event of default. As Hübner remarks, the cash settlement based on this assumption would be identical to the delivery of a security claim of the same credit standing, but on a smaller amount of underlying and this introduces the problem of "recurrent credit risk"[19].

- h and L are both functions of time and a state variable X, which is assumed to follow a risk-adjusted[20] mean-reverting process whose parameters are constant and specific to the defaultable counterparty, such that

---

[19]The problem of "recurrent credit risk" is even more visible in the case of credit derivatives. When a credit default swap is agreed by A with B, contingent on the default of the counterparty C, A still faces the default of B which would drive her/him back to the exposure to the default of C. This possibility, among others, makes credit risk a directly unhedgeable risk. The best way to hedge a credit risk still relies on the transformation of it into a market risk through collateralization.

[20]The risk adjustment is already made at this level for technical reasons, i.e. to be able to use the martingale approach directly with the risk-adjusted arrival rate.

$$d \ln X(t) = a_x(b_x - \ln X(t))dt + \sigma_x dZ_x(t), \qquad (7.47)$$

where

$$b_x = \frac{1}{a_x}\left(\mu_x - \frac{1}{2}\sigma_x^2\right),$$

Z_x is a Wiener process given the set of information available at t, and the correlation between Z_r and Z_x is given by ρ_{rx}.

Under the risk-neutral probability measure, and given a constant risk premia per unit of time of λ_x,

$$
\begin{aligned}
d \ln X(t) &= a_x(b_x' - \ln X(t))dt + \sigma_x dZ_x^*(t) \\
&= a_x b_x' - a_x \ln X(t)dt + \sigma_x dZ_x(t) \\
&= c_x - a_x \ln X(t)dt + \sigma_x dZ_x(t)
\end{aligned}
$$

with

$$b_x' = b_x - \frac{\sigma_x \lambda_x}{a_x},$$

$$c_x = \mu_x - \frac{1}{2}\sigma_x^2 - \frac{\sigma_x \lambda_x}{a_x}$$

$$Z_x^*(t) = Z_x(t) + \lambda_x t.$$

In the spirit of Duffie and Lando (1997), Hübner (1997b) notes that this state variable can be used as a way to reconcile the reduced-form framework with the structural approach by letting X represent the ratio of the value of assets over and economic threshold, in the sense of Longstaff and Schwartz (1995b).

Again, relying on subsection 7.3.1, leading to

$$R(r(t), X(t)) = r(t) + h(X(t))L(X(t)) = r(t) + s(X(t)),$$

the price of the bond at t, provided that default has not happened previously, is given by

$$D_t(r(t), X(t), T) = E_t^Q\left[\exp\left(-\int_t^T R(r(u), X(u))du\right)\right],$$

where E_t^Q denotes the expectation under the risk-neutral probability measure given information available at t. The ability to obtain a closed-form solution would rely on the possibility of $R(r(t), X(t))$ to be normally distributed. This requires that $s(X(t))$ should be a linear function of $\ln(X(t))$. Suitable properties should be therefore:

$$s(X(t)) \to \infty \quad \text{as } X(t) \to 0,$$

$$s(X(t)) = \hat{h}\hat{L} \quad \text{if } X(t) = 1,$$

$$s(X(t)) = 0 \quad \text{if } X(t) = B,$$

where $\hat{h}$, α, B are the referential arrival rate of default, the referential loss rate at default, and the "safety" threshold[21], respectively. Under these conditions, $s(X(t))$ would verify the following expression:

$$s(X(t)) = C_0 + C_1 \ln(X(t)), \tag{7.48}$$

with

$$C_0 = \hat{h}\hat{L},$$

$$C_1 = \frac{\hat{h}\hat{L}}{\ln(1/B)}.$$

Hübner (1997a) must then solve the following expression in order to obtain the pricing equation for a corporate discount bond at $t = 0$ maturing at T when credit risk is recurrent and given the definitions of $r(t)$, $X(t)$, and $s(X(t))$[22]:

$$D_0(r(t), X(t), T) = \exp[E_0^Q(y(T)) - \tfrac{1}{2}\mathrm{Var}_0^Q(y(T))],$$

where $y(T)$ is the yield of this bond for a maturity $\dot{T}$. Full computation of the expectation and the variance enable us to rewrite the last expression as

$$D_0(r(t), X(t), T) = \exp[\tfrac{1}{2}K_R^2(T) - N_R(r(t), X(t), T)],$$

where

$$K_R^2(T) = \kappa_1 e^{-a_r T} + \kappa_2 e^{-a_x T} + \kappa_3 e^{-2a_r T} + \kappa_4 e^{-2a_x T}$$
$$+ \kappa_5 e^{-(a_r + a_x)T} + \kappa_6 T + \kappa_7,$$

$$N_R(r(t), X(t), T) = (b_r' + C_1(c_x/a_x))T + \frac{1}{a_r}(1 - e^{-a_r T})(r - b_r')$$
$$+ \frac{1}{a_x}C_1(1 - e^{-a_x T})(\ln X(t) - (c_x/a_x)) + \hat{h}\hat{L}T,$$

$$\kappa_1 = \frac{2}{a_r^2}\left(C_2\rho_{rx}\sigma_r + \frac{\sigma_r^2(1 - \rho_{rx}^2)}{a_r}\right),$$

$$\kappa_2 = \frac{2}{a_x^2}C_1 C_2 \sigma_x,$$

---

[21] Or threshold of risklessness, in the terms of Hübner.
[22] See appendix 1 of Hübner (1997a) for a complete derivation.

$$\kappa_3 = \frac{-\sigma_r^2}{2a_r^3},$$

$$\kappa_4 = \frac{-C_1^2\sigma_x^2}{2a_x^3},$$

$$\kappa_5 = \frac{-2C_1\rho_{rx}\sigma_r\sigma_x}{a_r a_x(a_r + a_x)},$$

$$\kappa_6 = C_2^2 + \frac{\sigma_r^2(1 - \rho_{rx})}{a_r^2},$$

$$\kappa_7 = -(\kappa_1 + \kappa_2 + \kappa_3 + \kappa_4 + \kappa_5),$$

$$C_2 = \left(\frac{\rho_{rx}\sigma_r}{a_r} + \frac{C_1\sigma_x}{a_x}\right).$$

7.6   REFERENCES

Artzner, Philippe and Freddy Delbaen, 1995, "Default Risk Insurance and Incomplete Markets", *Mathematical Finance*, **5** (3), July, 187–95.

Bates, David S., 1991, "The Crash of '87: Was It Expected? The Evidence from Options Markets", *Journal of Finance*, **46** (3), July, 1009–44.

Dai, Q. and K. Singleton, 1998, "Specification Analysis of Affine Term Structure Models", *Working Paper*, Graduate School of Business, Stanford University.

Das, Sanjiv and Peter Tufano, 1996, "Pricing Credit Sensitive Debt when Interest Rates, Credit Ratings and Credit Spreads are Stochastic", *Journal of Financial Engineering*, **5** (2), June.

Duan, J. C. and J.-G. Simonato, 1998, "Maximum Likelihood Estimation of Deposit Insurance Value with Interest Rate Risk", *Working Paper*, November, 21 pp.

Duffee, Gregory R., 1997, "Estimating the Price of Default Risk", *Working Paper*, Federal Reserve Board.

Duffee, Gregory, 1999, "Estimating the Price of Default Risk", *The Review of Financial Studies*, **12** (1), Spring, 197–226.

Duffie, Darrell and Ming Huang, 1996, "Swap Rates and Credit Quality", *Journal of Finance*, **51** (3), July, 921–49.

Duffie, Darrell and Kan, Rui, "A Yield-Factor Model of Interest Rates", *Mathematical Finance*, **6** (4), October, 379–406.

Duffie, D. and K. Singleton, 1994, "Econometric Modeling of Term Structures of Defaultable Bonds", *Working Paper*, Graduate School of Business, Stanford University, November.

Duffie, Darrell and Ken Singleton, 1999, "Modeling Term Structures of Defaultable Bonds", *Review of Financial Studies*, Special 1999, **12**(4), 687–720.

Duffie, Darrell and David Lando, 1997, "Term Structures of Credit Spreads with Incomplete Accounting Information", Preliminary Draft, September 12, 39 pp.

Duffie, D., J. Pan and K. Singleton, 1999, "Transform Analysis and Asset Pricing for Affine Jump-Diffusions", *Working Paper*, Graduate School of Business, Stanford University, September, 44 pp.

Duffie, D., M. Schroder and C. Skiadas, 1996, "Recursive Valuation of Defaultable Securities and the Timing of Resolution of Uncertainty", *Annals of Applied Probability*, **6**, 1075–90.

Harrison, M. and D. Kreps, 1979, "Martingales and Arbitrage in Multiperiod Security Markets", *Journal of Economic Theory*, **20**, 381–408.

Harrison, M. and S. Pliska, 1981, "Martingales and Stochastic Integrals in the Theory of Continuous Trading", *Stochastic Processes and Their Applications*, **11**, 215–60.

Hübner, Georges, 1997a, "A Two-Factor Gaussian Model of Default Risk", *Working Paper 97/23/FIN*, INSEAD, Paris and University of Liège, Belgium, 84 pp.

Hübner, Georges, 1997b, "The Analytic Pricing of Asymmetric Defaultable Swaps", *Working Paper 97/24/FIN*, INSEAD, Paris and University of Liège, Belgium, 52 pp.

Iben, Th. and R. Litterman, 1991, "Corporate Bond Valuation and the Term Structure of Credit Spreads", *Journal of Portfolio Management*, **17** (3), Spring, 52–64.

Jarrow, Robert, 1992, *Lecture Notes: Recent Advances in the Pricing of Options on Financial Assets with Credit Risk*, June, 34 pp.

Jarrow, R. and Stuart Turnbull, 1995, "Pricing Derivatives on Financial Securities Subject to Credit Risk", *Journal of Finance*, **50** (1), 53–85.

Jarrow, R., David Lando and Stuart Turnbull, 1997, "A Markov Model of the Term Structure of Credit Spreads", *Review of Financial Studies*, **10** (2), Summer.

Keenan, Sean C., 1998, "Historical Default Rates of Corporate Bond Issuers, 1920–1997", *Moody's Special Comment*, Moody's Investors Service, Global Credit Research, February, 61 pp.

Lando, David, 1994, "On Cox Processes and Credit Risk Bonds", *Working Paper*, Institute of Mathematical Statistics, University of Copenhagen, 31 pp.

Lando, D., 1998, "On Cox Processes and Credit-Risky Securities", *Review of Derivatives Research*, **2**, 99–120.

Lehrbass, Frank, 1997, "Defaulters get intense", *Credit Risk Supplement*, Risk Publications, Financial Engineering Ltd, July, 56–9.

Longstaff, Francis and Eduardo Schwartz, 1995, "A Simple Approach to Valuing Risky Fixed and Floating Rate Debt and Determining Swap Spreads", *Journal of Finance*, **50** (3), July, 789–819.

Madan, Dilip and Haluk Unal, 1995, "Pricing the Risks of Default", *Working Paper*, September, 68 pp.

Moody's report by Keenan, Sean C., 1998, "Historical Default Rates of Corporate Bond Issuers, 1920–1997", *Moody's Special Comment*, Moody's Investors Service, Global Credit Research, February, 61 pp.

Ramaswamy, K. and Surech Sundaresan, 1986, "The Valuation of Floating-Rate Instruments", *Journal of Finance*, **17**, February, 251–72.

Schonbucher, P., 1997, "The Term Structure of Defaultable Bond Prices", *Working Paper*, University of Bonn.

Zhou, Chunsheng, 1997, "A Jump-Diffusion Approach to Modeling Credit Risk and Valuing Defaultable Securities", *Working Paper*, Federal Reserve Board, Washington, 47 pp.

Part Two
Credit Risk of Derivatives

8
Swap Credit Risk Pricing

Swaps are by far the most popularly issued and traded derivative instruments in the world. Their objective is very simple: interest rate swaps (IRS, thereafter) allow the conversion of a fixed-interest exposure into a floating one and vice versa, and currency swaps (CS, thereafter) permit the same transformation, but with respect to two different currency rates. Since swaps can be viewed as a series of long futures of maturities ranging from six months to the maturity of the swap contract, they can be used by the firm to:

- Hedge an upcoming stream of cash flows from a different country without having to change the location of the purchases.
- Diversify the exposure to worldwide currencies for a multinational.
- Enable the conversion of an otherwise unexchangeable currency.
- Modify the exposure of the debt financing of the company to the level and future evolution of interest rates.
- Take advantage of market asymmetries that may make the fixed form of borrowing compared to the floating one cheaper for firms with a high credit standing. We can cite the studies of Price and Henderson (1984) and their study focused on the arbitrage function of swaps of the imperfections in capital markets, Turnbull (1988) with a paper on the possibility offered by swaps to lower the borrowing costs which should not be possible if markets were perfectly integrated and complete, and others such as Wall and Pringle (1988) that use the "market incompleteness" or "agency costs" arguments to explain the continuous growth of this market.

Also, a financial institution can easily:

- manage its assets and liabilities (ALM);
- speculate against the evolution of the term structure of interest rates.

The ease in the dealing of swaps comes from very low costs and very tight spreads rendered possible by the huge volume being traded and therefore the high liquidity of this market, although it is an OTC market. This is the reason why swaps are of great interest in the credit risk literature. They are private transactions without any clearing house, which makes these operations very sensitive to the underlying credit quality of its counterparties to the trade. First concentrated only on AAA firms, the swap market, mainly because of its evident growth, has extended to lower credit quality firms. And therefore, beyond the traditional swap quotes supposed to be insensitive to the credit standing of the counterparty, academicians and practitioners have begun to think about:

- the reasons of the growth of this market,
- the real evidence on the pricing of credit risk behind the observed market quote,
- the real need to define a framework to price this risk despite other traditional mitigation techniques, and
- the way(s) to do so.

Pricing credit risk in swap contracts presents two major problems:

- First, the exchange of financial claims in risky swaps and the payment method at default must be characterized. Under the first "limited two-way payment" method, the net amount (positive or negative) of all open swaps, based on current market quotations, with the defaulted counterparty are added to the unpaid amounts owed to the nondefaulting counterparty. Unpaid amounts to the defaulting counterparty are subtracted. Should the amount be negative, i.e. in favor of the defaulting counterparty, the nondefaulting counterparty is not legally required to make any payment. However, as noted by Cooper and Mello (1991), because of their reputation in the financial place, non-defaulting parties were making at least some partial payment. That is why, in 1992, the swap market and the ISDA switched to the "full two-way payment" payment where all counterparties are required to honor the full payment of their commitment, even if they are on the nondefaulting side.

- Second, the two legs of the swap (fixed/floating or currency A/currency B) should not be priced separately.

Let us consider an IRS for a counterparty which is paying the floating rate r_t and receives the fixed rate k on a notional amount F from t to T. Suppose also that this swap is agreed by two riskfree counterparties. In a continuous-time perspective, with $P_t(s) = \exp(-\int_t^s r_u du)$, the value of this riskfree IRS could be formulated as

$$S_t(T, r_t, k) = E_t^Q \left[\int_t^T P_t(s)(k - r_t) F \, ds \right], \tag{8.1}$$

i.e. as the "risk-neutral" expectation of the net discounted exchange of interest payments between t and T. Here k is chosen such that, at time 0 of the contract, the value of the swap is null since it is an agreement between the counterparties entirely defined by the required fixed rate against LIBOR[1].

Because of the linearity of the expectation operator we can decompose equation (8.1) and add

$$\left(E_t^Q \left[\int_t^T P_t(s) F \, ds \right] - E_t^Q \left[\int_t^T P_t(s) F \, ds \right] \right)$$

such that it can be rewritten as

$$S_t(T, r_t, k) = \left(E_t^Q \left[\int_t^T P_t(s) k F \, ds \right] + E_t^Q \left[\int_t^T P_t(s) F \, ds \right] \right)$$
$$- \left(E_t^Q \left[\int_t^T P_t(s) r_t F \, ds \right] + E_t^Q \left[\int_t^T P_t(s) F \, ds \right] \right), \tag{8.2}$$

where $S_t(T, r_t, k)$ can be therefore viewed as an exchange of a FRN and a fixed-rate bond with coupon k. Many approaches use the same framework to price defaultable swaps. They consider the swap as being the exchange of two defaultable loans which avoids the fact that, in the presence of credit risk, the existence of each leg is conditional

---

[1] See Li (1996) for the pricing of swaps with default risk based on the same starting argument.

on the existence of the other. More precisely, taking one possible realization of the swap, supposing that a counterparty defaults on its leg, the swap ends up there and there is no reason why the second leg should include a credit risk premia for the rest of the time to maturity. Then, the credit risk premia embedded in each leg should be lowered by the existence of the credit risk on the other from the beginning. As Haitao Li (1996) shows, the use of equation (8.2) for defaultable swaps also implies that we are considering the principal amount while we know that it has only a notional role in the swap. Therefore, overall, using equation (8.2) will overestimate the credit risk embedded in the contract.

It has to be noted, however, that, although imprecise, this approach was used by the first attempts to price defaultable swaps because, with respect to previous studies, they introduced stochastic interest rates into the swap pricing framework. The next generation (Duffie and Huang, Li, Hübner, etc.) then tries to bring a solution that includes the real structure of the swap bearing default along with a nonflat and nonconstant term structure of riskfree interest rates.

8.1 SWAP CREDIT RISK PRICING MODELS

Although addressing the problem of the resolution of default, available structural models make the simplification that involves the presence of one riskless counterparty against a risky one. Reduced-form models allow relaxation of this important feature. All the models published at present analyze defaultable swaps free from any special covenant such as collateralization or any other credit risk mitigation technique which would considerably reduce or, at the limit, cancel the original exposure.

8.1.1 Cooper and Mello (1991)

The framework presented by Cooper and Mello (1991) has at least three main advantages. It enables the straight comparison with debt market default risk, it relates the swap pricing scheme to the payoff profiles of other claimholders in the firm, and it can be applied to both IRS and CS.

The Framework

Overall, the authors make the following main assumptions on the treatment of swaps at default, which seems to be in relation with what is mainly observed:

Assumption 1 Swaps are subordinate to debt in bankruptcy. Moreover, the value owed from a swap operation by a firm defaulting on its debt should be paid to it (the full two-way payment method is assumed in this case). Finally, the swap is treated as an exchange of net cash flows instead of the gross amounts such that the owned or owed value is that calculated after the netting of all unpaid positions.

And, as is the case with most of equilibrium or partial equilibrium pricing models:

Assumption 2 Capital markets are supposed to be complete, efficient and competitive, and frictionless with no additional deadweight costs at bankruptcy.

The first objective of their work is to provide a framework that allows the easy identification of the impact of alternative settlement rules. However, three main simplifications are made:

- The case is that of a *risky* firm (firm *A*) entering into a swap operation with a *riskfree* firm (firm *B*).

  Although this allows us to provide a clear identification of the source of total credit risk, this excludes the study of cross-effects between two risky counterparties and the importance in the reduction of the required spread for each counterparty given the credit standing of the other.
- The impact of stochastic interest rates is not considered here.
- The swap which is retained for the study is a single-period one, i.e. a swap with only one maturity remaining.

  Since the swap contract itself can be viewed as a succession of forward contracts, a single-period swap appears then as the simplest limiting case. However, as we will discuss further below, this is to ignore the conditionality on no prior default of the successive payments that should be taken into account once credit risk is present.

Firm *A* has an asset value of V_t which is stochastic. The funds have been raised thanks to the following capital structure:

- a floating-rate debt issue of maturity T with no coupon prior to T and a final stochastic face value $\tilde{M}_T$, given the evolution of the underlying structure of interest rates, and
- equity that pays no dividends before the maturity of the debt issue, in order to avoid problems of violations of the absolute priority rule.

As a counterparty to firm *A*, there is a riskless *B* firm with which firm *A* can enter into a swap transaction to transform its exposure to the floating rate into a fixed exposure where a fixed amount F is paid at T. This would be realized by a swap in which firm *A* would agree to pay the amount $(\tilde{M}_T - F)$ if positive. If negative, it would then be honored by firm B[2].

The next step is to examine the set of possible states of nature at time T depending on the credit status of firm *A* only, since firm *B* is riskfree, and on the realization of $\tilde{M}_T$. Table 8.1 summarizes the different payoffs for the different states of nature at T, for the bondholders (D_T) and equityholders (E_T) of firm *A* and the claim of their riskfree counterparty (B_T)[3].

Every line of this table should sum to V by the required *value preservation property*. Cooper and Mello show that, if we add the following payoff profiles of a European call option $C(V, F)$ on V_T with exercise price F, and an exotic European put $P^{VM}(V, M, F)$

---

[2]In the case of a currency swap, the realization of $\tilde{M}_t$, M_t, would stand as the fixed amount of foreign currency exchanged for dollars at maturity T at the exchange rate of that time, i.e. the payoff in dollars of a discount foreign bond maturing at T.

[3]For technical reasons, it is assumed that each state has a positive probability of occurrence.

Table 8.1   Payoff profiles for bondholders and equityholders of A and for their counterparty B depending on the state of nature for A at maturity

State of nature at T	D_T^s	E_T^s	B_T^s
1. $V > F > M$	M	$(V - F)$	$(F - M)$
2. $F > V > M$	M	0	$(V - M)$
3. $F > M > V$	V	0	0
4. $V > M > F$	M	$(V - F)$	$-(M - F)$
5. $M > V > F$	M	$(V - F)$	$-(M - F)$
6. $M > F > V$	$(V + M - F)$	0	$-(M - F)$

The s superscript states that these values are estimated in cases where a swap contract is agreed.
Source: Cooper and Mello (1991).

Table 8.2   Payoff profiles of a European call $C(V, F)$ and a special exotic European put $P^{VM}(V, M, F)$

State of nature at T	$C(V, F)$	$P^{VM}(V, M, F)$
1. $V > F > M$	$(V - F)$	0
2. $F > V > M$	0	$(F - V)$
3. $F > M > V$	0	$(F - M)$
4. $V > M > F$	$(V - F)$	0
5. $M > V > F$	$(V - F)$	0
6. $M > F > V$	0	0

Source: Cooper and Mello (1991).

on the maximum of V_T and M_T (see Table 8.2). Then D_t^s, E_t^s and B_t^s at time 0 can be respectively formulated as

$$D_0^s = V_0 - C(V_0, F) + M_0 - F_0 + P^{VM}(V_0, M_0, F),$$

$$E_0^s = C(V_0, F),$$

$$B_0^s = F_0 - M_0 - P^{VM}(V_0, M_0, F),$$

where F_0 and M_0 are the time 0 value of a default-free claim on F and M respectively. Again, it can be verified that $D_0^s + E_0^s + B_0^s = V_0$.

Let us define the values of equity and debt of firm A:

- if firm A issues floating rate zero-coupon debt with a reimbursement at maturity of M_T and does not swap it:

$$D_0^m = M_0 - P(V_0, M),$$

$$E_0^m = C(V_0, M),$$

- if firm A issues fixed rate zero-coupon debt of face value F and does not swap it:

$$D_0^f = F_0 - P(V_0, F),$$

$$E_0^f = C(V_0, F),$$

where $P(V_0, X)$ is a European put on V_T with exercise price X.

This will allow us to compare the value to each of the claimants of firm A with and without the swap contract since bondholders do not have any influence on the decision of undertaking the swap unless some debt covenant defines it.

In competitive markets, bondholders will then pay the minimum of D_0^m and D_0^s at the debt issue. Moreover, the equilibrium swap rate $\bar{F}$ will be such that the value of the swap is 0 to the riskfree counterparty:

$$B_0^s(\bar{F}) = \bar{F}_0 - M_0 - P^{VM}(V_0, M_0, \bar{F}) = 0. \tag{8.3}$$

The Wealth Transfer

The equilibrium swap. From this setting, Cooper and Mello show that any swap results in a value transfer to debtholders. Without the swap, debtholders have a claim that gives the $\min[V, M]$. With the swap, the payoff at T is $\min[\max[V, V + M - F], M]$[4]. And therefore $D_0^m < D_0^s$.

According to the equilibrium swap rate defined by equation (8.3), the loss in shareholders' value valued at time 0 is

$$C(V_0, M) - C(V_0, \bar{F}) \tag{8.4}$$

which corresponds exactly to the value gained by debtholders since the *value preservation property* is verified.

So, why would shareholders want to enter into swaps? First, if the swap has its origin in some pricing inefficiencies between the floating rate and the fixed rate markets, then it could add more value than the wealth that is being transferred to debtholders. If we stand on a perfectly efficient market, however, then two aspects should be still mentioned:

1. We have to note that the case presented above is only the one where floating debt is transformed into fixed debt. If the firm has a preference for the issuance of fixed rate debt, then swapping it could be profitable for shareholders under some circumstances[5].
2. Also, a covenant for the swapping of the floating debt at its issue would remove any wealth effect. Cooper and Mello also note that some authors such as Wall and Pringle (1988) and Arak et al. (1988) show that wealth can arise in the form of agency effects from the private knowledge that shareholders have and the swap would allow them to take advantage of it.

The equal value swap. Now suppose that we care about a swap that is not an equilibrium swap where there is an equal exchange of market values of debt, i.e. without any change in the value of equity. It is an exchange of two amounts $\hat{F}$ and M that, if they were issued as unswapped debt claims by the firm, would have an identical value. This rate $\hat{F}$ would be defined such that

$$C(V_0, M) = C(V_0, \hat{F}), \tag{8.5}$$

---

[4]Without the swap, states of nature 5 and 6 collapse to V which is lower than the payoff with the swap. As these states have a positive probability of occurrence, the conclusion follows straightforwardly.

[5]The proof to this proposition could be a good exercise.

and $D_0^m = D_0^{\hat{f}}$ by the *value preservation property* with and without a swap. However, this implicitly means that a wealth transfer then takes place from firm B to the debtholders of firm A. More precisely, Cooper and Mello show that this value is equivalent to $P^{VM}(V_0, \hat{F}, M)$, i.e. the value of a European put on the maximum of V_T and $\hat{F}$ with exercise price M_T[6], an option that will pay only in the natural state where both V_T and $\hat{F}$ are less than M_T.

It transpires that this "equal value swap" does not duly compensate firm B for the special way in which the swap is settled. And, because of assumption 1, firm B has no means to cut this transfer. Therefore, firm B would not enter into this contract unless they could be directly compensated for the difference $(\bar{F} - \hat{F})$.

The final deduction is that $\bar{F}$ is in fact greater than $\hat{F}$. The proof is provided by combining equations (8.4) and (8.5) which allows us to infer that $C(V_0, \hat{F}) > C(V_0, \bar{F})$.

The corollary for a swap where firm A would pay the floating leg and receive the fixed one is that the equilibrium rate $\bar{F}$ of this swap should be lower than $\hat{F}$. These two equilibrium rates could then be seen as a bid–ask spread around $\hat{F}$, which would be justified by the requirement by the bank of a compensation for taking a swap position at $\hat{F}$ regardless of the direction of the swap.

The credit or default spread. The default spread on each leg taken as a separate debt issue can be computed, for the fixed debt issue, as

$$cs^f = \frac{1}{T} \ln\left[\frac{\hat{F}_0}{D_0^{\hat{f}}}\right] \tag{8.6}$$

and, for the floating debt issue, as

$$cs^m = \frac{1}{T} \ln\left[\frac{M_0}{D_0^m}\right], \tag{8.7}$$

knowing that $D_0^{\hat{f}}$ and D_0^m are the default-exposed debt values. $\hat{F}_0$ simply corresponds to $\hat{F}e^{-rT}$.

Quotations in the market are fixed rates against LIBOR. Typically, a quoted 3% swap versus LIBOR could be finally arranged as a 2.9% swap versus LIBOR-10 bp (basis points).

Following this, the swap spread required by the market would be simply the complement to the riskless fixed interest rate to obtain the swap quote against the riskless variable rate. More precisely, if we consider the fixed side of the swap as F against the riskless side M_0, the swap spread will be such that

$$F = M_0^{(r+S)T}, \tag{8.8}$$

where

$$S = \frac{1}{T} \ln[F_0/M_0]. \tag{8.9}$$

---

[6]A proof to this proposition could again constitute a good review exercise of the methodology.

It follows then directly by the combination of previous equations that

$$S = cs^f - cs^m + \frac{1}{T}\ln[F_0/\hat{F}_0].\tag{8.10}$$

This result calls for three observations:

1. Expression (8.10) shows that the swap spread is not equal to the difference between equilibrium spreads in the fixed and variable interest rate markets unless the swap could be viewed as an exact exchange of cash flows from two types of risky debt. In the latter case, as shown above, an "equal value" swap would have a negative value to the riskless counterparty.
2. The third element of equation (8.10) compensates the swap counterparty for the incremental default risk arising from the way the contract is settled in the case of bankruptcy. Cooper and Mello call this the pure swap spread. Suppose that the swap rate is the equilibrium rate $\bar{F}$ previously defined, and knowing that $\bar{F} > \hat{F}$, the pure swap spread is positive and therefore we can conclude that $S > cs^f - cs^m$.
   Any violation of this rule would indicate an arbitrage opportunity.
3. The problem resides in that equation (8.10) is valid for where one of the legs is owned by a completely riskless counterparty. In this particular case, the swap spread arises from some linear combination of the credit spreads from both legs. Part of the criticism of these theories relies on the fact that, in the case of two defaultable counterparties, the swap cannot be priced as the combination of two legs independent from each other, since the existence of each leg as a commitment to one of the counterparties should be conditioned on the survival of the counterparty owning the other leg.

Alternative Settlement Rules

Cooper and Mello analyze three particular cases of swap treatment at default in order to provide a picture of the size of the risk given the uncertainty on this treatment. These rules are variants to assumption 1 and we can construct a table (Table 8.3) with the different states of nature similar to Table 8.2 introduced earlier:

1. Swap payments are only made if both counterparties are solvent prior to the swap payment. In another sense, counterparty B is riskless and is not committed to make any payment, if the swap could be in the money for A, if A falls into bankruptcy first.
2. The net payment is made prior to any payment to bondholders. The debt is subordinated to the swap contract[7] (Table 8.4).
3. The swap is treated as an exchange of gross amounts rather than an exchange of net cash flows[8] (Table 8.5).

---

[7] It is, however, difficult to assume that bondholders would not require a compensation for the "swapability" of their debt, should this possibility of violation exist.

[8] This is the case, for example, of currency swaps, where the amounts in each currency are exchanged at the origination of the contract and back again at its maturity. But, it would then involve a certain amount of risk given that the two amounts exchanged are in different currencies.

Table 8.3 Alternative settlement rules (version 1)

State of nature at T	D_T^s	E_T^s	B_T^s	$C(V, M) - C(V, F)$	$P((M-V)^+, F)$
1. $V > F > M$	M	$(V-F)$	$(F-M)$	$(F-M)$	0
2. $F > V > M$	M	0	$(V-M)$	$(V-M)$	0
3. $F > M > V$	V	0	0	0	0
4. $V > M > F$	M	$(V-F)$	$-(M-F)$	$-(M-F)$	0
5. $M > V > F$	M	$(V-F)$	$-(M-F)$	$-(V-F)$	$(M-V)$
6. $M > F > V$	V	0	0	0	0

Source: Cooper and Mello (1991).

Table 8.4 Alternative settlement rules (version 2)

State of nature at T	D_T^s	E_T^s	B_T^s	$(F_0 - M_0)$	$P(V+M, F)$
1. $V > F > M$	M	$(V-F)$	$(F-M)$	$(F-M)$	0
2. $F > V; F > M$ $V+M > F$	$(V+M-F)$	0	$(F-M)$	$(F-M)$	0
3. $F > M; F > V$ $V+M < F$	0	0	V	$(F-M)$	$(F-V-M)$
4. $V > M > F$	M	$(V-F)$	$-(M-F)$	$(F-M)$	0
5. $M > V > F$	M	$(V-F)$	$-(M-F)$	$(F-M)$	0
6. $M > F > V$	$(V+M-F)$	0	$-(M-F)$	$(F-M)$	0

Source: Cooper and Mello (1991).

Table 8.5 Alternative settlement rules (version 3)

State of nature at T	D_T^s	E_T^s	B_T^s	$(V_0 - M_0)$	$C(V, F)$
1. $V < F$	M	0	$(V-M)$	$(V-M)$	0
2. $V > F$	M	$(V-F)$	$(F-M)$	$(V-M)$	$(V-F)$

Source: Cooper and Mello (1991).

Under any of these rules, the value of equity is clearly the value of a call on the maximum between V and F, i.e. $C(V, F^i)$, where F^i is the equilibrium swap rate under the given rule. Before the swap operation, the value of equity is $C(V, M)$ and debt and equity sum to V_0. After the swap, debt, equity, and $B^S(F^i)$ sum to V_0. From the "equal value" swap, we know that $C(V, M) = C(V, \hat{F})$. Therefore, we can argue again that the shareholders' net wealth change is $C(V, \hat{F}) - C(V, F^i)$ which is a pure transfer to or from debtholders since, by definition, the equilibrium swap rate supposes that $B^S(F^i) = 0$ at the origin of the contract.

The equilibrium swap rates are provided straightforwardly under each rule:

1. In the case of "cross-default", F^c should verify that

$$C(V, M) - C(V, F^c) = P((M - V)^+, F^c), \tag{8.11}$$

i.e. a wealth transfer to debtholders of $P^{M-V}(V, M, F^c)$[9], since

---

[9]The value of an option is always positive.

$$\begin{cases} B^S(F^c) = C(V, M) - C(V, F^c) - P((M - V)^+, F^c) \\ B^S(F^c) = 0. \end{cases}$$

2. In the case of "prior settlement", F^p should verify that

$$V_0 - C(V + M, F^p) = 0, \qquad (8.12)$$

i.e. a transfer between debtholders and shareholders of $C(V, F^p) - C(V, M)$, where $C(V + M, F^p)$ is the value of a European call on the payoff $\max[V_T + M_T, F^p]$ at T. The sign of the transfer is not defined.

From the previous corresponding table, we can show that

$$B^S(F^p) = F_0^p - M_0 - P(V + M, F^p).$$

Again, at equilibrium, $B^S(F^p) = 0$ and, using the put-call parity condition

$$P(V + M, F^p) = C(V + M, F^p) - V_0 + F_0^p - M_0,$$

equation (8.12) is easily obtained. Moreover, it can be shown that $F^p < \bar{F}$.

Prior settlement is advantageous to the swap riskless counterparty and that is why it is possible for him/her to ask for a lower swap rate than the equilibrium rate $\bar{F}$. A priori, a wealth transfer occurs from debt to equity. But, as mentioned in an earlier footnote, if debtholders can believe that a swap will be arranged with a prior settlement rule, then they will adjust their debt conditions and the wealth transfer will turn out to be from shareholders to debtholders.

3. With the "gross settlement" rule, the gross payment by firm B of the variable leg of the swap will provide a full guaranty to debtholders of firm A while passing to B the claim on the assets that debtholders had on A before. F^g should verify that

$$V_0 - M_0 - C(V, F^g) = 0, \qquad (8.13)$$

which is obvious from the previous corresponding table and knowing that $B^S(F^g)$ is equal to 0 at time 0.

The wealth transfer in this last case is of

$$C(V, F^g) - C(V, \hat{F}) = C(V, F^g) - C(V, M),$$

which is equivalent to $V_0 - M_0 - C(V, M)$ by straight substitution of equation (8.13), or $-P(V, M)$ with the put–call parity relationship. Therefore, the swapping of the debt offers a guaranty to debtholders of a value $P(V, M)$ which they do not pay because it is an uncertain event since the swap is not part of the covenants of the debt contract. This value is thus on the behalf of shareholders.

Stochastic Swap Pricing

Cooper and Mello make then assumptions on the stochastic processes followed by the value of the firm V and the variable swap payment M, and they derive expressions for the currency swap and interest rate coupon-bearing swaps (please refer to their paper for the complete presentation).

Cooper and Mello (1991) have provided a clear vision of the scenarios and their impact on the final payoff profile for every claimant related to the swap operation. However, the three simplifications exposed at the beginning of the presentations reduce considerably the scope of the problem. Relaxing the first simplification (only one risky counterparty) would require to be able to condition every payoff presented from the perspective of one counterparty on the credit status of the other counterparty. Relaxing constant interest rates in defaultable debt contracts has been shown to be a major problem since the interactions between riskfree interest rates and credit spreads are still too simply modeled. Swaps offer then an additional difficulty since the final exposure at default would depend on the moneyness of the contract to each counterparty, i.e. on the dynamics of the riskfree interest rates themselves, in the case of an IRS. Finally, the use of a single-period swap excludes the impact of any strategic behavior from the risky counterparty with regard to the replacement cost for the riskfree firm in the case of default since, in reality, the latter firm will have to find an alternative contract in the market for the remaining maturity. And overall, when relaxing all these assumptions, it is clearly not obvious that the defaultable swap could be treated as a sum of forwards with exactly the same credit risk exposure characteristics.

Baz (1995) provides a framework similar to Cooper and Mello, the latter being viewed as a special case where the risky firm pays the value of a fixed rate loan and receives the value of a riskfree bond that is not necesarily zero-coupon. It remains a one-sided default risk model.

On the other hand, the option pricing framework applies in these models elegantly and allows for a clear overview of the settlement scenarios and how the value is extracted by each claimant from the total value of the firm.

8.2   ASYMMETRIC DEFAULTABLE SWAP PRICING

In the pricing literature such as in Longstaff and Schwartz (1994), the swaps are often analyzed as a netting of two legs. In the case of IRS, a floating leg and a fixed leg are valued under "defaultability" and then netted to give the value of the swap. This principle is the one commonly adopted by the regulatory recommendations on risk management. However, when including credit risk in this OTC contract, it becomes quite obvious that the pricing of both legs should be done simultaneously unless either one counterparty is totally riskfree (adopted by Cooper and Mello, 1991, or Baz, 1995) or both counterparties are in all points of identical credit quality[10].

Some studies have been developed on the pricing of asymmetric defaultable swaps, all from the reduced-form models side as the complexity of bilateral default has not yet been addressed in structural form models. As already mentioned in the earlier wrap-up, the first theoretical study in providing such a framework was the one by Duffie and Huang (1996). More recently, we can cite Hübner (1997). It has to be noted that these studies rely on a reduced-form approach for the arrival of default with some refinement for the possibilities of resolution specific to swap contracts.

---

[10]Since the literature is not very consensual on the large palette of determinants of credit risk, it is still difficult to define what "identical" means.

8.2.1 Duffie and Huang (1996)

In Duffie and Huang (1996), the promised cash flows of a swap are discounted at a switching discount rate that at any given state and time is equal to the discount rate of the counterparty for whom the swap is currently out of the money or a liability. This modeling idea is fruitful since it allows the evaluation of any derivative where there is credit risk stemming from both counterparts. But it should be noticed that it remains a framework for numerical analysis since no closed-form solution is provided. We then refer the reader to the published paper for the formulae and their details. Such expressions are better explained in the Hübner (1997) case since he provides a closed-form solution. We will only focus here on the intuition and the results on the behavior of the modelizations to changes of the difference of creditworthiness between the two counterparties, since the introduction of this asymmetry is the main contribution of Duffie and Huang (1996).

The model, as the previous ones, does not take into account the effect of marking-to-market, collateralization and the possibility of early termination, but Duffie and Huang argue that their model does not deter such extensions.

The discrete-time intuition provided by Duffie and Huang is helpful to easily encompass their methodology. Briefly, suppose that the value of the swap at any time to counterparty A is V_t, i.e. $-V_t$ for counterparty B. Typically, A faces some credit risk between t and $t+1$ when s/he is a net receiver into the swap, i.e. when $V_t > 0$. Therefore, under risk-neutral probabilities, V_t can be expressed by two components:

$$V_t = DP[V_t \mid \text{B defaults within } [t, t+1]]$$
$$+ (1 - DP)[V_t \mid \text{B does not default within } [t, t+1]],$$

where DP stands here for the default probability. Each of the conditional V_ts in the latter expression is a risk-neutral expectation:

- Of the present value of V_{t+1} plus the net payment received by A from B between t and $t+1$ for the no-default case.
- Of some fraction of the present value of V_{t+1}, for the default case.

Whenever market conditions change and the swap turns out to be in favor of B the same principles are applied to B for the risk s/he faces.

Then, in continuous time, the credit quality of a counterparty is represented by the spread s over the short-term interest rate for the debt commitments of that counterparty. This spread s is modeled as in Duffie and Singleton (1999), i.e. $s_t = (1 - \varphi_t)h_t$, where φ_t is the stochastic recovery process and h_t the risk-neutral hazard rate or intensity process. Remember from Duffie and Singleton (1999) that this formulation allows to write the risky interest rate R as the sum of the riskfree short-term interest rate r and the spread s and therefore all previous models of the riskfree term structure of interest rates can be used on R.

They consider either interest rate swaps with a square-root process for the short-term LIBOR rate (in the sense of CIR, 1985a) and currency swaps where the foreign exchange rate process follows a GBM. Their results for these two instruments are the following: for a 5-year IRS increasing the credit asymmetry by 100 bps on the fixed leg (i.e., the credit spread of the fixed-rate payer counterparty on the bond market) produces through the model an increase of the swap rate of around 1 bps[11]. For a 5-year currency swap (CS) on a foreign exchange that displays a 15% volatility the CS credit spread is of 8.7 bps. In the latter case, doubling the volatility would double the spread.

In accepting for the fixed leg a new counterparty whose bonds yield is trading 100 bps higher than the previous counterparty, the model gives an IRS rate that is 1 bps higher and a CS rate that is 10 bps higher.

Duffie and Huang consider cases where counterparty A is always of better credit-worthiness than B, which by the no-arbitrage argument leads to $s_A \leqslant s_B$, $\forall t \in [0, T]$. In this context, their model produces the following deductions:

- Netting across swap portfolios always increases (decreases) the market value of the portfolio to A (B), in addition to the risk diversification brought by the netting which is profitable to both counterparties.
- It is interesting to see that a delay in the price discovery process in the market that could have an effect on the swap value would be profitable to A. Indeed, Duffie and Huang (1996) provide a quantitative measure of the marginal impact on the swap of a change in the difference of the spreads of A and B, i.e. a change in the credit quality asymmetry since the credit spread is retained here as the key indicator of the creditworthiness.

8.2.2 Hübner (1997)

Hübner (1997) obtains analytical pricing of swaps with bilateral, asymmetric default. At present, structural models do not allow for the bilateral default present in swaps. The reduced-form model proposed by Duffie and Huang (1996), on the other hand, only leads to numerical approximations rather than to analytical solutions (that are easier to handle and simulate with different parameters). Hübner (1997) proposes fully analytical, option-like formulae for defaultable swaps that incorporate bilateral default in a reduced-form setup. It addresses the settlement issue by which, since the 1992 ISDA Master Agreement, swaps in case of default of one counterparty are terminated through full payment of the market value if the market value is positive to the defaulting counterparty and only a fractional payment if the market value is negative to the defaulting counterparty. This setup corresponds to the loss given default obtained in unilateral risk in Duffie and Singleton (1999) as described in Chapter 7. Jarrow and Turnbull (1995) in contrast propose a loss given default that is in proportion to a corresponding riskfree bond rather than to the market value of the contract before default. This does not correspond to default settlement defined in the current ISDA Masters Agreement on swaps.

---

[11] Duffie and Huang (1996) also provide a very interesting comparison with the naive approach of swap pricing subject to credit risk, i.e. the one that consists in treating each leg independently. The gap can be very big: for the case where LIBOR rates and credit spreads are uncorrelated, such a "pseudo"-credit swap rate of 26.4 bps would obtain.

Hübner (1997) decomposes the value of the swap to one of the counterparties as the net of two nonnegative components which correspond to the risk exposures of each counterparty. Each of these quantities is only exposed to one counterparty's credit risk. Arrival risk and magnitude risk are functions of a different state variable per counterparty, each following a lognormal mean reverting process and each correlated to the interest rate process.

Hübner (1997) supposes that the riskiness of each counterparty (A and B) is represented through the state variables X_j ($j = A, B$), which processes, under the risk-neutral probability measure, are defined as

$$d \ln X_j = (\bar{\gamma}_j - \tfrac{1}{2}\sigma_j^2 - a_j \ln X_j(t))\,dt + \sigma_j\,dZ_j(t),\ Z_j(t) \times Z_r(t) = \rho_j\,dt,$$

where $\bar{\gamma}_j$ and a_j are the parameters that define the mean reversion property of $d \ln X_j$ and $Z_j(t)$ is a Brownian motion correlated to $Z_r(t)$ the Brownian motion that intervenes in the short-term interest rate process. The resulting differential equation of the risky interest rate is[12]

$$R_j(t) = r(t) + C_{0j} + C_{1j} \ln X_j(t),$$

where C_{0j} and C_{1j} are coefficients used for the linear combination.

In the event of default the riskiness of the undefaulted party is not technically suppressed as the price of the swap still accounts for the fact that the undefaulted party still exhibits credit risk. A recursive solution can be found from there that leads to analytical solutions for both interest rate swaps and currency swaps, using a Vasicek process for the interest rate dynamics and an event-of-default process that follows an exponential distribution.

In particular, the solution obtained for the predefault interest rate swap price to party A is

$$V(t) = \sum_{i=1}^{n} P_c(r(t), X_B(t), t, t_i)[(\alpha(\tau) + \beta(\tau)m_B(t, t_i) - r_f)N(-d_{Bi}) + \beta(\tau)v(t, t_i)N'(d_{Bi})]\tau$$

$$- \sum_{i=1}^{n} P_c(r(t), X_A(t), t, t_i)[(r_f - \alpha(\tau) - \beta(\tau)m_A(t, t_i))N(-d_{Ai}) + \beta(\tau)v(t, t_i)N'(d_{Ai})]\tau,$$

where $P_c(r(t), X_j(t), t, T)$ is the price of a pure risky discount bond (the short-term riskfree rate is simply replaced by its risky version R in a very standard expression) such that

$$P_c(r(t), X_j(t), t, T) = E^Q\left[\exp\left(-\int_t^T R(r(u), X(u))\,du\right)\bigg|\mathcal{F}_t\right],$$

---

[12]This differential equation is also defined under the risk-neutral probability measure and comes from the requirement that $R(r(t), X(t))$ should be normally distributed to maintain tractability. This requires the spread $s(X(t)) = R(r(t), X(t)) - r(t)$, to be a linear function of $\ln X(t)$.

where $E^Q[\cdot]$ is the expectation operator under the risk-neutral probability measure, and

$$d_{ij} = \frac{r_f - \alpha(\tau) - \beta(\tau)m_j(t, t_i)}{\beta(\tau)v(t, t_i)}, \quad \text{for } j = A, B,$$

$$\beta(\tau) = \frac{B_1(\tau)}{\tau} = \frac{1 - e^{-a_r\tau}}{a_r\tau}$$

$$\alpha(\tau) = -\frac{1}{\tau}\left[\frac{(B_1(\tau) - \tau)(a_r^2\bar{r} - \sigma_r^2/2)}{a_r^2} - \frac{\sigma_r^2 B_1(\tau)^2}{4a_r}\right]$$

$$m_j(t, t_i) = r(t)\,e^{-a_r(t_i-t)} + \left(\bar{r} - \frac{\sigma_r^2}{a_r^2} - \frac{C_1\rho_j\sigma_r\sigma_j}{a_r a_j}\right)(1 - e^{-a_r(t_i-t)})$$

$$+ \frac{\sigma_r^2}{2a_r^2}(1 - e^{-2a_r(t_i-t)}) + \frac{C_1\rho_j\sigma_r\sigma_j}{a_j(a_r + a_j)}(1 - e^{-(a_r+a_j)(t_i-t)})$$

$$v^2(t, t_i) = \frac{\sigma_r^2}{2a_r}(1 - e^{-2a_r(t_i-t)}),$$

where a_r and a_j are the adjustment speeds of the mean reverting behavior of the processes for $dr(t)$ and $d\ln X(t)$, respectively. Similarly, σ_r and σ_j are the constant volatility parameters.

The analysis stresses the differences between interest rate and currency swaps, as well as the impact of netting rules (in the line of Duffie and Huang, 1996). Simulations lead to seemingly higher impact of changes in underlying variables than previous reduced-form models and allow a greater understanding of correlation effects on the prices of swaps.

As all the other theoretical papers in this chapter, this paper does not deal with the issue of collateralization, a methodology that seems to substitute to credit-risk pricing (as analyzed later in this book). Most practitioners seem to rely at least in part on collateralization, or on rationing, rather than only on pricing of credit risk in the swap market, as analyzed in the following sections.

8.3 EMPIRICAL INVESTIGATIONS OF SWAP CREDIT RISK

On the empirical side, research on swap credit risk is almost nonexistent, the papers of Sun et al. (1993) and Cossin and Pirotte (1997) being currently the only published references.

Sun et al. (1993) use quotations from two IRS dealers with different credit ratings (AAA and A) to examine the effect of dealers' credit reputation on swap quotations and bid–offer spreads assuming that the credit quality of the counterparties is the same for different swap dealers, and that the swap contracts do not differ in other characteristics such as the up-front fee and collateral. They analyze the relationship between the quoted swap rates and the estimated par bond yields in the interbank market. They obtain some important conclusions, including:

- Spreads between AAA swap offer rates and Treasury yields are significantly positive at all maturities irrespective of the shape of the Treasury yield curve.

- Spreads between swap rates and Treasury yields generally increase significantly with maturities, whereas the increase is much smaller when the Treasury yield curve is inverted.

- Bid–offer spreads of swap dealers are sensitive to their credit reputations. The A dealers' swap rates appear to be bracketed by the AAA dealers' swap rates. It must be remembered that it has been assumed here that the credit standing of the counterparties to the two dealers is the same.

Their work remains constrained by the fact they could not get more precise information than the swap quotes themselves.

Chen and Selender (1995) also study swap quotes and the impact of a number of factors on changes in swap spreads. Notably, Treasury level and the slope of the yield curve impact spreads for 5-year contracts; Eurodollar rates play a major role in explaining spreads for short-term rates; corporate AA minus AAA spreads are a major factor in explaining changes in spreads for long maturity contracts (over 5 years).

Cossin and Pirotte (1997)[13] analyze swap credit risk on actual transaction data and not from quoted bid and offer rates. They obtained a sample of interest rate and currency swaps actual transaction prices with some confidential counterparty information. It thus allows for a more precise treatment of credit risk than previously, even though the sample remains small.

8.3.1   Data Sample Description

Swap transaction details for 55 IRS and 201 CS were *generously* provided to us by a medium-size European bank (denoted by MSB for future references), a small operator on the swap markets. The sample is unfortunately quite small. It is nonetheless valuable as it is extremely rare to obtain confidential data from swap market participants. The confidential information we had available for each transaction was the type of transaction (currency or interest rate, bid or offer, . . .), the fixed rate (which corresponds to the swap transaction rate) with the initial LIBOR rate for IRS and the fixed forward exchange rate for CS, the referential currency for IRS or the currency pair for CS, the rating of the client (or the type of client when no rating is available), the amount traded, the starting date and the maturity date of the contract. The transactions considered did not involve collaterals (which became current practice only later). Our sample contains IRS initiated between March 7, 1990 and December 15, 1994 and CS initiated between March 1, 1994 and August 7, 1995. IRS data are available for maturities of 3 years up to 10 years, with an average of 8 years and for an average amount of close to $50 million. CS data are short term as the

[13]The present chapter is based on the research paper written by the authors, "Swap Credit Risk: An Empirical Investigation on Transaction Data", and published in the *Journal of Banking and Finance*, **21** (10) October 1997, 1351–73. For this research, we thank Profs Suresh Sundaresan, Ernst-Ludwig von Thadden, Jean-Luc Vila, Ton Vorst, Ben Sopranzetti, Ivo Welch, two anonymous referees, seminar participants at the FMA meetings in New Orleans, at the EFA meetings in Oslo, at the LINK conference, at George Washington University, and many professionals at major institutions for useful discussions. We also thank the bank that provided us with transaction data for its generosity. Financial support was provided by the FNRS (Swiss National Fund for Scientific Research).

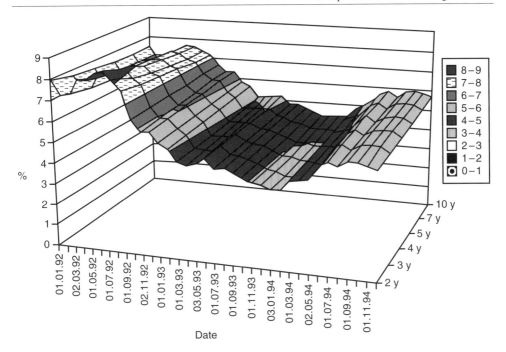

Figure 8.1 Quoted Swiss francs IRS offer rates between 1992 and 1994 for maturities of 2 years up to 10 years. Reproduced with authorization from Cossin and Pirotte (1997)

maturities available range from 1 month up to 20 months, with an average of 6 months, and for an average amount of close to $8 million. The behavior of these currency swaps is close to that of forwards, with the difference that principal amounts are exchanged at maturity.

Other data needed for the analysis were obtained mainly from Data Stream. They consist in forward exchange rates with respect to the US dollar, market IRS rates, Euro-currency rates, LIBOR and LIBID rates. Market IRS rates are available on Data Stream for 2-, 3-, 4-, 5-, 7-, and 10-year maturities. Euro-currency rates are available on Data Stream for 1-, 3-, and 6-month maturities and for 1-, 2-, 3-, 4-, and 5-year maturities. We checked the Data Stream swap Swiss francs IRS quotes against swap quotes provided for part of the period considered by a major swap broker (Gottex). No significant difference or clear outliers were found. Sun et al. (1993) compared Data Stream and DRI LIBOR and LIBID data and concluded that the two sources provided rates that are not "economically different from each other".

Next is the description of the data retained for the analysis made.

In order to assess graphically the swap rate structure over the period, Figure 8.1 provides the surface of the monthly quoted Swiss francs IRS offer rates for the different maturities available.

These transactions take place in a highly changing interest rate environment: monthly quoted Swiss francs IRS rates (bid and offer) between 1990 and 1994 show increasing as well as decreasing term structures, while for any maturity, the time evolution of the series displays an overall decreasing pattern.

The forward rates we use to calculate spreads are also obtained from Data Stream. The original source is Midland Bank quotes (long-term rating of Aa3). Quotes were also available from National Westminster Bank (Aa2) and Barclays Bank (Aa2), but included fewer of the maturities and currency pairs needed.

Collateralization, Credit Lines and Other Considerations

An important characteristic of our data is that they do not involve any collateralization. Collateralization has now become frequent and certainly obliterates part or all of the credit risk pricing. At the time of our operations though, MSB did not use collateralization. Daily marking-to-market and some netting by counterparty occurred. Counterparties of different credit risk were not treated differently regarding these two aspects. Because of marking-to-market and netting we can expect some distortion of the impact of credit risk on prices compared to simple pricing models. But according to professionals, the largest distortion should come from the use of credit lines.

Many professionals, when asked about the pricing of credit risk in swaps, have told us that they will not price swap contracts differently for differently rated banks or companies (a statement that makes it all the more important to test for the presence of credit risk spreads). They claim they actually use credit lines. Banks or companies that do not have a credit line with the intermediary concerned will have to open one, or post a guarantee. Banks or companies that have a credit line will be limited in their operations with that intermediary to the amount fixed by the credit line, with different multiplicative factors affecting the different product lines. In other words, the relatively limited credit risk of swaps, relatively to the size of the notional, will be rationed thanks to the credit line to this bank or company. For example, our medium-size bank can hold credit lines with proportional factors of 5% for IRS transactions of less than 12 months of maturity, 10% for longer maturities, 15% for CS transactions of less than 12 months, and 30% for CS of maturities longer than 12 months. Thus if bank AAA has a credit line with MSB of $20 million, of which $12 million are currently in use for other operations, no long-term IRS swap of more than $80 million will be allowed, save for negotiating a credit line revision.

How can a credit line substitute for credit risk pricing? It does if only homogeneous and extremely low credit risks are given out credit lines (an extreme form of rationing). It also does if the credit line reduces in itself the credit risk of the instrument, i.e. the credit risk of the counterparty is highly correlated to the operation considered and not correlated to any other operation (another extreme case, certainly not pertinent to the swaps considered, which will most often not be the basis of the credit risk of the counterparty involved; indeed swaps are rarely the major activity of a counterparty, be it a bank or a company). In other cases (i.e. in general), free credit lines cannot substitute for correct pricing of credit risk. And as markets become more complete, more diverse counterparties in regard to their credit risk are entering swap transactions and the pricing of credit risk becomes a critical issue.

Note that an equilibrium price for credit risk on swaps may arise from the market even if intermediaries do not price credit risk efficiently individually. Suppose, indeed, that credit lines are highly correlated to credit risk. A bank that has significant credit risk will soon face the limits of its credit lines with its main partners. It will then have to relax its pricing to be able to obtain credit lines with new intermediaries, with which it had no previous relationships. This effect may be particularly important for medium-size players that tend to be price takers, as our MSB often seems to be. But such an effect can only be temporary, before an efficient pricing of credit risk (or alternatively an efficient control via collateralization) sets in the markets.

Next we present the empirical evidence on swap credit risk pricing that arises from our data set.

8.3.2 Empirical Evidence

General Methodology

The primary goal of this study was to examine the presence of credit risk in the pricing of swap deals. In the next subsections, we present the results of our study for IRS and CS taken separately. It is known that CS are more subject to credit risk, as in CS the principal is actually exchanged at the beginning of the swap and again at maturity, while in IRS the notional is not exchanged. We would thus expect credit spreads to be higher on CS, all else being equal. Theoretical models pricing credit risk do obtain this result (see Duffie and Huang, 1996). On the other hand, the CS we consider are rather short term (up to 2 years) while the IRS are of longer maturity (up to 10 years). We would expect the longer maturity instrument (here the IRS) to be more credit-risk sensitive. Note also that the principal amount is generally larger in IRS. It thus makes sense to investigate the credit risk of each instrument separately. The reader will also find an analysis of the global sample in the last subsection (merged data), in order to take advantage of a larger sample to examine statistical tests of presence of credit risk in swap data overall.

The methodology of the study is designed as follows: for the whole study, we use spreads of transaction data to market quotes. We compare the transaction data available to the corresponding bid or offer swap rate quoted for the same day or currency forward rate quoted for the same day as given on Data Stream and described earlier (we do not have intraday data, so that some bias may arise there in highly volatile environments). These data correspond to quotes to the interbank market, for which the rating could be estimated to be a solid A, although this is a difficult issue. As noticed notably by Grinblatt (1994), because the interbank market is a group of banks and because there is no perfect correlation in the dynamics of bank ratings, some diversification effect exists: the rating of the portfolio is better than the average rating of the participants. The probability of being downgraded is stronger for a single bank than for the interbank market as a whole (which will be sensitive only to systemic downgrades). The interbank market will be downgraded only if the overall rating quality of banks goes down. If a bank is downgraded while its competitors are not, it will probably drop out of the interbank market and the downgrade will not affect the interbank market rating.

As an example, consider an IRS. If, in the transaction considered, MSB receives fixed payments, the relative spread considered will be the transaction rate minus the quoted offer rate of the same day. That gives the absolute difference in basis points which, divided by the quoted offer rate of the same day, gives the relative difference. If MSB receives the floating rate payments, the relative difference considered will be the quoted bid rate of the day minus the transaction rate divided by the quoted bid rate. This allows us to pool the two sides and have the counterparty risk theoretically affect relative differences in the same direction (lower credit risk should lead to lower absolute and relative differences). Note that the spreads considered are spreads to the interbank market and not spreads to riskfree securities as is the norm for US IRS (but is not the norm for Swiss francs swaps).

We first present statistical summary tables and robust test of differences for the given rating categories. This allows us to investigate closely differences in ratings and terms. Note that overall, the relative differences between transaction data for the pooled transaction counterparties of the whole sample and the interbank quoted rates are significantly different from 0, with a mean of -0.00304 and a standard error of 0.00104. On average, MSB's counterparties get a better rate than the quoted interbank rate.

In order to analyze further the raw data, we use then a straightforward regression of the type:

$$Y_n = \alpha + \beta \, \text{dummy}_n + \gamma \, \text{maturity}_n + \phi \, \text{amount}_n + \epsilon_n, \tag{8.14}$$

where $n \in [1, N]$, and where the dummy takes value 1 if the point belongs to group 2 and 0 if it belongs to group 1. Groups 1 and 2 are chosen to be of comparable size (as our sample is small) and of clearly different ratings. β is thus the difference of the mean in Y of group 2 and group 1. This enables us to check that some credit risk pricing exists and is not explained away by differences in contract terms (maturity, amount). We consider as a dependent variable the difference (absolute or relative) between the actual transaction price and the corresponding bid or offer side of the quoted rate for the same day, either the IRS quote of corresponding maturity or the currency forward rate of the corresponding maturity. Amounts are in Swiss francs and maturities are in years.

Interest Rate Swaps (IRS)

We first consider the IRS. We start thus with 55 data points representing differences in basis points between transaction data and interbank market quotes.

The IRS in which our nonrated medium-size bank participated consist in 24 operations with Aaa rated counterparties (Moody's rating), 7 with Aa1 rated counterparties, 12 with Aa2 rated counterparties, 4 with A1 rated counterparties, 1 with A3 rated counterparties, 1 with a nonrated bank, and 6 with nonrated companies. The companies tend to be local and medium size, and we would expect most of them to obtain a rather low rating (strictly lower than A) in case they would apply for one. The banks are a less unified mix as some medium-size state banks might be included, banks that may obtain a rather high rating if they applied for one. Some local banks with higher credit risk are probably present in the data too. In short, unrated banks can be of good quality (all are Swiss, some are state owned), but need not be so.

We first investigate the pricing differences among rating categories. Table 8.6 presents standard statistics on pricing, maturities, and notional amounts per rating group and Table 8.7 presents the p-values of tests of differences for the different variables over different rating groups. Tests of difference are done following standard Student

Table 8.6 Standard statistics per rating group for the difference in basis points (Diff bp), the maturity and the amount for the IRS transaction data. SE stands for standard error. UF stands for unrated firms and UB for unrated banks. Reproduced with authorization from Cossin and Pirotte (1997)

	# obs.	Diff bp		Maturity		Amount	
		Mean	SE	Mean	SE	Mean	SE
Aaa	24	−5.51	1.46	8.71	0.41	40 625 000.00	5 502 901.90
Aa	19	−4.35	2.07	8.32	0.56	64 105 263.16	7 156 110.93
A	5	−5.77	1.18	7.80	0.66	50 000 000.00	0.00
UF	6	5.89	2.88	8.50	0.81	46 666 666.67	13 017 082.79
UB	1	−1.00	0.00	4.00	0.00	25 000 000.00	0.00

Table 8.7 This table presents the p-values of tests of differences for the different variables over different rating groups. Diff bp stands for the difference in basis points of the transaction data with the market quoted rate. The first panel shows the results for the normal mean test, assuming a normal distribution of differences. Corrections for small sampling bias have been taken into account. The second panel shows the results computed by the mean of a nonparametric test, i.e. without making any assumption on the underlying distribution. This method is clearly useful when small samples are considered. Reproduced with authorization from Cossin and Pirotte (1997)

p-values obs.		Diff bp					Maturity					Amount			
		Aaa	Aa	A	UF		Aaa	Aa	A	UF		Aaa	Aa	A	UF
Normal	Aaa					Aaa					Aaa				
mean	Aa	0.64				Aa	0.57				Aa	0.01			
test	A	0.94	0.73			A	0.35	0.66			A	0.45	0.33		
	UF	0.00	0.02	0.01		UF	0.82	0.87	0.53		UF	0.64	0.25	0.82	
	UB	0.54	0.72	0.17	0.41	UB	0.03	0.10	0.08	0.09	UB	0.58	0.24	1.00	0.56
Non-	Aaa														
parametric	Aa	0.30													
	A	0.57	0.19												
	UF	0.11	0.17	0.00											
	UB	1.00	1.00	0.33	0.29										

procedures, as well as under a nonparametric framework to check the robustness of our results[14].

Except for the A group, the mean spread of each group is ranked in the expected order. The Aaa group has the lowest negative spread (when excluding the small sample of five As) while the unrated firm group has the highest spread to quotes (i.e. MSB can

[14]The small size of our samples makes standard Student tests of difference of distribution somewhat unreliable, even when adjusting for small sample bias as we do. We thus also use nonparametric tests based on the method of ranking runs (see Hogg and Craig, 1995, p. 517). On the other hand, nonparametric tests based on ranking are not good for testing distribution differences for noncontinuous distributions such as maturity and amounts (for example, the 24 Aaa take only six different values for amount and five for maturities). This is why we present the nonparametric tests for spreads only.

Table 8.8 Regression results on the sample of IRS. The dependent variable is the relative difference between the quoted Swiss francs IRS rate and the IRS of our transaction data for that day. Here α and β denote the constant and the coefficient of the dummy variable respectively. The dummy variable takes the value 0 for group 1 (ratings of Aaa) and 1 for group 2 (ratings of Aa2 and less). The maturity is in years and the amount in SF, p-values are given in parentheses under the variables concerned. Reproduced with authorization from Cossin and Pirotte (1997)

	α (constant)	β (credit risk dummy)	γ (maturity)	ϕ (amount)	# obs.	R-squared	Prob (F-stat)
1	−3.6241 (0.00)				47		
2	−5.5069 (0.00)	3.8475 (0.08)			47	0.065	0.083
3	−2.6822 (0.57)		−1.11 E-01 (0.84)		47	0.001	0.836
4	−6.1663 (0.01)			5.34 E-08 (0.18)	47	0.039	0.181
5	−5.4679 (0.26)	3.8453 (0.09)	−0.004482 (0.99)		47	0.065	0.227
6	−7.0641 (0.00)	3.2998 (0.15)		3.83 E-08 (0.35)	47	0.084	0.145
7	−9.5569 (0.16)		0.330154 (0.16)	6.59 E-08 (0.59)	47	0.045	0.358
8	−10.3232 (0.12)	3.2829 (0.16)	0.317797 (0.60)	5.04 E-08 (0.29)	47	0.089	0.251

extract much higher spreads from the unrated firm group than from the Aaa rated group). Table 8.8 reveals that the differences are not strong enough to be statistically significant though, except for the unrated firms. The transactions spreads do not differ significantly among the different rated groups (and this is valid in both parametric and nonparametric specifications). Our sample probably suffers from its small size at this point. On the other hand, the unrated firm spreads differ strongly from all the other rating groups. More aggregated tests of difference between the rated group and the unrated group, not reproduced here, show a highly significant difference. As far as maturity is concerned, we would expect the higher ratings to obtain longer maturities and this is what happens, with the exception of the unrated firm group. The unrated firms group, which is clearly segmented against as far as pricing goes, still obtains long maturities. Note that there is no statistically significant difference between the maturity of the differently rated groups. As far as amounts are concerned, except for the Aa group that stands out for large amounts, there is no significant difference between the differently rated groups. Different groupings of ratings on all the dimensions confirm these results.

Given the small size of our sample and the previous results, regression analysis in the way we defined it before will allow us to point out the main "spread ingredients" in our dataset and study the interaction of credit quality with amounts and maturities. Two groups were chosen to split the data about evenly. Group 1 consists in the Aaa rated operations, group 2 in the Aa2, A1, A3 and nonrated companies operations. Results are given out in Table 8.8. Regression #2 (with the constant and the credit risk dummy) is the only one where the F-statistic is valid at less than 10%. In all the combinations, the credit risk dummy is quite significant (even 16% as in regression #8 is a fair result, knowing the small number of observations and the large number of variables). The signs are in the expected direction: examining the estimated value for the constant shows that the fixed rate received in transactions with Aaa banks is lower than the fixed rate quoted on the same day in the interbank market. Because we consider the corresponding bid or offer side of the quoted rate, the constant does not measure some systematic bias that could exist between midmarket quotes and actual transaction prices. It does, however, represent a systematic bias between the actual transaction rate and the corresponding side of the quoted rate. This is instructive in itself: market quotes are not what MSB transacts at, at least when dealing with Aaas. A possible explanation for this is that Aaa banks obtain a "better" rate from MSB (or offer a less "good" rate to MSB) than banks or companies with a lower rating. The Aaa group thus distinguishes itself from the average sample and from the interbank market (possibly because of lower credit risk). An alternative explanation would be that MSB, because it is a relatively small player, must get smaller average spreads on its transactions in order to compete in the market[15].

This relationship is highly significant (except in regressions #3 and #5). The positive dummy coefficient shows that the fixed rate received from counterparties of rating lower than Aa2 is higher than the one received from Aaa counterparties on average. It is interesting to notice that the value of the coefficient does not change much from a regression to another. It is not very sensitive to the configuration of the regression (whether or not the terms of the swaps are integrated) and hence is probably a good measure[16]. Thus many elements seem to point towards a pricing of credit risk in interest swaps. Aaa banks differentiate themselves strongly from the interbank market. Highly rated companies differentiate themselves also from low or nonrated companies.

It is also interesting to look at the impact of the maturity of the contract and size of the notional. Computing correlations (see Table 8.9) directly shows little dependence between our credit risk dummy and the amount of the contract (0.25) or the maturity of the contract (-0.11). It also reveals a -0.50 correlation between maturity and size of contract: perhaps in order to limit its credit risk exposure, MSB tends to deal in smaller amounts in longer-term contracts. Neither of the two variables appear to have explanatory power on its own or in combinations with other variables, as can be seen in the regression table. Everything looks as if, as far as IRS are concerned, only credit risk affects the pricing. Terms of the contracts do not seem to have a significant impact on the swaps spreads to the interbank market, once credit risk has been taken into account.

We then look at the economic importance of the regression results found. Our regression results (#2) show that a difference in ratings of Aaa (group 1) to Aa2 or lower (group 2) leads to a difference in effective rate of 3.8 basis points. Although the number may seem small at first, in the highly competitive swap market, 3.8 basis points are economically very important.

---

[15]We thank an anonymous referee for stressing this point to us. MSB is not rated, but is considered as very low credit risk on the markets as it has an implicit state guarantee. It will be interesting to check if the same result is obtained with the combined sample.

[16]A general test for heteroskedasticity following White (1980) reveals a not-to-be-neglected probability of heteroskedasticity in some regressions. We implemented the White procedure for statistical correction. The results were not significantly affected (results not presented here but available from the authors).

Table 8.9 Correlations between amounts, the dummy variable (accounting for rating differences between Aaa rated companies and companies rated Aa2 or less) and the maturity of the swap, for the sample of IRS as defined in the previous regression. Reproduced with authorization from Cossin and Pirotte (1997)

	β (credit risk dummy)	γ (maturity)	ϕ (amount)
β (credit risk dummy)	1		
γ (maturity)	-0.116743	1	
ϕ (amount)	0.255332	-0.503497	1

We then investigate the impact of the interest rate volatility on the credit risk spreads. Theoretical models value credit risk as an option and thus find that credit spreads increase with interest rate volatility. We regress spreads on a constant and an interest rate volatility measure. Our results are qualitatively in that direction (negative coefficient to the interest rate volatility) and the statistical significance is good with a t-statistic of -1.81 (8% significance threshold; detailed results not reproduced here)[17].

In conclusion, there seems to be some pricing of credit risk in our sample of IRS[18]. We have apparently been able to separate the pricing from the impact of the swap terms themselves. Transactions carried out with rated counterparties are close in spreads to one another. But there is a strong difference of spreads with unrated companies. Unrated firms — that we suppose, along with professionals, to have higher credit risk — have much less favorable prices on the swap market but no worse terms (maturities and amounts are not significantly different from those of the rated firms).

Next we investigate whether these results are specific to IRS or hold for currency swaps as well.

Short-term Currency Swaps

In our IRS sample, we came to the conclusion that credit risk affects prices and that terms do not affect prices. We now look at the behavior of our sample of short-term CS. As previously mentioned, these so-called swaps behave much like forwards. Their maturities are short. We have 119 data points, including 7 operations with Aaa banks, 12 with Aa1 banks, 14 with Aa2 banks, 1 with AA rated counterparty (Standard and Poors' rating, no Moody's rating), 6 with A3 banks, 69 with nonrated banks and 10 with nonrated companies.

We operate the same tests as before and first analyze differences among the different rating groups. With the strong exception of the Aaa group, the ranking of the spreads is as expected: it increases with credit risk and the unrated banks actually do not present very high credit risk (possibly a Swiss particularity!). We cannot explain at this point

---

[17]Note that the level of the transaction rates (as opposed to the spreads, that we looked at before) is highly dependent on the volatility of interest rates, with a t-statistic of 8.5.

[18]A simple test also indicates that there seems to be significantly more credit risk pricing in our sample in 1994 than there was in 1992 (t-statistic of 1.75, or 8% significance for the difference), a possible indication that markets are becoming more efficient at pricing credit risk or that lower credit ratings are accessing the swap markets. We do not reproduce the regression here because of the small size of the sample.

Table 8.10 Standard statistics per rating group for the difference in percentage (Diff 100), the maturity, and the amount for the CS transaction data. SE stands for standard error, UF stands for unrated firms, and UB for unrated bank. Reproduced with authorization from Cossin and Pirotte (1997)

	# obs.	Diff bp Mean	Diff bp SE	Maturity Mean	Maturity SE	Amount Mean	Amount SE
Aaa	7	0.0049	0.0042	11.14	0.86	15 107 203.23	8 375 933.15
Aa	27	−0.0072	0.0038	9.48	0.67	16 259 064.84	2 823 939.51
A3	6	0.0026	0.0057	6.33	2.01	31 397 111.21	8 559 035.42
UB	69	−0.0023	0.0011	3.71	0.35	1 601 472.66	728 434.62
UF	10	0.0088	0.0047	4.9	0.97	15 524 383.11	6 916 515.40

Table 8.11 This table presents the *p*-values of test of differences for the different variables over different rating groups. Diff 100 stands for the difference in percent of the transaction data with the market quoted rate. The first panel shows the results for the normal mean test assuming a normal distribution of differences. Corrections for small sampling bias have been taken into account. The second panel shows the results computed by the mean of a nonparametric test, i.e., without making any assumption on the underlying distribution. This method is clearly useful when small samples are considered. Reproduced with authorization from Cossin and Pirotte (1997)

p-values obs.		Diff bp Aaa	Diff bp Aa	Diff bp A	Diff bp UF		Maturity Aaa	Maturity Aa	Maturity A	Maturity UF		Amount Aaa	Amount Aa	Amount A	Amount UF
Normal	Aaa					Aaa					Aaa				
mean	Aa	0.13				Aa	0.24				Aa	0.87			
test	A	0.74	0.26			A	0.04	0.07			A	0.61	0.48		
	UF	0.05	0.09	0.22		UF	0.00	0.00	0.05		UF	0.00	0.00	0.00	
	UB	0.56	0.02	0.42	0.00	UB	0.00	0.00	0.48	0.24	UB	0.97	0.91	0.61	0.00
Non-	Aaa														
parametric	Aa	0.79													
	A	0.88	0.79												
	UF	0.15	0.28	0.46											
	UB	0.55	0.30	0.96	0.03										

the strong unexpected spreads to Aaas. It should be noted that we have only seven Aaas in the CS sample though, and that the standard error is strong. We may just be facing a small sample problem. We find also very little difference between the rated groups but some difference between the unrated firms and the rated counterparties (although not with all rated groups). These differences have low statistical significance (see Tables 8.10 and 8.11). The unrated firms are less distinct in CS than they were in IRS swaps.

Interestingly, maturities evolve clearly and significantly toward lower maturities for higher credit risks (with the exception of the difficult-to-interpret unrated banks). Amounts are not significantly different from each other. It looks as if, as far as CS are concerned, credit risk affects terms (and especially maturity) more than pricing, even if some price impact remains. Different groupings of the ratings confirm these results.

Clearly, the size of the sample affects the statistical significance of the disaggregated data. Nonetheless, maturity seems to play an important role in CS while it did not in

Table 8.12 Regression results on the sample of currency swaps. The dependent variable is the relative difference between the quoted forward exchange rate and the CS rate. α and β denote the constant and the coefficient associated with dummy variables respectively (accounting for differences between the high-ratings group 1 and the low-ratings group 2). The maturity is in years and the amount in US\$, p-values are given in parentheses under the variables concerned. Reproduced with authorization from Cossin and Pirotte (1997)

	α (constant)	β (credit risk dummy)	γ (maturity)	ϕ (amount)	# obs.	R-squared	Prob (F-stat)
1	0.0004 (0.88)				35		
2	−0.0046 (0.26)	0.0111 (0.07)			35	0.096	0.070
3	−0.0029 (0.65)		4.56 E-4 (0.55)		35	0.011	0.546
4	0.0023 (0.57)			−1.20 E-10 (0.48)	35	0.015	0.483
5	−0.0177 (0.04)	0.0166 (0.02)	0.001404 (0.08)		35	0.177	0.044
6	−0.0024 (0.60)	0.0117 (0.06)		−1.53 E-10 (0.36)	35	0.119	0.130
7	−0.0003 (0.97)		0.000302 (0.61)	−9.50 E-11 (0.71)	35	0.019	0.733
8	−0.0159 (0.12)	0.0164 (0.02)	0.0013 (0.14)	−5.71 E-11 (0.74)	35	0.180	0.099

IRS. Some credit risk pricing also appears significant at the pooled data regression level, although it remains controversial at the disaggregated level.

As for the IRS case, we undertook regression analysis in order to analyze further the relationship between credit risk pricing and contract terms. We build a credit risk dummy on two groups with a similar number of companies and significant rating differences: group 1 consists of operations with ratings better than Aa1, and group 2 of companies with ratings of single A or no rating. The results are shown in Table 8.12. The difference in transaction rates between the higher-rated and the lower-rated group is positive as expected, and strongly significant across all the specifications considered, with a t-statistic of a minimum of 1.86[19]. The F-statistic gives overall statistical significance to all regressions where the credit risk dummy is included and the R2 remains over 10% each time the credit risk dummy is included. The regression results clearly strengthen the results of the previous tests on smaller ranking categories. Credit risk plays a significant role here. It is less easy to isolate the unrated firms as being the impetus for pricing differences as they seem to be in interest swaps. The notional amount of the contract does not play a significant role in explaining the spreads to the interbank market. The maturity does not play a role in itself, but becomes significant when considered with the credit risk dummy, and this whatever the configuration considered (regressions #5 and #8). The terms of the contract, and more precisely the

---

[19] We also checked that calculating heteroskedasticity consistent coefficients does not affect our results significantly.

Table 8.13   Correlations between amounts, the dummy variable (accounting for rating differences between companies better rated than Aa1 and companies less well rated than A) and the maturity of the swap, for the sample of currency swaps as defined in the regression analysis. Reproduced with authorization from Cossin and Pirotte (1997)

	β (credit risk dummy)	γ (maturity)	ϕ (amount)
β (credit risk dummy)	1		
γ (maturity)	-0.473521	1	
ϕ (amount)	0.101045	-0.367523	1

maturity, does impact spreads when considering CS, while it did not impact spreads for IRS.

We are dealing with a low credit risk portfolio of companies. Interestingly, it looks as if our intermediary may have tried to limit its credit risk exposure. It is mainly active in CS that are very short term, while CS are more default sensitive than IRS. By choosing short-term instruments, MSB may be limiting its credit risk exposure in CS.

The negative correlation between amounts and maturities shows also that exposure to longer maturities instruments, being more default sensitive, may have been limited by not taking large amounts in long maturities (see Table 8.13). Thus, credit risk may be stronger in larger samples than MSB's swap portfolio and may also become stronger as credit risk pricing becomes more efficient in the markets. Nonetheless, the economic significance of our regressions results should not be neglected as they mean that a counterparty of the lower rating group can obtain a rate 1.11% lower than a counterparty of the higher rating group (as a percentage of the higher rating group rate).

Results When Considering all Swaps

Finally, we consider the overall swap sample, with all types (currency and interest rates), sides (bid and offer), maturities (from 3 months to 10 years), and amounts mixed. Although we are pooling here instruments that are somewhat different, we are trying to overcome the small sample problems we had before and obtain confirmation of credit risk pricing in the swap markets. Using relative differences with interbank market quotes allows us to easily pool currency and IRS transaction data. We have thus 174 data points, including 31 Aaa counterparties, 19 Aa1, 26 Aa2, 1 AA, 4 A1, 7 A3, 70 nonrated banks and 16 with nonrated companies.

Because of the heterogeneity of the data, we only do the regression analysis. Group 1 consists in Aaa rated counterparties and group 2 in single A rated counterparties and nonrated companies (assumed as being of single A rating or less). The overall results are presented in Table 8.14[20]. First, our subsample of transaction data is not statistically different overall from the corresponding side (bid or offer) of market quotes (*p*-value of 0.63 in regression #1). By regressing the difference between transaction and quoted rates on a constant and a credit risk dummy, we find a highly significant regression regarding the *F*-statistic (probability of the set of coefficients being non-significant of only 0.01%).

---

[20]Correcting for possible heteroskedasticity through the White (1980) procedure confirms these results.

Table 8.14 Regression results on the overall sample (including IRS and CS). The dependent variable is the relative difference between the quoted Swiss francs IRS rate and the IRS rate of our transaction data for the IRS swaps (IRS) and the relative difference between the quoted forward exchange rate and the CS exchange rate of our transaction data for currency swaps (CS). The dummy variable takes the value 0 for Aaa-rated companies and 1 for the A rated companies and the nonbank unrated ones. The maturity is in years and the amount in SF, p-values are given in parentheses under the variables concerned. Reproduced with authorization from Cossin and Pirotte (1997)

	α (constant)	β (credit risk dummy)	γ (maturity)	ϕ (amount)	# obs.	R-squared	Prob (F-stat)
1	−0.0009 (0.63)				58		
2	−0.0054 (0.03)	0.0097 (0.01)			58	0.115	0.009
3	0.0056 (0.06)		−1.21 E-03 (0.01)		58	0.126	0.006
4	0.0016 (0.59)			−7.4 E-11 (0.29)	58	0.020	0.290
5	0.0008 (0.84)	0.0067 (0.09)	−0.000893 (0.06)		58	0.172	0.005
6	−0.0032 (0.36)	0.0094 (0.01)		−6.3 E-11 (0.35)	58	0.130	0.022
7	0.0062 (0.07)		−0.001169 (0.72)	−2.5 E-11 (0.01)	58	0.129	0.023
8	0.0015 (0.73)	0.0068 (0.08)	−0.000833 (0.09)	−3.1 E-11 (0.65)	58	0.176	0.015

The coefficient for the constant is strongly different from 0 and negative at −0.005. Our lower rating group presents a positive and highly significant difference with the higher rated group, as expected. The discussion made in the IRS case is then still topical. Overall, there seems to be a price element linked to credit risk as measured by ratings differences between our two groups. A R2 of only 11% shows that with credit risk, we capture only a small part of the variance of the spreads to the interbank market. This result could be expected as many other factors will enter the determination of swap spreads (see the study by Chen and Selender, 1995, for example).

To confirm this effect and/or look for alternative explanations to the difference found, we look into whether we could just be capturing the effect of missing variables, e.g. the terms of the contracts: the amount and the maturity of the contracts. It is possible that there would be a price discrimination based on quantities traded or simply a liquidity effect that would be captured indirectly by ratings. The correlation between the rating dummy and amounts is rather low at −0.11, while it is somewhat higher between the dummy and maturities (−0.40) and the amounts and maturities (0.36), this last number being mostly explained by the difference between CS and IRS.

Regressing the relative difference on the notional amount traded, however, provides us with a highly nonsignificant regression (regression #4). Hence, on the overall sample, the notional amount exchanged does not seem to explain the difference between quoted rates and actual transaction data. Maturity could also be a factor affecting the spreads. If there is credit risk, you expect this risk to grow with maturity (i.e. the option the

Table 8.15 Correlations between amounts, the dummy variable (accounting for rating differences between Aaa rated companies and A rated or unrated companies) and the maturity of the swap. Reproduced with authorization from Cossin and Pirotte (1997)

	β (credit risk dummy)	γ (maturity)	ϕ (amount)
β (credit risk dummy)	1		
γ (maturity)	−0.401283	1	
ϕ (amount)	−0.107595	0.369261	1

credit risk-taker is short increases in value with maturity). Regressing the usual relative difference on the maturity of the different contract is statistically significant, both at the regression and at the coefficients level (regression #3). Although the coefficient of the maturity variable is highly significant, its sign is opposite to the one we would first expect (we would expect longer maturities to have larger spreads). A possible explanation is that because of the very diverse mix of instruments considered, from 3-month CS (that look almost like forwards) to 10-year interest rate swaps, the maturity variable may actually capture the overall difference between our CS (which are short term) and our IRS (which are long term). The maturity coefficient is indeed positive for the CS sample (longer maturities obtain less good rates). The negative sign of the coefficient would follow if we have larger spreads for currency (an instrument highly sensitive to credit risk) than for interest rate swaps. A second explanation is that highly rated counterparties have longer maturity swaps than do lower rated counterparties (see the strong negative correlation of −0.4 between the dummy and the maturity): in that case, it would show that credit risk affects the terms (and here specifically the maturity) of the swap contracts one can obtain from dealers, and not only swap rates.

Next, we check whether swap terms can explain away the credit risk dummy impact. In other words, we check whether the terms choices by intermediaries take away the price impact of credit risk. We combine the different variables in the regressions. Note that different combinations always lead to the credit risk dummy being significant and all except #7 also lead to the maturity being significant[21]. We do not take away the explanatory power of the credit risk dummy by introducing the terms of the contracts (amount, maturity). Credit risk as represented by the dummy seems to affect swap pricing in a manner that cannot be reduced to swap terms. But swap terms (and maturity specifically) also seem to play an important role (see Table 8.15).

Market participants have told us that they do not price contracts differently depending on credit risk. The data seem to show that some credit risk pricing may actually occur in the market, even on data reflecting a low credit risk overall. There exists at least one solution to this puzzle. Suppose that traders of one firm do not offer different prices to different credit risk counterparties, but ration them depending on their credit quality. A low rating company will reach the maximum of its credit line faster than a high rating company. It will have to obtain a quote from a globally less favorable dealer. At equilibrium, in the market, participants may obtain different

---

[21]The behavior of regression #7 makes us suspect some problem such as multicolinearity between the constant, the amount and the maturity.

rates from different dealers even though no dealer gives different quotes to different companies.

The results on pooled data are interesting because they present significant amounts of data to test on. They also present the major disadvantage of resulting from very heterogeneous data, which can make interpretation difficult. Overall though, they confirm the presence of credit risk pricing we had found at a disaggregated level in both CS and IRS.

Conclusions

Cossin and Pirotte (1997) show support for the presence of credit risk in swap spreads during the period considered, confirming thereby the Sun et al. (1993) study. Credit ratings appear to be a significant factor affecting swap spreads not only for the pooled sample but for IRS and for CS separately as well. In IRS, the credit rating impact on prices seems to come largely to the detriment of the nonrated companies.

Overall credit risk pricing exists in the data. It does not appear to be strong statistically at the disaggregated level (although it has an important economic significance at the aggregated level). Many other factors certainly affect spreads. But the low impact of credit risk here may also be linked to sample bias: several elements seem to show that MSB may have tried to limit its credit risk exposure in its choice of instruments used.

Another interesting result is that swap terms, and especially maturity, also play an important role. Maturity is particularly important concerning the highly sensitive currency swaps (an impact very clearly obtained at the disaggregated level too). Amounts do not have a significant impact in any configuration. A better understanding of the interaction of swap terms and pricing and their relationship to credit risk is required at the empirical level. Unfortunately, recent practices, such as collateralization, will make it even more difficult to analyze credit risk in swaps, by adding another dimension to the already complex problem.

Current research is not far along as far as our empirical understanding of credit risk in swaps is concerned. Much more research is needed in this area. Tests of the theoretical models currently available will also help our understanding (see Cossin and Pirotte, 1998, for such a test). But in general, larger databases will be necessary for our understanding of market pricing and management of swap credit risk via collateralization to advance significantly. Hopefully, swap market operators will start trusting academics with large samples of confidential data, as empirical studies are still lagging behind theoretical work in this field.

8.4   REFERENCES

Altman, E. and D. L. Kao, 1992, "Rating Drift in High-Yield Bonds", *Journal of Fixed Income*, March.

Baz, Jamil, 1995, "Three Essays on Contingent Claims", Harvard PhD Thesis, August.

Black, F. and J. C. Cox, 1976, "Valuing Corporate Securities: Some Effects of Bond Indenture Provisions", *Journal of Finance*, **31**, 351–67.

Chen, Andrew and Arthur Selender, 1995, "Determination of Swap Spreads: An Empirical Analysis", *Working Paper*, Southern Methodist University, Edwin L. Cox School of Business, Dallas, Texas, February.

Cooper, Ian A. and Antonio S. Mello, 1991, "The Default Risk of Swaps", *Journal of Finance*, **46**, 597–620.

Cossin, Didier and Hugues Pirotte, 1997. "Swap Credit Risk: An Empirical Investigation on Transaction Data", *Journal of Banking & Finance*, **21** (10), 1351–73, October.

Cossin, D. and H. Pirotte, 1998, "How Well Do Classical Credit Risk Models Fit Swap Transaction Data?", *European Financial Management Journal*, **4** (1), March, 65–78.

Cox, J. C., J. E. Ingersoll and S. A. Ross, 1985a, "A Theory of the Term Structure of Interest Rates", *Econometrica*, **53**, 385.

Das, S., 1994, *Swap and Derivative Financing*, Probus Publishing, Chicago, Illinois.

Duffee, G. R., 1995a, "On Measuring Credit Risks of Derivative Instruments", *Working Paper*, Federal Reserve Board, February.

Duffee, G. R., 1995b, "The Variation of Default Risk with Treasury Yields", *Working Paper*, Federal Reserve Board, January.

Duffie, Darrell and Ming Huang, 1996, "Swap Rates and Credit Quality", *Journal of Finance*, **51** (3), July, 921–49.

Duffie, D. and K. Singleton, 1994, "Econometric Modeling of Term Structures of Defaultable Bonds", *Working Paper*, Graduate School of Business, Stanford University, November.

Duffie, Darrell and Ken Singleton, 1999, "Modeling Term Structures of Defaultable Bonds", *Review of Financial Studies*, Special 1999, **12** (4), 687–720.

Fama, Eugene F., 1984, "Term Premiums in bond returns", *Journal of Financial Economics*, **13**, 529–46.

Grinblatt, Mark, 1994, "An Analytic Solution for Interest Rate Swaps Spreads", *Working Paper*, UCLA AGSM, June.

Hogg, Robert V. and A. T. Craig, 1995, *Introduction to Mathematical Statistics*, Prentice-Hall, 5th edn, Englewood Cliffs, NJ.

Hübner, Georges, 1997b, "The Analytic Pricing of Asymmetric Defaultable Swaps", *Working Paper 97/24/FIN*, INSEAD, Paris and University of Liège, Belgium, 52 pp.

Iben, B. and R. Brotherton-Ratcliffe, 1994, "Credit Loss Distributions and Required Capital for Derivatives Portfolios", *Journal of Fixed Income*, June, 6–14.

Iben, Th. and R. Litterman, 1991, "Corporate Bond Valuation and the Term Structure of Credit Spreads", *Journal of Portfolio Management*, **17** (3), Spring, 52–64.

Jarrow, R. and Stuart Turnbull, 1995, "Pricing Derivatives on Financial Securities Subject to Credit Risk", *Journal of Finance*, **50** (1), March, 53–85.

Lando, David, 1994, "On Cox Processes and Credit Risk Bonds", *Working Paper*, Institute of Mathematical Statistics, University of Copenhagen.

Li, Haitao, 1996, "Pricing of Swaps with Default Risk", *Working Paper*, Yale School of Management, New Haven, 38 pp.

Longstaff, F. and E. Schwartz, 1994, "A Simple Approach to Valuing Risky Fixed and Floating Rate Debt and Determining Swap Spreads", *Working Paper* (22-93), Anderson Graduate School of Management, University of California, April.

Longstaff, Francis and Eduardo Schwartz, 1995b, "A Simple Approach to Valuing Risky Fixed and Floating Rate Debt", *Journal of Finance*, **50** (3), July, 789–819.

Lucas, D. J. and J. Lonski, 1992, "Changes in Corporate Credit Quality 1970–1990", *Journal of Fixed Income*, **2**, March, 7–14.

Merton, Robert C., 1974, "On the Pricing of Corporate Debt: The Risk Structure of Interest Rates", *The Journal of Finance*, **29**, May, 449–70.

Ramaswamy, K, and Suresh Sundaresan, 1986, "The Valuation of Floating-Rate Instruments", *Journal of Finance*, **17**, February, 251–72.

Sorensen, Eric H. and Thierry F. Bollier, 1994, "Pricing Swap Default Risk", *Financial Analysts Journal*, **50** (3), May–June, 23–33.

Sun, Tong Sheng, Suresh Sundaresan and Ching Wang, 1993, "Interest Rate Swaps: An empirical Investigation", *Journal of Financial Economics*, **34** (1), August, 77–99.

Wall, Larry D. and John J. Pringle, 1998, "Interest Rate Swaps: A Review of the Issues", *Federal Reserve Bank of Atlanta Economic Review*, **73** (November/December), 22–37.

White, H., 1980, "A Heteroscedasticity-Consistent Covariance Matrix Estimator and a Direct Test for Heteroscedasticity", *Econometrica*, **48**, 817–38.

9

Credit Risk in Options: Vulnerable Options

9.1 INTRODUCTION

Vulnerable options are those where the option writer may default and not honor the possible exercise. They should not be confused with options on a defaultable underlying[1], although the asset measuring the writer's credit rating can be correlated with the optioned asset price. As observed by Rich (1996), would these two reference assets be the same, for example would the equity in a levered firm be viewed as a vulnerable option, we get back to the Cox and Rubinstein (1985) paradigm as explained later.

9.2 JOHNSON AND STULZ (1987)

As Johnson and Stulz have pointed out, options subject to default risk do not present some well-established results of standard options and offer a totally new scope of possible outcomes. In particular:

1. The value of a vulnerable European option may decrease with the time to maturity, with the interest rate, and with the volatility of the underlying asset.
2. In the case of a vulnerable American option on a nondividend-paying asset, it could be optimal to exercise earlier than maturity.

In fact, many OTC options in the market are vulnerable options since there is no guarantee from a third counterparty such as a clearing house. Second, many contracts, such as insurance contracts can be assimilated to vulnerable derivative contracts[2]. Any private contract with an option payoff profile without the protection of a credit riskfree intermediary is a vulnerable option.

9.2.1 The Pricing Framework of such Options

As in the case of the structural approach described in earlier chapters, we assume that the optionholder receives the assets value of the option writer, should the latter not honor its commitments in case of exercise of the option. Also, standard assumptions apply again: markets are frictionless (no taxes, no transaction costs, no liquidity costs) and complete, and trading takes place continuously.

If the standard European call option has a profile at maturity of

$$c_T(S, K, T) = \max(S_T - K, 0),$$ (9.1)

---

[1] A typical example of an option on a defaultable underlying is the value of the debt being modeled as a put option on the value of the firm.

[2] There has been some default by insurance companies in the past. However, today, this risk is somewhat mitigated by the existence of reinsurance companies, which contribute to the overall risk-sharing.

where S_T is the underlying variable and K the exercise price, the value of the vulnerable European call at maturity is given by

$$c_T^v(S, V, K, T) = \min(V_T, \max(S_T - K, 0)), \tag{9.2}$$

i.e. it is at most equal to the standard European call value and pays the same payoff only if the option writer is solvent at the exercise time. The joint distribution of S_t and V_t is assumed to be insensitive to any change of S_t or V_t.

The idea of Johnson and Stulz was to rewrite equation (9.2) such that it would have the same form as equation (10.1). Let

$$A_t = \min(K + V_T, S_T),$$

then it is easy to show that

$$c_T^v = \min(V_T, \max(S_T - K, 0)) = \max(A_T - K, 0). \tag{9.3}$$

We can therefore work directly on the derivation of a European call option on A, a new option on the minimum of two assets.

9.2.2   Distribution-free Comparative Statics

Let $E(x, y, T)$ denote a European option to exchange an asset y for an asset x at date T. Then the value of our virtual asset A_t can be derived as

$$\begin{aligned}
A_t &= S_t - E(S_t, Ke^{-r(T-t)} + V_t, T) \equiv S - E^I \\
&= Ke^{-r(T-t)} + V_t - E(Ke^{-r(T-t)} + V_t, S_t, T) \\
&= Ke^{-r(T-t)} + V - E^{II}.
\end{aligned}$$

With the rule $E(x, y, T) = y\, c_T(x/y, 1, T)$, and using previous Merton's results, we obtain the following sensitivities:

$$\frac{\partial A}{\partial S} = -E_2^{II} > 0,$$

$$\frac{\partial A}{\partial V} = -E_2^{I} > 0,$$

$$\frac{\partial A}{\partial K} = -E_2^{I}e^{-r(T-t)} > 0,$$

$$\frac{\partial A}{\partial r} = (T-t)Ke^{-r(T-t)}E_2^{I} < 0,$$

$$\frac{\partial A}{\partial T} = rKe^{-r(T-t)}E_2^{I} - E_3^{I} < 0.$$

Therefore, A_t increases with S, V, and K, and decreases with R and T. Now we can derive the same comparative statics for the vulnerable call option:

$$\frac{\partial c}{\partial S} = c_1^v \frac{\partial A}{\partial S} > 0,$$

$$\frac{\partial c}{\partial V} = c_1^v \frac{\partial A}{\partial V} > 0,$$

$$\frac{\partial c}{\partial K} = c_1^v \frac{\partial A}{\partial K} + c_2^v < 0,$$

$$\frac{\partial c}{\partial r} = c_1^v \frac{\partial A}{\partial r} + \frac{\partial c^v}{\partial r} < 0,$$

$$\frac{\partial c}{\partial T} = c_1^v \frac{\partial A}{\partial T} + \frac{\partial c^v}{\partial T} \gtrless 0.$$

9.2.3 The Put–Call Parity

A vulnerable European put with exercise price K has the following payoff at maturity:

$$p_T^v(S, V, K, T) = \min(V_T, \max(K - S_T, 0)),\qquad(9.4)$$

Again considering an artificial asset, but this time of the form of $a_T = \max(S_T, K - V_T)$, we can make an analogous statement to equation (9.3):

$$p_t^v(S_t, V_t, K, T) = p_t(a_t, K, T).\qquad(9.5)$$

With the standard put–call parity and using expressions (9.3) and (9.5), we can easily derive the new put–call parity relationship. Let

$$M_T = \min(a_T, K + V_T) = \max(A_T, K - V_T).$$

It is straightforward to show that

$$M_t = a_t - E[a_t, Ke^{-r(T-t)} + V_t, T],$$
$$M_t = A_t - E[Ke^{-r(T-t)} - V_t, A_t, T].$$

The put–call parity is obtained as

$$p_t(a_t, K, T) = c_t(A_t, K, T) - M_t + Ke^{-r(T-t)}.\qquad(9.6)$$

Johnson and Stulz provide an easy proof: since the put is exercised only if $a_T < K$, and so is the call only if $A_T > K$, we can replace a_t and A_t by M_t in equation (9.6).

9.2.4 The Case of the American Put and the American Call

We assume that S_t and V_t are the prices of nondividend-paying traded assets. The American call (C) and the American put (P) can be exercised before maturity, but will respect the same rule as with standard American options:

$$C(S_t, V_t, K, T) \geqslant c(S_t, V_t, K, T),\qquad(9.7)$$

$$P(S_t, V_t, K, T) \geqslant p(S_t, V_t, K, T).$$

We know already that even the standard put can be exercised before maturity. But so can the vulnerable call option. This is consistent with the fact that the value of the vulnerable call may decrease with the time to maturity.

The exercise moment of our American vulnerable call before the original maturity is at the first instant that $S - K \geqslant V$. Effectively, we cannot have $C \geqslant V$, since V would dominate the call. And, if $C < V$, then we should have $S - K < V$ because $C \geqslant S - K$.

9.2.5   Applications and Extensions

In their article, Johnson and Stulz (1987) derive the value of their vulnerable option when the option writer offers a default-free bond or a fraction of the underlying asset as collateral. Standard derivations are provided for the underlying asset following either a lognormal diffusion process or a pure jump process, while the value of the firm is overall assumed to be lognormally distributed.

9.3   RICH (1996)

Another important contribution in this area is the paper by Don Rich. His framework allows the timing of default and the recovery value to be uncertain. Different recovery scenarios are provided. The model allows to evaluate the current margin requirements made for exchange-traded options.

In Johnson and Stulz (1987) default can only happen at specific points in time, while the present approach goes in the direction of the previous approach of Hull and White (1995) that allows the writer to default at any point in time[3]. Rich's (1996)[4] main purpose is to value European options subject to an intertemporal default risk. The former approach is said to be preferable if the option is the dominant security in the writer's liability portfolio, because default would be due only to the option's expiration. In cases where the writer has a mixed portfolio with commitments of different maturities, seniorities, and payoff profiles the present approach would be preferred.

Hull and White (1995), however, do not provide any idea regarding the hedging of these vulnerable options and obtain a closed-form solution only in the case of perfectly independent price risk (the risk on the potential payoff of the option) and credit risk (the risk that the option execution may not be honored if positive to the buyer).

Another refinement is that, contrary to previous modeling issued, it is not necessary in Rich (1996) to assume no violations of the absolute priority rule (APR).

9.3.1   First Setting: a No-recovery Framework

It is assumed that there exists a financial characteristic that can depict the writer's creditworthiness. Rich (1996) assumes that, generically, there exists an asset A_t

---

[3]We prefer to present the more recent Rich (1996) paper since it provides a fully analytical framework and it also provides a direct comparison with the Hull and White (1995) development.
[4]The working paper was already available and submitted in March 1995.

proxying the stochastic writer's creditworthiness which would force the firm to enter into bankruptcy, should it breach a critical level D_t that can also be stochastic through time[5].

Suppose for now that there is no recovery at default. Therefore the problem can simply be stated as follows: a European vulnerable call option would be written as

$$C_v(S_t, K, t, T, A_t, D_t),$$

which pays the $\max(S_T - K, 0)$ at T if $A_t > D_t$ for any t between the contract origination and T ($\forall t \in [0, T]$).

Define the behavior of S_t, A_t, and D_t. They are assumed to follow a GBM of the following form:

$$\frac{di_t}{i_t} = \beta_i(t, i_t)dt + \sigma_i dZ_t^i, \quad i \in \{S, A, D\},$$

where $\beta_i(t, i_t)$ is a general formulation for the expected return, σ_i the constant volatility parameter, and Z_t^is are standard Brownian motions. Furthermore it is generally accepted that the innovations of the three Brownian motions can be constantly correlated with parameters $\rho_{S,A}$, $\rho_{S,D}$, $\rho_{A,D}$. The vector $\{\mathbf{Z}_t\}$ represents the implicit three-dimensional Brownian motion.

Traditional Black–Scholes assumptions such as the market completeness and frictionlessness are made. The instantaneous interest rate r is assumed constant while it is accepted that any asset has a continuous payout rate d_i.

Using Itô's lemma to obtain the differential equation, considering the boundary conditions (for the payoff at default or at maturity if default does not occur), and the traditional hedging argument that lead to a portfolio which must generate the riskfree return r, Rich (1996) obtains the following closed-form solution for the European vulnerable call option price[6]:

$$C_v(S_t, K, t, T, A_t, D_t) = Se^{-d_s(T-t)}N_2(y_1, y_2; \rho) \tag{9.8}$$

$$- Ke^{-r(T-t)}N_2(y_1 - \sigma_S\sqrt{T-t}, y_2 - \sigma_S\rho\sqrt{T-t}; \rho)$$

$$- Se^{-d_s(T-t)}\left(\frac{D}{A}\right)^{\gamma_1+\gamma_2} N_2(y_3, y_4; \rho)$$

$$+ Ke^{-r(T-t)}\left(\frac{D}{A}\right)^{\gamma_1} N_2(y_3 - \sigma_S\sqrt{T-t}, y_4 - \sigma_S\rho\sqrt{T-t}; \rho)$$

with

---

[5]In reality, A_t can be initially above D_t if the latter is a minimum asset requirement, or below D_t if, for example, it is a maximum leverage level, etc.

[6]Please refer to Rich (1996) for the entire developments and justifications.

$$\sigma = \mathrm{Var}\left(\ln \frac{A_T}{D_T}\right)\Big/(T-t) = \sigma_A^2 + \sigma_D^2 - 2\sigma_A\sigma_D\rho_{A,D}$$

$$\rho = \mathrm{Corr}\left(\ln S_T, \ln \frac{A_T}{D_T}\right) \times (T-t) = \frac{\sigma_A\rho_{S,A} - \sigma_D\rho_{S,D}}{\sigma}$$

$$\gamma_1 = 2[d_D - d_A - 1/2(\sigma_A^2 - \sigma_D^2)]/\sigma^2$$

$$\gamma_2 = 2\sigma_S\rho/\sigma$$

$$y_1 = \frac{\ln(S/X) + (r - d_S + 1/2\sigma_S^2)(T-t)}{\sigma_S\sqrt{T-t}}$$

$$y_2 = \frac{\ln(A/D) + 1/2(\gamma_1 + \gamma_2)\sigma^2(T-t)}{\sigma\sqrt{T-t}}$$

$$y_3 = y_1 + 2\ln(D/A)\rho/\sigma\sqrt{T-t}$$

$$y_4 = y_2 + 2\ln(D/A)/\sigma\sqrt{T-t},$$

where

$$S \equiv S_t,\ A \equiv A_t,\ D \equiv D_t$$

and $N_2(c_1, c_2; \rho)$ is the bivariate standard cumulative normal distribution function with upper limits of integration c_1 and c_2 and a correlation coefficient of ρ.

The elegance of the development allows us quickly to explain some important issues:

- The Black and Scholes framework is subsumed into the following since it is the simpler case where $A_t \to \infty$ or $D_t \to 0$. In fact, the value of a vulnerable option is upward bounded by the value of its corresponding default-free version.
- The value of the vulnerable option does not depend on the expected return of the underlying assets.
- At default, because of the absence of recovery until here, the value of the formula is zero ($y_1 = y_3$, $y_2 = y_4$).

One could use this formula in the context of a levered firm, where the ratio $\ln(A/D)$ would be obtained from the writer's total asset value and its portfolio of liabilities. Rich warns against doing that because the vulnerable option itself is part of the liability of the writer. Therefore, we would have an option whose vulnerability would depend somewhere on its own value which leads us to a problem of simultaneity. Of course, it could be the case that the option is a tiny fraction of the liabilities and then could be assumed to be insignificant in the ratio $\ln(A/D)$.

If it is noticed that one can rewrite part of the equation above in terms of the Black and Scholes option price as

$$Se^{-d_s(T-t)}N_2(y_1, y_2; \rho) - Ke^{-r(T-t)}N_2(y_1 - \sigma_S\sqrt{T-t}, y_2 - \sigma_S\rho\sqrt{T-t}; \rho)$$

$$= [Se^{-d_s(T-t)}N_1(y_1) - Ke^{-r(T-t)}N_1(y_1 - \sigma_S\sqrt{T-t})] - [Se^{-d_s(T-t)}N_2(y_1, -y_2; -\rho)$$

$$- Ke^{-r(T-t)}N_2(y_1 - \sigma_S\sqrt{T-t}, -y_2 + \sigma_S\rho\sqrt{T-t}; -\rho)],$$

where $N_1(\cdot)$ is the standard cumulative normal distribution function. Then we can extract the default option value owned by the writer and write it as[7]

$$Se^{-d_s(T-t)}N_2(y_1, -y_2; -\rho) - Ke^{-r(T-t)}N_2(y_1 - \sigma_S\sqrt{T-t}, -y_2 + \sigma_S \rho\sqrt{T-t}; -\rho)$$

$$+ Se^{-d_s(T-t)}\left(\frac{D}{A}\right)^{\gamma_1+\gamma_2} N_2(y_3, y_4; \rho)$$

$$- Ke^{-r(T-t)}\left(\frac{D}{A}\right)^{\gamma_1} N_2(y_3 - \sigma_S,\sqrt{T-t}, y_4 - \sigma_S \rho\sqrt{T-t}; \rho). \tag{9.9}$$

The last expression is typically the sum of two potential payoffs: a first one which is the option that pays $\max(S_T - K, 0)$ if default occurs at T, and a second one which is the option with the same payoff, but if default occurs prior to T. Expression (9.9) also gives a quantitative idea of what should be the value of a variable collateral such that the OTC optionholder would be indifferent between such a covered alternative and the straight default-free option. Therefore, should these margin requirements be market determined, the value of the writer's default option would determine the margin required to sell an exchange-traded option. But, looking at the current institutional practices that require the writer to deposit the option premium plus a margin equivalent to 15% of the underlying stock value for at-the-money index options, Rich (1996) finds that current requirements are set at least 35–40% higher than the model predicts as being a fair market level.

Comparative statics in the simplified case of a constant default barrier are provided in Rich (1996). Roughly, it is found that the analytical properties of this vulnerable option can differ widely from the default-free one. This can have a great impact for hedging purposes. Rich (1996) explains it simply by looking at the price of the vulnerable call option as a default-free option minus the writer's option to default. An increase in one of these two arguments by a change in the parameters will be partially offset by an increase in the other argument. Numerical examples show the following results[8]:

- The deeper the option is initially in the money, the larger the default premium.
- The default premium is larger the longer the time to maturity.
- At the money vulnerable call options are nearly linear in σ_S, but nonlinear in σ_A.
- The default premium decreases as the correlation between the optional asset and the writer's creditworthiness increases toward 1.
- The value of the default option increases as the default boundary decreases (remember that we have no recovery in this part).
- The default-free delta and the vulnerable delta differ with the moneyness and are only similar for deep out-of-the-money options. This will have a great impact for hedge trading purposes.
- Longer default-free calls require investors to increase the initial size of their hedge position while longer-term vulnerable call options allow investors to decrease the size of their position.

---

[7]The relationship with the Black and Scholes formula can be directly provided remembering that, in the absence of any rebate when the barrier is reached, a traditional Black and Scholes option can be split into the sum of a down-and-out option and a down-and-in option.
[8]Directly taken from Rich (1996).

- The vulnerable gamma never exceeds the default-free gamma.

These unusual impacts on the hedging strategy have also been partly shown in the Johnson and Stulz (1987) framework as well.

Other Considerations

Some other issues and features linked to this first part of Rich (1996) are listed below:

- Foreign currency options can be valued with the present model by letting S_t stand for the foreign currency exchange rate and d_S denote the foreign currency interest rate. The relation is thus made to the Hull and White (1995) model, for the present one provides a closed-form solution when a fixed default barrier is assumed. Results show the accuracy obtained by Hull and White with their binomial methodology.
- Cox and Rubinstein (1985) consider firm valuation when the debt contains a safety covenant that allows debtholders to trigger bankruptcy if some standard is not satisfied. If the bondholder's position is viewed as holding the risky asset (the firm's assets), and granting a down-and-out call option to the shareholders, and the bondholders are assumed to have only this asset (the holding), then the asset measuring the writer's creditworthiness is also the asset on which the option is being written. Collapsing variables S and A into a sole one will give the solution for the valuation in such a scenario.
- Using the fact that the parity, that states that a default-free forward contract can be replicated by a portfolio of default-free European options, is also verified in the risky case, Rich (1996) easily provides the solution for the one-sided default-risky forward price. The equilibrium risky forward price is

$$X = \psi S e^{d_S - r} - (T - t),$$

where

$$\psi \equiv \frac{N_1(y_2) - N_1(y_4)(D/A)^{\gamma_1 + \gamma_2}}{N_1(y_2 - \sigma_S \rho_{S,A}\sqrt{T - t}) - N_1(y_4 - \sigma_S \rho_{S,A}\sqrt{T - t})(D/A)^{\gamma_1}}$$

$$\gamma_1 = 2(r - d_A)\sigma_A^{-2} - 1$$

$$\gamma_2 = 2\sigma_S \rho_{S,A}/\sigma_A, \text{ when the default boundary is fixed.}$$

9.3.2 Partial Recovery

Four scenarios are examined:

1. The option has a fixed default barrier D and is secured by a prespecified margin deposit, which is an exponential function of the time remaining until maturity.

    The buyer's recovery option at time $t = \tau$, i.e. the first passage time under the barrier, is defined as

    $$R_\tau^1 = M e^{-\xi\theta(T - \tau)},$$

    where M is a given constant, θ a constant rate of change through time, and ξ a binary variable that takes a value 1 (-1) if the margin deposit is decreasing (increasing) over time.

The expected discounted value of the recovery at time t is given by

$$R_t^1 = Me^{-\xi\theta(T-t)}\left[\left(\frac{D}{A_t}\right)^{1/2\gamma_1+\gamma_3}N_1(y_5) + \left(\frac{D}{A_t}\right)^{1/2\gamma_1-\gamma_3}N_1(y_5 - 2\gamma_3\sigma_A\sqrt{T-t})\right],$$

$$(9.10)$$

where

$$\gamma_1 = 2(r - d_A)\sigma_A^{-2} - 1$$

$$\gamma_3 \equiv \sqrt{2(r - \xi\theta) + 1/4\gamma_1^2\sigma_A^2}\Big/\sigma_A$$

$$y_5 \equiv \frac{\ln(D/A_t) + \gamma_3\sigma_A^2(T-t)}{\sigma_A\sqrt{T-t}}.$$

2. The option has a fixed default barrier D, A_t also denotes the writer's assets, and the optionholder receives a determined fraction α of the remaining assets at default. Here,

$$R_\tau^2 = \alpha A_\tau,$$

where $A_\tau = D$ by definition. The solution for R_t^2 is equivalent to formula (9.10), substituting αD and 0 for M and θ respectively.

3. The payoff of the recovery is the same as in case 2, but the barrier is stochastic. Rich (1996) obtains

$$R_t^3 = \alpha A_t\left[\left(\frac{A_t}{D_t}\right)^{1/2\gamma_4+\gamma_5}N_1(-y_6) + \left(\frac{A_t}{D_t}\right)^{1/2\gamma_4-\gamma_5}N_1(-y_6 + 2\gamma_5\sigma\sqrt{T-t})\right], \quad (9.11)$$

where

$$\sigma = \sigma_A^2 + \sigma_D^2 - 2\sigma_A\sigma_D\rho_{A,D}$$

$$\gamma_4 = 2(d_A - d_D)\sigma^{-2} - 1$$

$$\gamma_5 \equiv \sqrt{2d_A + 1/4\gamma_4^2\sigma^2}\Big/\sigma$$

$$y_6 \equiv \frac{\ln(A_t/D_t) + \gamma_5\sigma^2(T-t)}{\sigma\sqrt{T-t}}.$$

4. Let us suppose that we now want to tie the recovery value at default to the moneyness of the option. So, let us now apply the ratio α to the moneyness of the option. Therefore,

$$R_\tau^4 = \alpha\max[S_\tau - K, 0].$$

The time zero solution is written as

$$R_0^4 = \frac{2\alpha \ln(A/D)}{\sigma} \left[S\left(\frac{D}{A}\right)^{1/2\gamma_1 + 1/2\gamma_2 + \gamma_6} \int_{T^{-1/2}}^{\infty} N_1\left(\frac{y_{8,t} - \rho y_{7,t}}{\sqrt{1-\rho^2}}\right) \times n(y_{9,t})\,dt \right.$$

$$\left. - K\left(\frac{D}{A}\right)^{1/2\gamma_1 + \gamma_7} \int_{T^{-1/2}}^{\infty} N_1\left(\frac{(y_{8,t} - \sigma_S/t) - \rho(y_{7,t} - \rho\sigma_S/t)}{\sqrt{1-\rho^2}}\right) \times n(y_{10,t})\,dt \right], \quad (9.12)$$

where

$$\sigma = \sigma_A^2 + \sigma_D^2 - 2\sigma_A \sigma_D \rho_{A,D}$$

$$\gamma_6 \equiv \sqrt{2d_S + 1/4\sigma^2(\gamma_1 + \gamma_2)^2} \Big/ \sigma$$

$$\gamma_7 \equiv \sqrt{2r + 1/4\sigma^2\gamma_1^2} \Big/ \sigma$$

$$y_{7,t} \equiv \frac{t \ln(A/D) + 1/2\sigma^2(\gamma_1 + \gamma_2)/t}{\sigma}$$

$$y_{8,t} \equiv \frac{t \ln(S/K) + (r - d_S + 1/2\sigma_S^2)/t}{\sigma_S}$$

$$y_{9,t} \equiv \frac{t \ln(D/A) + \gamma_6 \sigma^2/t}{\sigma}$$

$$y_{10,t} \equiv \frac{t \ln(D/A) + \gamma_7 \sigma^2/t}{\sigma}.$$

The model relates nicely to the Merton–Black and Scholes setup while allowing for the complexity of vulnerability in options.

In conclusion, models of vulnerable options (or defaultable options) add to our understanding of OTC options pricing by integrating a dimension not well considered generally. Of course, portfolio effects will matter as well and should be the object of further research.

9.4   REFERENCES

Cox, J. and M. Rubinstein, 1985, *Options Market*, Prentice-Hall, Englewood Cliffs, NJ.

Hull, J. and A. White, 1995, "The Impact of Default Risk on the Prices of Option and Other Derivative Securities", *Journal of Banking and Finance*, **19**, 299–322.

Johnson, H. and R. Stulz, 1987, "The Pricing of Options with Default Risk", *Journal of Finance*, **42** (2), June, 267–80.

Rich, Don, 1996, "The Valuation and Behavior of Black–Scholes Options Subject to Intertemporal Default Risk", *Review of Derivatives Research*, **1**, 25–59.

Part Three
Theoretical Wrap-up and Empirical Evidence

10
Introduction

Credit risk is a matter of preoccupation for the management of the bank lending business in terms of allocation and diversification, the specific pricing of credit spreads over government bond yields for corporate bonds, the valuation of credit derivatives instruments, the measurement of the exposure of a portfolio and its components to this particular source of risk. This preoccupation has increased mainly because of the proliferation of financial derivatives and the rising complexity of the resulting payoffs of the portfolios and the globalization with the accessibility of (or recourse to) lower credit standing participants in the market. With the evolution of markets and growth requirements, investors have been looking toward solutions that can enable them to take on more positions while managing their exposures in a dynamic environment rather than through static rationing. Indeed, the credit term structure is a main input to many credit risk portfolio management systems.

As has been presented in earlier parts of this book, there is now a large literature on the pricing of credit risk with formulations for coupon-bearing bonds or zero-coupon bonds, in the context or not of a strategic behavior of lenders and borrowers and with different definitions for the default event, the liquidation procedure, and the recovered amount. This literature requires some wrap-up or common denominator in order to compare these approaches and understand why and in which cases some of them could be more suitable.

More precisely, credit risk can be decomposed into its main determinants, i.e. the probability of default and the recovery at default. All modeling approaches can be then analyzed in terms of these two components: the definition of the default event arrival, the valuation of the recovery, either deterministic, stochastic, or with some prespecified scenarios, and the assumptions on their joint behavior.

Generally, while the event of default is a main issue in credit risk modeling, the recovered amount at default remains a difficult issue to define. The resolution of default is cumbersome to modelize because it is difficult to have some consensus on it. There are many possibilities to define it, from a historical level of loss given some factors like seniority and the sector of industry, up to a completely detailed range of scenarios accounting for the delay between the time of default and the final recovery of "something". The trade-off is then made between the degree of sophistication and the possibility of estimating consistent parameters to enter back into the model for operational use. More fundamentally, when dealing with a portfolio of standard and complex positions like OTC derivatives, the availability of a common framework will be a natural requirement[1].

Chapter 11 will be dedicated to this comparison and to the emphasis on the useful insights of the literature presented, in the form of a wrap-up.

---

[1] Here is the basis of the criticism against the current programming solutions: in order to be global, they reduce the problematic substantially.

The reader is provided with up-to-date empirical evidence on the determinants of credit risk. Defaults, recoveries, and traditional ratings' data are analyzed to end up with what could be the most desirable features for a modeling system. At the end of Chapter 12 we have incorporated three typical empirical studies, one on the behavior of credit spreads (Duffee, 1998), the other on the implementation of a reduced-form model for the pricing of risky debt (Duffee, 1999). The third study is the one of Wei and Guo (1997) that depicts clearly some differences among structural models and provides some interesting empirical results.

10.1   REFERENCES

Duffee, Gregory, 1998, "The Relation Between Treasury Yields and Corporate Bond Yield Spreads", *The Journal of Finance*, **53** (6), December, 2225–41.
Duffee, Gregory, 1999, "Estimating the Price of Default Risk", *The Review of Financial Studies*, **12** (1), Spring, 197–226.
Wei, D. G. and D. Guo, 1997, "Pricing Risky Debt: An Empirical Comparison of the Longstaff and Schwartz and Merton Models", *The Journal of Fixed Income*, September, 9–28.

11

Literature Wrap-up

"Any scientific truth is an awaiting fallacy" (Karl Popper, 1904–94)[1]

Suppose we concentrate on the valuation of a riskfree amount equivalent (after the risk adjustment) to the exposure to credit risk of a long position in a zero-coupon bond with finite maturity with the final objective to obtain a term structure of credit spreads. Different approaches exist for the estimation of credit spreads. First, credit spreads can be estimated directly as an exogenous variable without any reliance on underlyings. Instead of trusting a model, some market values are used. Typically, a widespread proxy is the difference between a corporate bond yield and a government yield. Second, the credit spread can be expressed as the resultant of two components: a (risk-neutral) probability of default (P) and a recovery rate (ω) at default such that the riskfree equivalent (D) at time 0 of an owed amount F is equal to

$$D = F(1 - P) + \omega FP \tag{11.1}$$

under the assumption that there is no time value of money. The continuous credit spread is then simply $-\ln[D/F]$.

Rather than reviewing papers in the order of the presentation of the previous chapters, we provide here a discussion related to their formalization of the probability of default and of the recovery rates. We will relate in Chapter 12 empirical evidence on both dimensions.

11.1 THE PROBABILITY OF DEFAULT

The probability of default supposes that there is a nonambiguous definition of the event of default[2] which could be simply: "a missed contractual payment that produces a non-timely payment"[3]. The existing theories mainly follow from two branches: the

---

[1] It is the central axis of all Popper's epistemology, through his work entitled *The Logic of the Scientific Discovery*. A statement turns out to be scientific if it is falsifiable or forgeable. It is not a state but a disposition: whenever the theory is not yet falsified, it would not necessarily be scientific. In other domains an error becomes an exception to be nested into the proposed theory. In scientific research, a counter-example falsifies the theory and demands to be revisited (change of paradigm). That is certainly why theories in human sciences are encompassed by a set of hypotheses.

[2] This is a very important point to stress, since in practice the default event is sometimes not accepted as it is and it is a source of conflicts and legal suits. This is particularly the case for the "credit derivatives", where a certain payoff is conditional on a credit event, i.e. either a change in the rating as well as a default event. The problem is that whenever such an event occurs the parties may not agree on its correspondence with the contractual definition. This uncertainty in the "docs" reduces considerably the usefulness of the derivative instrument as an insurance product.

[3] Moody's definition of default is: "Any missed or delayed disbursement of interest and/or principal, bankruptcy, receivership, or distressed exchange where (i) the issuer offered bondholders a new security or package of securities that amounts to a diminished financial obligation (such as preferred or common stock, or debt with a lower coupon or APR amount) or (ii) the exchange had the apparent purpose of helping the borrower avoid default."

reduced-form approach as opposed to the *structural* approach. In the former, the default event is modeled as a surprise. The probability arrival of this surprise follows a jump process and therefore depends on an intensity parameter also called hazard rate. This hazard rate can be constant through time or allowed to move stochastically, thereby implying a term structure of probabilities of default. This "surprise" rate is either estimated to fit a historical probability or fitted to current market data (calibration).

The structural approach, instead, relates the *arrival* of this event to the dynamics of the underlying structure of the firm, giving thereby an economic significance to the establishment of the default rate. This stream of research emerged with Merton who saw here an application of option theory. The value of the firm is supposed to evolve continuously and to be shared by two broad categories of claimants: the shareholders and the debtholders. Relying on the Modigliani–Miller theorem, we assume that leverage does not have any effect on the value of the firm such that the latter is a pure exogenous variable which process triggers any other relationship by itself. Because of their limited liability, shareholders have a payoff which is positive whenever the face value owed to creditors can be reimbursed. Otherwise it is null or "out of the money". The shareholders' claim is then just a call on the value of the assets of the firm; a European call in the case of Merton[4]. In addition, a bond is simply a right of a face amount to be reimbursed with the sale of a put to shareholders on the assets of the firm, i.e. a put on the "collateral"[5].

A direct advantage of the structural approach is that credit default is not an unpredictable event here; there is a resolve to take into account the corporate conditions that lead to default. Relying on the evolution of the value of the assets of the firm gives a continuity of the credit standing evolution of the firm as a borrower. Default is not an incursion into the history of the firm but it is related to a financial variable which can be more or less directly related to traded data. From that perspective, it is difficult to believe that credit risk is unpredictable. The credit risk source being represented by a diffusion process, it is also easier to relate it to market risks' processes in the context of an overall portfolio perspective. Moreover, since debt is the instrument to be priced, it would be restrictive not to include the interest rate risk when estimating credit spreads from this class of models. Unfortunately, since the value of the firm is not a tradable asset, nor it is easily observable, the parameters of the standard structural model are difficult to estimate consistently[6]. Reduced-form approaches appeared mainly because of this limitation and the restrictive character of the Modigliani–Miller assumption which states that a higher leverage does not

---

[4]We can see a direct analogy with Black's derivation of the analytic price of an option on a stock's futures. While "reduced-form" approaches would be equivalent of taking the futures price as given, the structural one would start one step upstream. Although in the credit risk case, for a single counterpart, the reconciliation also exists and has been given by Duffie and Lando (1997). The intensity rate can be reconciled with the value of the firm and the threshold value, their initial "distance" implying some propensity to default.

[5]The notion of collateral is used here derogatively since the creditor does not have the ownership of the assets of the firm nor the usufruct, before the final liquidation. This problem of access to collateral is studied by Jarrow and Turnbull (1991) from a reduced-form perspective with their FOREX analogy.

[6]In fact, there exists an iteration procedure based on the complementarity of debt and traded stock into the value of the firm that makes use of the option pricing framework backwards to obtain the key-variable, namely the volatility of the value of the assets, as a function of stock market data. Thus, the estimation itself is not a pure calibration problem since it depends on the model and therefore still requires the fulfilment of the value preservation property which is the main underlying hypothesis of the Modigliani–Miller theorem.

increase the value of the firm. Also, the inclusion of some frictions like tax shields and liquidation costs would break the last rule. Encompassing these difficulties requires a refinement of the pricing derivation of the standard model and an explicit definition of the relationship that relates the assets value to the total value of the firm under certain hypotheses, better known under the name of "value preservation property".

On one hand, the use of option pricing theory is very appealing because of its elegance and significance. On the other hand, it requires further analysis into the underlying hypothesis that could reconcile the financial policy and the fundamentals of the firm with the option pricing framework.

Structural modeling has been founded by Merton with the introduction of the contingent claims approach (Merton, 1974, 1977), followed by Black and Cox (1976). Two main sophistications were then added, beyond numerous engineering refinements surveyed in the chapter on financial engineering: a construction including also the link with stochastic interest rates[7] (Shimko et al., 1993) and more complex bankruptcy definitions. One way to obtain different bankruptcy levels is via the possibility of the default occurring prior to the maturity with the definition of a constant threshold level that drives default whenever the value of the assets reaches it. This threshold acts as a barrier for a barrier option. The latter converts the Markovian case into a past-dependent problem. This is the case in the study of Longstaff and Schwartz (1995). The improvement of this model relies on the existence of a correlation between both stochastic processes resulting in credit spread shapes more in line with that observed in the market than with the pure Merton model. Yet we have seen in Chapter 4 that Longstaff and Schwartz (1995b) present some mathematical problems in its derivation[8]. Some refinements were recently introduced by Briys and Varenne (1997) and Saá-Requejo and Santa Clara (1997). Briys and de Varenne (1997) use a stochastic barrier option approach for more generality. Their barrier consists of a constant parameter (the threshold level) multiplying a function which is simply the price of a default-free zero-coupon bond, $P_0(T)$[9]. Boundary conditions imply that $P_T(T) = 1$, and therefore the "stochastic" barrier is just a trend function, the slope of which is given by the time remaining until maturity. We argue that this replaces one limitation by another, making an implicit relationship between the time to maturity and the expected distance to default through time. This kind of barrier option approach, however, has the merit of providing a closed-form solution and can be shown to be consistent with the significance of insolvency in a firm with a single debt issue. Saá-Requejo and Santa Clara (1997) assume that the process for the value of assets and the threshold value have a similar form. Then a new variable comes out of the ratio of both processes[10] with a new resulting process of the same form. The new threshold level is

---

[7] This consideration is crucial for an interest rate contingent security.

[8] It is indeed because of this kind of mathematical problems that subsequent studies have focused on a stochastic barrier in order to eliminate the problem posed by the estimation of the passage time of the underlying assets' process under the barrier in a bi-dimensional context, which has no derived mathematical solution until today.

[9] $P_0(T)$ stands for the today's price of one dollar to be delivered in T years.

[10] Longstaff and Schwartz (1995) have already derived their model in terms of the ratio of the value of the assets (V) and the threshold value. This has the advantage of encompassing the problem of the nontradability of V. The ratio as a variable then implicitly represents some distance to default.

simply 1 and we return to a constant barrier framework[11] and a closed-form solution is again derivable.

The last four referenced models do include a correlation factor between a *one-factor* interest rate process and the value of the assets' process. Very recently, an extended analysis has been provided by Chang and Sundaresan (1999) through a general equilibrium framework in which asset prices, default-free term structure, and default premia are determined simultaneously. The linkage between riskfree and risky rates comes from the equilibrium and not from an *ad hoc* correlation.

In the case presented in Chapter 15 we will take into account a two-factor model of the term structure of interest rates justified below in Chapter 12 on the empirical evidence.

Another important extension of the structural approach is the endogenous determination of the threshold value when its level can be chosen by the firm and under the assumption of no explicit time dependence, by Leland (1994). Optimal structure considerations are also presented in the papers of Leland and Toft (1996) and Leland (1998). Net cash outflows from the firm can be financed in two ways: either by selling additional equity or by selling assets. In the first alternative, Leland (1994) shows that this immediately defines an endogenous level of bankruptcy. By the limited liability property of equity, there is a non-trivial level of the assets of the firm where the equity will fall to zero, preventing the barrier level from being arbitrarily small. In the second alternative, the possibility of selling assets is often accompanied by a barrier level imposed by a safety covenant in order to limit agency costs of debt, making possible the assumption of the absolute priority rule (APR) and avoiding bizarre behaviors by shareholders. Again, these essential considerations can be only tackled in a structural approach that relates to the fundamentals of the firm. The branch of research dedicated to game-theoretic issues, i.e. to the strategic behavior of both shareholders and debtholders, leads to the idea that default can be a desired and voluntarily triggered event. Also, when bankruptcy is declared, the claimants may want to renegotiate the debt because liquidation can be an inefficient resolution if default is a liquidity problem of the firm rather than a real insolvency. If all parties know that this is part of their strategic set and may make use of it, this should be priced by the market *ex ante*. These strategies are so many additional decisional options that have a positive value. The research in this area is well represented by the work of Anderson and Sundaresan (1996, 1998), and Anderson et al. (1996).

The reduced-form approaches are well documented by the contributions of Jarrow and Turnbull (1995), Jarrow et al. (1997), and Duffie and Singleton (1999)[12]. The key hypothesis made by reduced-form models is that default is an event that happens by surprise. Jarrow and Turnbull conceive credit risk through a FOREX analogy where

---

[11]Or 0 in "ln(·)" terms. Contrary to some of these studies, the barrier is still differentiated, in the model that will be presented in Chapter 15, from the nominal face value of debt which defines the capital structure of the firm and *it is not stochastic*. In Saá-Requejo and Santa Clara, the construction obeys the fact that the default event is entirely dependent on the dynamics of the value of the firm, V and that the stochasticity of the barrier will firstly constitute an additional degree of freedom rather than a well-justified economic random variable.

[12]Other proposed "reduced-form" modelizations include the works of Das and Tufano (1996), Lando (1998), Iben and Litterman (1991), Madan and Unal (1993), Schönbucher (1997) and Zhou (1998) among others.

the expected credit loss rate can be viewed as a corporate exchange rate, where the credit spread is just the expression of the discount applied to \$1 of value inside the firm to have its riskfree equivalent: the default of a corporate zero-coupon bond at time t implies the recovery of an exogenously specified fraction of a default-free bond of the same maturity. Their methodology is worked out through the use of matrices of historical transition probabilities from original ratings and recovery values at each terminal state. Duffie and Singleton (1999) use back standard models of the term structure of interest rates, replacing the short riskfree rate r by a default adjusted rate $R = r - hL$, where h is the hazard rate and L is the expected fractional loss if default occurs[13]. They propose and compare several econometric inference procedures out of current market data, either focusing directly on R or parametrizing its components r, h, and L separately. One of the criticisms relies here on the following: for econometric estimations purposes, they have to either estimate h and L jointly or consider them as independent and make assumptions on which financial series will be used to estimate each parameter. This is particularly visible in Das and Tufano (1996). Indeed, Izvorski (1997) provides empirical evidence on the cobehavior of the probability of default and the recovery rate. Wei and Guo (1997) provide a theoretical comparison of structural models of default and show that even in the basic setting of Merton (1977) this relationship can inherently obtain from the model (see section 12.5).

11.2   THE RECOVERY

The next step is the review of the literature for the recovery[14]. Unfortunately, no tractable model can capture all the particularities and possible scenarios that take place during bankruptcy proceedings. Most of the models substantially summarize this process through a straight formula for the recovery rate at default, and can still preserve an uncertain behavior if designed as a function of the assets value[15]. While it is not explicitly defined in Merton's model, it can be shown that the recovery implicit in his model is in fact stochastic. This has been provided by Crouhy and Galai (1997), whose study stresses some very useful interpretations from Merton's model[16] (see Chapter 3).

Longstaff and Schwartz (1995) assume a constant recovered amount equal to a constant times the price of a riskfree zero-coupon bond. Briys and de Varenne (1997) point out that, due to the assumptions of exogenous threshold value and recovery rate, their pricing equations do not assure that the payment to bondholders is not greater than the firm value upon default[17]. Moreover, even if the firm is in a solvent position at maturity, the value of the firm can be lower than the face value of the bond. Briys and de Varenne (1997) propose a constant recovery "fraction" of the value of the firm with

---

[13]This is a perfect analogy with equation (12.1) but at the rate level.

[14]An important remark must be made here. The recovery is the *overall amount* reimbursed at default, while the recovery rate is the *fraction* of the remaining quantity or of some security that is given back to the creditor. Even if this recovery rate is assumed to be some constant, the resulting recovery can be still time varying should the recovery rate apply to the underlying stochastic variable.

[15]Duffie and Singleton (1997) make the same remark when comparing different alternatives for the recovery.

[16]A good interpretation is also provided by Ericsson and Reneby (1995).

[17]It can also be seen as merely a matter of calibration of the recovery rate since the value of the firm intervenes only in the derivation of the default probability.

a differentiation between the recovery taking place when default occurs at maturity (the value of assets remaining at the maturity is a stochastic variable) and the recovery taking place when default occurs because of the triggering of the barrier level (here the value of assets remaining is known with certainty and equal to the defined barrier level). As mentioned in Chapter 4, however, this differentiation does not hold economically. This will give an overall time-varying recovery for this type of model and such a form will be held in the methodology we provide later.

We find the same discussion in the "reduced-form" literature. Duffie and Singleton (1999) look at the practical implementation of a "loss-of-market-value" assumption compared to:

- a "loss-of-face-value" assumption (Brennan and Schwartz, 1980, and Duffee, 1998).
- a "recovery-of-Treasury" assumption. The creditor receives immediately upon default an exogenous fraction of an otherwise equivalent riskfree bond (approach by Jarrow and Turnbull, 1995).

As is well presented by Duffie and Singleton (1997), the final choice merely depends on the legal structure of the contract (product) to be priced[18].

Also the stochasticity of the recovery in Merton is due to the continuous behavior of the value of the firm up to the maturity where the option can end up "in" or "out of the money". The future distance of the firm value to the debt face value is therefore uncertain at the contract origination. In Zhou (1997) this uncertainty is related to the unpredictable magnitude of the jump that may trigger default.

11.2.1 Theoretical Specifications in the Literature

Credit-risk modeling studies can be categorized depending on the following characteristics:

1. Structural framework (a) versus intensity-based approach (b).
2. Integration of strategic behaviors or optimizing schemes (a) versus a completely exogenous setting (b).
3. Integration (a) or not (b) of stochastic interest rates and possible cross-correlations with other processes in the modeling framework.
4. Discrete (a) versus continuous-time (b) pricing model.
5. Econometric fitting (a) or not (b) with current financial and economic data.

---

[18]In the case that the APR is perfectly respected, the "loss-of-face-value" assumption is unique in that it implies that bonds of the same seniority and of the same issuer have the same recovery. Even if a "loss-of-market-value" assumption is often preferred for the reasons mentioned earlier, the "loss-of-face-value" assumption can be important when considering firms with multiple debt issues and a cross-default clause that assures the APR.

Tables 11.1 and 11.2 present a representative set of researches, making a reference to the categories presented above.

Table 11.1 This table enumerates the most representative research studies in terms of *structural* frameworks proposed to the integration of credit risk in our pricing models as well as in the definition of the optimal policy of the firm. For the structural approaches, the default event is a precise boundary condition. For intensity-based approaches, the expected time of default is the resultant of a "surprise" discounting process. And other models are a mixture of these two main branches. Reproduced with authorization from Pirotte (1999a)

Theoretical specifications — structural approaches (panel A)	
Reference	Specification of the event of default/discount for default
Merton (1977) 1(a), 2(b), 3(b), 4(b), 5(b)	$V \leqslant F$, at maturity T
Shimko et al. (1993) 1(a), 2(b), 3(a), 4(b), 5(b)	$V \leqslant F$, at T, with stochastic interest rates, which dynamics are correlated to those of V
Leland (1994) 1(a), 2(a,b), 3(b), 4(b), 5(b)	$V \leqslant K$ where K can be exogenously or endogenously determined
Longstaff and Schwartz (1995b) 1(a), 2(b), 3(a), 4(b), 5(b)	$V \leqslant F$, between 0 and T, with stochastic interest rates, which dynamics are correlated to those of V
Das (1995) 1(a), 2(b), 3(a), 4(b), 5(b)	$V \leqslant F$, between 0 and T. Compound option pricing. Ho and Lee term structure
Anderson et al. (1996) 1(a), 2(a), 3(b), 4(a,b), 5(b)	The default process is not solely the resultant of an exogenous process but linked also to the opportunistic behavior of the parties
Saá-Requejo and Santa Clara (1997) 1(a), 2(b), 3(a), 4(b), 5(b)	$V \leqslant K$, between 0 and T, K following a diffusion process with diffusion components linked to the randomnesses of the short-term interest rate and V
Briys and de Varenne (1997) 1(a), 2(b), 3(a), 4(b), 5(b)	$V \leqslant \alpha.F.P(t, T)$, between 0 and T, with stochastic interest rates whose dynamics are correlated to those of V. $V \leqslant F$ at maturity if no prior default
Zhou (1997) 1(a), 2(b), 3(a), 4(b), 5(b)	$V \leqslant F$, between 0 and T, where dV/V is a jump-diffusion process
Notation V = value of the firm F = face value of the debt contract B = a trigger independent of F	T = maturity of the contract $P(t, T)$ = price at t of \$1 riskfree delivered at T α = arbitrary discount value

Table 11.2 This table enumerates the most representative research studies in terms of *reduced-form* frameworks proposed to the integration of credit risk in our pricing models, as well as in the definition of the optimal policy of the firm. For the structural approaches, the default event is a precise boundary condition. For intensity-based approaches, the expected time of default is the resultant of a "surprise" discounting process. And other models are a mixture of these two main branches. Reproduced with authorization from Pirotte (1999a)

Theoretical specifications — reduced-form approaches (panel B)	
Reference	Specification of the event of default/discount for default
Jarrow and Turnbull (1991, 1995) 1(b), 2(b), 3(a), 4(a,b), 5(b)	In discrete time, there is a particular martingale default probability for each discrete time interval. In continuous time, the credit term structure relies on a τ^*, the first time of bankruptcy which is exponentially distributed with an intensity parameter resulting in a jump process
Madan and Unal (1993) 1(b), 2(b), 3(a), 4(a,b), 5(a)	First paper in modeling the default risk as composed of arrival and magnitude risks. "The two components are explicitly priced as if they were traded in the futures market and the spot price of the risky debt is derived as a consequence"
Longstaff and Schwartz (1995a) 1(b), 2(b), 3(a), 4(b), 5(a)	Mean reverting process for credit spreads. Credit spread call and put valuations
Das and Tufano (1996) 1(b), 2(b), 3(a), 4(b), 5(a)	Similar to Jarrow et al. (1997), but with stochastic recovery rates
Jarrow et al. (1997) 1(b), 2(b), 3(a), 4(a,b), 5(b)	First model to explicitly incorporate the credit rating information into the valuation methodology
Duffie and Lando (1997) 1(b), 2(b), 3(a), 4(b), 5(b)	The hazard-rate process is a function of V conditional on accounting data
Duffie and Singleton (1999) 1(b), 2(b), 3(a), 4(b), 5(a)	The defaultable claim is discounted at a default-adjusted short-term interest rate for the risk-neutral, mean-loss rate (see Madan and Unal, 1993)
Duffee (1999) 1(b), 2(b), 3(a), 4(b), 5(b)	One $ at T is discounted at a default-adjusted short-term interest rate for the intensity which follows a one-factor square-root process

Notation
V = value of the firm T = maturity of the contract
F = face value of the debt contract $P(t, T)$ = price at t of $1 riskfree delivered at T
B = a trigger independent of F α = arbitrary discount value

11.3   REFERENCES

Anderson, Ronald and Suresh Sundaresan, 1996, "Design and Valuation of Debt Contracts", *The Review of Financial Studies*, **9** (1), Spring, 37–68.

Anderson, Ronald W., Suresh Sundaresan and Pierre Tychon, 1996, "Strategic Analysis of Contingent Claims", *European Economic Review*, **40** (3–5), April, 871–81.

Briys, Eric and François de Varenne, 1997, "Valuing Risky Fixed Rate Debt: An Extension", *Journal of Financial and Quantitative Analysis*, **32** (2), June, 239–49.

Black, F. and J. C. Cox, 1976, "Valuing Corporate Securities: Some Effects of Bond Indenture Provisions", *Journal of Finance*, **31**, 351–67.

Brennan, M. and E. Schwartz, 1980, "Analyzing Convertible Bonds", *Journal of Financial and Quantitative Analysis*, **15**, 907–29.

Chang, Ganlin and Suresh Sundaresan, 1999, "Asset Prices and Default-Free Term Structure in an Equilibrium Model of Default", *Working Paper*, Graduate School of Business, Columbia University, March, 49 pp.

Crouhy, Michel and Dan Galai, 1997, "Credit Risk Revisited: An Option Pricing Approach", May 1997, *Working Paper* 97-2, Canadian Imperial Bank of Commerce/Market Risk Management/Global Analytics, 18 pp.

Das, S. R., 1995, "Credit Risk Derivatives", *Journal of Derivatives*, Spring, 7–23.

Das, Sanjiv and Peter Tufano, 1996, "Pricing Credit Sensitive Debt when Interest Rates, Credit Ratings and Credit Spreads are Stochastic", *Journal of Financial Engineering*, 5 (2), June.

Duffee, Gregory R., 1998, "The Relation Between Treasury Yields and Corporate Bond Yield Spreads", *Journal of Finance*, 53, 2225–42.

Duffee, Gregory, 1999, "Estimating the Price of Default Risk", *The Review of Financial Studies*, 12 (1), Spring, 197–226.

Duffie, Darrell and David Lando, 1997, "Term Structures of Credit Spreads with Incomplete Accounting Information", Preliminary Draft, September 12, 39 pp.

Duffie, Darrell and Ken Singleton, 1999, "Modeling Term Structures of Defaultable Bonds", *Review of Financial Studies*. Special 1999, 12 (4), 687–720.

Ericsson, Jan and Joel Reneby, 1995, "A Framework for Valuing Corporate Securities", *Working Paper*, Stockholm School of Economics, November, 35 pp.

Iben, Th. and R. Litterman, 1991, "Corporate Bond Valuation and the Term Structure of Credit Spreads", *Journal of Portfolio Management*, 17 (3), Spring, 52–64.

Izvorski, Ivailo, 1997, "Recovery Ratios and Survival Times for Corporate Bonds", International Monetary Fund, *Working Paper*, Research Department, WP 97/84, July, 32 pp.

Jarrow, Robert, David Lando and Stuart Turnbull, 1997, "A Markov Model of the Term Structure of Credit Spreads", *Review of Financial Studies*, 10 (2), Summer.

Jarrow, R. and Stuart Turnbull, 1991, A Unified Approach for Pricing Contingent Claims on Multiple Term Structures: The Foreign Currency Analogy, Working Paper.

Jarrow, R. and Stuart Turnbull, 1992, Lecture Notes: Recent Advances in the Pricing of Options on Financial Assets with Credit Risk, 34 pp.

Jarrow, R. and Stuart Turnbull, 1995, "Pricing Derivatives on Financial Securities Subject to Credit Risk", *Journal of Finance*, 50 (1), March, 53–85.

Lando, D., 1998, "On Cox Processes and Credit-Risky Securities", *Review of Derivatives Research*, 2, 99–120.

Leland, Hayne E., 1994, "Corporate Debt Value, Bond Covenants and Optimal Capital Structure", *Journal of Finance*, 49 (4), September, 1213–52.

Leland, Hayne E., 1998, "Agency Costs, Risk Management, and Capital Structure", Presidential address presented at the AFA meeting in Chicago, December, 43 pp.

Leland, H. E. and K. B. Toft, 1996, "Optimal Capital Structure, Endogenous Bankruptcy and the Term Structure of Credit Spreads", *Journal of Finance*, 51 (3), July, 987–1019.

Longstaff, F. and E. Schwartz, 1995a, "Valuing Credit Derivatives", *Journal of Fixed Income*, June, 6–12.

Longstaff, Francis and Eduardo Schwartz, 1995b, "A Simple Approach to Valuing Risky Fixed and Floating Rate Debt", *Journal of Finance*, 50 (3), July, 789–819.

Madan, D. and H. Unal, 1993, "Pricing the Risks of Default", *Working Paper*, College of Business, University of Maryland.

Merton, Robert C., 1974, "On the Pricing of Corporate Debt: The Risk Structure of Interest Rates", *The Journal of Finance*, 29, May, 449–70.

Merton, Robert C., 1977, "On the Pricing of Contingent Claims and the Modigliani–Miller Theorem", *Journal of Financial Economics*, 5, 241–9.

Pirotte, H., 1999a, "Implementing a Structural Valuation Model of Swap Credit-Sensitive Rates", *Working Paper*, Institute of Banking and Finance, Ecole des HEC, University of Lausanne, December, 32 pp.

Saá-Requejo, Jesús and Pedro Santa Clara, 1997, "Bond Pricing with Default Risk", *Working Paper*, John E. Anderson Graduate School of Management, UCLA, Los Angeles, 23 pp.

Schaefer, Stephen and Eduardo Schwartz, 1984, "A Two–Factor Model of the Term Structure: An Approximate Analytical Solution", *Journal of Financial and Quantitative Analysis*, 19 (4), December, 413–24.

Schönbucher, P., 1997, "The Term Structure of Defaultable Bond Prices", *Working Paper*, University of Bonn.

Shimko, David, Naohiko Tejima and Donald Van Deventer, 1993, "The Pricing of Risky Debt When Interest Rates are Stochastic", *The Journal of Fixed Income*, September, 58–65.

Wei, D. G. and D. Guo, 1997, "Pricing Risky Debt: An Empirical Comparison of the Longstaff and Schwartz and Merton Models", *The Journal of Fixed Income*, September, 9–28.

Zhou, Chunsheng, 1997, "A Jump-Diffusion Approach to Modeling Credit Risk and Valuing Defaultable Securities", *Working Paper*, Federal Reserve Board, Washington, 47 pp.

12
Empirical Evidence

"The Heisenberg uncertainty"[1].

It would be presumptuous to pretend that the models proposed here bring any improvement if no consideration is given to recent empirical studies. While very scarce up to a few years ago, empirical literature is today more extensive, thanks notably to credit risk management which has largely relied in the past upon the use of ratings.

12.1 DEFAULT PROBABILITIES

12.1.1 Appraisal and Estimation

Ratings have been extensively used as a probability of default indicator[2] and therefore they deserve to be analyzed with respect to our structural approach. The approach of ratings is thereby used by important programming developments, such as CreditMetrics[TM][3].

For three main reasons, however, ratings are a strong reduction of the creditworthiness universe. First, whatever is their sector of activity and their specific functions, firms and claims on these firms are ranked into these rating classes. And all firms within the same rating class therefore have the same default rate. That strongly assumes that no specific risk is being priced and, moreover, that each rating rank corresponds to a deterministic level of systematic credit risk. In a market perspective, this provides some ambiguity: suppose that we observe that a bond of a AA firm is being priced with a significantly lower credit spread than the AA category requires. Should we assume that this is a good market opportunity? Or that this firm will be upgraded because of new information disseminated on the marketplace? Or that it integrates some favorable features (for example on the recovery side) that are not well captured by the rating? Or that the rating is just plain wrong? Transitions between these classes are defined overall for each class, and therefore the categorization scheme and the attachment of a company to this scheme already conforms to some deterministic decomposition, while we would prefer the same kind of approach as used for market risks. Ratings also take little account of recoveries which are a major determinant of default pricing.

Second, except for the econometric approaches that infer default rates implicitly from market spreads (for example, Duffee, 1999), the actual default rate is assumed to be equivalent to the historical average which can greatly weaken the accuracy of the

---

[1] The uncertainty of Heisenberg (1901–76) lays down that the sole observation of the matter alternates the parameters. Moreover, a change in one of them modifies at least one other.

[2] Following the definitions of ratings' categories by Moody's, ratings are a straight representative of (historically) estimated levels of default probabilities.

[3] See Chapter 23.

calculations. Because of this, KMV[4] has shown that strong overlaps in default probability ranges can exist between different categories of ratings. Indeed, a Monte Carlo simulation of the average default rate ran by KMV (see Crouhy et al., 2000) starting from a true default rate, obtained a right-skewed distribution which means that the mean value is higher than the median or typical value of the rating class. This verifies the fact that the average historical default rate overstates the true default rate.

Third, ratings induce a discreteness problem. Their revisions are not so frequent as those to which we are used to in the context of market risks[5]. Since the final goal of any risk measurement and monitoring system is to be able to provide the risk manager with techniques that integrate both market risks and credit risk into a single measure, we would prefer a more dynamic (reactive) and practical handling of credit risk. The survey of CFOs and investors by Ellis (1997) reveals that, on the one hand, investors would like to see ratings updated immediately to reflect all relevant information while, on the other hand, issuers regret that unsolicited ratings are forcing them to obtain ratings from several agencies. Altman and Kishore (1996a) have shown the existing lag between the revisions of ratings and the real evolution of the creditworthiness of a firm. In a sample of defaulted issues in the period 1970–94, 6.8% of the firms were still ranked as investment grade[6] and only 1.1% ranked as C (the lowest rating), six months prior to default. The comparison between changes in ratings and changes in measures provided by KMV's contingent claims approach can be seen in Crouhy et al. (2000). KMV's model provides *expected default frequencies* (EDFs) based on Merton's approach which tend to sharply increase between one year and two years prior to default, sometimes more than one year before the downgrading of the issuer by Moody's or Standard & Poors. This discreteness problem also exacerbates the difference between the historical average default rate and the true one, while producing transition probabilities that are too small. Mapping the EDFs backwards into ratings categories and observing the history of changes, KMV obtains large differences compared to the Standard & Poors transition matrix. As an example, except for CCC obligors, the KMV probability of staying in the same class over a one-year horizon can be half of the historical one. And, the probability of an upgrade of one class is around 20% which is considerably higher than the historical average which is in the 0.70–6.48% interval when CCC obligors are not taken into account[7].

---

[4]KMV Corporation is a company founded by Stephen Kealhofer, John McQuown and Oldrich Vasicek that has developed a framework for credit risk pricing and monitoring based on Merton's model. Two main items of their approach is the inference of the volatility of assets and the value of the firm from stock market data and the mapping of their "structural" distances-to-default (DD) to the actual probabilities of default for a given time horizon. Indeed, DDs allow them to recategorize firms into classes and to compare this classification with that of Moody's or Standard & Poors.

[5]This fortifies our first remark on the relevance of credit classes as classes of systematic levels of risk.

[6]For the sake of completeness, it has to be mentioned that 94% of them were rated as BBB. Furthermore, the remark on the "uncompleteness" of past history still applies.

[7]However objectively, two remarks must be made about these transition matrices. First, the KMV transition matrix presents quite similar values along the top left to bottom right diagonals. For example, the one-year probability of staying at the same rating is in the interval 42.54–69.95% and four of seven values are comprised between 42.54% and 44.41%. The one-year probability of a one-class downgrade is in the close interval 20.58–25.83%. This would mean that the behavior around the current rating is quite homogeneous whatever is the original class. It is much less the case with historical averages.

Second, except for the B and CCC rankings, the cumulated probability of a downgrading is higher than for an upgrading (for the KMV matrix as well as for that of Standard and Poors). This is obvious for upper classes since the rankings are discrete and truncated upwards and downwards. However, the same result is evidenced with BBB and BB obligors, the central categories.

KMV assessments may not be statistically better (we lack serious studies on the topic), but they certainly are statistically different, which questions historical ratings in themselves.

It should also be noted that we do not know at today's date of strong academic studies that explore the difference between the different rating agencies' evaluation of credit risk in a formally consistent econometric setup. Moon and Stotsky (1993) come close to such a study, but in the municipal market field. They do a joint analysis of a municipality's decision to obtain a bond rating, and of the determinants of the municipality's rating for each of the major rating agencies. Their model provides a formal framework for differential analysis of the rating agencies, and the system of simultaneous equations obtained is estimated via smooth simulated maximum likelihood, a manipulation that allows estimation of such a complex system. They find interesting results for the municipal market: self-selection is important in Moody's ratings but not in that of Standard & Poors. Split ratings occur because agencies differ in the mix of the determinants of the ratings, but also differ in their rating classification. Rating classification between agencies does not correspond exactly, contrary to the practical use of equivalences today. For example, the best Moody's rating (Aaa) contains the best Standard & Poors rating (AAA), while the worst Moody's rating (Baa) is contained within the worst Standard & Poors rating (BBB). The replication and improvement of such a study on the corporate market would certainly help professionals grasp the institutional implications of ratings on prices.

More evidence is provided by Hite and Warga (1997) who study the effect of bond-rating changes on bond price performance[8] based on a transition matrix of downgrades and upgrades for a total of 1283 events. Surprisingly, the ending rating can diverge substantially from the original one, in particular for noninvestment grades (except on 166 original B issues, 38 were downgraded to CC, i.e. five subclasses lower). Second, the reaction is particularly negative in the six months prior to a downgrade to a non-investment grade. Unfortunately, no causality study is provided and thus the anticipation of the market can simply reflect the lag of adjustment in the ratings. Thus we would conclude that rating methods offer a stability in the measurement that can be unrespecting of the real dynamic of the credit risk exposure. Indeed, several old studies have already concluded that bond rating changes do not carry new information: Katz (1974), Hettenhouse and Sartoris (1976), Weinstein (1977) and Pinches and Singleton (1978) that confirm Weinstein's results on the fact that a lag exists and ensures that the information is largely integrated by the month of the change. Based on analysts' forecast revisions, Clark et al. (1997) conclude that the new informational content of ratings changes is only significant for small firms diminishing, therefore, information asymmetries. This is an important result since it shows that unexpected forecast revisions occur for small, illiquid, and not frequently traded firms, while the information is already integrated for large firms. This gives support to the need of obtaining information from stock market prices as the structural approach enables it in the case of publicly and frequently traded firms (see assumptions in Chapter 3).

It is also important to note that neither ratings nor their volatility are static in the long term. Lucas and Lonski (1993) find both a general trend toward a lower average

---

[8]The authors note that there is a sample bias towards noninvestment grade bonds in terms of listing, volume, and trading frequency.

quality over the period 1970–90 and a trend towards higher volatility of the ratings. Whether this is linked to real factors or to statistical ones, historical ratings may not be a good representation of future ratings and their dynamics.

The probabilities of default for a continuous set of maturities correspond precisely to an expected time to default for a given type of counterpart. Unfortunately, in the case of the historical ratings' approach, past data are clearly not sufficient to be able to provide us with the probability estimates for a continuum of term horizons. In the structural approach, the one-factor model of the assets value will drive the whole structure of default probabilities. Investors can then confront this term structure to their investment horizon.

Finally, there exists a number of empirical bond pricing models that use the credit ratings of Moody's or Standard & Poors in a set of variables to explain cross-sectional spreads over Treasury yields. Evidence, however, shows that these two families of ratings can differ[9] for a substantial number of issues. Cantor et al. (1997) integrate both ratings in the same study to compare the efficiency of alternative pricing rules using multiple ratings: 2405 issues out of 4399 were split-rated[10] between 1983 and 1993 and both ratings systems proved not to be redundant.

12.1.2   Evidence on Default Probabilities Behavior

Three important studies have been carried out by Altman and Kishore (1996a,b) and Izvorski (1997). Altman and Kishore (1996a) show that the history of defaults and the resulting default rate (either as an average of the total number of firms or as a compounded average of the total par value of outstanding debt) of high-yield bonds are too dependent on specific defaulted issues. Moreover, the exclusion of ongoing defaults underestimate the average[11] default loss rate of principal and coupon.

Izvorski's (1997) study is very complete in terms of analyzed relationships. It reveals that seniority, the maturity of the original contract, and the state of the economy at default can be considered as main determinants of firm-specific contracts[12]. The model presented in Chapter 15 integrates these three variables. Maturity, whose significance seems obvious, offers an interesting paradox corroborated by both empirical and theoretical researches. A credit risk averse investor can be thought to prefer shorter maturities and will rely on more liquid assets to commit on lending (see Duffee, 1998). On the other side, if the lending investor has a longer-term horizon, it is not clear that s/he would prefer a rollover of short-term contracts rather than a straight longer one.

---

[9]The explanation is simple. While Standard and Poors risk ratings represent default probabilities only, Moody's factors also include some measure of the expected recovery.

Bloomberg provides one of the rules to price split-rated issues when trader quotes are unavailable. It is an algorithm where the value 1 is assigned to the lower rating in the case of a one-notch differential, to a rating one notch above the lower rating in the case of a three-notch differential, and to the average rating in the case of even-notch differentials.

[10]After controlling for gross issuances below $10 million and special features such as government guarantees, variable coupon rates, significant equity characteristics, etc.

[11]Weighted by par value of amount outstanding.

[12]It stems from the fact that determinants and their behavior are different if we consider credit risk at the industrial level or at the firm-specific level. However, the lack of sufficient data across the different sampling methods is critical. Even taking back a large history of defaults, it is nearly impossible to construct sufficiently stratified samples that could help us in determining the level at which credit risk is specific.

This characteristic is present even in the simple setting of Merton (1974) (mainly because of the assumption of no default before the maturity) and it is confirmed by the results of Izvorski (1997). Indeed, firms in higher recovery ratio industries tend to issue bonds with longer maturities. If we agree on the idea that "longer" bonds should default later because it also means a lower debt burden for the borrower, then we have a relationship between the recovery rate, the maturity and the expected survival time. This relationship is well presented, in the case of Merton, by Wei and Guo (1997) and will therefore be also implicit in the model proposed later.

12.2 ON RECOVERY RATES

12.2.1 Estimation

There exists a practical method to estimate recovery rates that is rather cumbersome. It consists in recording all payments made on a defaulted debt, expressing them first as a percentage of the par value of the contract. A separate discount rate must be defined for each payment. Moreover, the recovery can be articulated through other types of issues rather than just a discount on a cash payment. Some maturities can be rescheduled and some options on surviving or sold claims can be given. This depends on the conclusions of the renegotiation process. For many of the features, it is difficult to put a price on them, even more when the liquidity of these securities has plunged[13]. In our case, we assume that the recovery obtains through cash. Should it be in the form of securities, the parameter accounting for the liquidation costs could also integrate an expectation for the "liquidity cost" incurred when converting them into cash.

Research has evidenced that historical recovery rates estimated on long-term horizons are inconsistent with their dynamic behavior. Moreover, not only market conditions change through time but also some features of debt contracts. Much more bond issues were secured in the past, thereby influencing the realized recovery.

On the practical side, we can cite Moody's methodology which consists in using the trading price at approximately one month after default of the firm as a proxy for the present value of the ultimate recovery. They argue that, whenever it is an estimate, it has the advantage of corresponding to the recovery rate obtained by debtholders who quickly liquidated their position after default. This price is finally related to the par value to provide the estimate[14].

---

[13] In some sense, the lack of liquidity at default reflects the unwillingness of investors to take on bad risks (see Duffee and Zhou, 1998, where the event of default is seen as a breakdown of the existing loan-sharing rule in the market). Even if debt prices mainly express the repayment capacity of the debtor, some additional premia seems to be required to accept that risk which information set has been updated to "defaulted debt". Again, the change of regime of the debt instrument has a strong impact on the perception of the risk by investors. Credit risk is the risk to incur a definitive loss on a part of the investors' portfolio. Contrary to market risks, at default, the underlying Markov chain is being reduced to the new state. Default therefore implies a real cash loss. The problem with recession and cold markets is the risk of propagation of default in the economy. In the case of an overall credit crisis, the availability of cash is valuable and the required premia to convert defaulted but still tradable debt into cash increases. The analogy with the stochastic convenience yield of Gibson and Schwartz in the pricing of oil contingent claims is straightforward.

[14] Several kind of ratios exist. Izvorski (1997) mentions three of them: R/P, R/F, $R/(F + AI)$, where R is the dollar amount recovered, P is the price of a riskless bond with coupon, principal, and maturity identical to the risky one, F is the face value of the bond, and AI is the accrued interest from the date of default to the date of consummation. Because of the time value of money, the first definiton of the recovery ratio provides the most consistent interpretation.

We do not think that the reason given for the use of this proxy is fairly valid. On the one hand, we can argue that it corresponds to some mean recovery as most debtholders try to terminate their positions. Then, the time length chosen is the only refuted parameter. But, on the other hand, this is omitting the falling liquidity of the defaulted instrument. Even if this rate is a mean rate, it is not the one really received by all debtholders. Given the demand and offer readjustment in our case, it would be clearly more realistic to use the marginal trading price for some level of dismissal by debtholders. In fact, if too large a number of debtholders decide to cancel their position at the same time, then prices will plummet and will be close to the residual value of assets upon liquidation.

12.2.2   Evidence

Altman and Kishore (1996a,b) provide a strong evidence that the industrial sector is a significant explanatory variable of the level of recovery on defaulted bonds, even when controlling for seniority which has an undeniable impact[15]. Altman and Kishore (1996b) show that original ratings have no explanatory power on recoveries once seniority is taken into account. This provides support to our remark on the use of ratings and their reduction of the credit environment, and gives evidence on the link of the recovery to the structure of the economy.

However, more in line with the model proposed in Chapter 14, the state of the economy seems to be important in explaining the fluctuations in recovery rates[16]. Izvorski (1997) demonstrated that firms defaulting in good times (high growth of GNP) suffer lower recovery ratios than firms defaulting in bad times (low growth of GNP). Izvorski is careful at defining recovery rates, a quality not present in all the studies on recovery rates. He defines recovery rates as the proportion recovered of the riskfree market value of the bond (rather than the face value of the bond). His methodology, although more complex than using simple face value, has the advantage of answering the true concern of investors, i.e. how much they will recover of the value of what they have, and allows for consistent comparison across bonds of recovery rates. Izvorski points out that interest rates and interest rate spreads have been widely used to predict times of slow-growth of recession (see also Fridson et al. (1997) for high-yield bonds). He also finds that the type of industry, especially the growth of the industry, the seniority of the debt as well as the type of restructuring used in case of default, are important variables determining the level of the true recovery rate. For example, firms that are in high-growth industries and restructure informally (rather than through the formal bankruptcy procedures) tend to have lower recovery ratios, while firms in high growth industries that go bankrupt tend to have higher recovery ratios. This could happen because investors are ready to concede more during informal negotiations with firms that have high-growth perspectives than with firms that have low-growth perspectives. Interestingly also, recovery ratios seem to be a significant negative determinant of the survival time. Lower recovery leads to higher survival time,

---

[15] Even if violations of the absolute priority rule are frequently observed.

[16] The use of interest rate dynamics in an economic setting has already been illustrated by Sussman and Zeira (1995) who provide a theoretical model of banking development where financial series of interest rates are a good proxy for the influence of economic behavior on financial indicators.

probably because creditors are willing to provide financial relief to financially distressed firms for a longer period if they have less to gain from forcing default.

More recent empirical works include Duffee (1998) and Alessandrini (1998)[17], although both studies are on credit spreads and not on recovery rates precisely. Both find that yield spreads and credit spreads, respectively, are negatively correlated to short interest rates and the term spread. They also find that lower rated bonds react more significantly to changes in the term structure. Alessandrini's (1998) main drawn conclusions are that credit risk cannot be managed independently from interest rate risk and that long-term interest rates seem to capture most of the business cycle effect on credit spreads[18]. Other conclusions are that credit risk seems to be more systematic than the stock market risk and that the impact of the term structure on credit spreads is stronger during recessions. In particular, Izvorski (1997) concludes that there is a deeper scrutiny of bond issues in times of low GDP growth and that creditors are willing to provide financial relief to financially distressed firms for a longer period of time if these firms operate in high recovery ratio industries. However, these last studies do not state whether this cross-effect is on probabilities of default or on recovery rates.

12.3 DUFFEE (1998): A STUDY ON TREASURY YIELDS VERSUS CORPORATE BOND YIELD SPREADS

The objective of the next three sections is to emphasize the methodologies used in recent empirical studies to further the analysis of relationships presented above.

In this first investigation, Duffee observes that the existing indexes of corporate bond yields comprise both callable and noncallable bonds. Moreover, from the mid-1980s, the "mixture" has evolved and we have now a much higher proportion of noncallable bonds. As an example, in the dataset of Duffee, only 271 out of 5297 straight bonds were noncallable for life by January 1984. This proportion increased dramatically up to 2814 out of 5291 by March 1985.

Therefore Duffee's interest is about the pertinence in calculating yields on these indexes without isolating the effect of the call attached to these bonds. This effect is certain and the indicated variations of the yields over time can be due only to the variation of the value of the embedded options or to a change into the mixture of callable and noncallable bonds in these indexes. In particular, in a fall of yields, callable bonds are not expected to rise as much as the noncallable ones because of the value of the embedded short call which also rises. And, given that these embedded options alter the perception of credit risk in these bonds, testing the differences between callable and noncallable bonds can provide us with interesting evidence on the way the market really prices credit risk.

Studying the relationship between corporate yield spreads over Treasury yields and noncallable Treasury yields will inform us about the joint behavior of default riskfree rates and the market perception of corporate default. However, in the case of callable corporate

---

[17]Evidence on the negative relationship between credit spreads and the term structure of interest rates is also discussed in Chang and Sundaresan (1999).

[18]Alessandrini's (1998) results show also that stock returns help in predicting future credit spreads which is helpful since the implementation of the structural model will be in part to estimate the parameters of the assets' value indirectly from stock market data.

bonds this can just tell us that the high value of *T*-bonds are associated with high values of the embedded call. This can make the latter relationship even more negative.

Duffee obtained a database of all prices and yields of the bonds constituting the Lehman Brothers Bond Indexes with additional information on their rating (Standard & Poors and Moody's), their coupon and maturity, their business sector affiliation, and indications on special features such as calls, puts, and sinking funds. All bonds are investment grade. Only quoted prices effectively established by a trader are used because of the illiquid character of the remaining prices.

Because of the insignificant proportion of noncallable bonds before 1985, only those after January 1985 are considered.

12.3.1 Preliminary to the Empirical Study

First, Duffee constructs bond indexes from bonds without any particular call, put, or sinking fund feature. These indexes were computed of monthly corporate yields, spreads over Treasuries and changes in the latter spreads, for four rating categories (Aaa, Aa, A and Baa), four business sectors (all, industrials, utilities and financials) and three maturity ranges (2–7 years, 7–15 years and 15–30 years).

Thanks to these indexes, Duffee computes mean spreads for each time t and mean yield spreads for each t to $t+1$ period with all bonds from the same rating/sector/ maturity sample. It is important to note on the construction of these variables that the bonds that are being downgraded, or change of maturity range between t and $t+1$, are not included in their old group for the computation of $SPREAD_t$, while they are still considered in the estimation of $\Delta SPREAD_{t,t+1}$. As stressed by Duffee, it is important not to "refresh" all indices. In the case of the index of changes in spreads, holding constant some dimension in the index will typically be problematic because the changes will be somewhat upward biased. In any case, Duffee points out that such cases in which a bond changes of rating over a 1-month horizon are so infrequent that the method retained has not a great impact in fact. Aggregate yield spreads are weighted averages of mean yield spreads over the four sectors by the number of bonds present in each of them.

In order to document the changes in the Treasury term structure, Duffee chooses the 3-month Treasury bill yield and the spread between the 30-year Treasury yield and the latter 3-month yield. An increase in this spread would mean an increase on the yields of a more than 3-month maturity.

12.3.2 Empirical Evidence with Noncallable Corporate Bonds

A First Regression

The relationship between yield changes on corporate yield spreads and the determinants of the Treasury term structure is analyzed through the following regression estimated by ordinary least squares (OLS):

$$\Delta SPREAD_{s,r,m,(t,t+1)} = \alpha_{s,r,m} + \beta^1_{s,r,m} \Delta Y_{t,t+1} + \beta^2_{s,r,m} \Delta TERM_{t,t+1} + \epsilon_{s,r,m,t+1}, \quad (12.1)$$

where $\Delta SPREAD_{s,r,m,(t,t+1)}$ is the change in the spread (corporate bond yield–Treasury yield of the same maturity) between month t and month $t+1$, $\Delta Y_{t,t+1}$ the contemporaneous change in the 3-month Treasury yield, and $\Delta TERM_{t,t+1}$ the contemporaneous change in the slope of the Treasury term structure. The variance–covariance matrix has been corrected for the possible impact of heteroskedasticity and two lags of moving average residuals.

The following results could be seen with all business sectors' bonds:

- An increase in the 3-month bill yield (the short rate) is accompanied by a decrease in the corporate yield spread.

- This relationship is even stronger as the credit rating is lower: a 4.2 bps increase for long-term Baa rated bonds for a 10 bps decrease in the 3-month T-bill yield[19].

- The same conclusion arises with respect to the Treasury term spread.

  Indeed, for the long-term bonds, the coefficients on the Treasury slope (the Treasury spread represented by the *TERM* variable) are very similar to the coefficients attached to the 3-month Treasury yields. In fact, the short-term Treasury yield and the Treasury spread sum to the 30-year Treasury yield. Therefore, the fact that the relationship of the long-term bonds is significant and similar with both of these components simply means that the changes in the corporate yield spread on the long-term bonds is influenced by the changes in the yield of long-term Treasuries, the latter summarizing the information of the Treasury term structure for long-term corporate bonds.

  However, this seems no longer true for short- and medium-maturity corporate bonds where the coefficient on the slope of the Treasury term structure is of weaker significance. It has been tested that the coefficient attached to this slope is clearly not similar to that of the short-term bill yield for these maturities. Therefore, in these cases the information of the Treasury term structure is summarized mainly by the short-term bill yield.

- Duffee remarks that the negative relation is the opposite of the one we would expect when focusing on the different tax rates that apply to corporate and Treasury bonds. The tax wedge between both of them increases when bond yields increase. Therefore, to offset this, corporate bond yields should more than increase when Treasury yields increase.

Macroeconomic Effects and Differences Among Business Sectors

No theory states precisely what should be the reaction of corporate yields across sectors, and it would be surprising to find that all sectors are equally influenced by a given set of macroeconomic variables. Given the separation in three sectors, Duffee has run a joint estimation of equation (12.1) for the three sectors using the generalized method of moments (GMM), and this for every one of the 12 combinations of rating and maturity.

The test of equality between the coefficients of the three sectors does not reject the hypothesis of equal coefficients across sectors, for any combination. Moreover, there is no real economic difference between the value of the estimates. Therefore, all subsequent results are obtained looking at indexes computed on all sectors together.

---

[19] It is statistically insignificant for long- and medium-maturity Aaa bonds.

The Persistence of Yield Changes

The persistence of the indicated relationships is tested thanks to the iterative use of fourth-order vector autoregression (VAR) on the 3-month yield, the slope of the term structure, and the corporate yields on Baa rated bonds (the most reactive sample), for each maturity band. The ordering of these three variables is shown not to alter the conclusions on the impact of the innovations of the 3-month yield and the slope on the Baa rated yield. Although we do not reproduce here the figures of the impulse response functions[20], they provide interesting results:

- The two-standard-deviation bounds around the values of the impulse response function show that the VAR coefficients are too unstable (even more for horizons greater than 3 months in some graphs) to conclude on any persistence of the response of changes in corporate yields to changes in the term structure variables.
- Responses to the 3-month bill yield are not really reversed within 1 to 2 months.
- The half-life of the responses is in the interval of 8–10 months, depending on the bond maturities.
- For the response of the Baa yield spread to innovations of the slope of the term structure or of the Baa yield spread itself, the figures present a hump-shaped form, important for the first 10 months.

The main conclusion is that if it is the laggish behavior of corporate yield spreads that explains the indicated relationships in the last subsection, then it also means that the quotes stemming from bond traders require many months to include the new information.

The Effect of Coupons

The fact that yields on low-rated bonds display a strong relationship to the slope of the term structure of the Treasury yield curve when of a long maturity only, can have two alternative explanations. First, it can be argued that this is just to reflect the fact that corporate bond yields are not compared to government bond yields of the same maturity. Duffee argues that it is rather related to the presence of coupons. Since coupons lower the duration of the corporate bond which have higher coupons than Treasuries have, and short-duration assets are more sensitive to short-term discount rates, an increase in the Treasury slope (holding constant the zero-coupon bond yield) will decrease the yield spread between corporate and Treasury bonds.

Duffee tries to verify this empirically. Suppose that the yield at time t of a zero-coupon Treasury bond with a T maturity, $Y_{t,T}^{g}$, satisfies the following linear equation[21]:

$$Y_{t,T}^{g} = 0.066 + 0.0014\,T. \tag{12.2}$$

Similarly, the yield spread between zero-coupon corporate and Treasury bonds, $S_{t,T}$, after the matching on certain coupon-bond data points, is assumed to have the following behavior:

---

[20]A good presentation of the vector autoregression as an econometric estimation procedure is provided in Hamilton (1996).

[21]This equation is estimated such that some chosen yields on coupon bonds are matched when this structure is applied to them.

$$S_{t,T} = 0.012 + 0.0005\,T. \tag{12.3}$$

These structures allow us to estimate prices and yields on coupon-bearing bonds. Assuming the following update of equation (12.2) for time $t + 1$:

$$Y^g_{t+1,T} = 0.0659085 + 0.0017664\,T,$$

it can be found that it produces a yield for a 30-year 8.4% coupon-bearing Treasury bond 50 bps higher than before, while the yield on a 3-month T-bill does not change. Assuming that equation (12.3) has not changed, yield spreads between corporate and Treasury coupon-bearing bonds are calculated for different coupons and the 22, 9.5, and 4 year maturities (the averages of the long, medium, and short maturity bands of the sample).

This shows a result of a 5.5 bps decrease in the yield spread for the maturity of 22 years[22] while the effect is almost null for the shorter maturities. The difference between long and short low-rated corporate bonds can be therefore explained by a duration effect independently of any credit risk perception.

12.3.3 Comparing with Callable Bonds

When using the Moody's Aaa Industrials Index which contains callable and noncallable bonds, over the same sample period, the estimated coefficients are eight times those estimated previously, showing a strong negative relationship to the short-term level and to the slope of the Treasury yield curve. Moreover, the coefficients for these two explanatory variables are statistically equal. This simply means that it is the long-term behavior of the Treasury yield curve that influences the yield spreads with corporate bonds, even the shorter ones.

This can be explained by the callability feature of part of the bond sample. The call option value of a corporate bond is clearly related to the yield of a maturity-equivalent Treasury bond. Indeed, Duffee has shown that the correlation of monthly changes in the constant-maturity 5-year Treasury yield with the 30-year Treasury bond is 0.91 instead of 0.67 for the correlation with the 3-month bill yield. Overall, this explains why the call option value is influenced mostly by the long-term end of the Treasury yield curve, reflected by the fact that the coefficients of the corporate yield to the short-term yield and the term slope are equal.

The next step for Duffee was to test if this sensitivity was significantly stronger for callable bonds and was affected by the moneyness of the call option. Duffee retained six samples of Aa rated bonds, three for currently callable bonds, and three for bonds that will still remain at least call-protected for 1 year. Then, they are further separated in three groups depending on their moneyness. Four conclusions arise:

1. The sensitivity is positively related to the price of the bond, which is consistent with the option pricing theory.
2. The out-of-the-money sample presents the same sensitivity as for noncallable bonds of the same rating category.

---

[22] For example, a coefficient of -0.11 for the $\Delta TERM$ variable in equation (12.1).

3. The negative sensitivity is very strong for the in-the-money sample and it is not significantly different for the short-term yield compared to that to the term slope, which implies straightfowardly that it is a sensitivity with respect to the long-term Treasury yield.

4. The sensitivity for call-protected bonds is nearly the same, although a little bit lower than the sensitivity for currently callable bonds.

Thus the conclusion of Duffee who stresses that it is not acceptable to use the yield on a call-protected bond for the yield on an otherwise noncallable bond.

12.3.4   Conclusions

Other conclusions are as follows:

- The negative sensitivity of corporate yields to short-term bill yields seems to be initially related to the rating of the issue, but
- the evident persistence of these changes is accompanied by a great deal of dispersion, and
- the sensitivity seems to be clearly linked to the callable feature of the bond which is an important result for previous and further "data mining studies".

12.4   DUFFEE (1999): THE ESTIMATION OF THE PRICE OF DEFAULT RISK

Credit risk is not only important from an *ex post* econometric point of view but also *ex ante* for traders wanting to accurately price instruments subject to it. Duffee's idea is to test the implementability and the accuracy of reduced-form modelizations[23]. Reduced-form models, which stand on a mathematical basis without high economic modeling constraint, can be tested like any other econometric calibration problem.

12.4.1   The Model

Under the equivalent martingale measure, the price at time t of a default-free zero-coupon bond maturing at time T is given by

$$P(t, T, c = 0) = E^Q \left[\exp \left(- \int_t^T r_u \, du \right) \right]$$ (12.4)

with the following translated two-factor model for the instantaneous interest rate:

$$r_t = \alpha_r + s_{1,t} + s_{2,t},$$ (12.5)

---

[23]Again, we have to make some definitions here. Reduced-form models are preferred because their mathematical form does not rely on a financial framework that must also match some corporate reality. On the other hand, when their economic content is put into question, researchers in this area say that the probabilities of default and recoveries can always be matched to some underlying corporate relationships. Duffie and Lando have provided a development of this correspondence, but no test has been run to analyze the remaining pricing power of the model. "Double-sided objectives" like the present one can therefore present some contradictions.

where each $s_{i,t}$ factor is assumed to follow a square-root diffusion process of the form

$$ds_{i,t} = \kappa_i(\theta_i - s_{i,t})dt + \sigma_i\sqrt{s_{i,t}}dZ_{i,t}. \tag{12.6}$$

Both factors are considered to be independent from each other and therefore $dZ_{1,t}.dZ_{2,t} = 0$. Under the equivalent martingale measure, this generic process can be rewritten as

$$ds_{i,t} = (\kappa_i\theta_i - (\kappa_i + \lambda_i)s_{i,t})dt + \sigma_i\sqrt{s_{i,t}}d\hat{Z}_{i,t}, \tag{12.7}$$

with the same independency assumption. Pearson and Sun (1994) provide a closed-form solution to this modelization.

For the definition of the event of default, it is assumed that it happens as an unpredictable jump in a Poisson process. The intensity of this process under the equivalent martingale measure for firm j at time t is denoted $h_{j,t}$. That means that the probability under the equivalent martingale measure of the j firm defaulting in the interval $\{t, t+dt\}$ is $h_{j,t}dt$[24]. If we denote as $V(t, T, c = 0, 1 - L = 0)$ the price of a zero-coupon defaultable bond with maturity T and 0 recovery, then it can be valued as an expectation under the equivalent martingale measure as in equation (12.4), but now applied to an adjusted instantaneous discount rate $r_t + h_{j,t}$ such that

$$V(t, T, 0, 0) = E^Q\left[\exp\left(-\int_t^T (r_u + h_{j,u})du\right)\right]. \tag{12.8}$$

Similarly to the instantaneous interest rate, the intensity of default $h_{j,t}$ is modeled as a translated one-factor model plus two terms accounting for its link with the two interest rate factors such that

$$h_{j,t} = \alpha_j + h_{j,t}^* + \beta_{1,j}(s_{1,t} - \overline{s_{1,t}}) + \beta_{2,j}(s_{2,t} - \overline{s_{2,t}}), \tag{12.9}$$

where $h_{j,t}^*$ also follows a square-root model of the form

$$dh_{j,t}^* = \kappa_j(\theta_j - h_{j,t}^*)dt + \sigma_j\sqrt{h_{j,t}^*}dZ_{j,t}. \tag{12.10}$$

where $Z_{j,t}$ is independent from $Z_{1,t}$ and $Z_{2,t}$. Under the equivalent martingale measure, this process can be rewritten as

$$dh_{j,t}^* = (\kappa_j\theta_j - (\kappa_j + \lambda_j)h_{j,t}^*)dt + \sigma_j\sqrt{h_{j,t}^*}d\hat{Z}_{j,t}. \tag{12.11}$$

This form is very important for the behavior that will be evidenced in the results of the implementation below. For the moment, it has to be noticed that all processes are mean-reverting processes. It means that we have the risk that if the estimation procedure does not produce stochastic parameters of significant magnitude, then we will end up with a trivial and deterministic model where the mean which the process reverts to will be the key determinant of the level of the default risk. The results obtained will thus be explicit rather than implicit from the model.

---

[24]This intensity will not be the same under the true probability measure unless the market price of risk associated with the jump risk is null.

Apart from this caveat, the particular definition of $dh^*_{j,t}$ provides us with three advantages:

1. The obtained yield spreads will be stochastic.
2. Even yield spreads of very high-rated firms will be positive. There is a minimum spread given by α_j, whatever the level of $h^*_{j,t}$. Duffee argues that this can be justified by the existence of liquidity effects or state taxes, unrelated to the default itself, or by the fact that a major economic or legal event can push the healthiest firm into default. But then Duffee makes the assumption that this can be directly assimilated into the default intensity parameter $h_{j,t}$.
3. Even if the process for $h^*_{j,t}$ is assumed to be unrelated to innovations in the term structure factors, the correlation between $h_{j,t}$ and $s_{1,t}$ and $s_{2,t}$ will be entirely represented by the coefficients $\beta_{1,t}$ and $\beta_{2,t}$. This allows us to be consistent with the evidence presented in Duffee (1998) above. And, given the absence of correlation directly between the processes themselves the setup allows a closed-form solution for the price of $V(t, T, 0, 0)$ with yields that are linear in $h^*_{j,t}$, $s_{1,t}$ and $s_{2,t}$.

However, a final remark can be made on this third advantage which will show us two limitations that the reduced-form models impose. The precision is entirely available in Duffee (1999).

1. We could have written equation (12.9) as

$$h_{j,t} = \alpha^*_j + h^*_{j,t} + \beta_{1,j}s_{1,t} + \beta_{2,j}s_{2,t},\tag{12.12}$$

where the new α^*_j absorbs the differences with respect to the mean values of $s_{1,t}$ and $s_{2,t}$. Let us compare two firms that are differentiated only by their $\beta_{1,j}$ value. In equation (12.9) this will not change anything to the mean value of $h_{j,t}$, while in equation (12.12) a higher $\beta_{1,j}$ will correspond to a higher mean $h_{j,t}$ as long as the mean value of $s_{1,t}$ is positive. But, as stressed by Duffee, "the model is not rich enough to allow us to infer from corporate bond data whether a firm with a high $\beta_{1,j}$ has a high mean $h_{j,t}$ because of this $\beta_{1,j}$ or because it happens to have a high α_j". However, in structural models such as the model of Longstaff and Schwartz (1995b) the relationship between the likelihood of default and the correlation between the bond price and the asset value of the firm is clearly settled by the model. It is shown, indeed, that a negative correlation will stabilize the asset value and therefore reduce the default spread.
2. The empirical evidence of Duffee below shows that even though we obtain a positive value for α_j we do obtain values for the βs which are negative. Therefore the model does not prevent us from producing negative intensities. This a general problem, however, for an accurate pricing of the riskfree and risky bonds, we must obtain suitable values from the calibration.

A final element to define is now the recovery which was assumed to be null until here. Suppose, as in Jarrow and Turnbull's model, that we want to allow a recovery ratio $\delta > 0$ of an otherwise riskfree bond at default maturing at T[25]. Moody's evidence

---

[25]This is compatible with the absence of arbitrage after default.

retained by Duffee is that this ratio is indeed of 44% for senior unsecured debt issues. Prior to default, the absence of arbitrage requires that

$$V_j(t, T, 0, \delta) = \delta \, P(t, T, 0) + (1 - \delta) \, V_j(t, T, 0, 0). \tag{12.13}$$

This framework allows us to easily derive bond prices as functions of zero-recovery prices and riskfree bonds while the nonstochasticity of δ allows us to avoid additional estimation problems that arise when both h and δ are stochastic. The estimation procedure would not be able to distinguish between both. That is why Duffie and Singleton (1999) propose to modelize jointly the product $(1 - \delta)h$. Duffee stresses the fact that, since we are not able to directly observe δ (and also because of the liquidity and tax effects evocated earlier), we have to be careful when interpreting h directly as the equivalent martingale probability of instantaneous default.

12.4.2 The Data

Initially, 40 270 month-end observations (indicative bid quotes of traders) of non-callable bonds across 161 firms from January 1985 to December 1995, mostly investment-grade. These bonds are also nonputable, senior unsecured with no sinking fund provision with constant semiannual coupons and original maturities of under 35 years but above 1 year. One-third of the sample is constituted by bond issues of financial firms and for each firm there are at least 36 months where bond quotes are available from at least two traders, after dropping similar maturity bonds. Finally, the median number of observations for a firm is of 92 data points. When looking at the median number of bonds per month and per firm, i.e. 2.5, we notice already that the term structure will have to be derived with sometimes a tiny sample.

12.4.3 The Estimation

Duffee (1999) uses an extended Kalman filter method for the estimation of cross-sectional and time-series properties of the bonds in the sample. Since bond prices depend on the processes of h, s_1, and s_2 it would be preferable to estimate simultaneously the default-free interest rate and default probability processes parameters. But since it is not feasible to do it cross-sectionally for all firms at once, the method is finally run firm by firm. This gives us 162 Kalman filter estimations.

12.4.4 The Results

The Default-free Process

The results coming out from the Kalman filter applications show clearly that α_r is negative but has a great dispersion. Duffee then follows the approach of Pearson and Sun (1994) and arbitrarily fixes the value of α_r to a lower boundary, say -1.

Here s_1 is clearly highly correlated to the spread between long and short bond yields (-0.97). The correlation of the first differences of these two series remains very high. Its mean-reverting behavior is also important: its half-life is less than 1.5 years. Similarly, the correlation between s_2 and the series of long bond yields (in first differences) is 0.97. But, contrary to s_1, its half-life is more than 20 years. As concluded by Duffee, this latter variable is close to a martingale.

These results clearly go in the same direction as those of previous studies, focusing on the application of the Kalman filter approach for multifactor problems of the term structure, namely Chen and Scott (1995), Geyer and Pichler (1996), and Duan and Simonato (1998).

The negativity of α_r implies that negative interest rates are not precluded. On the other hand, this negativity ensures that the model is able to generate a wide variety of term structure shapes with a coherent level of volatility.

The estimated two-factor model is shown to be quite inaccurate for short-term bills, but does a pretty good job for long-maturity instruments. Fortunately, corporate bonds in our sample are of a maturity longer than 1 year. Part of the poor results for the short end of the term structure should be related to a misspecification in the estimation which assumes that s_1 and s_2 are uncorrelated, while the empirical correlation coefficient amounts to -0.37.

The Default Intensity Processes

Looking at the results of the estimated $h_{j,t}$ and $h^*_{j,t}$ ranked by quartile it is noticeable that the results of the extreme quartiles differ widely. The two possible explanations are a high uncertainty in the estimates or a high cross-variation into the sample of firms. Taking back the comments in the data section above, the high uncertainty in the estimates is highly plausible. Duffee retains, therefore, the median values only.

Taking a more precise look at some median values, we observe that the median α_j is of 0.0075. Taking the median values for the processes of s_1 and s_2, and regardless of the health of the firm (suppose $h_{j,t} = 0$), assuming a 44% recovery at default, the obtained yield spread for a near-zero maturity corporate discount bond is downward bounded at 41.9 bps. Because of the construction of the model this cannot be assumed to be nonrelated to default risk.

Default intensities seem to be quite stationary with a half-life of less than 3 years. The negative median for λ_j means that investors are particularly interested by assets that pay when the default probabilities rise. Because the negative median λ_j is higher in absolute value than the median κ_j, we are in the presence of negative mean reversion, which means that higher levels of risk can lead to larger growth in the risk itself.

The median annual firm's mean fitted default probability is of 1.4%, which is higher than the historical value[26].

Results by Credit Rating

Owing to the small precision obtained on a firm-by-firm basis, the stability of default intensities can be tested through the study of the variation across rating categories[27]. The resulting spread curves by rating[28] as a function of the remaining time to maturity are in the expected order and present an upward-sloping shape. This slope is indeed stronger for lower-rated bonds; $h^*_{j,t}$ and α_j values are higher for lower-rated bonds,

---

[26] This is compatible with the survivorship bias in the overall sample of firms through time.
[27] The instability of the parameters could also be driven by the fact that the firms could update their choice of capital structure when bonds were already outstanding.
[28] Remember that the sample is solely constituted of investment-grade bonds.

thereby explaining the behavior of the spread curves. To obtain a steeper curve with a higher $h_{j,t}^*$ we need a negative $\kappa_j + \lambda_j$ value.

Also, "because $\kappa_j + \lambda_j$ is more negative for lower-rated firms, default risk is more explosive under the equivalent martingale measure for low-rated firms".

Last but not least, lower-rated firms appear to be more sensitive to the slope of the default-free term structure of interest rates.

When sorting the firms, not by their initial rating but by the rating prevailing at time t of the estimation, $h_{j,t}$ values are again inversely related to the firms' credit ratings. Aaa rated firms have a median annual default probability of 0.79%, while it is 1.83% for Baa rated firms. There is also a general pattern of higher default risk volatilities for lower-rated counterparts (this ordering is, however, violated for two categories).

12.4.5 Conclusions

The study gives good insights about the behavior of default probabilities and the spread curve by credit rating. However, there is a great instability of the parameters across ratings. The latter conclusion may be driven by the form of the diffusion processes which are all mean-reverting.

12.5 WEI AND GUO (1997)

Wei and Guo (1997) compare the two models of Merton (1974) and Longstaff and Schwartz (1995b) in terms of tractability and performance. Again, they focus on the fact that default risk is constituted of the probability of default and the recovery, and it is the treatment of these two components that is studied. The main refinements of Longstaff and Schwartz (1995a) are that interest rates are stochastic and correlated with the asset value process and default can happen before the maturity of the contract. Longstaff and Schwartz also assume that a firm's capital structure is irrelevant to firm value, allowing us to imagine liability structures with different maturities and coupon payment profiles. But, contrary to what we could think of, Merton (1974) is not subsumed in Longstaff and Schwartz (1995b).

Indeed looking at the recovery rate, Longstaff and Schwartz (1995b) assume an exogenously specified recovery rate of an otherwise riskfree bond, making implicitly the assumption that the absolute priority rule (APR) can be violated. In fact, such violations would be more consistent with a random recovery rate[29].

Wei and Guo (1997) provide two useful expressions to easily compare the two models. The credit term structure of credit spreads ($cs(\tau)$) in Merton (1974) can be viewed as given by

$$cs(\tau) = -\frac{1}{\tau} \ln \left[1 - \left(1 - \frac{1}{X} \right) Q + \sigma_{\alpha, DP} \right],$$

where τ is the time remaining to maturity, X the "quasi" debt-to-firm value ratio, Q the risk-neutral probability of default, and $\sigma_{\alpha, DP}$ the covariance between the recovery rate α and the default probability DP.

---

[29] Some criticisms around the economic meaning of a constant recovery of an otherwise identical riskfree bond have been provided by Briys and de Varenne (1997).

The equivalent expression in Longstaff and Schwartz's case would be

$$cs(\tau) = -\frac{1}{\tau} \ln \left[1 - \omega Q \right],$$

where $\alpha = 1 - \omega$, ω being the constant writedown in case of default.

Wei and Guo (1997) use Eurodollars as risky debt and US Treasury bills as riskless debt for the estimation of the parameters and the comparison of the behavior of both models. Data is taken for 53 Thursdays in 1992. Continuously compounded yields to maturity are calculated from the difference in the yields of the initial time series. They obtain a credit term structure of Eurodollars. All structural models provided until here implicitly produce a hump-shaped term structure of credit spreads, while Wei and Guo find an empirical N-shaped term structure in the Euromarket. Das's (1995) model explained in the chapter on financial structuring with credit derivatives, obtains an "N-shaped" term structure of credit spreads.

The Wei and Guo paper is also interesting for the way they estimate the different parameters. The Longstaff and Schwartz (1995b) paper is more demanding, regarding this estimation because of some of their restrictions, a higher number of parameters than in Merton, and the number of calculations that must be made.

The results are, however, the following: both models are rejected in three out of five cases when parameters are held constant. When a variable asset volatility is allowed for Merton the rejection is only of one case out of five. The conclusion is that, even if the Longstaff and Schwartz model seems to be more flexible to adjust to real data with more variables and thus more degrees of freedom, Merton (1974) has a significantly higher performance. The Longstaff and Schwartz model is more general regarding the default probability, while Merton (1974) is more general for the recovery issue and is not subsumed in the Longstaff and Schwartz framework.

This also shows that simple models may still perform well compared to seemingly more sophisticated ones.

12.6   CONCLUSION

The empirical literature on credit risk, while getting stronger, is still lacking compared to the theoretical literature. A better understanding of the dynamics of recovery rates and of probabilities of default is still required. The first true tests of models are coming through and show the way for more work to be done in this area.

12.7   REFERENCES

Alessandrini, F., 1998, "Credit Risk, Interest Rate Risk and the Business Cycle", Masters Thesis, Master of Science in Economics, HEC, Lausanne University, n. 98, November, 62 pp.

Altman, Edward and Vellore Kishore, 1996a, "Defaults and Returns on High Yield Bonds: Analysis through 1995", New York University Salomon Center *Special Report*.

Altman, Edward and Vellore Kishore, 1996b, "Almost Everything You Wanted to Know about Recoveries on Defaulted Bonds", *Financial Analysts Journal*, November/December, 57–64.

Anderson, Ronald and Suresh Sundaresan, 1996, "Design and Valuation of Debt Contracts", *The Review of Financial Studies*, Spring, **9** (1), 37–68.

Anderson, Ronald W., Suresh Sundaresan and Puni Tychon, 1996, "Strategic Analysis of Contingent Claims", *European Economic Review*, **40** (3–5), April, 871–81.

Black, F. and J. C. Cox, 1976, "Valuing Corporate Securities: Some Effects of Bond Indenture Provisions", *Journal of Finance*, **31**, 351–67.

Brennan, M. and E. Schwartz, 1980, "Analyzing Convertible Bonds", *Journal of Financial Quantitative Analysis*, **15**, 907–29.

Briys, Eric and François de Varenne, 1997, "Valuing Risky Fixed Rate Debt: An Extension", *Journal of Financial and Quantitative Analysis*, **32** (2), June, 239–49.

Cantor, Richard, Frank Packer and Kevin Cole, 1997, "Split Ratings and the Pricing of Credit Risk", Research Update from The Federal Reserve Bank of New York, Number 9711, March, pp. 77–82.

Chang, Ganlin and Suresh Sundaresan, 1999, "Asset Prices and Default-Free Term Structure in an Equilibrium Model of Default", *Working Paper*, Graduate School of Business, Columbia University, March, 49 pp.

Chen, Ren-Raw and Louise Scott, 1995, "Interest Rate Options in Multifactor Cox-Ingersoll-Ross Models of the Term Structure", *The Journal of Derivatives*, **3** (Winter), 53–72.

Clark, Corolyn, Paul Foster and Waqar Ghani, 1997, "Differential Reaction to Bond Downgrades for Small vs. Large Firms: Evidence from Analysts' Forecast Revision", *The Journal of Fixed Income*, December, 94–99.

Crouhy, Michel and Dan Galai, 1997, "Credit Risk Revisited: An Option Pricing Approach", May 1997, *Working Paper* 97-2, Canadian Imperial Bank of Commerce/Market Risk Management/Global Analytics, 18 pp.

Crouhy, Michel, Dan Galai and Robert Mark, 2000, "A Comparative Analysis of Current Credit Risk Models", *Journal of Banking and Finance*, **24** (1–2), 59–117.

Das, Sanjiv and Peter Tufano, 1996, "Pricing Credit Sensitive Debt when Interest Rates, Credit Ratings and Credit Spreads are Stochastic", *Journal of Financial Engineering*, **5** (2), June.

Duan, J. C. and J.-G. Simonato, 1998, "Maximum Likelihood Estimation of Deposit Insurance Value with Interest Rate Risk", *Working Paper*, November, 21 pp.

Duffee, Gregory R., 1998, "The Relation Between Treasury Yields and Corporate Bond Yield Spreads", *Journal of Finance*, **53**, 2225–42.

Duffee, Gregory, 1999, "Estimating the Price of Default Risk", *The Review of Financial Studies*, **12** (1), Spring, 197–226.

Duffee, Gregory R. and Chunsheng Zhou, 1999, "Credit Derivatives in Banking: Useful Tools for Managing Risk?", *Working Paper*, Federal Reserve Board, September, 38 pp.

Duffie, Darrell and David Lando, 1997, "Term Structures of Credit Spreads with Incomplete Accounting Information", Preliminary Draft, September 12, 39 pp.

Duffie, Darrell and Ken Singleton, 1999, "Modeling Term Structures of Defaultable Bonds", *Review of Financial Studies*, Special 1999, **12** (4), 687–720.

Ellis, David, 1997, "Different Sides of the Same Story: Investors' and Issuers' Views of Rating Agencies", *Working Paper*, Finance Division, Babson College, August, 18 pp.

Ericsson, Jan and Joel Reneby, 1995, "A Framework for Valuing Corporate Securities", *Working Paper*, Stockholm School of Economics, November, 35 pp.

Fridson, Martin, Christopher Garman and Sheng Wu, 1997, "Real Interest Rates and the Default Rate on High-Yield Bonds", *The Journal of Fixed Income*, September, 29–34.

Geyer, Alois L. J. and Stefan Pichler, 1999, "A State-Space Approach to Estimate and Test Multifactor Cox-Ingersoll-Ross Models of the Term Structure", *The Journal of Financial Research*, **22**, Spring, 107–30.

Gibson-Asner, Rajna, 1990, *Obligations et Clauses Optionnelles*, Presses Universitaires de France, Paris, 243 pp.

Hamilton, James D., 1996, *Time Series Analysis*, Princeton University Press, 799 pp.

Hettenhouse, George W. and William L. Sartoris, 1976, "An Analysis of the Informational Value of Bond-Rating Changes", *Quarterly Review of Economics and Business*, **16**(2), Summer, 65–78.

Hite, Gailen and Arthur Warga, 1997, "The Effect of Bond-Rating Changes on Bond Price Performance", *Financial Analysts Journal*, May/June, 35–47.

Iben, T. and R. Litterman, 1991, "Corporate Bond Valuation and the Term Structure of Credit Spreads", *Journal of Portfolio Management*, Spring, 52–64.

Izvorski, Ivailo, 1997, "Recovery Ratios and Survival Times for Corporate Bonds", International Monetary Fund, *Working Paper*, Research Department, WP 97/84, July, 32 pp.

Jarrow, R. and Stuart Turnbull, 1991, "A Unified Approach for Pricing Contingent Claims on Multiple Term Structures: The Foreign Currency Analogy", Working Paper.

Jarrow, R. and Stuart Turnbull, 1995, "Pricing Derivatives on Financial Securities Subject to Credit Risk", *Journal of Finance*, **50** (1), 53–85.

Jarrow, R., David Lando and Stuart Turnbull, 1997, "A Markov Model of the Term Structure of Credit Spreads", *Review of Financial Studies*, **10** (2), Summer.

Jones, E. Philip, Scott P. Mason and Eric Rosenfeld, 1984, "Contingent Claims Analysis of Corporate Capital Structures: An Empirical Investigation", *The Journal of Finance*, **39** (3), July, 611–27.

Katz, Steven, 1974, "The Price Adjustment Process of Bonds to Rating Reclassifications: A Test of Bond Market Efficiency", *Journal of Finance*, **29**(2), May, 551–9.

Longstaff, F. and E. Schwartz, 1995a, "Valuing Credit Derivatives", *Journal of Fixed Income*, June, 6–12.

Longstaff, Francis and Eduardo Schwartz, 1995b, "A Simple Approach to Valuing Risky Fixed and Floating Rate Debt", *Journal of Finance*, **50** (3), July, 789–819.

Lucas, D. J. and J. Lonski, 1992, "Changes in Corporate Credit Quality 1970–1990", *Journal of Fixed Income*, **2**, March, 7–14.

Madan, D. and H. Unal, 1993, "Pricing the Risks of Default", *Working Paper*, College of Business, University of Maryland.

Merton, Robert C., 1974, "On the Pricing of Corporate Debt: The Risk Structure of Interest Rates", *The Journal of Finance*, **29**, May, 449–70.

Merton, Robert C., 1977, "On the Pricing of Contingent Claims and the Modigliani–Miller Theorem", *Journal of Financial Economics*, **5**, 241–9.

Merton, Robert C., 1994, *Continuous-Time Finance*, Blackwell, 732 pp.

Moon, Choon-Geol and Janet G. Stotsky, 1993, "Testing the Differences Between the Determinants of Moody's and Standard & Poors' Ratings: An Application of Smooth Simulated Maximum Likelihood Estimation", *Journal of Applied Econometrics*, **8** (1), Jan.–March, 51–69.

Musiela, Marek and Marek Rutkowski, 1997, *Martingale Methods in Financial Modelling*, Springer-Verlag, 512 pp.

Pearson, N. D. and T.-S. Sun, 1994, "Exploiting the Conditional Density in Estimating the Term Structure: An Application to the Cox, Ingersoll and Ross Model", *The Journal of Finance*, **49**, 1279–304.

Pinches, George E. and J. Clay Singleton, 1978, "The Adjustment of Stock Prices to Bond Rating Changes", *Journal of Finance*, **33** (1), March, 29–44.

Saá-Requejo, Jesús and Pedro Santa Clara, 1997, "Bond Pricing with Default Risk", *Working Paper*, John E. Anderson Graduate School of Management, UCLA, Los Angeles, 23 pp.

Schaefer, Stephen and Eduardo Schwartz, 1984, "A Two-Factor Model of the Term Structure: An Approximate Analytical Solution", *Journal of Financial and Quantitative Analysis*, **19** (4), December, 413–24.

Schönbucher, P., 1997, "The Term Structure of Defaultable Bond Prices", *Working Paper*, University of Bonn.

Shimko, David, Naohiko Tejima and Donald Van Deventer, 1993, "The Pricing of Risky Debt When Interest Rates are Stochastic", *The Journal of Fixed Income*, September, 58–65.

Sussman, Oren and Joseph Zeira, 1995, "Banking and Development", Centre for Economic Policy Research, Financial Economics and International Macroeconomics, n. 1127, February, 42 pp.

Wei, D. G. and D. Guo, 1997, "Pricing Risky Debt: An Empirical Comparison of the Longstaff and Schwartz and Merton Models", *The Journal of Fixed Income*, September, 9–28.

Weinstein, Mark I, 1977, The Effect of a Rating Change Announcement on Bond Price, *Journal of Financial Economics*, **5** (3), December, 329–50.

Zhou, Chunsheng, 1997, "A Jump-Diffusion Approach to Modeling Credit Risk and Valuing Defaultable Securities", *Working Paper*, Federal Reserve Board, Washington, 47 pp.

Part Four
A Proposition for a Structural Model

13

Introduction

As has been presented in the earlier parts of this book, there is now a large literature on the pricing of credit risk with formulations for perpetual coupon-bearing bonds or zero-coupon bonds, in the context or not of a strategic behavior of lenders and borrowers and with different definitions for the default event, the liquidation procedure, and the recovered amount. Here we will present the approach developed in Pirotte (1999b) and focus on an implementable model for the pricing of a straight corporate defaultable bond[1] with finite maturity, i.e. the riskfree equivalent at time 0 of a $1 cash flow due at maturity by an industrial firm under the main assumption that the lender faces the risk of a nonstrategic default from the firm until the reimbursement date. This is performed through an extended structural modeling of the event of default that makes use of the option pricing theory. A term structure of credit spreads for a given counterparty is then derived.

Pirotte (1999b) concentrates on the hypothesis underlying Merton's basic structural framework that treats bonds and stock as contingent claims on the assets of the firm, and then refine the classical specifications of the event of default and the recovery at default. A particular emphasis is made on the role played by the existence of a threshold value[2], the impact of interest rates and the business cycle, the time horizon of the investor, and the existence of the dividend payout rate as a mean for shareholders to extract cash out of the firm before the maturity of the debt contract.

Indeed, given previous empirical evidence, there is an incentive to relate the amount that the creditor recovers at default with the state of the economy prevailing at that time. Theoretical models and recent empirical studies (see Altman and Kishore, 1996a,b), Izvorski, 1997, Duffee, 1998, Alessandrini, 1998 and others) have shown that we can relate the evolution of interest rates and, in particular, the long rate and the term spread with the evolution of the business cycle. A two-factor model of the term structure of interest rates is thus chosen for the price of the riskfree zero-coupon bond and, in particular, for the evolution of the threshold value that can trigger default before the maturity horizon.

The appeal of a structural model resides in the valuation being linked to economic fundamentals of the firm and its stochastic output where default is not a purely unpredictable event as it is assumed in the *reduced-form* approaches which models are either too parsimonious or with many state variables that require too many restrictions to be still computable. In the presence of an investment opportunity, the price of corporate debt and its structure should be settled simultaneously[3]. In the spirit of Black

---

[1]Since credit risk deals with counterparty risk and is therefore present in any contract, we have to be aware of the usual mitigating techniques or "bypassing strategies", such as the use of netting, covenants, collateralization, the foundation of AAA pass-through trusts, etc. These possibilities should not be undermined since they modify considerably the profile of the overall exposure. We will therefore concentrate on a single corporate bond free from any of these mitigating features.

[2]Acting as a protective covenant (in the sense of Leland, 1994) or as a flow insolvency threshold.

[3]This obeys one of the first principles of economics.

and Cox (1976), the threshold value as a safety covenant will be optimally fixed by debtholders. At the same time, shareholders will define their desired dividend payout knowing that a higher rate will also mean a shorter expected life of the firm and therefore a shorter dividend stream, given the existence of the safety covenant. This will allows us to endogenize these two parameters and provide consistency to our pricing model.

In former structural approaches like Merton and Black and Cox, default is restricted to happen only at maturity. Then, Longstaff and Schwartz (1995b) proposed a model for a non-perpetual zero-coupon bond and a floating rate bond where the structurally defined event of default can take place at any point between the origination of the contract and the maturity while correlated to the dynamics of the term structure of interest rates. The absolute amount recovered at default is, however, constant contrarily to Merton's setting. Briys and de Varenne (1997) provide a more consistent approach to this kind of problem. They also relaxed the idea of a fixed default threshold allowing it to be itself dependent on the term structure of interest rates but the economic implications of this definition remain unexplored. Also, up to now, only one-factor arbitrage models of the term structure of interest rates have been used in conjunction with the process of the value of the firm.

Next, Chapter 14 presents the pricing approach developed in Pirotte (1999b) and its closed-form solution. Chapter 15 provides comparative statics along with the term structure of credit spreads, against earlier structural studies. Relating these results to the fundamentals of the firm, the problem of the contractual design of the contract is viewed as a clear extension of the work presented here and it is available in Pirotte (1999b). Chapter 16 reproduces a tractable implementation procedure that relates the debt pricing model to traded stock market data, using, in reverse, the barrier option pricing framework presented earlier.

13.1 REFERENCES

Alessandrini, F., 1998, "Credit Risk, Interest Rate Risk and the Business Cycle", Master Thesis, Master of Science in Economics, HEC, Lausanne University, n. 98, November, 62 pp.

Altman, Edward and Vellore Kishore, 1996a, "Defaults and Returns on High Yield Bonds: Analysis through 1995", *New York University Salomon Center Special Report.*

Altman, Edward and Vellore Kishore, 1996b, "Almost Everything You Wanted to Know about Recoveries on Defaulted Bonds", *Financial Analysts Journal*, November/December, 57–64.

Briys, Eric and François de Varenne, 1997, "Valuing Risky Fixed Rate Debt: An Extension", *Journal of Financial and Quantitative Analysis*, **32** (2), June, 239–49.

Duffee, Gregory R., 1998, "The Relation Between Treasury Yields and Corporate Bond Yield Spreads", *Journal of Finance*, **53**, 2225–42.

Leland, Hayne E., 1994, "Corporate Debt Value, Bond Covenants and Optimal Capital Structure", *Journal of Finance*, **49** (4), September, 1213–52.

Longstaff, Francis and Eduardo Schwartz, 1995b, "A Simple Approach to Valuing Risky Fixed and Floating Rate Debt", *Journal of Finance*, **50** (3), July, 789–819.

Izvorski, Ivailo, 1997, "Recovery Ratios and Survival Times for Corporate Bonds", International Monetary Fund, *Working Paper*, Research Department, WP 97/84, July, 32 pp.

Pirotte, H., 1999a, "Implementing a Structural Valuation Model of Swap Credit-Sensitive Rates". *Working Paper*, Institute of Banking and Finance, Ecole des HEC, University of Lausanne, December, 32 pp.

Pirotte, H., 1999b, "A Structural Model of the Term Structure of Credit Spreads with Stochastic Recovery and Contractual Design", *Working Paper*, Institute of Banking and Finance, Ecole des HEC, University of Lausanne, December, 85 pp.

14
The Pricing Model

The intention here is to present the price a zero-coupon bond issued by the defaultable firm in a more refined setup such as in Pirotte (1999b) which also integrates the stochasticity of interest rates and the possibility of earlier default, before the maturity of the contract, while remaining coherent with the main principles presented in Chapter 12 in order to complete previous modelizations such as those of Longstaff and Schwartz (1995b), Briys and de Varenne (1997), and Saá-Requejo and Santa Clara (1997). The model is rooted in the contributions of Merton (1974, 1977) and Black and Cox (1976).

The presentation that follows is derived from a pure pricing perspective where all driving parameters are by now considered to be exogenously specified. This hypothesis can be relaxed when considering optimal initial debt contracting in the same framework[1].

In this model, the standard assumptions presented in the context of Merton (1974) are completed as follows[2]:

Assumption 1 *All assets can be traded continuously without any restriction in a perfectly liquid and frictionless financial market.*

This summarizes briefly assumptions 1 and 2 previously presented.

Assumption 2 *The firm is founded by the equityholders and has not yet defaulted when the new debt is contracted.*

It must be noted that the will of creating the firm comes from equityholders who therefore must have some incentive function to ensure the initial existence of the firm itself. Since the event of default is analogous to an absorbing state in a Markov chain, the debt contracting supposes that the firm is not already at default.

In addition, the following assumptions are newly introduced:

Assumption 3 *The asset value of the firm, denoted by V, follows the lognormal diffusion process*

$$\frac{dV_t}{V_t} = (\mu - \delta)\,dt + \sigma_v\,dZ_t^v \tag{14.1}$$

with μ standing for the constant instantaneous expected return or drift on the value of the assets' gross of δ, the overall continuous payout rate, and σ_v representing the constant instantaneous volatility of the returns of assets. The cash payout at any time is δV_t; dZ_t is a standard Wiener process.

---

[1] Although Pirotte (1999b) presents this extension, it remains a model with no strategic behavior since these parameters will be deduced from the model assuming that the participants fix them once at the beginning of the contract without modifying them during the life of the contract, i.e. as if investors were "myopic" in their behavior.
[2] From Pirotte (1999b).

We consider only cash outflows that are proportional to the firm asset value.

Under the risk-neutral probability measure, with stochastic interest rates, expression (14.1) becomes

$$\frac{dV_t}{V_t} = (r_t - \delta)dt + \sigma_v dZ_t^v, \qquad (14.2)$$

where r_t is the time-varying instantaneous interest rate, the dynamics of which are described below in assumption 8.

Assumption 4 *Equityholders perceive a continuous dividend rate, as long as the firm does not default, equivalent to the entire cash payout δ.*

Dividends are then implicitly financed by asset sales. This ensures that the limited liability rule for shareholders is verified at any level of the threshold value B_t defined in assumption 6 below.

Assumption 5 *The firm's capital structure consists of equity and a single noncallable zero-coupon bond of finite maturity, both of them being continuously traded.*

Assumption 6 *There exists a threshold level or barrier B_t such that default is triggered, should it be reached by the asset value of the firm at any time t between the origin of the contract and the maturity T.*

In the present setting, the put option held by shareholders is a "stopping barrier" put option, where the effective maturity is the time that the underlying process takes to reach the triggering point, B_t, or at least the maturity T of the contract itself, should it be earlier than the expected time to default.

For now, the barrier level B_t is considered to be defined exogenously as

$$B_t = H P_t(T) = \phi F P_t(T), \qquad (14.3)$$

i.e. some constant fraction ($0 \leqslant \phi \leqslant 1$) of the face value of debt F times a riskfree discount bond $P_t(T)$ maturing at T, whose dynamics are presented in assumption 8 below (see equation (14.8)); B_t is therefore stochastic. This form is borrowed from that used by Briys and de Varenne (1997). In this setting, B_t can be viewed as the safety covenant introduced by Black and Cox (1976), but now extended to a stochastic interest rate environment. This specification could have the drawback, as mentioned earlier in Chapter 5, to make the barrier to be strongly dependent on the time to maturity of the bond which is being priced. On the other hand, it allows us to view the passage time as purely related to a problem of asset insolvency and to be mathematically rigorous when computing the density of the passage time as a one-dimensional problem. More precisely, the default passage time is in this kind of framework a function of the distance between V_t and B_t, i.e. their ratio. Thanks to the dynamics of B_t, the drift in expression (14.2) will be offset with the drift of the process presented in equation (14.8)[3]. Without this particularity, the distance would be also directly influenced by the

---

[3]Indeed, from Itô's lemma, the drift of the log of this solvency ratio can be shown no longer to depend on the spot interest rate.

Notice that the volatility parameter of the solvency ratio will still be a function of the individual volatilities of V_t and B_t, plus a correlation effect due to the co-behavior of the processes presented in equations (14.2) and (14.8).

term structure of interest rates and the expected passage time would remain a bidimensional problem, i.e. a point on a surface of possible passage times. Avoiding this problem is helpful since there is presently no mathematical solution to the expected passage time in a bidimensional framework. And economically, assuming that the firm has a sole debt issue, the form of B_t is coherent with the definition of insolvency, that is when the assets of the firm are not sufficient to cover the current value of the liabilities. If the drift r_t was not eliminated, the passage time could not be thought of as a pure insolvency problem unless we assume that the liabilities have a payout rate of r_t.

Hence, the time of default, τ_b, is an event simply defined as

$$\tau_b = \inf\{u \geqslant t, V_u \leqslant B_u\} \tag{14.4}$$

with the following property:

$$P(\tau_b \leqslant T) > 0 \quad \text{a.s.,} \quad \tau_b > t_0,$$

where t_0 is the starting date of the contract. τ_b is therefore a stopping time. Notice that the maturity is a stopping time for alternative reasons: either default is triggered precisely at maturity or the contract matures normally. The only admissible exercise times are τ_b and T. Therefore, the resulting ending date of the contract would be bounded by T such that

$$\tau = \min[\tau_b, T]. \tag{14.5}$$

Assumption 7 *The firm can be liquidated only at a cost (similarly to the study of Fan and Sundaresan, 1997) and the rule of strict priority at default applies. If default happens at maturity (the Mertonian case) or earlier, an exogenous cost of $(1 - \varphi)$ is taken away by outsiders from the value of assets at that time.*

As in Merton's model, the recovery value at the moment of default conditional on its occurrence (*Rec*) is of the form

$$Rec = \begin{cases} \varphi V_T, & \text{at } T \\ \varphi V_{\tau_b} = \varphi B_{\tau_b}, & \text{at } \tau_b \end{cases}, \tag{14.6}$$

where φ is an exogenously specified recovery rate on the assets value available at the moment of default, should it be prior or at T. Given *Rec*, the expected discounted recovery value will not be a constant but will keep varying as a function of the time to maturity, the value of the firm's assets and the evolution of the term structure of interest rates (see assumption 8). This finding is similar to that presented in Merton's setting in expression (3.18).

For the internal consistency of the model (because of its continuous-time nature), the liquidation cost has to take the same value should the default happen at maturity or earlier. Compare the following two cases: a firm default at maturity with $F > V_T = (B_T + \epsilon)$, where ϵ is an infinitesimal difference, and a firm that defaults earlier at time $T - \epsilon$, with $V_{T-\epsilon} = B_{T-\epsilon}$. The two cases are so close to each other that it is not economically sustainable to specify a different liquidation factor in each case[4].

---

[4]Moreover, the default time is far from being a precise time in practice. Would a difference exist in the φs the participants would try to force a type of liquidation rather than the other.

Variation. A brief note can be made here on the value of φ since practitioners find it difficult to give a value to what occurs after default. An alternative way to model this loss incurred by bondholders would be to take into account the fact that even though the default occurs at τ_b, the final liquidation will take place later. This elapsed time is therefore an open option to shareholders to steal value from the firm. Thus, the value finally recovered would be a subsequent evolution of the value from default, i.e. from B_{τ_b}. An assumption implicit in any continuous model like the present one is that we have continuous monitoring such that we know exactly when the threshold value has been reached, and only the value B_{τ_b} is relevant since τ_b is perfectly revealed. Then, whatever is the choice of the distribution for the evolution after τ_b, we can work directly through the expectation of this additional loss (φ) since the distribution is, in any case, independent of past values of V[5]. Therefore, this additional loss, called φ here, could be related to an implicit expectation about the time from default to final liquidation.

Assumption 8 *There exists a riskfree asset $P_0(T)$ whose value depends on a term structure of interest rates $R_t(T)$ governed by a two-factor model following a bidimensional Ornstein–Uhlenbeck process. The two underlying processes are those of the long-term rate and the spread between the short-term and the long-term rate with the following specifications*

$$ds = a_s(b_s - s)\,dt + \sigma_s\,dZ_t^s \tag{14.7}$$

$$dl = a_l(b_l - l)\,dt + \sigma_l\,dZ_t^l$$

where $r = s + l$, with s standing for the interest rate spread and l for the long-term interest rate. Here b_s and b_l are the two long-run averages to which s and l revert with adjustment speeds a_s and a_l respectively; σ_s and σ_l are the two respective diffusion parameters. The asset value of the firm is assumed to be correlated to the structure of spot interest rates which can be decomposed into these two risk factors. Moreover, $dZ_t^s.dZ_t^l = \rho_{sl}$.

The dynamics under the risk-neutral probability of this bond are given by

$$\frac{dP_t(T)}{P_t(T)} = r_t\,dt + \sigma_{P_t(T)}dZ_t^p, \tag{14.8}$$

where Z_t^p is a linear combination of Z_t^s and Z_t^l, $dZ_t^p.dZ_t^v = \rho_{vp}\sigma_v\sigma_{P_t(T)}$, and

$$\sigma_{P_t(T)} = \sqrt{\eta_s^2 + \eta_l^2 + 2\rho_{sl}\eta_s\eta_l}$$

$$\eta_s = \sigma_s \frac{1}{P_t(T)}\frac{\partial P_t(T)}{\partial s}$$

$$\eta_l = \sigma_l \frac{1}{P_t(T)}\frac{\partial P_t(T)}{\partial l}.$$

Proof. Under the risk-neutral probability measure, we have that:

---

[5]That means that even if the same process of dV/V is used for this small period of time, because of the property of independent increments, knowing B and τ_b is sufficient.

$$\frac{dP_t(T)}{P_t(T)} = r_t dt + \frac{\partial P_t(T)}{\partial s}\frac{1}{P_t(T)}\sigma_s dZ_t^s + \frac{\partial P_t(T)}{\partial l}\frac{1}{P_t(T)}\sigma_l dZ_t^l \qquad (14.9)$$

$$= r_t dt + (\eta_s dZ_t^s + \eta_l dZ_t^l).$$

Taking into account the correlation ρ_{sl}, we can decompose Z_t^l into two orthogonal Brownians as

$$Z_t^l = \rho_{sl} Z_t^s + \sqrt{1 - \rho_{sl}^2} Z_t^0,$$

where Z_t^0 is a Brownian motion uncorrelated with Z_t^s. Now,

$$(\eta_s dZ_t^s + \eta_l dZ_t^l) = \eta_s dZ_t^s + \eta_l\left(\rho_{sl} dZ_t^s + \sqrt{1 - \rho_{sl}^2} dZ_t^0\right)$$

$$= (\eta_s + \rho_{sl}\eta_l) dZ_t^s + \sqrt{1 - \rho_{sl}^2}\,\eta_l Z_t^0$$

Therefore

$$\mathrm{Var}\left(\frac{dP_t(T)}{P_t(T)}\right) = (\eta_s + \rho_{sl}\eta_l)^2 + \left(\sqrt{1 - \rho_{sl}^2}\,\eta_l\right)^2$$

$$= \eta_s^2 + \eta_l^2 + 2\rho_{sl}\eta_s\eta_l,$$

which allows us to write expression (14.8).   ∎

The integration of interest rates in the current proposition is twofold. First, it is difficult to talk about credit-risk bond pricing, assuming constant interest rates. Second, the stochasticity of interest rates and the mean reversion property of the spread are indirectly linked to the integration of business cycle effects in the present framework, since the dynamics of recovery rates have been shown to be related to macroeconomic variables (see Chapter 12). The long-term rate, l, captures mostly the business cycle effect. Indeed, Alessandrini (1998) shows that positive changes in the level of the long-term rate are compatible with negative changes in credit spreads, as well as for the term spread as defined here. Here, a higher discounting rate would mean a lower barrier but also a lower discounted value to recover if the barrier is touched. So, it will have the desired impact on credit spreads through its effect on the probability of default, but not directly through the recovery rate. On the other hand, we know that, given the mean reverting behaviour of the processes for s and l, high values of s and l can lead to a reversion in their levels if well above their long-run average. Together with the higher volatility of the long rate in times of upheaval, a forthcoming recession could translate in the term structure with the desired effect on the expected recovery value.

The objective is thus to show the individual effect of the long rate and the interest rate spread on the credit spread, knowing that these effects will have a different impact depending on the location of the current levels with respect to their long-term average. It will be shown that this specification presents indeed a similar behavior to the evidence submitted in Chapter 12. The choice of two Ornstein–Uhlenbeck processes allows us to decompose the interest risk source into two components that have been shown to have a particular relationship with the business cycle of the economy, which in turn has been shown to be relevant in credit risk pricing.

A last motivation is that the choice of the two-factor model with two Ornstein–Uhlenbeck processes allows us to recover a variance of the riskfree zero-coupon bond that is deterministic, which is essential for the derivation proposed below.

In the forthcoming derivations, $P_0(T) = \exp(-R_0(T))$ is the price of a zero-coupon bond at time 0 for \$1 default-free being delivered at T.

Given the proposed assumptions, all the cash flows of the project are paid out in the form of dividends. In the eventuality of a default, given assumption 7, some bankruptcy costs are taken away from the collateral by outsiders, debtholders receive the remaining amount, and shareholders receive nothing[6]. The model thus satisfies the following *value preservation property* that enables us to treat the value of assets, V, as an exogenous variable:

$$V_t = E_t + D_t + L_t(V) - C_t(V), \tag{14.10}$$

where E_t is the value of equity, D_t is the debt value, $L_t(V)$ is the present expected value of bankruptcy costs and $C_t(V)$ is the present expected value of the dividend stream[7]. V_t remains unaffected by the leverage of the firm and the particular value attributed to φ. The value of the assets of the firm is thus differentiated from the total value of the firm, $v_t(V)$, which does depend on the leverage and bankruptcy parameters:

$$v_t(V) = V_t - L_t(V) + C_t(V). \tag{14.11}$$

14.1 FORMULATIONS

The value of the corporate bond at maturity (set of information $\mathcal{F}_T$), given the payoffs in the different states, can be expressed as

$$D_T(V, s, l, T) = F\mathbf{I}_{\{\tau_b > T, V_T > F\}} + \varphi V_T \mathbf{I}_{\{\tau_b > T, V_T < F\}} + \varphi\phi F\mathbf{I}_{\{\tau_b < T\}},$$
$$0 < \tau_b \leqslant T. \tag{14.12}$$

The payoff of the third term in the previous equation comes directly from the definition of the barrier (see expression (14.3) in assumption 6) together with the description of the payoff in the case of early default (see expression (14.6) in assumption 7). At τ_b, $B_{\tau_b} = H P_{\tau_b}(T) = \phi F P_{\tau_b}(T)$.

It is further assumed that the market is complete and, by the no-arbitrage principle, that all continuously traded securities can then be priced in terms of the short rate process and a risk-neutral — or equivalent martingale — probability measure Q (see Harrison and Kreps, 1979, and Harrison and Pliska, 1981). This implicitly supposes that the asset value is a traded asset which could be relaxed if V can be sustainably assumed to be fully observable (see Merton, 1994). Since debt and equity are traded

---

[6]Assumption 6 states that $B \leqslant F$, which rules out any possibility for the shareholders to recover some positive value at any default time.

[7]The framework proposed can be easily generalized to include the possibility of violations of the absolute priority rule at default simply by allowing part of the costs to go to shareholders as additional dividends. Outsiders would only receive then a fraction ω of the costs related to φ. This would mean that a part currently comprised in $L(V)$ would have to be withdrawn. Reverting equation (14.10) to isolate E_t would therefore imply that the fraction $(1 - \omega)$ would go straight to shareholders.

assets[8], and as far as liquidation costs and the dividend payout rate are common knowledge, V can be theoretically observed by a straight use of equation (14.10). Thus, we argue that, under Q and making the usual completeness assumption:

$$D_0(V, s, l, T) = E^Q\left[e^{-\int_{t_0}^{T} r_t dt}(F\mathbf{I}_{\{\tau_b>T, V_T>F\}} + \varphi V_T\mathbf{I}_{\{\tau_b>T, V_T<F\}} + \varphi\phi F\mathbf{I}_{\{\tau_b<T\}})\right]. \quad (14.13)$$

After some computations presented in Pirotte (1999b), the price at time 0 of this defaultable zero-coupon bond can be obtained as

$$D_0(V, s, l, T) = FP_0(T) - \text{default put} \qquad\qquad\qquad (14.14)$$

$$= FP_0(T) - FP_0(T)[N(-d_2) + (B_0/V_0)^{2\gamma-2}(N(l_2))]$$

$$+ \varphi V_0 e^{-\delta T}[N(-d_1) - N(-k_1) - (B_0/V_0)^{2\gamma}(N(h_1) - N(l_1))]$$

$$+ \varphi HP_0(T)[N(-k_2) + (B_0/V_0)^{2\gamma-2}N(h_2)]$$

with

$$B_0 = HP_0(T) = \phi FP_0(T),$$

$$\gamma = 1/2 - (\delta T)/T^*,$$

$$T^* = \Sigma(T)^2 = \int_0^T [\sigma_v^2 + \sigma_p^2(u, T) + 2\rho\sigma_p(u, T)\sigma_v]du,$$

$$d_1 = \frac{\ln\left(\dfrac{V_0 e^{-\delta T}}{FP_0(T)}\right)}{\sqrt{T^*}} + \frac{1}{2}\sqrt{T^*} = d_2 + \sqrt{T^*},$$

$$h_1 = \frac{\ln\left(\dfrac{B^2 e^{-\delta T}}{V_0 HP_0(T)}\right)}{\sqrt{T^*}} + \frac{1}{2}\sqrt{T^*} = h_2 + \sqrt{T^*},$$

$$k_1 = \frac{\ln\left(\dfrac{V_0 e^{-\delta T}}{HP_0(T)}\right)}{\sqrt{T^*}} + \frac{1}{2}\sqrt{T^*} = k_2 + \sqrt{T^*},$$

$$l_1 = \frac{\ln\left(\dfrac{B^2 e^{-\delta T}}{V_0 FP_0(T)}\right)}{\sqrt{T^*}} + \frac{1}{2}\sqrt{T^*} = l_2 + \sqrt{T^*}$$

and, given the developments presented in Sharp (1987), the value of the riskless bond has the following closed-form solution under the context defined in assumption 8:

---

[8] Although the debt market is not as liquid as is the stock market. That is one of the reasons of the estimation of the volatility of assets through the stock market volatility, analyzed in section 16.1.

$$P_t(T) = \exp[H(T-t) - sG_s(T-t) - lG_l(T-t)], \tag{14.15}$$

$$G_i(T-t) = \frac{1}{a_i}[1 - \exp(-a_i(T-t))],$$

$$H(T-t) = G_s(T-t)\left[N_s - \frac{1}{a_s}U_{sl}\right]$$

$$+ G_l(T-t)\left[N_l - \frac{1}{a_l}U_{ls}\right]$$

$$- (T-t)\left[N_s + N_l - \frac{1}{2}\frac{\rho_{sl}\sigma_s\sigma_l}{a_sa_l}\right]$$

$$- G_s(T-t)^2\frac{\sigma_s^2}{4a_s}$$

$$- G_l(T-t)^2\frac{\sigma_l^2}{4a_l}$$

$$- \frac{1}{2}U_{sl}G_s(T-t)G_l(T-t),$$

where

$$N_i = b_i - \frac{\lambda_i\sigma_i}{a_i} - \frac{\sigma_i^2}{2a_i^2},$$

$$U_{sl} = \frac{\rho_{sl}\sigma_s\sigma_l}{a_s + a_l},$$

λ_i being identified as the market price of risk, which, for the solution, is assumed not to depend on the maturities.

Then $\sigma_P(t, T)$ reduces to

$$\sigma_{P_t(T)} = \sqrt{\eta_s^2 + \eta_l^2 + 2\rho_{sl}\eta_s\eta_l},$$

$$\eta_s = \sigma_s G_s(T-t),$$

$$\eta_l = \sigma_l G_l(T-t).$$

Equation (14.14) is quite explicit and contains four terms. The first term is the value of a riskfree amount F delivered at T. The second term is the expectation of the loss of this amount whenever the barrier is reached or the process of $V(t)$ finishes under F at maturity. The third and the fourth terms then add the recovered amount in each scenario: φV_0 at maturity if the barrier is never crossed or φB_{T_b} at T_b if it is the case.

It could be interesting to regroup terms in order to be able to isolate the terms equivalent to Merton's approach from the remaining ones. Using the same terminology as Merton, we define the "quasi-leverage ratio" and the "quasi-distance-to-default" as

$$q^F = \frac{V_0 e^{-\delta T}}{FP_0(T)} \quad \text{and} \quad q^H = \frac{V_0 e^{-\delta T}}{HP_0(T)}. \tag{14.16}$$

Equation (14.14) can be then rewritten as

$$D_0(V, T) = FP_0(T).[1 - \text{expected cost of default (ECD\%)}] \tag{14.17}$$

$$= FP_0(T).\left[1 - (N(-d_2) - q^F N(-d_1)) + \left(\frac{q^F}{q^B} N(-k_2) - q^F N(-k_1)\right)\right.$$

$$- (1 - \varphi)\left[q^F(N(-d_1) - N(-k_1)) + \frac{q^F}{q^H} N(-k_2)\right] - (B_0/V_0)^{2\gamma-2} N(l_2)$$

$$\left. + \varphi q^F(-(B_0/V_0)^{2\gamma}(N(h_1) - N(l_1))) + \varphi \frac{q^F}{q^H}((B_0/V_0)^{2\gamma-2} N(h_2))\right],$$

where

- The first term is the value of a riskfree bond.
- The second term is a traditional Black and Scholes European put option. The lender may lose $F - V_0$ at maturity.
- The third term is a *European put* with a strike price equal to the barrier level. It gives the value of the covenant for the extreme scenario where the barrier is just touched at maturity only. It helps in mitigating the loss incurred with the previous put.
- The fourth term expresses the expected value of *bankruptcy costs* associated with a default at maturity. This completes the standard Merton's option.
- The last three terms are focused on the expected value of the default occurring prior to T. In that case: (a) the fifth term accounts for the possibility of losing F between t_0 and T; (b) and therefore not getting φV at T (seventh term); (c) in exchange for a value of $\varphi HP_{\tau_b}(T)$ at τ_b (eighth term).

The sum of these three last components gives the value of a *special hitting put* allowed to shareholders.

Moreover, following KMV's terminology, we have here two distances to default (under the risk-neutral probability measure), expressed in units of asset return standard deviation at T: d_2 for the propensity to default at T, k_2 for the propensity to default between 0 and T.

14.2 REFERENCES

Alessandrini, F., 1998, "Credit Risk, Interest Rate Risk and the Business Cycle", Master's Thesis, Master of Science in Economics, HEC, Lausanne University, n. 98, November, 62 pp.

Black, F. and J. C. Cox, 1976, "Valuing Corporate Securities: Some Effects of Bond Indenture Provisions", *Journal of Finance*, **31**, 351–67.

Brennan, M. and E. Schwartz, 1980, "Analyzing Convertible Bonds", *Journal of Financial and Quantitative Analysis*, **15**, 907–29.

Briys, Eric and François de Varenne, 1997, "Valuing Risky Fixed Rate Debt: An Extension", *Journal of Financial and Quantitative Analysis*, **32** (2), June, 239–49.

Fan, Hua and Suresh Sundaresan, 1997, "Debt Valuation, Strategic Debt Service and Optimal Dividend Policy", *Working Paper*, Graduate School of Business, Columbia University, March, 47 pp.

Geman, H. and M. Yo, 1993, "Bessel Processes, Asian Options and Perpetuities", *Mathematical Finance*, **4** (3).

Geman, H. and M. Yo, 1996, "Pricing and Hedging Double-Barrier Options: A Probabilistic Approach", *Mathematical Finance*, **6** (4).

Geman, H., N. El Karoui and J. C. Rochet, 1995, "Changes of Numeraire, Changes of Probability Measure and Pricing of Options", *Journal of Applied Probability*, **32**, 443–58.

Harrison, M. and D. Kreps, 1979, "Martingales and Arbitrage in Multiperiod Security Markets", *Journal of Economic Theory*, **20**, 381–408.

Harrison, M. and S. Pliska, 1981, "Martingales and Stochastic Integrals in the Theory of Continuous Trading", *Stochastic Processes and Their Applications*, **11**, 215–60.

Longstaff, Francis and Eduardo Schwartz, 1995b, "A Simple Approach to Valuing Risky Fixed and Floating Rate Debt", *Journal of Finance*, **50** (3), July, 789–819.

Merton, Robert C., 1974, "On the Pricing of Corporate Debt: The Risk Structure of Interest Rates", *The Journal of Finance*, **29**, May, 449–70.

Merton, Robert C., 1977, "On the Pricing of Contingent Claims and the Modigliani–Miller Theorem", *Journal of Financial Economics*, **5**, 241–9.

Merton, Robert C., 1994, "Pricing and Hedging Contingent-Claim Securities When the Underlying Security is Not Continuously Traded or Observable", *Class Teaching Notes*.

Pirotte, H., 1999b, "A Structural Model of the Term Structure of Credit Spreads with Stochastic Recovery and Contractual Design", *Working Paper*, Institute of Banking and Finance, Ecole des HEC, University of Lausanne, December, 85 pp.

Saá-Requejo, Jesús and Pedro Santa Clara, 1997, "Bond Pricing with Default Risk", *Working Paper*, John E. Anderson Graduate School of Management, UCLA, Los Angeles, 23 pp.

Schaefer, Stephen and Eduardo Schwartz, 1984, "A Two-Factor Model of the Term Structure: An Approximate Analytical Solution", *Journal of Financial and Quantitative Analysis*, **19** (4), December, 413–24.

Sharp, Keith, 1987, "Bond and Bond Option Prices Dependent on n Correlated Stochastic Processes", *Working Paper in Actuarial Science*, Department of Statistics and Actuarial Science, University of Waterloo, Ontario, 11 pp.

15
Comparative Statics

Here are some comparative statics extracted from Pirotte (1999b) for some sets of parameters that will allow a straight comparison with the Mertonian case and other more advanced modelizations, again from a pure mathematical pricing perspective. This will also tell us if the model verifies some of the empirically observed regularities.

From expression (14.17), we can see that the model does not provide only a formula but also a set of components that can provide a picture of the default character of a counterpart or a contract. It also helps in identifying credit risk through the sensitivity of a particular firm or contract to each of the sources. This expression allows us, for example, to isolate completely the effect of the barrier level and therefore the risk in its estimation.

Figures 15.1–15.4 present a complete picture of this composite behavior for different values of the volatility of assets and the barrier level and for two main leverage scenarios (Figures 15.3 and 15.4 versus Figures 15.1 and 15.2). We mainly observe that the reduction in leverage strongly reduces the differential impact of the other parameters. The other main deductions are as follows:

- The European Black and Scholes put is the only component to be insensitive to the barrier level.
- The risky debt value is always equal to or lower than the riskfree debt.
- It is not obvious that this model will always provide values lower than the standard Merton case and vice versa.

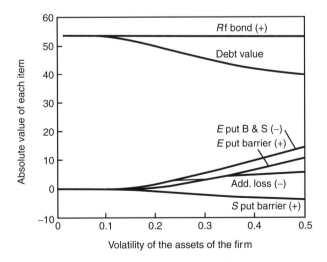

Figure 15.1 $V = 100$, $F = 70$, $H = 60$, $R = 5.43\%$, $\sqrt{T^*}$ between 1% and 50%, $\delta = 2\%$, $\varphi = 0.75$, $T = 5$. Reproduced with authorization from Pirotte (1999b)

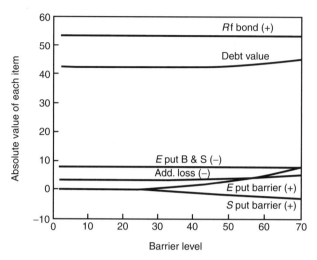

Figure 15.2 $V = 100$, $F = 70$, H between 2 and 70, $R = 5.43\%$, $\sqrt{T^*} = 35\%$, $\delta = 2\%$, $\varphi = 0.75$, $T = 5$. Reproduced with authorization from Pirotte (1999b)

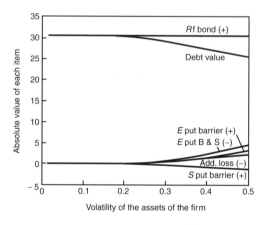

Figure 15.3 $V = 100$, $F = 40$, $H = 34$, $R = 5.43\%$, $\sqrt{T^*}$ between 1% and 50%, $\delta = 2\%$, $\varphi = 0.75$, $T = 5$. Reproduced with authorization from Pirotte (1999b)

- The *special hitting put* component is the only one to be monotone, decreasing with the barrier level as well as with the volatility of assets.
- The European put with a strike equal to the barrier, and the component accounting for the bankruptcy costs are of opposite signs and always cross each other.

Therefore, these components provide an explanation of much of the compensating behavior of the variables inherent to the specification of the overall expected cost of default (*ECD*). (Chapter 16 is devoted to the identification of the parameters and the ways to infer them.)

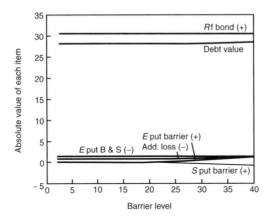

Figure 15.4 $V = 100$, $F = 40$, H between 2 and 40, $R = 5.43\%$, $\sqrt{T^*} = 35\%$, $\delta = 2\%$, $\varphi = 0.75$, $T = 5$. Reproduced with authorization from Pirotte (1999b)

15.1 THE CORPORATE YIELD AND THE CORPORATE CREDIT SPREAD

The corporate credit spread, $cs(T)$, is the difference between the corresponding corporate yield, $y_0(T)$, and the riskfree yield for the same maturity computed with the two-factor model of the term structure of interest rates, namely $R_0(T)$:

$$y_0(T) - R_0(T) = -\frac{1}{T} \ln \left[\frac{D_0(V, s, l, T)}{F P_0(T)} \right]$$

and, using the related equations (14.14) and (14.16), we simply obtain the following formulation:

$$
\begin{aligned}
cs(T) = -\frac{1}{T} \ln \Big[& N(d_2) + (B_0/V_0)^{2\gamma-2} N(l_2) + \varphi q^F [N(-d_1) - N(-k_1)] \\
& - (B_0/V_0)^{2\gamma}(N(h_1) - N(l_1))] + \phi \frac{q^F}{q^H} [N(-k_2)] \\
& + (B_0/V_0)^{2\gamma-2} N(h_2)] \Big],
\end{aligned}
$$

(15.1)

where the effect of the leverage is again well represented through the ratios presented in expression (14.16). With $\delta = 0$ and $\varphi = 1$, in order to have a direct comparison with the Black and Scholes formula, Figures 15.5 and 15.6 show that, depending on the values of the parameters and changing only the level of the barrier or the variability of the assets, it is possible to obtain credit spreads that are higher or lower than Merton's spread, but always lower for high levels of the barrier or the volatility. Combining previous figures with Figure 15.5 gives us an important insight into the modeling. The level of the barrier has two major impacts that compensate each other. First, the higher the barrier,

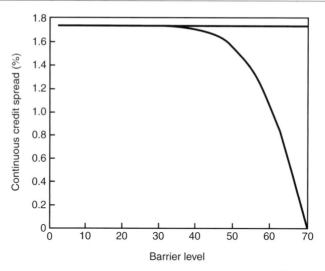

Figure 15.5 $V = 100$, $F = 70$, H between 2 and 70, $R = 5.43\%$, $\sqrt{T^*} = 30\%$, $\delta = 0\%$, $\varphi = 1$, $T = 5$. The straight line is Merton's credit spread. Reproduced with authorization from Pirotte (1999b)

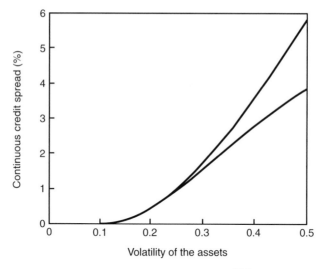

Figure 15.6 $V = 100$, $F = 70$, $H = 70\%$ of F, $R = 5.43\%$, $\sqrt{T^*}$ between 1% and 50%, $\delta = 0\%$, $\varphi = 1$, $T = 5$. The monotone increasing curve is Merton's credit spread. Reproduced with authorization from Pirotte (1999b)

the higher will be the probability of default, i.e. the earlier will be the expected first hitting time of the barrier by the process $V(t)$. Second, the higher the barrier, the higher is the level of remaining assets and the higher will be the recovery. The case of Merton can be nested in this model setting the barrier to 0, which is equivalent to assuming that there is a null chance of defaulting before T and recovering then a null amount since default in Merton is a binary event at T. Figure 15.5 also tells us that, depending on the values of the other parameters, this compensation is not monotone decreasing. There

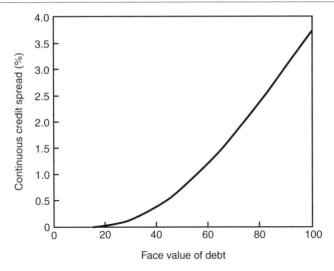

Figure 15.7 $V = 100$, F between 2 and 100, $H = 30\%$ of F, $R = 5.43\%$, $\sqrt{T^*} = 30\%$, $\delta = 0\%$, $\varphi = 1$, $T = 5$. Merton's credit spread coincides with Pirotte's values. Reproduced with authorization from Pirotte (1999b)

can be an area which actually gives higher spread values than the standard case. It is a local behavior where neither the probability is sufficiently low, nor the barrier is sufficiently high. It corresponds to the worst case for the creditors.

Figure 15.6 shows that the credit spread increases more slowly for high levels of volatility and does not explode as in the Merton approach.

Should the barrier be endogenously determined, it would depend on leverage ($0 \leqslant B \leqslant F$; see also Leland, 1994). It would be interesting then to see the impact of the leverage (F/V) for constant relative levels of the barrier. Figures 15.7 and 15.8 present this behavior when H is 30% and 90% of the face value respectively[1]. The implicit *protective function* of the default trigger is distinctly observable here.

The behavior shown in Figure 15.5 is particularly dependent on the value taken by φ as it is presented in Figures 15.9 and 15.10. Indeed, there seems to be some trade-off when φ remains high, but it disappears completely when φ becomes too small. This is a very important insight for the discussion on endogenous design.

15.2 THE AGGREGATED PROBABILITY OF DEFAULT, THE OVERALL RECOVERY AND THE EXPECTED COST OF DEFAULT

Credit risk is one of the risk domains where the term "loss aversion" would be more convenient than "risk aversion". From Chapter 3, we know that the expected cost of default (*ECD*) is essentially equivalent to the default probability (*DP*) times the expected discounted loss given default (*ELGD*). Rearranging the expected cost of

---

[1]Extreme values are chosen for the purpose of clarity in the visualization. A face value of 70 is equivalent to a *quasi-debt leverage ratio* of 53.36% in Merton's terminology which corresponds to q_F following the current notation.

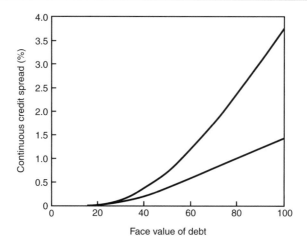

Figure 15.8 $V = 100$, F between 2 and 100, $H = 90\%$ of F, $R = 5.43\%$, $\sqrt{T^*} = 30\%$, $\delta = 0\%$, $\varphi = 1$, $T = 5$. The highest curve is Merton's credit spread. Reproduced with authorization from Pirotte (1999b)

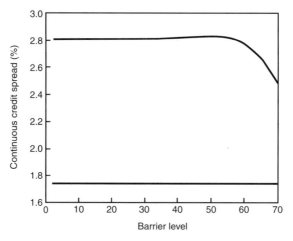

Figure 15.9 $V = 100$, $F = 70$, H between 2 and 70, $R = 5.43\%$, $\sqrt{T^*} = 30\%$, $\delta = 0\%$, $\varphi = 0.75$, $T = 5$. The straight line is Merton's credit spread. Reproduced with authorization from Pirotte (1999b)

default, presented in equation (14.14), which is simply the value of the *default put* option, we obtain:

$$ECD = [N(-d_2) + (B_0/V_0)^{2\gamma-2}N(l_2)]\left[FP_0(T)\right.$$

$$- \varphi V_0 e^{-\delta T} \frac{N(-d_1) - N(-k_1) - (B_0/V_0)^{2\gamma}(N(h_1) - N(l_1))}{N(-d_2) + (B_0/V_0)^{2\gamma-2}N(l_2)}$$

$$\left. - \varphi H P_0(T) \frac{N(-k_2) + (B_0/V_0)^{2\gamma-2}N(h_2)}{N(-d_2) + (B_0/V_0)^{2\gamma-2}N(l_2)}\right], \tag{15.2}$$

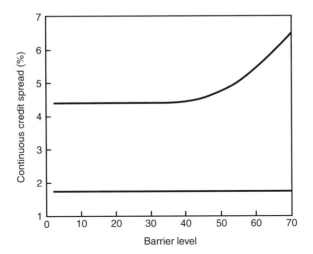

Figure 15.10 $V = 100$, $F = 70$, H between 2 and 70, $R = 5.43\%$, $\sqrt{T^*} = 30\%$, $\delta = 0\%$, $\varphi = 0.4$, $T = 5$. The straight line is Merton's credit spread. Reproduced with authorization from Pirotte (1999b)

where the first parenthesis is the overall probability of default while the second and third terms in the second parenthesis are expected discounted recovery values.

Therefore,

$$\frac{N(-d_1) - N(-k_1) - (B_0/V_0)^{2\gamma}(N(h_1) - N(l_1))}{N(-d_2) + (B_0/V_0)^{2\gamma-2}N(l_2)}$$

and

$$\frac{N(-k_2) + (B_0/V_0)^{2\gamma-2}N(h_2)}{N(-d_2) + (B_0/V_0)^{2\gamma-2}N(l_2)}$$

are two particular rates that, once multiplied by $\varphi V_0 e^{-\delta T}$ and $\varphi H P_0(T)$ respectively, correspond to the overall amount that can be expected to be recovered from the event of default[2].

If we compare the Merton approach to the present model on the same figure (see Figure 15.11) for an equivalent set of interest rate values (for s and l), φ (suppose a Merton framework with some extra liquidation cost), and firm asset value parameters (except that the variability of interest rates and the barrier do not exist in Merton's framework), we obtain analogous results to those of Figures 15.5 and 15.6 with the credit spread. Figures 15.13 and 15.14 show that we can emphasize the sensitivities to the barrier level through a change in the parameter φ. In particular, we can see on Figure 15.14 that the effect of the variation in the barrier level can be totally inverted

---

[2]Dividing them by $FP_0(T)$, we obtain two individual recovery rates such that their sum would produce the *aggregated expected discounted recovery rate* (*AEDR*),

$$ECD = FP_0(T).[DP(1 - AEDR)]$$

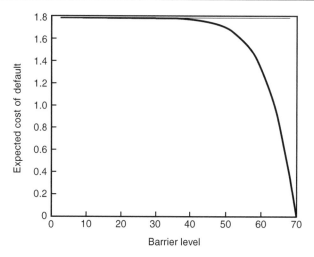

Figure 15.11 $V = 100$, $F = 70$, H between 2 and 70, $R = 5.43\%$, $\sqrt{T^*} = 20\%$, $\delta = 2\%$, $\varphi = 1$, $T = 5$. Reproduced with authorization from Pirotte (1999b)

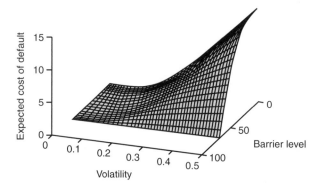

Figure 15.12 $V = 100$, $F = 70$, H between 2 and 70, $R = 5.43\%$, $\sqrt{T^*}$ between 1% and 50%, $\delta = 2\%$, $\varphi = 1$, $T = 5$. Reproduced with authorization from Pirotte (1999b)

with a change in the additional discount variable. At low levels of the bankruptcy cost, i.e. φ near 1, the expected cost of default decreases with the value of the barrier, while this is nearly a minimum for a lower level of φ. Additional considerations can straightforwardly be obtained when assigning a different value to φ.

Based on equation (15.2), Figures 15.15 and 15.16 show the dynamics of the components of the aggregated expected discounted recovery versus the probability of default against the change of either the barrier level or the variability of the assets of the firm. It is interesting to note that the two recovery rates and the probability of default almost cross each other[3] at some level of the barrier, namely here 40.81. This level almost coincides with the highest value of the expected cost of default. We can also see that the stabilizing behavior of the credit spread as the volatility increases shown in Figure 15.6 is explained mainly by the stabilization of the component recovery rates.

---

[3] Not with good precision for the probability (34.20% versus 34.35% for the two recovery rates).

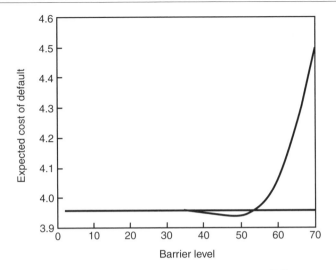

Figure 15.13 $V = 100$, $F = 70$, H between 2 and 70, $R = 5.43\%$, $\sqrt{T^*} = 30\%$, $\delta = 2\%$, $\varphi = 0.7$, $T = 5$. Reproduced with authorization from Pirotte (1999b)

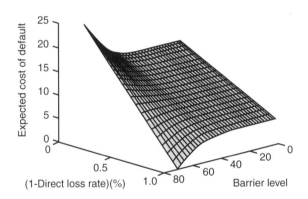

Figure 15.14 $V = 100$, $F = 70$, H between 2 and 70, $R = 5.43\%$, $\sqrt{T^*} = 30\%$, $\delta = 2\%$, φ between 1% and 100%, $T = 5$. Reproduced with authorization from Pirotte (1999b)

As seen in equation (14.14), k_2 is a useful intermediate value, since it represents the number of asset returns volatilities for a time horizon T that separates the current value of the process $V(t)$ from the threshold value. As an example of its importance, this is the key variable that KMV uses for the mapping of firms to expected default frequencies (*EDFs*) and then to a ratings' ranking system.

As could be expected, this distance is shorter, the higher the threshold value and the larger the volatility which is the unit measure (see Figures 15.17 and 15.18).

15.3   THE TERM STRUCTURE EFFECTS

Based on the two-factor model of the term structure of interest rates presented in assumption 8, and with the methodology of Sharp (1987), we know the theoretical value

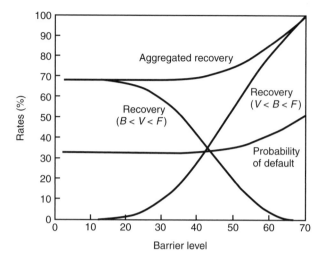

Figure 15.15 $V = 100$, $F = 70$, H between 2 and 70, $R = 5.43\%$, $\sqrt{T^*} = 30\%$, $\delta = 2\%$, $\varphi = 1$, $T = 5$. Reproduced with authorization from Pirotte (1999b)

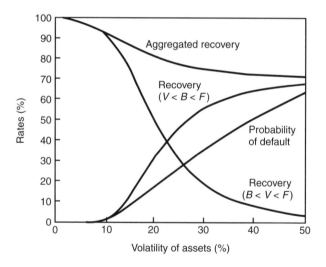

Figure 15.16 $V = 100$, $F = 70$, $H = 50$, $R = 5.43\%$, $\delta = 2\%$, $\varphi = 1$, $T = 5$. Reproduced with authorization from Pirotte (1999b)

of the credit riskfree zero-coupon bond (as a function of the time to maturity, the term spread s and the long-term rate l). This bond is valuable since it intervenes in the discounting factors of the payoffs in the pricing model and, more importantly, in the definition of the default threshold. First, without assuming any variability in the term structure of interest rates, we can already visualize the effect of a different $R_0(T)$ on the debt values of the model with respect to Merton's model. In this simple context, the threshold value has again a strong impact on the sensitivity to the interest rates compared to the standard contingent claims' case (see Figures 15.19 and 15.20). Figures

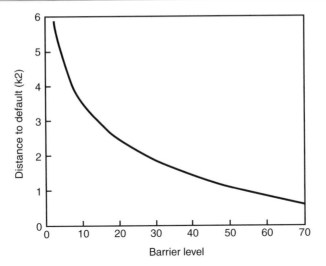

Figure 15.17 $V = 100$, $F = 70$, H between 2 and 70, $R = 5.43\%$, $\sqrt{T^*} = 30\%$, $\delta = 0\%$, $\varphi = 1$, $T = 5$. Reproduced with authorization from Pirotte (1999b)

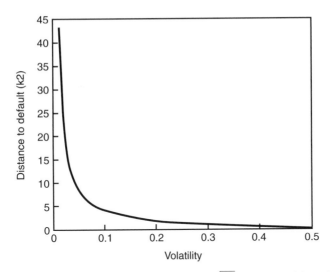

Figure 15.18 $V = 100$, $F = 70$, $H = 50$, $R = 5.43\%$, $\sqrt{T^*}$ between 1% and 50%, $\delta = 0\%$, $\varphi = 1$, $T = 5$. Reproduced with authorization from Pirotte (1999b)

15.19 and 15.20 prove that Merton's case is nested into the present one. The combined effect of the threshold value and the level of interest rates come from the definition of the recovery at an early default: $Rec_{T_b} = \varphi H P_0(T)$.

Rec_{T_b} is a function of R over the remaining time to T among other parameters. In fact, the classical barrier option, which has a null value if the barrier has been previously touched, and the barrier option which stops at the hitting time, are equivalent by a factor $P_{T_b}(T)$.

Focusing, therefore, on the definition of the threshold value which leads to the value recovered at default, it would be interesting to investigate the effect of a change in the

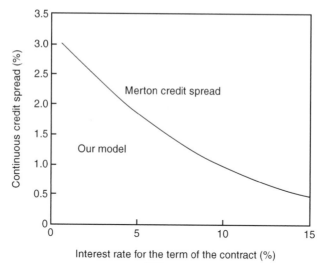

Figure 15.19 $V = 100$, $F = 70$, $H = 30$, $\sqrt{T^*} = 30\%$, $\delta = 0\%$, $\varphi = 1$, $T = 5$. Reproduced with authorization from Pirotte (1999b)

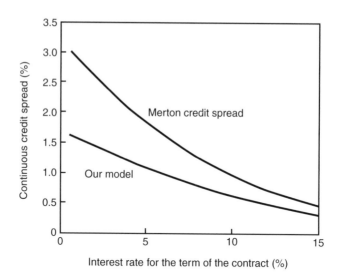

Figure 15.20 $V = 100$, $F = 70$, $H = 60$, $\sqrt{T^*} = 30\%$, $\delta = 0\%$, $\varphi = 1$, $T = 5$. Reproduced with authorization from Pirotte (1999b)

parameters of the term structure of interest rates since it is assumed to be the link to the business cycle dependence of the final credit spread. The next two figures (15.21 and 15.22) provide evidence of the impact of a change in the volatility of the spread (σ_s) and a change into the expected spread (b_s) for realistic parameters (a spread of -4% between the long rate and the short rate ($r \leqslant l$), a long-term rate volatility of $\frac{1}{2}\%$) and a spread risk premia of 0%. Should the structure become inverted ($r \geqslant l$) and correspond to a recession, the recovered value would plunge.

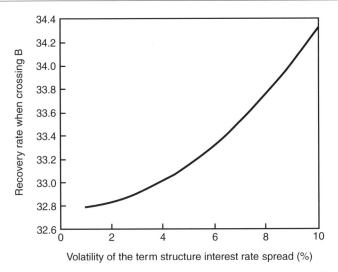

Figure 15.21 $\varphi = 0.8$, $H = 50$, $\lambda_1 = \lambda_s = 0$, $a_s = 0.5$, $a_l = 0.7$, $b_s = -0.02$, $b_l = 0.07$, σ_s between 0.01 and 0.1, $\sigma_l = 0.005$, $s = -0.04$, $l = 0.06$, $T = 5$, $\rho_{sl} = 0$. Reproduced with authorization from Pirotte (1999b)

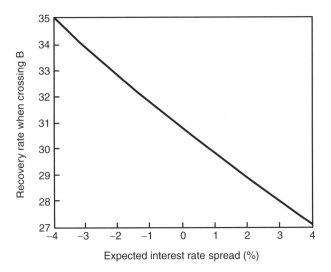

Figure 15.22 $\varphi = 0.8$, $H = 50$, $\lambda_1 = \lambda_s = 0$, $a_s = 0.5$, $a_l = 0.7$, b_s between -0.04 and 0.04, $b_l = 0.07$, $\sigma_s = 0.015$, $\sigma_l = 0.005$, $s = -0.04$, $l = 0.06$, $T = 5$, $\rho_{sl} = 0$. Reproduced with authorization from Pirotte (1999b)

These two figures are far from sufficient to describe the entire set of possibilities. The location of the spot spread above or below the long-term expected value has a strong impact on the resulting behavior of the term structure, reflecting back into credit spreads through the obtained continuous rate R. Therefore, as mentioned in assumption 8, the business cycle effect will indirectly propagate through the term structure, but the final effect on the credit spread is a priori difficult to predict without knowing the relative positions of s and l with respect to their long-run averages.

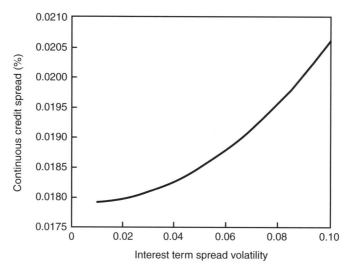

Figure 15.23 $\varphi = 0.75$, $H = 50$, $\lambda_1 = \lambda_s = 0$, $a_s = 0.5$, $a_l = 0.7$, $b_s = -0.02$, $b_l = 0.07$, σ_s between 0.01 and 0.1, $\sigma_l = 0.005$, $s = -0.04$, $l = 0.06$, $T = 5$, $\rho_{sl} = 0$. $\sigma_v = 0.2$, $\rho_{vp} = 0.15$. Reproduced with authorization from Pirotte (1999b)

Much more interesting now is to examine the impact of the same changes of the term structure on the credit spread. The variability in the interest rates will then also reflect in the value of T^* through $\sigma_p(t, T)$ and through the correlation between the value of the riskfree bond and the assets value of the firm.

The results with the same parameter values than in the previous figures when changing either the volatility of the spread or the correlation between the riskfree bond price and the asset value of the firm, are respectively presented in Figures 15.23 and 15.24.

15.4   CREDIT TERM STRUCTURE COMPARISONS WITH PREVIOUS LITERATURE

One of the most important issues in credit risk pricing is the computation of term structures that allow straight comparisons with standard term structures of interest rates available in financial markets. However, comparing different models cannot be a rigorous task since Merton, Briys and de Varenne, and Pirotte make divergent assumptions on the modeling of the term structure of riskfree rates: a constant short interest rate for Merton, an Ornstein–Uhlenbeck process for the short-term interest rate for Briys and de Varenne[4], and a two-factor term structure for Pirotte (1999b). We have chosen a sample of parameters that allows us to have structures beginning near to each other and then look at their behavior for longer term horizons. Figure 15.25 shows this behavior for a middle leverage level with a traditional hump-shaped structure, and Figure 15.26 completes the comparison for a high leverage case with a standard

---

[4]Briys and de Varenne (1997) in fact propose a more general form where the parameters are time dependent in the way of the extended Vasicek of Hull and White (1990). However, in their numerical example, they also use constant parameters.

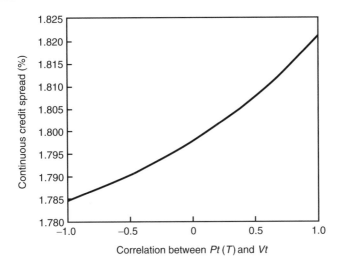

Figure 15.24 $\varphi = 0.75$, $H = 50$, $\lambda_1 = \lambda_s = 0$, $a_s = 0.5$, $a_l = 0.7$, $b_s = -0.02$, $b_l = 0.07$, $\sigma_s = 0.015$, $\sigma_l = 0.005$, $s = -0.04$, $l = 0.06$, $T = 5$, $\rho_{sl} = 0$. $\sigma_v = 0.2$, ρ_{vp} between -1 and 1. Reproduced with authorization from Pirotte (1999b)

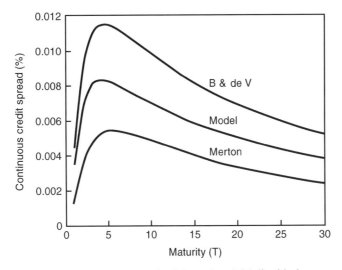

Figure 15.25 $V = 100$, $F = 60$, $H = 40$, r (for Merton) $= 0.06$, liquidation costs of 0.2, $\delta = 0.02$, $\sigma_v = 25\%$. The two-factor interest rate model parameters are: $a_s = 0.5$, $a_l = 0.2$, $b_s = 0.015$, $b_l = 0.055$, $\sigma_s = 0.02$, $\sigma_l = 0.005$, $l = 0.08$, $s = 0.02$, $\rho_{sl} = 0.4$. For B and de V, Vasicek's parameters are: $a = 0.3$, $b = 0.06$, $\sigma_r = 0.02$, and $\rho_{vp} = 0.25$ and $\alpha = B/F$. Reproduced with authorization from Pirotte (1999b)

inverted shape. Interest rate parameters are such that the constant interest rate used in Merton is 6%, coinciding with both the sum of s and l of the present two-factor model and with r following the Vasicek process assumed in the approach of Briys and de Varenne. Also, both adjustment speeds are equal. The difference comes from the two-factor model with a long-run average term spread ($r - l$) of 1.5%. With this inverted

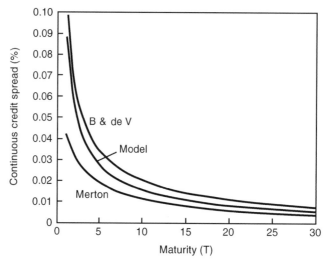

Figure 15.26 $V = 100$, $F = 90$, $B = 40$, r (for Merton) $= 0.06$, liquidation costs of 0.1, $\delta = 0.8$, $\sigma_v = 25\%$. The two-factor interest rate model parameters are: $a_s = 0.5$, $a_l = 0.2$, $b_s = 0.015$, $b_l = 0.055$, $\sigma_s = 0.02$, $\sigma_l = 0.005$, $l = 0.08$, $s = 0.02$, $\rho_{sl} = 0.4$. For B and de V, Vasicek's parameters are: $a = 0.3$, $b = 0.06$, $\sigma_r = 0.02$, and $\rho = 0.25$ and $\alpha = B/F$. Reproduced with authorization from Pirotte (1999b)

spot term structure, we obtain significant credit spreads that are comprised between those of the two other models. Again, these figures should be taken as an example of the behaviors of the credit spread term structure implied by the models rather than as a consistent comparison of them.

It can also be noticed in the Figure 15.25 that both the Briys and de Varenne (1997) and the Pirotte (1999b) credit term structures converge to that of Merton in the long term. This is due to the particular choice of interest rate structure parameters, and to the particular definition of the barrier level which depends on a discount bond which slope is softer for longer maturities (see Chapter 11, section 11.1). We see that the Pirotte (1999b) model produces credit spreads that seems to converge to some long-term value when the maturity increases.

Besides these results, other sets of parameters have been tested, and depending on the location of the spot term interest spread with respect to the long-term trend and if the latter is negative (inverted term structure) or positive, we can obtain shapes that can be much higher than the other two referenced models or even obtain a shape for a middle leverage level that is slowly increasing up to a convergence level instead of being hump-shaped. The latter occurs, for example, where there is a current upward-sloping term structure of interest rates, while some risk to become inverted is present, and therefore it corresponds to a recession context. Very high shapes are also obtained when δ is raised at higher levels[5].

---

[5]This is mainly due to the drift of the barrier that offsets the positive part of the drift of V_t.

15.5 REFERENCES

Briys, Eric and François de Varenne, 1997, "Valuing Risky Fixed Rate Debt: An Extension", *Journal of Financial and Quantitative Analysis*, **32** (2), June, 239–49.

Crouhy, Michel, Dan Galai and Robert Mark, 2000, "A Comparative Analysis of Current Credit Risk Models", *Journal of Banking and Finance*, **24** (1–2), 59–117.

Hull, John and A. White, 1990, "Pricing Interest Rate Derivative Securities", *Review of Financial Studies*, 573–92.

Leland, Hayne E., 1994, "Corporate Debt Value, Bond Covenants and Optimal Capital Structure", *Journal of Finance*, **49** (4), September, 1213–52.

Merton, Robert C., 1994, "Pricing and Hedging Contingent-Claim Securities When the Underlying Security is Not Continuously Traded or Observable", *Class Teaching Notes*.

Pirotte, H., 1999b, "A Structural Model of the Term Structure of Credit Spreads with Stochastic Recovery and Contractual Design", *Working Paper*, Institute of Banking and Finance, Ecole des HEC, University of Lausanne, December, 85 pp.

Ronn, Ehud and Avinash Verma, 1986, "Pricing Risk-Adjusted Deposit Insurance: An Option-Based Model", *The Journal of Finance*, **41** (4), September, 871–95.

Sharp, Keith, 1987, "Bond and Bond Option Prices Dependent on *n*-Correlated Stochastic Processes", *Working Paper in Actuarial Science*, Department of Statistics and Actuarial Science, University of Waterloo, Ontario, 11 pp.

16

The Practical Implementation and Final Issues

The added value of any model comes also from its implementability. In particular, the proposed model would be attractive for purposes of pricing and credit risk monitoring. Given the formulation proposed above (see equation (14.14)), the use of the model in a straight pricing perspective would require the identification of a certain amount of parameters. Table 16.1 presents them as well as the data source and the way to infer them from the data.

The next section is attached to the estimation of the major factor driving the source of risk in structural modeling, namely the volatility of the assets of the firm, here in the particular context of an exotic option pricing.

16.1 PRICING IN TERMS OF THE TRADED VARIABLE

16.1.1 Introduction

So far we have made the unrealistic assumption that the asset value of the firm is a continuously traded asset. Its intangibility renders difficult the implementation of structural models. Conversely, bonds and equity shares are traded[1]; a very liquid market exists *de facto* for the latter (see Leland, 1994, footnote 11). A common practice is thus to revert the pricing equation of debt in terms of the stock value and infer the asset returns' volatility from the volatility of equity returns (see Table 16.1 for the identification of the parameters to be estimated). In the Mertonian case, we obtain:

$$D_0 = \frac{1}{N(d_1)} \left[\underbrace{Fe^{-rT}N(d_2) - E_0 N(d_1) + E_0}_{\text{covered call}} \right], \qquad (16.1)$$

where the probabilities ($N(\cdot)$) are still a function of σ_v among others. E_0 is the value of equity or the stock capitalization at time 0. The debt value can thus be interpreted as the inverse of the *option delta* times the sale of a covered call.

As presented in the literature review, this exercise has the main advantage of including all the information stemming from a liquid and efficient marketplace giving rise to credit risk management models with fairly good anticipative properties (see Crouhy and Mark, 1998 for example). One of the first formulations toward this idea in the context of a simple structural approach was provided by Ronn and Verma (1986).

---

[1] Depending on firm specificities, V can be estimated through the market value of traded equity and traded bonds, but in some cases, this estimation is not better than a classical book value. Either the bonds are not traded or the debt is constituted by private loans and other untradable claims. For the current proposition to hold, it is not necessary that debt is a traded asset because the calculations will end up in the value of the debt as a function of uniquely traded equity.

Table 16.1 Data sources and inference of the parameters. Reproduced with authorization from Pirotte (1999b)

Parameter(s)	Source/Method
1 Interest rate structure	SURE fitting methods with discount bond or stripped bond data
2 V, F	Only the ratios V/F, B/V, V/B, B^2/VF must be computed. Levels are not required since all these variables are used through their ratios. Only the ratios V/F, V/B are needed
3 φ, ϕ	Expected value of direct and indirect bankruptcy costs. It seems that this could be also related to the seniority of the issue
4 δ, B	Endogenous target dividend payout ratio and safety covenant resulting from the numerical optimization, assuming σ_v is known
5 T	Maturity of the contract or average duration if the measures are calculated for credit risk monitoring purposes
6 σ_v	Implicitly computed from stock market data. It is the main goal of section 16.1

Hence, by Itô's lemma and because $v(V) = V$ in Merton's setting, the volatility of equity returns is simply

$$\sigma_E = \frac{V}{E} \cdot \left(\frac{\partial E}{\partial V} \right) . \sigma_v.$$

Then it follows that

$$\sigma_v = \sigma_E \left[1 - \frac{N(d_2)}{XN(d_1)} \right], \qquad (16.2)$$

where $X = V/Fe^{-rT}$ is the relative distance to loss and $N(d_1)$ is the standard call option delta. Substituting iteratively equation (16.2) into the expressions of d_1 and d_2 provides convergence to the implicit true volatility of asset returns:

$$d_1^i = \frac{\ln(X)}{\sigma_E \left[1 - \frac{N(d_2^{i-1})}{XN(d_1^{i-1})} \right] \sqrt{T}} + \frac{1}{2} \sigma_E \left[1 - \frac{N(d_2^{i-1})}{XN(d_1^{i-1})} \right] \sqrt{T}, \qquad (16.3)$$

$$d_2^i = d_1^i - \sigma_E \left[1 - \frac{N(d_2^{i-1})}{XN(d_1^{i-1})} \right] \sqrt{T},$$

where i stands for the ith iteration.

There is, however, still a point on which to make a precision. Reverting the pricing equation as a function of the stock price and the stock volatility is like assuming that there is no risk premia in doing this. Because the previous development is a straightforward use of the put–call parity relationship where we try to replicate the payoff of the value of assets with a call on it. A straight replacement would indicate that the investor is indifferent between the two alternatives which is still sustainable only in the case where the value of the assets is fully observable, even though it is not traded (see Merton, 1994)[2].

---

[2] It can be shown that we could find a process $Y(t)$ such that $V(T) = Y(t)E(t)$. Then, writing a simple European contingent-claim $F(E, t)$ instead of $F(V, t)$ will change the boundary condition from $F(V, T) = h[V]$ to $F(E, T) = E^Y[h[EY]]$.

Application to the Present Model

Defining the following ratios:

$$\left\{k_F = \frac{F}{V}\right\}, \left\{k_B = \frac{B}{V}\right\}, \left\{k_{BF} = \frac{B}{F}\right\},$$

and representing the overall stock amount at time t_0 as E_0, equation (14.14) can be re-expressed as

$$D_0(V, T) = \frac{1}{1 - \varphi e^{-\delta T}[N(-d_1) - N(-k_1) - (k_B)^{2\gamma}(N(h_1) - N(l_1))]}$$

$$\cdot \left[\begin{array}{c} FP_0(T)[N(d_2) + (k_B)^{2\gamma-2}N(l_2)] \\ +\varphi E_0 e^{-\delta T}[N(-d_1) - N(-k_1) - (k_B)^{2\gamma}(N(h_1) - N(l_1))] \\ +\varphi H P_0(T)[N(-k_2) + (k_B)^{2\gamma-2}N(h_2)] \end{array} \right], \qquad (16.4)$$

where V/F, B/V, V/B, B^2/VF are substituted by $1/k_F$, k_B, $1/k_B$ and $k_B.k_{BF}$ respectively in the formulations of d_1, h_1, k_1, l_1. Although this expression seems to be much more complex than expression (16.1), it is in fact completely analogous. If we recover more or less the same context as in Merton's approach, i.e. $\varphi = 1$ and $\delta = 0$, equation (16.4) can be rewritten as

$$D_0(V, T) = \frac{1}{\underbrace{[N(d_1) - N(-k_1) - (k_B)^{2\gamma}(N(h_1) - N(l_1))]}_{d*}}$$

$$\cdot \left[\begin{array}{c} \overbrace{FP_0(T)[N(d_2) + (k_B)^{2\gamma-2}N(l_2)]}^{-\text{covered call}*} \\ -E_0[N(d_1) + N(-k_1) + (k_B)^{2\gamma}(N(h_1) - N(l_1))] + E_0 \\ \underbrace{+ \varphi H P_0(T)[N(-k_2) + (k_B)^{2\gamma-2}N(h_2)]}_{\text{special rebate}} \end{array} \right]. \qquad (16.5)$$

The last expression mainly states that the value of the corporate debt is equivalent to $1/d*$ times a written exotic covered call on E_0 with a special rebate in case of default triggering, where the $N(\cdot)$s are still functions of the ratios with respect to V and the volatility of assets. But, as with the Merton's case, we can express the latter as an iterated function of the stock market volatility which allows the model to be entirely specified by the dynamics of the stock market and the interest rate term structure.

The derivation of the volatility of the asset returns in the present approach is more complex because of the differentiation made between the value of assets and the total value of the firm, and the eventuality of default prior to T. In this context, equation (16.2) becomes

$$\sigma_v = \frac{E}{V}\left(\frac{\partial E}{\partial V}\right)^{-1} \cdot \sigma_E \tag{16.6}$$

$$= \frac{E}{V}\frac{1}{\Delta_E} \cdot \sigma_E$$

$$= \frac{V - L(V) + C(V) - D(V)}{V}\frac{1}{\Delta_E}\sigma_E,$$

where Δ_E is the sensitivity of equity to firm's returns. After the computation of $\partial E/\partial V$ and some rearrangements, it can be found that Δ_E verifies the following equation[3]:

$$\Delta_E = (1 - e^{-\delta T})\,[1 - N(-k_1) - V_0 N(-k_1)' - V_0(B_0/V_0)^{2\gamma}N(h_1)' + (2\gamma-1)(B_0/V_0)^{2\gamma}N(h_1)]$$

$$- (FN(l_2) - HN(h_2))(P_0(T)/V_0)(B_0/V_0)^{2\gamma-2}(2\gamma - 2)$$

$$- e^{-\delta T}(B_0/V_0)^{2\gamma}(N(h_1) - N(l_1))(2\gamma - 1) - e^{-\delta T}(N(-d_1) - N(-k_1))$$

$$+ B\int_0^T (e^{\delta T} - 1)\frac{1}{\sqrt{2\pi}V\,\Sigma(\tau_b)}e^{-1/2(h_2(\tau_b))^2}\left(\frac{1}{\tau_b^2} - \frac{\ln(V_0/B)}{\Sigma(\tau_b)\tau_b}h_2(\tau_b)\right)d\tau_b \tag{16.7}$$

where $N(-k_1)'$ and $N(h_1)'$ are the inner derivatives of $N(-k_1)$ and $N(h_1)$ respectively.

When δ gets closer to 0% and the threshold value is not high enough, we do obtain values for Δ_E that are very close to those of the Merton's basic case. For reasonable levels of dividend payouts, Figure 16.1 shows that a higher B produces a gap between both deltas that decreases whenever the probability of earlier default decreases (V increases). However, when the dividend rate is raised, Δ_E can present an inverted shape that stays well above the Δ_E of Merton's equity. The existence of the dividend payout stresses the sensitivity of shareholder's payoff to the firm's asset evolution.

Once again, following the methodology already described in the introduction of the present section, we iterate σ_v from the computed volatility of the returns of the stocks of the company using backwards equation (16.6). At each step, the computed equity value[4] and Δ_E are used in this equation to find the next σ_v which is substituted back into the debt pricing equation to find the new debt value. Table 16.2 provides analogously root mean square errors between debt values, knowing the true σ_v versus debt values computed with iterated sigmas after "i" steps.

16.2   ENDOGENOUS DESIGN

Given that the current model relies upon two parameters linked to the agency problem between shareholders and debtholders, i.e. the dividend payout level and the threshold value, it would be interesting to imagine that both claimants would fix a pair $\{\delta^*, H^*\}$ at time 0, given a desired project.

---

[3]The complete derivation is available upon request.
[4]One possibility could be to substitute the ratio E/V in equation (16.6) by (1 − the target leverage ratio of the company) if known.

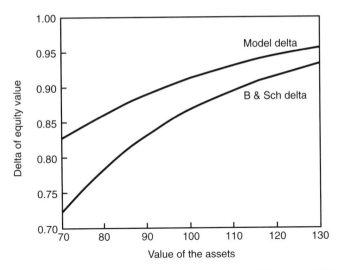

Figure 16.1 V between 70 and 130, $F = 70$, $B = 50$, $r = 5.43\%$, $\sigma_v = 30\%$, $\delta = 0\%$, $T = 5$. Reproduced with authorization from Pirotte (1999b)

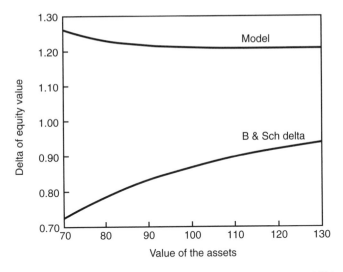

Figure 16.2 V between 70 and 130, $F = 70$, $B = 50$, $r = 5.43\%$, $\sigma_v = 30\%$, $\delta = 5\%$, $T = 5$. Reproduced with authorization from Pirotte (1999b)

Suppose that a particular project requires an investment of I_0 financed by a zero-coupon debt issue[5]. Debtholders are promised a payment of F in T years and will fix a safety covenant H, in the pure sense of Black and Cox (1976), that allows them to counter somehow the fact that the dividend yield that shareholders are getting is in

---

[5]In the model despite its possible inefficiencies because alternative forms of financing such as pure equity can convey agency costs that can exceed those of debt.

Table 16.2 This table presents the root mean square errors (RMSEs) between the debt value computed under the present model with an iterated estimate of σ_v from the original σ_E, versus the same value calculated with the true σ_v. The series on which the RMSEs are calculated contain 99 values of volatilities in the range 1%–50%. Other parameters are: $V = 100$, $F = 70$, $B = 50$, $r = 5\%$, $T = 10$, $\varphi = 75\%$. Reproduced with authorization from Pirotte (1999b)

Iterations	Dividend payout $\delta = 2\%$
0 (σ_E)	0.9518
1	0.0385
2	0.0029
3	0.0003
4	0.0000
5	0.0000
6	0.0000
7	0.0000
8	0.0000
9	0.0000
10	0.0000
11–20	0.0000

fact financed by asset sales[6]. The optimal set of variables will include the optimal dividend yield for shareholders[7] and the optimal barrier level for debtholders.

Pirotte (1999b) does not introduce a context of "strategic gaming" since this part is only an extension of the paper to illustrate the economic meaning behind such a structural model. Of course, this supposes that investors have a myopic behavior: it is assumed that the optimal pair $\{\delta^*, H^*\}$ fixed by the two counterparties is common knowledge at time 0 and fixed for the entire contractual period (this requirement could be part of the bond indenture provisions).

Similar to Myers and Majluf (1984), the incentive condition for debtholders to finance the investment will be to assure them that the expected reimbursement will cover the investment proceedings[8]. By the absence of arbitrage, we should have

$$D_0(V, T) \geqslant I_0, \tag{16.8}$$

so that debtholders will fix the threshold value conveniently, raising it from 0, but not too much because of the existence of inefficient bankruptcy costs if default occurs. The shareholder's incentive rule will make equation (16.8) binding.

---

[6]The following alternative definitions are provided in the literature for δ and B, respectively:

- $\delta\{1, 2\}$: {financed by selling additional equity, financed by asset sales}
- $B\{1, 2\}$: {liquidity threshold, safety covenant}

Then, because of the limited liability property of equity and the absolute priority rule, $\delta(1)$ allows $B(1)$ and $\delta(2)$ requires $B(2)$.

[7]This is analogous to the equilibrium setting of Chang and Sundaresan (1999) where the borrower is assumed to choose his optimal rate of dividends so as to maximize his expected lifetime utility of consumption.

[8]As pointed out by Anderson and Sundaresan (1996), optimal design may not prevent us from inefficient solutions where some positive NPV projects may not be undertaken. For some funding requirements, it will not be possible to write a debt contract valuable enough to meet the incentive condition for debtholders.

Bankruptcy costs preclude debtholders of fixing a barrier equal to F so that the debt would be riskfree.

On the other hand, shareholders will realize that, given the barrier required by debtholders, if they lower their high dividend rate, they will be able to expect a longer life for the firm and therefore also a longer payout of dividends, since the absolute priority rule prevents them from recovering some value at default. This is a typical case where the maximization of the equity value leads also to a higher debt value. Lenders and borrowers will successively revise their requirements until an optimal set of values is reached.

The numerical procedure that solves the program for the optimal pair $\{\delta^*, H^*\}$ is entirely described in Pirotte (1999b). For its implementation, it has to be remembered that the expression of the equity value, because of the value preservation property,

$$E_t(V) = v_t(V) - D_t(V) = V - L_t(V) + C_t(V) - D_t(V), \tag{16.9}$$

will require the valuation of the expected discounted amount of bankruptcy costs and the expected discounted continuous stream of dividends, knowing that the firm can default prior to the maturity of the contract.

As stated earlier in this book, structural approaches present a main difficulty. Since they can be directly related to real economic aspects of the life of the firm, structural modelizations must provide a multitude of behaviors that, ideally, should be consistent with the economic rationale of the firm. Indeed, if the approach supposes that some bargaining could take place, it should be integrated to the model and the model should provide values for $\{\delta^*, H^*\}$ that are "reasonable". Pirotte (1999b) partly answers this worry by providing the necessary expressions and numerical estimates for the "myopic" case.

16.3 REFERENCES

Anderson, Ronald and Suresh Sundaresan, 1996, "Design and Valuation of Debt Contracts", *The Review of Financial Studies*, **9** (1), Spring, 37–68.

Black, F. and J. C. Cox, 1976, "Valuing Corporate Securities: Some Effects of Bond Indenture Provisions", *Journal of Finance*, **31**, 351–67.

Chang, Ganlin and Suresh Sundaresan, 1999, "Asset Prices and Default-Free Term Structure in an Equilibrium Model of Default", *Working Paper*, Graduate School of Business, Columbia University, March, 49 pp.

Crouhy, Michel, Dan Galai and Robert Mark, 2000, "A Comparative Analysis of Current Credit Risk Models", *Journal of Banking and Finance*, **24** (1–2), 59–117.

Leland, Hayne E., 1994, "Corporate Debt Value, Bond Covenants and Optimal Capital Structure", *Journal of Finance*, **49** (4), September, 1213–52.

Longstaff, Francis, 1990, "Pricing Options with Extendible Maturities: Analysis and Applications", *Journal of Finance*, **45** (3), July, 935–56.

Myers, S. and M. Majluf, 1984, "Corporate Financing and Investment Decisions When Firms Have Information that Investors Do Not Have", *Journal of Financial Economics*, **13**, 187–222.

Pirotte, H., 1999b, "A Structural Model of the Term Structure of Credit Spreads with Stochastic Recovery and Contractual Design", *Working Paper*, Institute of Banking and Finance, Ecole des HEC, University of Lausanne, December, 85 pp.

Ronn, Ehud and Avinash Verma, 1986, "Pricing Risk-Adjusted Deposit Insurance: An Option-Based Model", *Journal of Finance*, **41** (4), September, 871–95.

Shalev, Jonathan, 1997, "Loss Aversion Equilibrium", Working Paper, CORE, Université Catholique de Louvain-la-Neuve, Belgium, 26 pp.

Part Five

Collateralization, Marking-to-Market, and their Impact on Credit Risk

17

Introduction

Starting with Merton (1974), research has approached credit risk mostly as a pricing issue. Although many credit risk pricing models exist today, as seen in the previous chapters, from structural to reduced-form models, very little attention has been paid to the impact of risky collateral on credit risk. It is nonetheless well known that practitioners often mitigate credit risk with collateral, using so-called "haircuts" for collateral level determination, rather than fully price credit risk. It is often more practical to ask for collateral and/or to mark-to-market than to precisely price the credit risk of an instrument. But collateral usage clearly mitigates the credit risk issue, as exposure is reduced via collateral. Analyzing the value of the credit risk when risky collateral is present thus becomes essential, for credit risk pricing as well as for collateral management (or haircut determination).

Cossin and Hricko (1999) analyze the value of credit risk when there is collateral in a range of different situations, including dual-default in a simple setting, stochastic collateral, stochastic bond collateral with stochastic interest rates, continuous and discrete marking-to-market, and margin calls. The basic structure of their work and some of the results are briefly presented here. They pay particular attention to the situation of forwards, although the models could be extended in the same spirit to other instruments. The models confirm many practical intuitions, such as the impact on the haircut level required of the risks of the collateral asset and of the underlying asset to the forward as well as the impact of their correlation. The models also stress the possibly unexpected magnitude of these factors. More importantly, they give actual solutions to determining the value of the credit risk depending on the haircut chosen and the frequency of marking-to-markets, results not presented before in the literature. The models are also a good basis to understand the portfolio effect of collateral management. Finally, they illustrate how differences in prices may arise from pure differences of credit risk management, as illustrated here in the case of futures and forwards.

Cossin and Aparicio (1999) make the problem more general by formulating the auditing and controlling functions of the collateral holder as an impulse control problem. The goal of their work is to determine the optimal times and the optimal controls (i.e. margin calls, equity infusions) that should apply to a credit risky instrument. This second approach frames the collateral control problem as an impulse control problem and proposes a solution based on a numerical approximation of quasi-variational inequalities, a methodology prone to making a complex situation simple. This general model is presented in the second half of this chapter.

17.1 REFERENCES

Cossin, D. and F. Aparicio, 1999, "Control of Credit Risk Collateralization using Quasi Variational Inequalities", *IGBF Working Paper*, University of Lausanne.

Cossin, D. and T. Hricko, 1999, "Pricing Credit Risk With Risky Collateral: A Methodology for Haircut Determination", *Working Paper*, HEC, University of Lausanne.

Merton, Robert C., 1974, "On the Pricing of Corporate Debt: The Risk Structure of Interest Rates", *The Journal of Finance*, **29**, May, 449–70.

18

A Structural Methodology for Haircut Determination and the Pricing of Credit Risk With Risky Collateral

Collateralization has become the favourite way for practitioners and regulators alike to handle credit risk. As stressed in Cossin and Pirotte (1997, 1998) for example, collateralization affects swaps' and other derivative instruments' credit risk and thus puts into question the academic models of credit risk pricing that tend not to incorporate collateralization.

It is thus interesting to notice that while many theoretical models of credit risk pricing have arisen lately, much less work has been done in order to achieve a good theory of pricing credit risk with risky collateral. Determination of haircuts on collaterals asked for by banks, notably in a portfolio setting, has been left to rules of thumb rather than to advanced analysis. The goal of this chapter is to participate in filling that theoretical gap and to analyze the issue of pricing credit risk with risky collateral.

Notice that the issue of pricing an instrument that is collateralized with another risky instrument is not trivial and becomes complex when marking-to-market or margin calls are considered. Margrabe (1978) has mentioned the analogy between an exchange option and a margin account and provides the pricing for a very simple framework with no marking-to-market. Stulz and Johnson (1985) have priced secured debt using contingent claim analysis and study the use of collateralization in a corporate finance framework, analyzing the impact of collateralization on the value of the firm. The rest of the economic literature has addressed the rationale behind the use of collateral in debt contracts and is an extension of the questions arising in the theory of debt (see Benjamin, 1978, Plaut, 1985, Bester, 1994), but has not been concerned with pricing the credit risk with collateral or with evaluating the impact of haircut levels on the credit risk value. Our goal of pricing credit risky instruments with risky collateral is thus fundamentally different and has not yet been fully addressed.

While the finance academic world has focused on the issue of pricing credit risk, practitioners and regulators have used collateralization extensively rather than pricing to manage credit risk exposures. Collateralization is an elegant way of transforming a credit risk issue into that of a market risk. For example, it is well known in practice that pricing of swap contracts bears little or no dimension of credit risk (a problem examined in Cossin and Pirotte, 1997), notably because collateralization is today used extensively. Many securities can in practice be used for collateralization of risky contracts. The amount of collateral required typically differs depending on the risk of the security being used in the collateral. This is why practitioners traditionally use so-called "haircuts", that determine how much collateral is required, depending on the type of security used as collateral, a phenomenon not well incorporated in current research (nor in current regulation).

Table 18.1 Typical collateral policy. Reproduced with authorization from Cossin and Hricko (1999)

Collateral	Acceptable types	Valuation post-haircut (%)
Cash	G10 countries	100
US treasuries	Under 1 year	100
	Less than 5 years	97
	5–10 years	95
G10 gov. bonds (except otherwise specified)		90
US agencies	GNMA, FNMA	90
Mortgage backed pass throughs issued by:	FHLMC, SLMA, FHLB	90
	ARMs	90
Listed bonds issued by banks		90
Listed bonds issued by corporates		80
Listed warrants/convertibles		60
Unlisted notes		50
Letters of credit	AA rated or better	90
Japanese straight bonds		80
Investment trusts		50
European equities		50
US equities		50
Japanese equities		50

Note: Maturities referred above refer to residual maturity.

Typically, cash and short-term US Treasuries will have traditionally post-haircut valuations of 100% (meaning that 100% of the current value of the assets is considered collateral), 5–10 years US Treasuries post-haircut valuations of 95%, listed bonds issued by corporates post-haircut valuations of 80%, US equities may have post-haircut valuations of 50%, etc. We reproduce in Table 18.1 a haircut schedule by Security Type of a major global player.

We follow here Cossin and Hricko (1999) and aim at providing in this chapter a framework to analyze haircut determination and the impact of risky collateral on credit risk and look precisely at the case of risky forwards, analysis that could be generalized to swaps, and other instruments.

Cossin and Hricko (1999) follow a structural methodology and begin by analyzing different stylized situations. We proceed similarly here. Firstly, we study the simple situation of a nonstochastic collateral. We then present an analysis of collateralizing an instrument with stochastic equity when there is no marking-to-market, followed by an analysis of collateralizing with bonds when interest rates are stochastic. Finally, we briefly describe, in a structural approach, the problem of pricing a credit risky instrument with collateral when there are marking-to-market and margin calls.

18.1 MODEL WITH DUAL DEFAULT AND NONSTOCHASTIC COLLATERAL

In this very simple setup, and before studying the more pertinent situation of risky collateral, we analyze the value of the collateralized credit risk (CCR) for two credit-risky agents that engage in a contract subject to credit risk (for example, one takes the long side of a forward while the other takes the corresponding short side: this stylistic simplification would also correspond to pricing collateralized credit risk for a bank with exact book matching). In order to manage their respective credit risk exposure both agents require the counterparty to deposit some collateral, either with their counterparty or with a neutral institution, for example a clearing house. There is no intermediate marking-to-market between initiation of the contract and its expiration. Hence the only time when default can occur is at maturity. The collateral deposited by both agents is cash (and thus is not risky itself). We assume that the decision to default depends only on the value of the original contract and the value of the collateral. We thus consider default to be endogenous. Extension to exogenous default could be the work of future research, but the assumption of endogenous default may be stronger than it first appears. Indeed, we assume here that an agent defaults if the loss of the collateral and the underlying contract is worth less than the future payments s/he had committed to make. One might object that a company or an individual might default for a wide variety of reasons. Some of them might be totally unrelated to the specific contract considered. For example a company might have to file for bankruptcy for some liquidity reasons. In the case of bankruptcy though, creditors will take over control and behave optimally by maximizing the contract value, as described in our model. Therefore they will take the same decisions as the company would have taken, namely they will not default if default is costlier than honoring the contract. We also assume no external costs to default (for simplification), which means that both agents will exercise their options if they are in the money at expiration.

We consider a forward contract to illustrate the decomposition. At time 0 the contract is initiated. The agents fix the price at which the stochastic asset will be traded in the future. This price remains fixed until the expiration of the contract. We will refer to it as the forward price. Agent 1 has the obligation to buy the asset for the forward price at expiration (hereafter called time T), while agent 2 must sell the asset at time T. The forward price is set at time 0 so as to make the value of the forward contract equal to zero. We assume that the storage cost of this asset can be neglected and that it pays no dividend (and that there is no convenience yield). By using the classical cash-and-carry arbitrage argument we know that the forward price that yields a forward contract value of zero at time 0 is given by

$$H = S_0 \cdot e^{rt}. \tag{18.1}$$

The collateral posted by each agent is denominated M_1 and M_2. The following variables are used in the subsection 18.1.1:

S_0 Value of the underlying of the forward contract at time 0
S_T Value of the underlying of the forward contract at time T
H Forward price
M_1 Cash amount that agent 1 has to give as collateral
M_2 Cash amount that agent 2 has to give as collateral.

We assume that the price of the underlying of the forward contract follows a geometric Brownian motion (GBM) process. The interest rate is assumed to be constant for the time being.

Table 18.2 Payoffs at maturity. This table provides payoffs for various values of the underlying of the forward contract at maturity. Reprinted with authorization from Cossin and Hricko (1999)

Stock price	$S \leqslant H_T - M_1$	$H_T - M_1 \leqslant S_T \leqslant H_T + M_2$	$H_T + M_2 \leqslant S_T$
Riskless forward	$S_T - H_T$	$S_T - H_T$	$S_T - H_T$
Risky forward	$-M_1$	$S_T - H_T$	M_2
Short call	0	0	$-(S_T - (H_T + M_2))$
Long put	$(H_T - M_1) - S_T$	0	0

18.1.1 The Basic Model

Under the above assumptions, the value of the credit-risky forward with collateral to the agent having the long position in the forward is, as can be seen from Table 18.2:

$$\text{Risky forward} = \text{riskless forward} + \text{put}(S_t, H - M_1) - \text{call}(S_t, H + M_2). \quad (18.2)$$

The term risky (and riskless) in the above formula means with (without) default risk.

The value of the forward contract with two-sided default risk can be smaller, larger, or equal to the situation without the possibility of default. Agent 1 with the long position gains because s/he has the possibility of defaulting if the price of the underlying of the forward contract drops. On the other hand, s/he loses because the counterparty might not honor its obligation if the contract evolves in agent 1's favour. S/he loses due to the presence of the implicit call option. The resulting value of the long position in the credit-risky forward contract can be bigger or smaller than the riskfree forward contract.

As mentioned previously, the amount of collateral demanded from both agents must not be the same. In order to obtain a risky forward contract with a value of zero at time 0, the value of both options must be the same. As a consequence of the limited liability assumption the price of the underlying of the forward contract cannot be negative. This implies that agent 1's loss is bounded. On the opposite the loss of agent 2 with the short position is unbounded. Hence the possibility to default is of greater value to her/him. In order to obtain the same value for both options agent 2 must deposit a higher amount.

The following example illustrates the decomposition:

$$S_0 = 100,$$
$$H = 100 \cdot \exp(r * (T - t)) = 102.532,$$
$$M_1 = 20.5063(20\% \text{ of } H),$$
$$M_2 = 20.5063,$$
$$r = 0.1,$$
$$\sigma = 0.3,$$
$$T - t = 0.25.$$

If the forward price is chosen in a way as to make the value of the forward contract at time zero equal to zero, the value of the risky forward contract at time 0 is just the sum of the two options:

$$\text{Risky forward} = \text{put}(S_t, H - M_1) - \text{call}(S_t, H + M_2), \tag{18.3}$$
$$\text{Risky forward} = 0.403599 - 0.891276 = -0.487677.$$

In order to make the value of the credit risky forward contract equal to zero at initiation, i.e. to give both options the same value, the party with the short position in the forward contract would need to deposit a higher margin. In the above example the necessary value of M_2 for a 0 contract value at initiation is equal to 27% of the forward price (versus 20% for the long position).

18.2 MODEL WITH STOCHASTIC COLLATERAL

We now generalize our model to the more realistic situation of one credit-risky agent giving a risky asset as a collateral to a third party, considered riskfree, corresponding to a bank or another financial intermediary. The credit riskfree assumption for the bank can be justified by the fact that the forward contract constitutes only a small fraction of the bank's obligations. Reputational damage of defaulting on one contract when it has many others prevents the bank from defaulting. In this setting the credit-risky agent can be seen as the client. For example, the buyer of a forward on an exchange rate can post a collateral of a certain amount of a portfolio of stock with the bank doing the forward. The only cost of default for the client is considered to be here, for simplification, the loss of the collateral. Hence the client will always choose to default when the expected gain (or loss) from the forward contract is bigger than the collateral he had to put up until that moment. We assume that the price of the underlying asset to the forward contract and the price of the asset given as collateral follow two separate GBM processes. The two processes are correlated. There is no marking-to-market and hence no default before maturity. This type of result is known in the literature.

18.2.1 The Model

The client's position corresponds to the following decomposition

$$\text{Risky forward} = \text{riskless forward} + \text{put}(-M, S - H) \tag{18.4}$$

where the put option is an option to exchange the loss of the collateral for the forward contract, M stands for the value of the asset given as collateral, S_t for the value of the underlying of the forward contract, and H is the forward price.

The payoff of the implicit option at expiration is given by

$$\text{Option} = (-M - (S - H))^+ = (H - S - M)^+. \tag{18.5}$$

The collateralized credit risk can be compared to an exchange option. The simplest situation involving the possibility of exchanging one stochastic asset for stochastic asset was analyzed by Margrabe (1978). He mentioned the situation of a margin account as a possible use for his model. The situation described above is different. In the case of Margrabe the client just exchanges one asset for another, here he exchanges the difference of the forward and the spot price for the collateral. Hence the implicit option is a spread option. Similar pricing results are known in the literature. The value of the CCR option is as shown in Cossin and Hricko (1999):

$$\text{CCR option} = \int_{-\infty}^{+up(v)} \int_{-\infty}^{-d-\phi(v)} [H - Se^{(\mu_S-\frac{1}{2}\sigma_S^2)\tau+\sigma_S\sqrt{\tau}u} - Me^{(\mu_M-\frac{1}{2}\sigma_M^2)\tau+\sigma_M\sqrt{\tau}v}] \quad (18.6)$$

$$\cdot f(v) \cdot f(u \mid v) \, du \, dv.$$

The value of the CCR at time zero is given by the following formula:

$$CCR = He^{-r\tau}A_3 - SA_1 - MA_2, \quad (18.7)$$

$$A_1 = \int_{-\infty}^{+up(v+\rho\sigma_S\sqrt{\tau})} f(v) N\left(\frac{-d - \phi(v + \rho\sigma_S\sqrt{\tau}) - \rho v - \sigma_S\sqrt{\tau}}{\sqrt{1-\rho^2}}\right) dv, \quad (18.8)$$

$$A_2 = \int_{-\infty}^{+up(v+\sigma_M\sqrt{\tau})} f(v) N\left(\frac{-d - \phi(v + \sigma_M\sqrt{\tau}) - \rho v - \rho\sigma_M\sqrt{\tau}}{\sqrt{1-\rho^2}}\right) dv,$$

$$A_3 = \int_{-\infty}^{+up(v)} f(v) N\left(\frac{-d - \phi(v) - \rho v}{\sqrt{1-\rho^2}}\right) dv.$$

Assume H is the riskfree forward price. We will compare different collaterals as well as different levels of collateral demanded and analyze the influence of the various parameters on the option value and interpret the different parameters in the context of collaterals and the setting of optimal haircuts. The benchmark is the use of non-stochastic collateral.

Figures 18.1 and 18.2 illustrate the influence of changes in the various parameters.

The value of the CCR is comparable to the value of a spread exchange option. An intuitive result is that the value of the credit risk increases if the amount of collateral that is requested decreases. The effect of the value of the underlying security to the forward may seem less obvious. One would expect that the credit risk would be decreasing if the value of the underlying increases. This would be true if the strike price (the amount of collateral asked for) of the option would be fixed. In the case of the forward contract the bank will increase the strike price with a rising level of the underlying, by keeping in our example a constant proportional value of the forward as collateral (i.e. proportional haircuts). The value of the CCR increases if the maximum possible loss from the underlying contract increases. This effect dominates if the bank uses the cash-and-carry arbitrage price in setting the forward price (and the strike price of the option). Figure 18.2 shows the credit risk for different levels of σ_S, σ_M, and ρ. The riskier the underlying contract, the higher is the value of the possibility to default. This also implies that regulations on margin requirements have to be different for various risky assets underlying the original contract. The riskier the asset taken as collateral the higher the credit risk. This justifies the fact that assets that exhibit little or no market risk (which is captured by σ_M) tend to require lower haircuts. However, it is important to stress the fact that the influence of the volatility of the underlying seems to be at least as important as the influence of the volatility of the collateral assets. It seems to be the case in practice that the volatility of the collateral asset seems to be considered of greater importance than the volatility of the underlying contract for haircut determination. In our example the volatility of the underlying of the original contract actually has stronger influence. One can see further that the value of the possibility to default is higher for more positive values

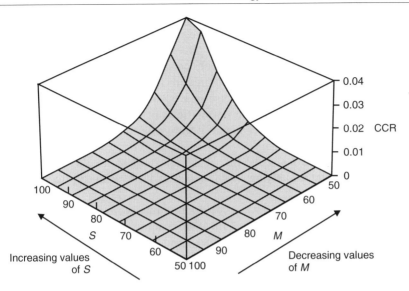

Figure 18.1 Collateralized credit risk for various levels of S and M. This figure gives the value of CCR for different levels of the values of S (the underlying asset of the forward) and M (the collateral) at time 0. The values for the fixed parameters are: $r = 0.1$, $\sigma_1 = 0.3$, $\sigma_2 = 0.3$, $\rho = 0.2$ and $T - t = 0.5$ (called CCR). Reprinted with authorization from Cossin and Hricko (1999)

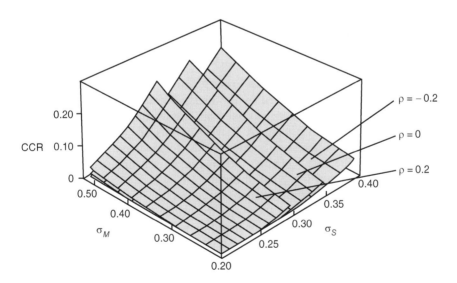

Figure 18.2 Collateralized credit risk and the correlation of collateral and underlying. This graph shows the CCR for different levels of σ_S (the volatility of the underlying asset of the forward), σ_M (the volatility of the collateral), and ρ (the correlation of the underlying asset and collateral). The values for the fixed parameters are: $S = 100$, $H = 100 \cdot \exp(r*(T-t)) = 102.532$, $M = 20.5063$ (20% of H), $r = 0.1$ and $T - t = 0.5$. Reprinted with authorization from Cossin and Hricko (1999)

of the correlation coefficient and can be highly sensitive to the correlation. This underlines the necessity to consider correlation effects in order to determine collateral requirements.

If the asset given as collateral is negatively correlated with the asset underlying the forward contract the CCR can be lower than with riskfree collateral of the same sizes. CCR is lower (in our example) in the case of stochastic collateral than in the case of nonstochastic collateral with negative correlations of about −0.2 and a volatility of 15% of the collateral asset. This means that negative haircuts may indeed be optimal in this situation.

The influence of σ_S and ρ suggest that it is important to take into account equally the source of risk in the underlying asset as well as its relationship to the risk of the collateral asset.

The present framework also allows us to address one more practical issue related to the design of collateral determination. In most cicumstances the client will not only have one contract with the bank. On the other hand, the collateral will be a portfolio of assets rather than a single asset. How should the bank structure collateral use when asset portfolios are concerned? Should one asset serve as collateral for some use or should all the assets of the collateral portfolio serve jointly as collateral for all the liabilities? In the context of our framework the answer would depend on the value of the implicit options. We have seen that the collateralized credit risk is influenced by the volatility of both the underlying contracts and the collateral portfolio. Because of diversification effects, the variance of both sides will be reduced when the portfolio view is adapted. The effect on the correlation cannot be unambiguously given a sign. Therefore the optional structure has to be designed case by case. The present framework is well suited to perform this analysis.

18.3 BONDS AS COLLATERAL

It has been shown in section 18.2 that a lower volatility of the asset used as collateral may lead to a lower haircut required by the bank. Because of this phenomenon, the asset class, which is used most often as collateral, is government bonds. The preceding setup is not well adapted to pricing CCR when bonds are used as collateral as we considered nonstochastic interest rates and a GBM for collateral value.

We still assume for the time being that there are no intermediate marking-to-markets. The asset given as collateral is a bond of maturity U, where $U > T$. We give the basic structure of the analysis of the valuation equation for the CCR with bonds and stochastic interest rates in order to show that the principles of the solution remain the same. The valuation methodology can be based on results by Cossin and Hricko (1999) for the specific application, Geman et al. (1995) for the change of numeraire, and Harrison and Pliska (1981, 1983) for the martingale pricing.

The example of setup proposed here comes from Cossin and Hricko (1999). They assume that the price process of the underlying of the forward contract follows GBM. The interest rate follows a Vasicek process:

$$dr = a \cdot (b - r)dt + \sigma_r dW_r. \tag{18.9}$$

The dynamics of a bond with maturity u at time t is given by

$$\frac{dB(U, t)}{B(U, t)} = (r + \lambda_r \cdot \sigma_u) dt + \sigma_u \cdot dW_r \tag{18.10}$$

or written equivalently under a different probability measure

$$\frac{dB(U, t)}{B(U, t)} = r \cdot dt + \sigma_u \cdot dW_r, \tag{18.11}$$

where

$$\sigma_u = \frac{\sigma_r (1 - \exp(-a \cdot (U - t)))}{a}. \tag{18.12}$$

The price of the underlying asset of the forward contract follows a GBM process with two sources of randomness:

$$\frac{dS_t}{S_t} = r \cdot dt + \rho \cdot \sigma_s \cdot dW_r + \sqrt{1 - \rho^2} \cdot \sigma_s \cdot dW_s. \tag{18.13}$$

We also assume the existence of a riskless bank account or accumulation factor, which is given by

$$\beta(t) = \exp\left(\int_0^t r(s) \, ds\right). \tag{18.14}$$

18.3.1 Valuation of the Collateralized Credit Risk Option

The gain from defaulting corresponds to

$$\text{Gain}(t) = \beta(t)\mathbb{E}_t\left[\left(\frac{1}{\beta(T)}(F - S_T - M \cdot B(T, U))\right)^+\right], \tag{18.15}$$

where $B(T, U)$ is the value of a zero-coupon bond with a face value of 1 and M represents the number of zero-coupon bonds. Cossin and Hricko (1999) show that by splitting the above expression into three parts, one can evaluate them separately.

$$\text{Part 1} = \beta(t)\mathbb{E}\left[\left(\frac{1}{\beta(T)}F \cdot \mathbf{I}_A\right)\right], \tag{18.16}$$

$$\text{Part 2} = \beta(t)\mathbb{E}_t\left[\left(\frac{1}{\beta(T)}S_T \cdot \mathbf{I}_A\right)\right], \tag{18.17}$$

$$\text{Part 3} = \beta(t)\mathbb{E}_t\left[\left(\frac{1}{\beta(T)}M \cdot B(T, U) \cdot \mathbf{I}_A\right)\right]. \tag{18.18}$$

By using the forward measure approach (change of numeraire) and some ordinary changes of measure Cossin and Hricko (1999) are thus able to derive the full solution to the above equation. There is no fundamental difference in the structure of the result from that in the previous section. The value of the option would certainly be lower for a comparable set of parameters. However, the values obtained cannot be compared directly as the model in this section works with stochastic interest rates, whereas the previous results assumed constant interest rates. This result allows us to extend all the conclusions of the preceding sections to situations when bonds are used as collateral.

Note that the mean level of the interest rate does not enter in the valuation equation. This result can be intuitively understood by realizing that the CCR is derived in a classical contingent claims setting.

We have shown in the previous section that the volatility of the underlying contract can have a larger impact on the CCR than the volatility of the underlying asset, and also that the correlation matters. Therefore it is important to see that the conclusion that bonds lead to lower haircuts compared to other assets with more market risk does not hold unconditionally. The effect of the higher market risk of other assets can be partially offset by the correlation effect.

18.4   MARKING-TO-MARKET: ON FORWARD AND FUTURES CONTRACTS

Up to this point, all the analysis has been done by assuming that there was no marking-to-market. In practice, credit risk is often managed by requiring collateral and by introducing marking-to-market and margin calls. In the literature the effect of marking-to-market has been most often seen as merely replacing the multiperiod decisions by a series of one-period decisions. Within this series all the decisions have been considered as being identical. It will become clear that this view is not correct. It is true that one of the benefits of marking-to-market and margin calls is to replace the option to default by the sum of options of shorter maturity. Therefore the benefit of introducing a marking-to-market procedure stems from the fact that the period during which the credit risk exposure builds up is shorter. This is, however, not the only benefit. Agents are not myopic. Therefore they consider all the effects of their actions. When taking the decision whether or not to default the agent will take into account that s/he will lose the contract and all the possibilities to default in the future. This will cause the probability of default to be lower than in the myopic case. Technically speaking the range of integration will be smaller than in the myopic case.

We will use our framework to show that price differences between forward and futures prices can arise from differences in the management of credit risk. It has been shown by Cox et al. (CIR) (1981) that without the possibility of default under nonstochastic interest rates the forward price is the same as the futures price. We will show that this is only true in a setting without credit risk. Futures contracts have been invented especially to deal with credit risk. An analysis which is conducted in a framework without the possibility of defaulting is lacking the most important feature of the contract. This section is organized as follows. We will first repeat the classical argument of CIR. Afterwards we will show that the payoff of the two strategies contracts is not the same, even in a setting without stochastic interest rates.

We model the situation between a bank and a client. The bank is assumed to be free of default. Therefore, it does not have to provide any collateral. The client has to provide a cash amount M.

The following variables will be used:

S_i Price of the underlying of the forward contract
r Continuously compounded interest rate

Table 18.3 Resulting positions and cash flows from the futures strategy. Reprinted with authorization from Cossin and Hricko (1999)

Time	0	$T/2$	T
Futures price	F_0	$F_{T/2}$	F_T
Futures position	$e^{(T/2)r}$	$e^{(T)r}$	0
Gain/loss	0	$(F_{T/2} - F_0)e^{(T/2)r}$	$(F_T - F_{T/2})e^{(T)r}$
FV gain/loss	0	$(F_{T/2} - F_0)e^{(T)r}$	$(F_T - F_{T/2})e^{(T)r}$

F_i Value of the futures contract maturing at T
G_i Value of the forward contract maturing at T.

18.4.1 The CIR Argument Without Credit Risk

The CIR argument is based on the following strategy:

1. At time 0, take a long position of $\exp(T/2)(r)$ in the futures contract maturing at time 2.
2. At time $T/2$ increase the futures position to $\exp((T)r)$.

The resulting cash flows and positions are shown in Table 18.3.
At time T the payout of this strategy will be given by

$$(F_{T/2} - F_0)e^{(T)r} + (F_T - F_{T/2})e^{(T)r} = (F_T - F_0)e^{(T)r}. \tag{18.19}$$

The value of the futures at time T with delivery at time T is obviously S_T, the spot price of the underlying at time T. If you combine this strategy with an investment of F_0 in the riskfree bond at time 0 you obtain:

$$(S_T - F_0)e(T)r + F_0 e^{(T)r} = S_T e^{(T)r}. \tag{18.20}$$

Consider now the alternative strategy. Take a position of $e^{(T)r}$ in a forward contract with maturity T and buy a bond with a face value of G_0 with the same maturity. The payoff at time T is

$$(S_T - G_0)e^{(T)r} + G_0 e^{(T)r} = S_T e^{(T)r}. \tag{18.21}$$

The payoff from both strategies is the same. Therefore the capital required to implement them must be the same. Hence we conclude that

$$F_0 = G_0. \tag{18.22}$$

18.4.2 Taking Into Account Credit Risk

In this step we introduce default risk. We use the strategy proposed by CIR and show the structure of the implicit options. We assume that the amount that needs to be given as collateral is directly proportional to the exposure taken and that there is marking-to-market and margin calls at maturity as well as at the intermediate period in the case of the futures, while this only happens at maturity in the case of the forward.

Assume that the client has to provide a cash amount of M as collateral. The present value of the credit risk implicit in the forward strategy is obtained as

$$e^{-r(T)}\mathbf{E}[(-M - (S_T e^{(T)r} - G_0 e^{(T)r}))^+] = \text{put}(S_T e^{(T)r}, G_0 e^{(T)r} - M). \qquad (18.23)$$

Hence this value can be seen as a put option on $Se^{(T)r}$ with maturity T and a strike price equal to $G_0 e^{(T)r} - M$.

Now we turn to the futures strategy. We will again assume that the client has to give an amount of cash equal to M as collateral. At time $T/2$ s/he faces the following decision: s/he can exchange the payment that s/he is supposed to make (which is given by $(F_{T/2} - F_0)e^{((T)/2)r}$) for the loss of the collateral, the second futures contract, and the possibility to default later. At the time when the decision is taken, the second futures position has a value of zero. The client will choose to default if the money s/he saves is more than the loss of the collateral and the implicit default option.

$$(F_{T/2} - F_0)e^{((T)/2)r} \leqslant -M - \text{future cash flows}. \qquad (18.24)$$

The term "future cash flows" refers to the value of the possibility of defaulting later. It is important to note that the strategy requires us to increase the futures position. We assume that the amount of collateral needs to be increased proportionally. The gain from defaulting at time T is

$$(-e^{(T)r/2}M - (S_T - F_{T/2})e^{(T)r})^+. \qquad (18.25)$$

This value is equal to the following option at time $T/2$:

$$\text{Put}(S_T e^{(T)r}, F_{T/2}e^{(T)r} - e^{(T/2)r}M). \qquad (18.26)$$

The range of integration for $S_{T/2}$ and/or u is obtained by finding the value of $S_{T/2}$ that makes the inequality (18.24) a strict equality. The gain from defaulting at time $T/2$ does not include the value of the default at time T. The distinction of the equation that determines the relevant range and the payoff of the option is quite important. This is the effect of the nonmyopic behavior of the agent. When taking the decision to default he takes into account that he will lose the future cash flows. This implies that he will not default in some range even if the value of the option at time $T/2$ is in the money.

The value of the option to default at time $T/2$ is a function of $S_{T/2}$. This price, however, is not known at time 0. The expected value at time 0 is

$$\text{Put}_1 = e^{-r((T)/2)} \int_0^{S_{\text{crit}}} (-M - (F_{T/2} - F_0)e^{((T)/2)r})^+ f(S_{T/2}) dS_{T/2} \qquad (18.27)$$

$$= e^{-r((T)/2)} \int_0^{S_{\text{crit}}} (-M - (S_{T/2}e^{r((T)/2)} - F_0)e^{((T)/2)r}) f(S_{T/2}) dS_{T/2}.$$

At time T the client has the possibility to default given that he did not default at time $T/2$. The value of this option is given by

$$\text{Put}_2 = e^{-r((T)/2)} \int_0^\infty \text{put}(S_T e^{(T)r}, F_{T/2} e^{(T)r} - e^{((T)/2)r}M)\cdot \mathbf{I}_{\text{no def at } T/2} f(S_{T/2}) dS_{T/2} \quad (18.28)$$

$$= e^{-r((T)/2)} \int_{S_{\text{crit}}}^\infty \text{put}(S_T e^{(T)r}, F_{T/2} e^{(T)r} - e^{((T)/2)r}M) f(S_{T/2}) dS_{T/2}.$$

In order to compare the result to one obtained without default risk we look at the future value of the strategy.

$$\text{Futures position} = (F_{T/2} - F_0)e^{(T)r} + \text{put}_{T/2} e^{(T)r}$$
$$+ (F_T - F_{T/2})e^{(T)r}\mathbf{I}_{\text{no def at } T/2}$$
$$- \text{put}_2(F_T, F_{T/2} - e^{((T)/2)r}M)e^{(T)r} + F_0 e^{(T)r}. \quad (18.29)$$

We can do the following simplifications: F_T is again equal to S_T. We know that the futures contract from $T/2$ to T has no more intermediate marking-to-market periods: it is identical to a forward contract. The futures price at time $T/2$ is therefore

$$F_{T/2} = S_{T/2} e^{((T)/2)r}. \quad (18.30)$$

The future value of the forward strategy is

$$\text{Forward position} = (S_T - G_0)e^{(T)r} + \text{put}(S_T e^{(T)r}, G_0 e^{(T)r} - e^{(T)r/2}M)e^{(T)r} + G_0 e^{(T)r}. \quad (18.31)$$

Without credit risk the value of the forward price is

$$G_0 = S_0 e^{(T)r}. \quad (18.32)$$

It is obvious that the value of the two positions will no longer be the same if the forward price is equal to the futures price. In order to determine explicitly the value of the two strategies at time 0, Cossin and Hricko (1999) take the expectation of the above flows under the risk-neutral probability and calculate its present value. Detailed calculations of the discounted expected values of the various positions in the futures strategy are skipped here, but Cossin and Hricko (1999) show that the value of the futures position at time 0 is equal to

$$\text{Value futures position} = \mathbf{E}[S_{T/2} e^{(T)/2r} - F_0] + \mathbf{E}[\text{put } 1]$$
$$+ e^{-r((T)/2)} \mathbf{E}[\text{put}(F_T e^{(T)r}, F_{T/2} e^{(T)r} - e^{(T)r/2}M)] + F_0. \quad (18.33)$$

The value of the forward position at time zero is given by

$$\text{Value forward position} = \text{put}(S_T e^{(T)r}, G_0 e^{(T)r} - e^{(T)r/2}M) + G_0. \quad (18.34)$$

It is obvious that the value of the two positions will no longer be the same if forward and futures prices are equal.

We will illustrate this with the following example: if the forward and the futures prices were the same the value of the two positions would be:

$$\text{Value futures position} = 106.318$$

$$\text{Collateralized credit risk} = 1.191$$

$$\text{Value forward position} = 106.717$$

$$\text{Collateralized credit risk} = 1.589$$

for the following parameters:

$$S_0 = 100$$

$$\sigma = 0.3$$

$$F_0 = G_0 = 105.127$$

$$M = 21.0254$$

$$T = 0.5.$$

The difference in the value of the two strategies comes uniquely from the difference in managing the credit risk exposures. The credit risk implicit in the forward strategy is higher compared to the credit risk in the futures strategy, despite the amount of collateral set at the beginning being the same. We would assume that the amount of collateral required will be lower in a situation with marking-to-market. In order to obtain the same value of the option to default the required margin for the futures contract needs to be nearly 9% lower than for the futures contract. This shows clearly how collateral can be replaced by dynamic strategies like the simple marking-to-market procedure used in the above example.

We have demonstrated in a simple framework that futures and forward prices need not to be the same in the presence of credit risk. We have also modeled the decision of the agent by taking explicitly into account that s/he will consider the loss of the second option when s/he decides whether or not to default. From this consideration it follows that it is incorrect to model the situation with marking-to-market as a series of independent put options. The effect of neglecting the more restricted ranges of the underlying variable is to overestimate the value of the default option under marking-to-market. The value of the marking-to-market procedure comes from the fact that it splits the longer maturity option into options of shorter maturities and that it introduces the dependence among the successive decisions to default.

18.5 DYNAMIC COLLATERAL MANAGEMENT

Cossin and Hricko (1999) also analyze a model with nonstochastic collateral but dynamic collateral management. In section 18.4 we have analyzed a situation with discrete marking-to-market using the contingent claim framework. The resulting collateralized credit risk values have a structure which is comparable to nonstandard compound options. In order to generalize the results one could use the same kind of setup and increase the number of marking-to-market times, but pricing becomes cumbersome quickly as option numbers increase exponentially. It is nonetheless possible to use an approximation that was first described by Broadie et al. (1997) and used there for the pricing of barrier options with discrete monitoring. The basic idea is that the value of a discretely monitored barrier option corresponds to a continuously monitored barrier option with a lower (for a down option) barrier. The uncertainty about the price at the next marking-to-market instant is therefore translated into a lower barrier. The valuation exercise of Cossin and Hricko (1999) leads to some conclusions on the optimal strategy of the bank. Using the models the bank can calculate the incremental benefit of an additional marking-to-market time and compare it with the marginal costs. Hence the optimal marking-to-market frequency could be determined conditional on the collateral and the marking-to-market costs. The optimal marking-to-market frequency will be an increasing function of the volatility of the underlying. The value of the option to default will be higher during turbulent times. One way of achieving a lower value of the option to default would be to adopt a strategy with nonconstant time intervals between the different marking-to-market times. The frequency would obviously have to be an increasing function of the volatility.

Readers interested in the problematic are referred back to the original paper for more details.

18.6   CONCLUSION TO STRUCTURAL CCR PRICING

We have shown the influence of collateral on the valuation of credit risk in some stylized situations using the example of forwards. We have explored the effect of different asset classes serving as collateral. The analysis underlines the necessity to think of collateral valuation jointly with the source of risk. Correlation matters. CCR depends obviously on all the characteristics of the assets involved. Therefore the decision on margin requirements and haircuts needs to take all of them into account at the same time. The models proposed give a technical solution to the problem of determining haircut levels across different classes of assets.

Next we approach the collateral control problem as an impulse control phenomenon, in order to try and get solutions directly useable in practice for control policies.

18.7   REFERENCES

Benjamin, Daniel K, 1978, "The Use of Collateral to Enforce Debt Contracts", *Economic Inquiry*, **16** (3), July, 333–59.

Bester, Helmut, 1994, "The Role of Collateral in a Model of Debt Renegotiation", *Journal of Money, Credit & Banking*, **26** (1), February, 72–86.

Broadie, M., P. Glasserman and S. Kou, 1997, "A Continuity Correction For Discrete Barrier Options", *Mathematical Finance*, **7** (4), October, 325–49.

Cossin, D. and F. Aparicio, 1999, "Control of Credit Risk Collateralization using Quasi Variational Inequalities", IGBF *Working Paper*, University of Lausanne.

Cossin, D. and F. Aparicio, 2000, "Optimal Control of Credit Risk, Security Collateralization, Deposit Insurance and Other Financial Guarantees", Advances in Computational Management Science series (AICM), Kluwer, forthcoming.

Cossin, D. and T. Hricko, 1999, "Pricing Credit Risk With Risky Collateral: A Methodology for Haircut Determination", *Working Paper*, HEC, University of Lausanne.

Cossin, Didier and Hugues Pirotte, 1997, "Swap Credit Risk: An Empirical Investigation on Transaction Data", *Journal of Banking & Finance*, **21** (10), October, 1351–73.

Cossin, D. and H. Pirotte, 1998, "How Well Do Classical Credit Risk Models Fit Swap Transaction Data?", *European Financial Management Journal*, **4** (1), March, 65–78.

Cox, J. C., Ingersoll, J. E and S. A. Ross, 1981, "The Relation between Forward Prices and Futures Prices", *Journal of Financial Economics*, **2**, December, 321–46.

19
Credit Risk Collateral Control as an Impulse Control Problem

We present here a different attempt at modelizing what should impact the decision to ask for more or less collateral during the lifetime of a credit-risky contract. We follow Cossin and Aparicio (1999). We show how the model can be thought of as an impulse control problem and present the Cossin and Aparicio approach to solve it. It is not a full structural model, but some structural parts of credit risk pricing can be incorporated. The general model presented here can be applied to a wide range of specific situations, for the control of credit risk or of any short position in financial guarantees. It can be used for ongoing control (i.e. impulse control) or for optimal seizure timing (i.e. stopping time). There are many other examples of optimal stopping/ impulse control problems in the finance literature and elsewhere. The more well-known applications include portfolio selection with transaction costs (Duffie and Sun, 1990, Grossman and Laroque, 1990, Eastham and Hastings, 1988, Hindy and Huang, 1992). Other applications include American option pricing (optimal stopping), exchange rate regulation (Flood and Garber, 1989), quality control problems (Anderson and Friedman, 1977), and inventory management (Harrison et al., 1983). This model is the first one we know of that applies the concept to credit risk and guarantee control problems.

Credit risk pricing, following Merton's terminology, corresponds to the pricing of a short position in a financial guarantee. Any long position in a credit-risky contract can be considered identical to a portfolio of a long position in a riskless contract and a short position in a guarantee (Merton and Bodie, 1992). As such, the pricing research on credit risk is valid, with slight modification to fit the institutional context, for pricing the guarantees that pervade financial contracts, such as letter-of-credit guarantees, mortgage guarantees, swap guarantees, public guarantees (such as for deposit insurance, pension benefits, etc.), and all the implicit embedded guarantees that appear in a risky contract (see Hirtle, 1987 for a survey of guarantees). Many applications using traditional financial engineering on the Merton approach to pricing credit risk and guarantees have been developed for each of these situations (e.g. Jones and Mason, 1980 on classical debt, Cooper and Mello 1991 on swap credit risk, Hsieh et al., 1994 on PBGC insurance premiums, Marcus and Shaked, 1984 and Crouhy and Galai, 1991 on deposit insurance).

Cossin and Aparicio (1999) use the methodology of quasi-variational inequalities (as developed in Bensoussan and Lions, 1982, Glowinski et al., 1981, and Hlaváćek et al., 1988). They also provide the numerical analysis of a simple setup of the problem and discuss the type of results our analysis provides. This chapter thus presents a framework that should be thought of as a basis to be refined for practical use. As a first try at handling the problem, the Cossin and Aparicio (1999) paper does not pretend to offer a solution to all the dimensions of a rather complex problem. Many refinements and extensions could be the topic of further research.

The chapter is organized as follows: we first introduce the model's setup and different approaches available to tackle the problem. Next we develop the quasi-variational inequality (QVI) in the full observation case, followed by its numerical analysis in a simple situation. We then analyze some basic results on this example, before describing the important and most pertinent case of partial observations, as in practice observations will not always be cost-free.

19.1   THE MODEL'S SETUP

Cossin and Aparicio (1999) consider one party exposed to the credit risk, also called the guarantor (the agent that is short the guarantee) and one party that provides the credit risk, also called the guaranteed party (long the guarantee). The guarantor is thus the credit risk-exposed agent, while the guaranteed party is the party giving the credit risk exposure. We use this guarantee terminology to stress the wide range of applications of the models and to keep the Merton terminology. This credit risk exposure is homogeneous to the guarantor issuing a guarantee to the guaranteed party with a lifetime of T, where T might be infinite. T can also be considered as the maturity of the financial contract on which the credit risk bears.

Suppose formally that the guaranteed party has net assets (i.e. assets less liabilities) securing the contract with aggregate market value at time t given by $y(t)$. Here $y(t)$ is thus the value of the collateral to the credit risk at any time t; $y(t)$ is stochastic as the collateral can consist of a number of different assets (stocks, bonds, derivatives) or any portfolio of these.

Cossin and Aparicio (1999) consider at this stage a situation in which a number of simplifying assumptions occur that make calculations easier (although many could be relaxed, as discussed later):

• The *guarantor*, the party exposed to the credit risk, does not present credit risk itself. We thus avoid the problem of two-sided credit risk, as it appears in swaps for example.
• The contract considered is a bullet contract and the *credit risk*, or the *guarantee*, bears on a payment at time T (a setup similar to Merton, 1974).
• The contract also bears on the *value of the collateral* so that the only stochastic process that affects its credit risk at this point is $y(t)$ (a setup also similar to Merton, 1974, and valid, for example, for debt secured by the assets of the issuer).
• We consider a situation where the value of the collateral $y(t)$ has *well-known dynamics* that we define later.
• There is *no gaming*. This is a major assumption in the partial observations case. Posting collateral with a third party would satisfy this assumption.

19.1.1   The Cost of the Guarantee or Credit Risk Cost

We assume that the credit risk-exposed party's objective is to control the evolution of its credit risk cost or the cost of the guarantee over time. Cossin and Aparicio (1999) define the instantaneous evolution of the cost to the guarantor of covering the guarantee as $f(y(t), t)$. The running cost $f(y(t), t)$ depends on the level of the collateral, $y(t)$. Although we are not explicit at this stage what the instantaneous cost of credit risk is, and thus derive general results, one should rely on the credit risk pricing literature as quoted above to define the objective function more precisely. We give a numerical example of analysis later relying on a simple interpretation of Merton (1974). The programs developed below are not dependent on the specific choice of the objective function.

The expected evolution of the cost to the credit risk-exposed party of the guarantee over its lifetime with no audits and no action to control the assets' behavior, and with $y(0) = x$, is therefore:

$$E_x \int_0^T f(y(t), t)dt, \tag{19.1}$$

where the expectation operator E_x carries over all possible trajectories of the process $y(t)$ starting at $y(0) = x$.

19.1.2   The Cost of Information

The optimal program will be different for situations in which information involves costs and when it does not. The cost of information can be divided between the cost of knowing which assets the guarantor can control and knowing how these assets behave (i.e. how much they are worth). There are some pertinent cases where there is actually almost no cost to gathering information: for example, when the collateral is well defined and consists of traded assets (e.g. a portfolio of publicly traded stocks securing a loan). The credit risk-exposed party can then obtain the market value of the assets traded at virtually no cost. This is our full observation case.

In other cases, the credit risk-exposed party will not have free access to the collateral's valuation. This is our partial observations case. In that case, the guarantor will obtain what is assumed to be reliable information through costly audits. Under these conditions, the guarantor cannot monitor the assets continuously (at finite cost). Instead the guarantor faces a trade-off between the high costs of more audits versus the costs of a decision based on less information.

We first work out the full observation case, including a numerical analysis example of a simple situation, and then show how the framework can be extended to the partial observations situation.

19.1.3   Forms of Control

Cossin and Aparicio (1999) formalize the control part as an impulse given on the level of the collateral's dynamics by the credit risk-exposed party (guarantor) with some cost. At discrete times, the credit risk-exposed party can ask for extra collateral (as in a margin call). The cost of doing this (both administrative and competitive costs) limits the credit risk-exposed party's opportunity to lower its credit risk exposure.

Note that some control could theoretically be effected on the variance of the collateral rather than on its level: for example, the credit risk-exposed party could ask for extra collateral in government bonds rather than in stocks. At this point we do not model this form of control. It is here assumed that control is effected on the level of the assets, not on their variance.

19.2   SOLUTION APPROACHES

Cossin and Aparicio (1999) handle the control of credit risk via collaterization using *stochastic control* techniques. We focus on two particular forms of stochastic control: *impulse control* and *optimal stopping*. In this section, we briefly define our problem, discuss two different avenues of approach to impulse control, and finally we focus on a characterization of optimality in terms of the so-called QVIs, following the Bensoussan and Lions (1982) methodology.

19.2.1   Defining the Problem in the Full Observation Case

The problem consists in deciding when to intervene on the fully observable value of CCR exposure along its lifetime, T (in the partial observation case, where the guarantor can only monitor the value of the guarantee through costly audits, the problem consists also in deciding when it is best to audit). First of all, we have the value of the collateral at time t, $y(t)$, modeled as a *diffusion* with drift and diffusion parameters, $\alpha(y(t), t)$ and $\sigma(y(t), t)$, respectively, and which depend on the underlying process. This means that when no control is exerted one has

$$dy(t) = \alpha(y(t), t)dt + \sigma(y(t), t)dz(t),$$

where $z(t)$ denotes the standard Wiener process. When control can be exerted through the parameters, we obtain for the *controlled diffusion* the model

$$dy(t) = \alpha(y(t), e(t), t)dt + \sigma(y(t), e(t), t)dz(t), \tag{19.2}$$

where $e(t)$ is an admissible control law, that is one which is nonanticipative with respect to the process $z(t)$. Note that unless $\sigma(y, t) \equiv 0$, realizations of the process $y(t)$ cannot be forced to be nonnegative with this model. To make sure that $y(t)$ is always positive, we can choose a GBM for $y(t)$.

In the impulse control problem, the control law will take the form of a *jump process*, which means that we can write $y(t)$ as

$$y(t) = y(0) + \int_0^t \alpha(y(s), e(s), s)ds + \int_0^t \sigma(y(s), e(s), s)dz(s) + J(t),$$

where the jump intensity at time t, $J(t)$, will depend on the value of the process just before t, $y(t^-)$. The jump process can be represented by a sequence of jump amplitudes, ϕ_i, and of *stopping times*, θ_i, at which the jumps affect the evolution of the process. In the optimal stopping problem, the control law will consist in seizing the assets at a given instant $\tau \leqslant T$, which is again a *stopping time*. As a consequence, the guarantee will have an effective lifetime of $T \wedge \tau = \min(T, \tau)$.

The credit risk-exposed party's decision criterion can be put into the form of minimizing a cost, part of which is a continuous cost at a rate $f(y(t), t)$. As the evolution of the value of the assets $y(t)$ is unknown, the guarantor's criterion consists in minimizing the expected cost over the lifetime of the guarantee.

In the impulse control case, there is a discrete control cost, $c(\phi_i, \theta_i)$, which depends on the required increase in $y(t)$, that is, ϕ_i, incurred at the chosen intervention or control times, θ_i. The objective function becomes therefore

$$E_x\left(\int_0^T f(y(t),\,t)\,dt + \sum_{i=1}^N c(\phi_i,\,\theta_i)\,\exp(-r\theta_i)\right) \tag{19.3}$$

with

$$dy(s) = \alpha(y(s),\,s)\,ds + \sigma(y(s),\,s)\,dz(s) + \sum_{i=1}^N \delta(s - \theta_i)\phi_i,$$

where y is the controlled process, with $y(0) = x$, where $\delta(s)$ is the delta of Dirac at time s, where r denotes the time value of money, and N is the number of jumps required, which together with ϕ_i and θ_i, are control variables. Here, the summation term has the effect of discouraging too frequent interventions. Note that the cost of the control at any time must be discounted back to its present value, hence the term $\exp(-r\theta_i)$.

In the optimal stopping problem, there is a single undiscounted discrete cost, $g(y(T \wedge \tau),\, T \wedge \tau)$, which is the cost of seizure at time τ. The cost to be minimized corresponds in this case to

$$J' = E_x\left(\int_0^{T \wedge t} f(y(t),\,t)\,dt + g(y(T \wedge \tau),\,T \wedge \tau)\,\exp(-r(T \wedge \tau))\right),$$

where the only control parameter is τ, that is, the set of admissible controls is a set of stopping times.

Given the previous variables, our impulse control problem can be stated as the minimization of the given objective function with constraints. According to *Bellman's principle of optimality*, this amounts to determining $\forall x,\,t$, the function $u(x,\,t)$, defined as

$$u(x,\,t) = \min_{\theta_i,\,\phi_i,\,N}\, E\left(\int_t^T f(y(s),\,s)\,ds + \sum_{i=1}^N c(\phi_i,\,\theta_i)\,\exp(-r(\theta_i - t))\right), \tag{19.4}$$

subject to

$$dy(s) = \alpha(y(s),\,s)\,ds + \sigma(y(s),\,s)\,dz(s) + \sum_{i=1}^N \delta(s - \theta_i)\phi_i$$

with $y(0) = x$, and where $\delta(s)$ is the delta of Dirac at time s. We must bear in mind that all control variables, $\{\theta_i,\,\phi_i,\,N\}_i$, depend on T.

Similarly, our optimal stopping problem amounts to determining:

$$\min_\tau E\left(\int_t^{T \wedge \tau} f(y(t),\,t)\,dt + g(y(T \wedge \tau),\,T \wedge \tau)\,\exp(-r(T \wedge \tau - t))\right), \tag{19.5}$$

subject to

$$dy(s) = \alpha(y(s),\,s)\,ds + \sigma(y(s),\,s)\,dz(s) + dJ(s),$$

where $J(s)$ is the jump process associated with the particular stopping problem.

In both problems, we decide to exert some "discrete control" over the continuous process $y(t)$ as soon as it hits a target set. This is accomplished by introducing one or more jumps at some optimally determined stopping times.

19.2.2 Iteration of a Single Jump Operator

The "single jump operator approach" seems to be the most direct method, but it usually requires a substantial amount of computation.

Let $u(x) = u(x, 0)$, that is, the minimum cost of the guarantee or credit to the guarantor at time 0, knowing that optimal control will be enforced later and that $y(0) = x$. In the more general case of an impulse control problem, this method, proposed in Davis (1993), consists in the iteration of an operator, L, as follows:

$$Lu(x) = \inf_{t < T} E_x \left(\int_0^t f(y(s), s)\, ds + \exp(-rt)\mathbf{M}u(y) \right), \tag{19.6}$$

where $y(t)$ is modeled as a *piecewise-deterministic Markov process* (essentially, a process which is deterministic in between stochastic jumps, where the jump mechanism is determined by two functions, namely, the jump rate and a transition probability measure), x is the initial state of the process, and $\mathbf{M}$ is a nonlinear operator having the form

$$\mathbf{M}u(y) = \inf_z c(z - y) + u(z).$$

Under certain regularity conditions (Davis, 1993), L gives rise to a monotonically decreasing sequence $u_n(x)$, given by $u_{n+1}(x) = Lu_n(x)$, and whose generic term represents the cost of the guarantee to the guarantor when at most n interventions are allowed. This sequence admits an infimum limit value, u_∞, the fixed-point operator of L, whose existence and unicity is shown in Davis (1993). This limit value is called the *value function*, and represents the minimum cost of the guarantee to the guarantor obtained by requiring increases in the value of the assets at a discrete set of optimally chosen stopping times. These intervention times cannot be determined along with the different terms of the guarantee cost sequence, v_n, but need to be obtained as those times at which the present value of the guarantee equals the value function. In the optimal stopping problem, the procedure is similar. Once the value function is determined via iteration of a monotone nonlinear operator, the optimal stopping time is obtained as the instant of time at which the cost function equals the value function (see Davis, 1993, for details).

19.2.3 The Quasi-variational Inequalities (QVIs)

Let $u(x, t)$ denote the minimum cost to the guarantor at time t, knowing that optimal control will be enforced after t, and that $y(t) = x$. An alternative solution approach begins by characterizing the value function of the impulse control or optimal stopping problem as the unique solution of a system of QVIs. This approach was suggested by Bensoussan and Lions (1982) in a theoretical context. Cossin and Aparicio (1999) derive the QVI characterization of the problem. They obtain the correct QVI to consider in order to determine u, which is merely one of stochastic partial differential equations (SPDEs) having the form:

$$\mathbf{A}u - f \leqslant 0, \tag{19.7}$$
$$u - \mathbf{M}u \leqslant 0,$$
$$(\mathbf{A}u - f)(u - \mathbf{M}u) = 0,$$
$$u(y, T) = 0, \forall y \in S,$$

where **M** is a monotone nonlinear operator defined as

$$\mathbf{M}u(y(t), t) = \min_{\phi} \{c(\phi, t) + u(y(t^-) + \phi, t)\} \text{ (impulse control)},$$

$$\mathbf{M}u(y(t), t) = g(y(t), t) \text{ (optimal stopping)},$$

and where **A** is a second-order differential operator having the form

$$Au(y, t) \equiv -\partial u(y, t)/\partial t - \alpha(y, t)\partial(y, t)/\partial y - 1/2\sigma^2(y, t)\partial^2(y, t)/\partial y^2 + r. \quad (19.8)$$

Recall that $u(x, t)$ is the function representing the minimum cost to the guarantor of the guarantee or credit at time t, assuming that optimal control is enforced after this instant of time, and that $y(t) = x$. This function could be defined recursively as

$$u(x, t) = \begin{cases} \min E_x \int_t^{t+\tau} f(y(s), s)\,ds + u(y(t+\tau), t+\tau)\exp(-r\tau), \\ \qquad\qquad\qquad\qquad\qquad \text{if no control in } (t, t+\tau) \\ \min_{\phi} \{c(\phi, t) + u(y(t^-) + \phi, t)\}, \quad \text{if control is needed at } t. \end{cases}$$

The problem is to find the minimum cost of the credit to the guarantor, $u(x, t)$, for any value $x \in S$ of the process at time t, as well as the controls $\{\phi_i, \theta_i\}_i$ achieving that value. This can be solved in two steps. First of all, we obtain the function $u(x, t)\forall t$, $\forall x \in S$, and then we determine the *continuation set*, $\mathcal{C}_{ic}$, defined as

$$\mathcal{C}_{ic} = \left\{(y, t); u(y, t) < \min_{\phi, \phi \neq 0} \{c(\phi, t) + u(y(t^-) + \phi, t)\}\right\}.$$

Secondly, once $\mathcal{C}_{ic}$ has been obtained, the guarantor can, at any time, ascertain whether $y(t)$, the current value of the assets, is such that $(y(t), t) \in \mathcal{C}_{ic}$. If this is the case, the guarantor lets the process evolve naturally (without control). Otherwise, s/he requests an amount of collateral equal to

$$\arg \min_{\phi} \{c(\phi, t) + u(y(t^-) + \phi, t)\}.$$

By proceeding in this way, we can obtain the set of controls needed. In the optimal stopping case, the continuation set has the form

$$\mathcal{C}_{os} = \{(y, t); u(y, t) < g(y, t)\}.$$

In this case the controller or guarantor seizes the assets affecting the credit or guarantee as soon as $(y(t), t)$ is in $\mathcal{C}_{os}$.

It can be shown that the solution to this set of inequalities is the unique fixed point of a concave and monotonically increasing operator, **T**, defined as follows:

$$z \leqslant \int_0^t \exp(-\alpha s)\Phi(s)\,f\,ds + \exp(-\alpha t)\Phi(t)z,$$

$$z \leqslant \mathbf{M}v,$$

$$\mathbf{T}v = z,$$

where Φ denotes a semigroup operator, that is

$$\Phi(0) = \mathbf{I},$$
$$\Phi(t + s) = \Phi(t)\Phi(s),$$
$$\Phi(s)f = E_x(f(y(s), s)),$$
$$\Phi(t)z = z(y(t), t),$$

with $\mathbf{I}$ denoting the identity operator. In other words we must find the unique fixed point of the operator mapping v to z, which, as stated, corresponds to the solution u of

$$\mathbf{A}u - f \leqslant 0, \tag{19.9}$$
$$u - \mathbf{M}u \leqslant 0,$$
$$(\mathbf{A}u - f)(u - \mathbf{M}u) = 0$$

with boundary condition $u(y, T) = 0$, $\forall y \in S$.

19.3   NUMERICAL ANALYSIS OF THE QVI APPROACH

Cossin and Aparicio (1999) use the convergence of a decreasing iterative numerical scheme to find this fixed point as established in Glowinski et al. (1981, lemma 1.2, p. 313). This scheme can be implemented by the so-called *regularization* or *penalization approach* (Bensoussan and Lions, 1973). Under this approach, given a positive real number ξ, we must look for the solution to the equation

$$\mathbf{A}u_\xi + \frac{1}{\xi}(u_\xi - \mathbf{M}u_\xi)^+ = f \tag{19.10}$$

with boundary condition $u(y, T) = 0$, $\forall y \in S$, and where $(a)^+ = \max(a, 0)$.

The penalized numerical scheme based on iterating the solution to

$$\mathbf{A}u_\xi^{(k)} + \frac{1}{\xi}(u_\xi^{(k)} - \mathbf{M}u_\xi^{(k-1)})^+ = f$$

on k, leads to an approximation from above to the expected minimum cost solution, u, that tends toward the latter as $\xi \to 0$ (see Bensoussan and Lions, 1973, Theorem 3).

Cossin and Aparicio (1999) show how to solve numerically our system of QVIs following an appropriate finite-difference approximation scheme. All numerical schemes first proceed by discretizing both the state-space, S, and the time interval $[0, T]$. Our continuous-time process for the assets, $y(t)$, must then be approximated by a *Markov chain*. In this chapter, we consider the uncontrolled process of the value of assets to be a GBM with zero drift, that is, the solution to the SDE:

$$dy(t) = \sigma(y(t), t)dz(t),$$
$$y(0) = x.$$

We can approximate this solution arbitrarily close by letting k be large enough in the discretized process

$$y_t^{(k)} = y_{t-1}^{(k)} + k^{-1/2}\sigma(y(t), t)\epsilon_t,$$
$$y_0^{(k)} = x,$$

where $\{\epsilon_i\}_i$ is an i.i.d. sequence of standard Normal random variables. If we further require that the discretized state-space $S_{\Delta y}$ (where Δy stands for the state-space stepsize) be finite dimensional then we may need to consider a reflecting boundary for the finite state Markov chain, since otherwise the latter could leave $S_{\Delta y}$. This reflecting boundary would project the approximating chain back into $S_{\Delta y}$ as soon as its sample paths leave it. Moreover, this must be done in a way that is consistent with the dynamics of the process. Obviously, considering a reflecting boundary in our problem translates into imposing an additional boundary condition, which we obviate by restricting our analysis to time intervals where the chain remains within $S_{\Delta y}$.

At each iteration (with k denoting the iteration index) we may use two different schemes:

1. The resolution of a variational equality by solving in reverse the SPDE:

$$\mathbf{A}(t_j)u^{(k)}(y_i, t_j) + \frac{1}{\xi_k}(u^{(k)}(y_i, t_j) - \mathbf{M}u^{(k-1)}(y_i, t_j))^+ - f(y_i, t_j) = 0,$$

for a sequence of positive real numbers ξ_k such that $\lim_{k\to\infty} \xi_k = 0$, and for each j on a grid $0 \leqslant i \leqslant n-1$, $1 \leqslant j \leqslant m$, where $y_i < y_{i+l}$, for $l > 0$, and where $t_1 = 0$ and $t_m = T$. This amounts to solving in reverse the system of linear equations,

$$\bar{\mathbf{A}}^{(k)}(t_j)U_j^{(k)} = D_j^{(k)},$$

for each j on the grid $0 \leqslant i \leqslant n-1, : 0 \leqslant j \leqslant m-1$, and where $\bar{\mathbf{A}}$ is the regularized second-order differential operator of the parabolic PDE:

$$\bar{\mathbf{A}}_j = \begin{pmatrix} b_{0,j} & c_{0,j} & 0 & 0 & \cdots & 0 \\ a_{1,j} & b_{1,j} & c_{1,j} & 0 & \cdots & 0 \\ \vdots & \vdots & \vdots & \vdots & \cdots & \vdots \\ 0 & \cdots & 0 & a_{n-2,j} & b_{n-2,j} & c_{n-2,j} \\ 0 & \cdots & 0 & 0 & b_{n-1,j} & c_{n-1,j} \end{pmatrix}$$

and, following the *Crank–Nicholson* discretization scheme:

$$U_j^{(k)} = (u^{(k)}(y_0, t_j), \ldots, u^{(k)}(y_{n-1}, t_j))',$$

$$D_j^{(k)} = (d^{(k)}(y_0, t_j), \ldots, d^{(k)}(y_{n-1}, t_j))',$$

$$d^{(k)}(y_0, t_j) = b_{1,j}^{(k)}u^{(k)}(y_0, t_j) + c_{1,j}u^{(k)}(y_1, t_j),$$

$$d^{(k)}(y_{n-1}, t_j) = a_{n-1,j}u^{(k)}(y_{n-2}, t_j) + b_{n-1,j}^{(k)}u^{(k)}(y_{n-1}, t_j),$$

$$d^{(k)}(y_i, t_j) = -a_{i,j}u^{(k)}(y_{i-1}, t_{j+1}) + \beta_{i,j}u^{(k)}(y_i, t_{j+1}) + T, \quad 0 < i < n-1, \qquad (19.11)$$

$$\text{with } T = -c_{i,j}u^{(k)}(y_{i+1}, t_{j+1}) + f(y_i, t_j) + \frac{1}{\xi_k}\mathbf{1}_{\mathbf{M}u^{(k)}(y_i, t_j) < u^{(k)}(y_i, t_j)}, \qquad (19.12)$$

$$a_{i,j} = -\alpha(y_i, t_j)/4\Delta y + \sigma^2(y_i, t_j)/4(\Delta y)^2,$$

$$b_{i,j}^{(k)} = -1/\Delta t - \sigma^2(y_i, t_j)/2\Delta y^2 + \frac{1}{\xi_k}\mathbf{1}_{\mathbf{M}u^{(k)}(y_i, t_j)<u^{(k)}(y_i, t_j)},$$

$$c_{i,j} = \alpha(y_i, t_j)/4\Delta y + \sigma^2(y_i, t_j)/4\Delta y^2,$$

$$\beta_{i,j} = -1/\Delta t + \sigma^2(y_i, t_j)/2\Delta y^2,$$

and $\Delta y = y_i - y_{i-1}$, $\Delta t = t_j - t_{j-1}$, and with

$$\mathbf{1}_{\mathbf{M}u^{(k)}(y_i, t_j)<u^{(k)}(y_i, t_j)} = \begin{cases} 1, & \text{if } \mathbf{M}u^{(k)}(y_i, t_j) < u^{(k)}(y_i, t_j) \\ 0, & \text{otherwise.} \end{cases}$$

2. The projection of the solution on a constraint set defined by the obstacle. Recall that the obstacle has, in our case, the form

$$\mathbf{M}u(y(t), t) = \inf_\phi [c(\phi) + u(y(t^-) + \phi, t)].$$

The projection is done by selecting at each instant j the solution

$$u_{i,j}^* = \min\{u_{i,j}, \mathbf{M}u_{i,j}\},$$

where $u_{i,j} = u(y_i, t_j)$ is the solution obtained in (1), and $\mathbf{M}u_{i,j} = \inf_\phi [c(\phi) + u(y_i + \phi, t_j)]$.

The method requires a few iterations. At each iteration the two operations (1) and (2) are carried out for each j. The number of iterations required for convergence is usually small (between 5 and 10 iterations were enough for convergence in the experiments). Some convergence results for this iterative method can be found in Glowinski et al. (1981, pp. 181–3). Denoting by $u_{i,j}^{(k)}$ the solution obtained after the kth iteration of the previous two-step procedure, and by $u_{i,j}^{(k+1/2)}$ the Crank–Nicholson solution of step (1), the strategy above ensures that the original variational inequality is satisfied at each iteration, that is,

$$(u_{i,j}^{(k)} - u_{i,j}^{(k+1/2)})(u_{i,j}^{(k+1/2)} - u_{i,j}^{(k)}) \leqslant 0.$$

19.4   SOME NUMERICAL ANALYSIS RESULTS[1]

Cossin and Aparicio (1999) consider an exposure of 100 periods (e.g. 100 days), and, for simplicity, we assume that the exposed party faces a default from the other party when the underlying matures at a level lower than its initial level. Otherwise, the exposed party recovers the initial level of the underlying.

For f, the instantaneous cost function of the guarantee, we rely on the Merton (1974) valuation of credit risk (as Merton's setup is fully compatible with ours) and thus use the theta of a classical Black and Scholes European put. Of course, the vast literature on credit risk previously presented in this book could be a basis of refinement for the target cost function, but we provide here a simple experimentation rather than a definite solution. We consider the impact of changes in economic environment (volatility, interest rates) on the optimal control policy followed by the

---

[1]This part is reproduced by permission from Cossin and Aparicio (1999).

credit risk-exposed party and then analyze the impact of different control cost functions on this optimal policy.

Cossin and Aparicio (1999) analyze the impact of volatility and interest rate changes when the control cost function is $c(\phi) = a + b.\phi$ with $a = b = 0.2$, the maturity of the guarantee is 100 and the GBMs used for the simulation have 0-drift and start at value 1. Statistics are derived on 20 GBM realizations for each change of variable.

19.4.1 Impact of Volatility Changes

Cossin and Aparicio (1999) set $r = 8\%$ and study the impact of increasing the volatility of the underlying GBM from 0.01 to 0.29. An extract of the results is given in Table 19.1. From option theory, we know that the credit risk exposure increases with the volatility. For the same cost function for controls, jumps therefore become relatively less expensive. We would thus expect controls to either become more frequent or larger when volatility increases. Table 19.1 shows that with this cost function both happen. Frequency (total number of jumps/total number of periods) increases markedly from 0.012 to 0.057. The size of the jumps increases from -0.010 to 0.740. (Negative jumps can be expected with this type of cost function, as explained below.) The standard deviation of the size becomes smaller at the same time so that the ratio mean size/ standard deviation increases: jumps become larger and positive. The negative skewness shows that controls smaller than average tend to happen more often than jumps larger than average, and this phenomenon becomes somewhat stronger with increases in volatility. The increase in kurtosis shows that extreme jumps (very small or very large ones) appear more often for higher volatilities. However, neither skewness nor kurtosis appear to be monotonic. Option pricing theory does not give us much insight in arrival times for the controls. Simulations show that the first two moments of arrival times do not seem to be clearly affected by the increase in volatility. The skewness statistic shows that early controls (compared to the mean) happen more with high volatility than with low volatility. The kurtosis statistic also shows a slight increase in extreme values. In other words, controls do not happen earlier on average when volatility increases, but there are more frequent early controls.

19.4.2 Impact of Interest Rate Changes

Using the same control cost function and the same economic environment, but with a volatility of the GBM of 0.02, Cossin and Aparicio (1999) analyze the impact of the increase of interest rates from 0.04 to 0.4 (see Table 19.2 for results). Because the costs of the jumps are discounted to today, we expect an increase in late jumps with an increase in interest rates. Because the cost of the guarantee is decreasing in interest rates, controls become relatively more expensive as interest rates increase, and we thus expect less or smaller jumps with an increase in interest rates. Note that the two effects may interact and fool our expectations. Our results show that control frequency is clearly not affected by the increase in interest rates. The size tends to decrease on average, in line with our second expectation (the ratio mean size/standard deviation decreases even more significantly). Controls tend to become smaller and less significant with an increase in interest rates. The high kurtosis for intermediate values of r shows that extreme jumps occur more often for these values. The arrival time of the controls

Table 19.1 Impact of volatility changes. Impact of changes in volatility of the GBM (with 0 drift) on the frequency, size and arrival time of jumps imposed by the optimal control policy ($T = 100$, 0-drift, $r = 0.08$, $C(\phi) = 0.2 + 0.2\phi$, $y(0) = 1$, statistics taken over 20 different Brownian motions with the same characteristics). Reprinted with authorization from Cossin and Aparicio (1999)

		Mean	Standard deviation	Skewness	Kurtosis
$\sigma = 0.01$	Frequency	0.012			
	size	−0.01	0.541	−2.266	3.517
	Arrival time	53.79	32.6	0.101	−1.61
$\sigma = 0.03$	Frequency	0.016			
	size	−0.147	0.838	−1.137	−0.652
	Arrival time	51.59	37.61	0.115	−1.72
$\sigma = 0.05$	Frequency	0.019			
	size	0.041	0.802	−1.54	0.454
	Arrival time	50.49	35.28	0.043	−1.59
$\sigma = 0.07$	Frequency	0.023			
	size	0.128	0.784	−1.64	0.781
	Arrival time	52.11	35.08	0.051	−1.56
$\sigma = 0.09$	Frequency	0.023			
	size	0.343	0.673	−2.42	4.06
	Arrival time	49.26	34.09	0.115	−1.53
$\sigma = 0.11$	Frequency	0.245			
	size	0.493	0.544	−3.49	10.83
	Arrival time	48.04	32.08	0.149	−1.42
$\sigma = 0.13$	Frequency	0.027			
	size	0.557	0.597	−3.64	11.81
	Arrival time	46.87	30.41	0.124	−1.32
$\sigma = 0.15$	Frequency	0.029			
	size	0.622	0.543	−3.776	13.15
	Arrival time	48.07	29.71	0.091	−1.25
$\sigma = 0.17$	Frequency	0.032			
	size	0.635	0.585	−3.93	14.4
	Arrival time	48.78	29.55	0.028	−1.29
$\sigma = 0.19$	Frequency	0.036			
	size	0.699	0.376	−4.73	24.99
	Arrival time	49.34	28.76	−0.018	−1.25
$\sigma = 0.21$	Frequency	0.39			
	size	0.694	0.442	−4.37	20.79
	Arrival time	49.46	28.74	−0.057	−1.26
$\sigma = 0.23$	Frequency	0.045			
	size	0.644	0.556	−3.64	12.99
	Arrival time	51.67	29.23	−0.077	−1.26
$\sigma = 0.25$	Frequency	0.048			
	size	0.718	0.425	−4.43	20.43
	Arrival time	49.652	28.28	−0.016	−1.22
$\sigma = 0.27$	Frequency	0.052			
	size	0.715	0.494	−4.17	17.95
	Arrival time	50.38	28.28	−0.043	−1.21
$\sigma = 0.29$	Frequency	0.057			
	size	0.74	0.422	−3.77	15.73
	Arrival time	50.92	28.63	−0.045	−1.26

Table 19.2 Impact of interest rate changes. Impact of changes in interest rates on the frequency, size, and arrival time of the jumps imposed by the optimal control policy ($T = 100$, 0-drift, $\sigma = 0.02$, $C(\phi) = 0.2 + 0.2\phi$, statistics taken over 20 different Brownian motions with the same characteristics). Reprinted with authorization from Cossin and Aparicio (1999)

		Mean	Standard deviation	Skewness	Kurtosis
$r = 0.04$	Frequency	0.015			
	size	0.403	0.789	−0.37	−1.88
	Arrival time	53.65	41.09	0.073	−1.84
$r = 0.08$	Frequency	0.012			
	size	−0.112	0.62	−1.444	0.23
	Arrival time	49.13	34.06	0.393	−1.45
$r = 0.12$	Frequency	0.012			
	size	0.115	0.243	−4.145	16
	Arrival time	51.3	27.64	0.318	−1.22
$r = 0.16$	Frequency	0.012			
	size	0.098	0.24	−4.125	15.9
	Arrival time	55.44	26.51	0.201	−1.25
$r = 0.20$	Frequency	0.01			
	size	0.088	0.256	−3.802	13.18
	Arrival time	61.4	24.3	−0.157	−0.971
$r = 0.24$	Frequency	0.01			
	size	0.082	0.255	−3.775	13.05
	Arrival time	69.5	21.01	−0.53	−0.112
$r = 0.28$	Frequency	0.011			
	size	0.077	0.248	−3.885	13.94
	Arrival time	71.9	19.99	−0.448	−0.575
$r = 0.32$	Frequency	0.011			
	size	0.024	0.331	−2.64	5.23
	Arrival time	74.32	19.69	−0.529	−0.429
$r = 0.36$	Frequency	0.01			
	size	0.068	0.259	−3.67	12.198
	Arrival time	74.53	19.54	−0.629	−0.346
$r = 0.40$	Frequency	0.012			
	size	0.02	0.31	−2.804	6.18
	Arrival time	79.71	19.02	−0.919	0.151

increases even more markedly, while its standard deviation decreases monotonically. As interest rates increase, jumps occur later and later. The skewness of arrival times decreases and becomes negative. Although controls tend to happen later on average, early outliers also become more frequent.

19.4.3 Impact of the Cost Function on the Optimal Control Policy

Here f and c are linked and somewhat endogenous: a guarantor may trade off a higher insurance premium (f smaller) for a higher cost of imposing jumps (c larger). A credit risk-exposed party may trade off a more lax collateral policy for a more aggressive pricing of credit risk. We study the impact of the shape of c on the optimal policy, which will help us understand the tradeoff between f and c and the endogeneity that follows. We consider simple cost functions of the shape $c(\phi) = a + b.\phi$ (a fixed cost + a proportional cost, for example a cost of capital on the new capital required) and $c(\phi) = a + b.|\phi|$ (a fixed cost + a transaction cost similar to those observed in trading). Note that the programs can be used with more complex functions. When there are no fixed costs to control (e.g. $c(\phi) = 0.2.|\phi|$) a case similar to proportional costs in a portfolio management setting, the number of jumps is high and their size is small as can be expected. Because there are no fixed costs, very small and frequent controls can occur. As we use discretization, we may not actually obtain, through our analysis, the smallest jumps involved. Note also that the discretization of the numerical analysis does not show jumps as discontinuities while they actually are discontinuous in a continuous setting. Because the credit risk-exposed party always faces positive costs at controlling, jumps are always positive. This situation may not be realistic in our case. When there is a positive cost of capital, there may be advantages of decreasing the amount of collateral as the capital can be used for other purposes. Negative jumps would then occur and a cost function of the type $c(\phi) = a + b.\phi$ may be preferable. One can then compare the different simple forms possible and the impact of higher fixed costs (intuitively we should obtain less controls), higher variable costs (intuitively we should obtain smaller controls), and symmetric versus asymmetric cost function. One can, for example, look at how increasing fixed costs affects the optimal control policy. When there are fixed and proportional costs ($c(\phi) = a + b.\phi$ with $a.b \neq 0$), the controls can become negative. Indeed, the gain in cost of capital from having a lower collateral may overcome both the fixed cost of the control and the increase in cost of the guarantee linked to a lower underlying process. At a low fixed cost the guarantor could profit from negative jumps. For example, an A rated company could take out some capital from its AAA subsidiary while the guarantee of the assets in place in the subsidiary would still be enough to obtain the AAA rating. Theoretically, a change in premium raised by the credit risk-exposed party (a change in f) may be compensated by a change in the costs of control (a change in c) so that the choices of f and c are interdependent. One can use these models to try and test this empirically by studying how a fixed increase in f may be compensated by a change in c. The programs designed can therefore be used by the credit risk-exposed party to compensate for a change in premiums raised by a change in collateralization control costs.

Cossin and Aparicio (1999) also show how the analysis can be extended to the situation of partial observations. In many situations the credit risk-exposed party or guarantor will need to invest an amount of money or management time in order to obtain information on the current position of the collateral's value (or the guaranteed party's assets). This situation changes the program in two different dimensions:

1. The dynamics of the controlled value of the assets, $y(t)$.
2. The costs faced by the guarantor.

Because of these auditing costs, the guarantor will be led to observe the assets' value process, $y(t)$, at only some optimally selected time instants. Clearly, the programs derived under full observation can no longer be used here. A simple change of variable (i.e. considering time elapsed since the last observation and the value at the last observation) make it possible to approach the optimal impulse control problem in a partial observation context as an analogy to the full observation programs.

19.5 CONCLUSIONS

A general framework for the optimal control of credit risk collateralization was developed. The methodology of QVIs as developed by Cossin and Aparicio (1999) was adapted to our problem, and exemplifies a possible approach to impulse control problems in credit risk modeling.

The problem is a complex one. Some assumptions and simplifications were made that may not be fully realistic, but were deemed necessary at this point. Refinements can be added to the model, that would relax these assumptions. Stochastic interest rates, dependence on multiple processes (different risk classes for the credit risk and the collateral risk, or stochastic variance as in Nelson, 1990) or delayed responses to control or audit can be built as interesting extensions. Integrating a full game may also be of interest, as strategic behaviors should affect collateralization policies in some situations.

In brief though, it should appear clear to the reader that rules of thumb for collateral determination, haircut levels, marking-to-market times, and margin calls decisions can rely on a more sophisticated approach than currently carried out. Taking this sophistication to an area where little is yet done can provide a significant competitive advantage.

19.6   REFERENCES

Altman, E. and D. L. Kao, 1992, "Rating Drift in High-Yield Bonds", *Journal of Fixed Income*, March.

Anderson, R. F and A. Friedman, 1977, "A Quality Control Problem and Quasi-Variational Inequalities", *Archive for Rational Mechanics and Analysis*, pp. 205–52.

Anderson, R. W. and S. M. Sundaresan, 1996, "The Design and Valuation of Debt Contracts", *Review of Financial Studies*, **9**, 37–68.

Benjamin, Daniel K, 1978, "The Use of Collateral to Enforce Debt Contracts", *Economic Inquiry*, **16** (3), July, 333–59.

Bensoussan, A. and J. L. Lions, 1973, "Nouvelle formulation de problèmes de contrôle impulsionnel et applications", *C. R. Acad. Sci. Paris*, **276**, 1189–92.

Bensoussan, A. and J. L. Lions, 1982, *Contrôle Impulsionnel et Inéquations Quasi-Variationnelles*, Dunod.

Bester, Helmut, 1994, "The Role of Collateral in a Model of Debt Renegotiation", *Journal of Money, Credit & Banking*, **26** (1), February, 72–86.

Broadie, Mark and Paul Glasserman, 1997, "A Continuity Correction For Discrete Barrier Options", *Mathematical Finance*, **7** (4), October, 325–49.

Cooper, Ian A. and Antonio S. Mello, 1991, "The Default Risk of Swaps", *Journal of Finance*, **46**, 597–620.

Cossin, D. and F. Aparicio, 1999, "Control of Credit Risk Collateralization using Quasi Variational Inequalities", IGBF *Working Paper*, University of Lausanne.

Cossin, D. and F. Aparicio, 2000, *Optimal Control of Credit Risk, Security Collateralization, Deposit Insurance and Other Financial Guarantees*, Advances in Computational Management Science series (AICM), Kluwer, forthcoming.

Cossin, Didier and Hugues Pirotte, 1997, "Swap Credit Risk: An Empirical Investigation on Transaction Data", *Journal of Banking & Finance*, **21** (10), October, 1351–73.

Cossin, D. and H. Pirotte, 1998, " How Well Do Classical Credit Risk Models Fit Swap Transaction Data?", *European Financial Management Journal*, **4** (1), March, 65–78.

Crouhy, M. and D. Galai, 1991, "A Contingent Claim Analysis of a Regulated Depositary Institution", *Journal of Banking and Finance*, **15**, 73–90.

Davis, M. H. A., 1993, *Markov Models and Optimization*, Chapman & Hall, pp. 188–204.

Duffee, G. R., 1995a, "On Measuring Credit Risks of Derivative Instruments", *Working Paper*, Federal Reserve Board, February.

Duffee, G. R., 1995b, "The Variation of Default Risk with Treasury Yields", *Working Paper*, Federal Reserve Board, January.

Duffie, Darrel, 1988, *Security Markets: Stochastic Models*, Academic Press.

Duffie, D. and T. Sun, 1990, "Transactions Costs and Portfolio Choice in a Discrete-Continuous-Time Setting", *Journal of Economic Dynamics and Control*, **14**, 35–51.

Duffie, Darrel and Ming Huang, 1996, "Swap Rates and Credit Quality", *Journal of Finance*, **51** (3), July, 921–49.

Duffie, Darrell and Kenneth J. Singleton, 1997, "An Econometric Model of the Term Structure of Interest-Rate Swap Yields", *Journal of Finance*, **52** (4), September, 1287–321.

Eastham, J. F. and K. J. Hastings, 1988, "Optimal Impulse Control of Portfolios", *Mathematics of Operations Research*, **13** (4).

Flood, R. P. and P. M. Garber, 1989, "The Linkage between Speculative Attack and Target Zone Models of Exchange Rates", *NBER Working Paper*, no. 2918.

Geman, H., N. El Karoui and J. C. Rochet, 1995, "Changes of Numeraire, Changes of Probability Measure and Pricing of Options", *J. Appl. Probab.*, **32**, 443–58.

Glowinski, R., J. L. Lions and R. Trémolières, 1981, *Numerical Analysis of Variational Inequalities*, North-Holland.

Grossman, S. J. and G. Laroque, 1990, "Asset Pricing and Optimal Portfolio Choice in the Presence of Illiquid Durable Consumption Goods", *Econometrica*, **58** (1), 25–51.

Harrison, J. M. and S. R. Pliska, 1981, "Martingales and Stochastic Integrals in the Theory of Continuous Trading", *Stochastic Process. Appl.*, **11**, 215–60.

Harrison, J. M. and S. R. Pliska, 1983, "A Stochastic Calculus Model of Continuous Trading: Complete Markets", *Stochastic Process. Appl.*, **15**, 313–16.

Harrison, J. M., T. Selke and A. Taylor, 1983, "Impulse Control of Brownian Motion", *Mathematics of Operations Research*, **8**, August, 454–66.

Hindy, A. and C. F. Huang, 1992, "Intertemporal Preferences for Uncertain Consumption: A Continuous Time Approach", *Econometrica*, **60** (4), 781–801.

Hirtle, B., 1987, "The Growth of the Financial Guarantee Market", *FRBNY Quarterly Review*, Spring, 10–28.

Hlaváček, I., J. Haslinger, J. Necas and J. Lovísek, 1988, *Solution of Variational Inequalities in Mechanics*, Springer-Verlag.

Hsieh, S-J., A. H. Chen and K. R. Ferris, 1994, "The Valuation of PBGC Insurance Premiums Using an Option Pricing Model", *Journal of Financial and Quantitative Analysis*, **29** (1), 89–99.

Iben, B. and R. Brotherton-Ratcliffe, 1994, "Credit Loss Distributions and Required Capital for Derivatives Portfolios", *Journal of Fixed Income*, June.

Iben, Th. and R. Litterman, 1991, "Corporate Bond Valuation and the Term Structure of Credit Spreads", *Journal of Portfolio Management*, Spring.

Jarrow, Robert and Stuart Turnbull, 1995, "Pricing Derivatives on Financial Securities Subject to Credit Risk", *Journal of Finance*, **50** (1), March, 53–85.

Jarrow, Robert A., David Lando and Stuart M. Turnbull, 1997, "A Markov Model for the Term Structure of Credit Risk Spreads", *Review of Financial Studies*, **10** (2), Summer, 481–523.

Jones, E. P. and S. P. Mason, 1980, "Valuation of Loan Guarantees", *Journal of Banking and Finance*, **4**, 89–107.

Kunitomo, Naoto and Masayuki Ikeda, 1992, "Pricing Options With Curved Boundaries", *Mathematical Finance*, **2** (4), October, 275–98.

Leland, H. and K. Toft, 1996, "Optimal Capital Structure, Endogenous Bankruptcy, and the Term Structure of Credit Spreads", *Journal of Finance*, **51**, July, 987–1019.

Longstaff, F. and E. Schwartz, 1995, "A Simple Approach to Valuing Risky Fixed and Floating Rate Debt", *Journal of Finance*, **50** (3), July.

Longstaff, F. and E. Schwartz, 1995, "Valuing Credit Derivatives", *Journal of Fixed Income*, June, 6–12.

Lucas, D. J. and J. Lonski, 1992, "Changes in Corporate Credit Quality 1970–1990", *Journal of Fixed Income*, March.

Marcus, A. J. and I. Shaked, 1984, "The Valuation of FDIC Deposit Insurance Using Option-pricing Estimates", *Journal of Money, Credit, and Banking*, **16** (4), 446–60.

Margrabe, W., 1978, "The Value of an Option to Exchange One Asset for Another", *Journal of Finance*, **33**, March, 177–87.

Mella-Barral, P. and W. Perraudin, 1997, "Strategic Debt Service", *Journal of Finance*, **52** (2), June, 531–56.

Merton, Robert C., 1974, "On the Pricing of Corporate Debt: The Risk Structure of Interest Rates", *Journal of Finance*, **29**, 449–70.

Merton, R. C. and Z. Bodie, 1992, "On the Management of Financial Guarantees", *Financial Management*, **22**, Winter.

Nelson, D. B., 1990, "Stationarity and Persistence in the Garch (1,1) Model", *Econometric Theory*, **6**, pp. 318.

Plaut, Steven E., 1985, "The Theory of Collateral", *Journal of Banking & Finance*, **9** (3), September, 401–19.

Rich, Don R., 1994, "The Mathematical Foundations of Barrier Option-Pricing Theory", *Advances in Futures and Options Research*.

Shimko, David C., Naohiko Tejuna and Donald Von Deventer, 1993, "The Pricing of Risky Debt When Interest Rates are Stochastic", *The Journal of Fixed Income*, September, 58–65.

Sorensen, Eric H. and Thierry F. Bollier, 1994, "Pricing Swap Default Risk", *Financial Analysts Journal*, May–June, 23–33.

Stulz, René and Herb Johnson, 1985, "An Analysis of Secured Debt", *Journal of Financial Economics*, **14**, 501–21.

Part Six
Management of Credit Risk

20
Advanced Management Tools

20.1 INTRODUCTION

Once made the extensive presentation of existing modeling alternatives for the pricing of credit spreads and the derivation of credit term structures for individual defaultable bonds and other credit-sensitive instruments, assessing the credit risk exposure of an overall portfolio is certainly the next necessary step.

In fact, credit risk in a portfolio is difficult to assess and even to define. From a credit perspective, a portfolio can be risky because it is highly concentrated in some markets and industries, or geographically. As an example, we can think of some specific regional banks in the US[1] or of local banks in Europe (such as the Raiffeisen banks in Switzerland) which are traditionally located in agricultural areas. Their portfolios are naturally concentrated, and in order to diversify their risks, they will try to sell them against others. Which others? What kind of choice do we have to make? What is a diversified portfolio in credit risk terms? A natural answer is to look at credit rating migrations computed by Standard & Poors or Moody's. Also, portfolio analysis will require not only the migrations themselves but the correlation of the migrations as well. Thus, standing on credit ratings, a diversified portfolio would mean having counterparties from different classes, with optimization on the correlation side. On the one hand, this is admitting that all counterparties in the same rating class have the same creditworthiness and credit behavior, whatever their activity and their size. On the other hand, this is forgetting that credit risk is more a loss aversion issue than a risk aversion issue[2]. Setting apart the problems of liquidity, with a pure "market-risky" position, you just know that you take a bet on having more with the possibility of having less at the end. With a pure "credit-risky" position, if you invest in a risky bond, you will earn a known spread under the condition of no default prior to the maturity. More precisely, what does a negative correlation between the migration behavior of an AAA counterparty to another class and the behavior of a B counterparty really represent? Moreover, nothing safeguards us from having these two counterparties defaulting at the same time, even if their probabilities of such an event are very different from each other. And here is where credit risk is inherently linked to liquidity. From this perspective, credit risk is the risk of collusion, and managing it is more an insurance problem than a hedging problem. In fact, whenever it is easy to relate market risks to interest rate, foreign exchange and stock market exposures, credit risk can appear to us as quite specific. Hedging perfectly a particular credit risk would be finding a claim in which the payoff is perfectly related to the payoff profile of this position, namely through credit derivatives, position by position, instead of on the overall portfolio credit exposure.

---

[1] The general bankruptcy of pension funds in the US and the management of such stress situations by the Federal Deposit and Insurance Commission (FDIC) is a good example of a typical unwanted scenario.

[2] See Jonathan Shalev's paper entitled "Loss Aversion Equilibrium" (1997).

There seems to be, however, some systemacy in credit risk which could be explained by the state of the economy or business cycle effects. This dependence is unfortunately missing in almost all of the models that will be presented here, as well as the use of stochastic interest rates. Interactions between market and credit risks are still not offered by any of the available approaches although covered in the works of several authors. The dependence on the state of the economy has already been documented in Chapter 12. The use of deterministic interest rates is quite controversial since many of the instruments subject to credit risk are in fact interest-rate sensitive ones. For individual stocks, we have already seen that some modeling approaches include a correlation parameter, as if interest rates could have an influence on the creditworthiness of the firm. But, relying on equilibrium considerations as in Sundaresan (1999), we know that the existence of a systematic credit risk in the corporate bond market will induce offer and demand effects on the term structure of interest rates itself[3].

There is still another source of great complexity when trying to develop an integrated portfolio management method for credit risk. A portfolio of a certain size will only be rarely composed of linear exposures to credit risk. Many of the positions can include special covenants, with different degrees of priority at default, the specification of guarantees and collateral, the use of marking-to-market, netting provisions, and also a linkage to investment activities which makes difficult to isolate the impact of credit risk.

20.1.1   The Regulatory Requirements

Now that the major G-10 banks have adopted the BIS 98 (the "Capital Accord") principles for market risks purposes, "general" and "specific", and for capital requirements with respect to the trading book, the time has come to develop some kind of credit VaR framework. Under BIS 98, capital requirements for "specific" risk are not very precise and it is merely argued that an internal model should appropriately take into account "concentration risk", "downgrade risk", and "spread risk". For this specific risk the required capital was equal to four times the sum of the VaRs (at the 99% confidence level) over a 10-day time horizon for "spread risk", "downgrade risk", and "default risk". Some preliminary observations can be made with respect to this restrictive view of credit risk:

- Since markets risks and credit risk are interconnected, we know from earlier chapters that the spreads would result from a mixture of them. In particular, the spreads are not constant across the whole term structure of interest rates. On the other side, downgrade risk is purely related to the credit component of the credit spread. Whenever a firm is downgraded, its required spread over the riskfree government rate increases in the market[4]. This will lead to a double-counting problem, as noted by Crouhy et al. (2000). Note also that BIS 98 assimilates the market component of the "spread risk" to credit risk while attributing to it a multiplier of four instead of three as with other market risks.
- While these different risks are different overlapping facets of the same problem, i.e. the risk of migrating to another credit standing, "default risk" should also be

---

[3]Therefore, implicitly assuming that traditional term structure modeling misses some informational content.
[4]Nothing preserves the overall market from suffering a general downgrade given a particularly strong recession phase of the economy.

considered. It is, however, easy to see "default risk" as a particular stage of migration, i.e. an absorbing state in Markovian jargon. Default is the only state where migration to another credit standing has a null probability of occurring. As an example, structural models work on the "default risk" and the path of the assets value of the firm until maturity with respect to some threshold value, defines a continuous evolution of the credit standing[5]. The term structure of credit spreads obtains as a consequence of this expected behavior. In reduced-form models, the spread behavior is directly modeled, and Duffie and Lando (1997) have shown that default and migration characteristics can be recovered in reverse. In the models that we will be studying, the credit state space is discretized (through rating classes) and "default" is one of the states to migrate to.

- The final observation comes from the empirical evidence already presented in Chapter 12. Ratings are laggish and markets seem to be more efficient in integrating new credit information than rating agencies. The advantage of this is that markets offer then a reliable source of continuous information that a model could use in turn to infer some implicit structure. The disadvantage is that this urges us to be able to disentangle market and credit risk components in financial time series.

With its new document release in April 1999, the Task Force of the Basle Committee has opened the door for discussion on the potential offered by credit risk modeling approaches to be used in the "supervisory oversight of banking organisations" (see BIS, 1999). This new orientation comes out because of the increasing use by world leading banks of such portfolio models for their credit risk monitoring and management processes, risk-based pricing, customer profitability analysis, credit value of customers' investment portfolios, and so forth. These models are imposing a new standard for internal management and therefore the Basle Committee has recognized that some gap exists with respect to previous BIS 98 principles for capital requirements, from a credit risk perspective. However, before the acceptance of such models, the Task Force of the Basle Committee must be assured that:

- the models "are conceptually sound", and "empirically validated", and that
- they will produce comparable requirements across the different institutions, since the objective should not be to favour any one institution.

For these reasons, this Task Force has presented a summary of the available methodologies asking for more precision on the problem of data availability when implementing these models and pointing out the necessary process of model validation. These two problems are seen as the main impediments to the incorporation of credit risk models into capital regulatory requirements, as has been the case with market risks. In terms of data availability, the scarcity of historical data, the survivorship bias in this data, the longer time horizon on which credit risk operates, etc. require assumptions and proxies that could largely reduce the reliability on these models in providing consistent estimates and sensitivities. In terms of model validation, the longer time horizons require unaffordable long time series where the potential existence of switching regimes reduce considerably the validity of backtesting. The report is therefore a

---

[5]Continuous in time and in state space.

submission to open the dialog with a survey on the internal modeling practices of 20 large banks in 10 countries.

20.1.2 Available Approaches to Portfolio Credit Risk

In contrast to BIS 98, the Task Force expects from these models to:

- Offer to the bank a framework to examine credit exposures across geographical regions and product lines in a timely manner, "centralizing data on global exposures and analysing marginal and absolute contributions to risk".
- Provide estimates of credit risk reflecting the diversification of concentration risk compared to nonportfolio approaches.
- Be designed in such a way that they are sensitive to "shifts in business lines, credit quality, market variables, and the economic environment".
- Offer "the incentive to improve systems and data collection efforts, a more informed setting of limits and reserves, more accurate risk and performance-based pricing for a more transparent decision-making process, and a more consistent basis for economic capital allocation".
- Provide overall "rigor and consistency of the risk management processes". The Task Force thinks that capital requirements will be more aligned with the perceived riskiness of the portfolio of the institution. This will also give a clearer picture of the sources of capital requirements while distributing more efficiently the capital in the business operating cycle of the financial institution. Finally, they argue that the flexibility of these models in adapting to the environment will deter "regulatory capital arbitrage".

The main methodologies which the Task Force refers to are:

- CreditMetrics^{TM} initially from JP Morgan in partnership with Bank of America, BZW, Deutsche Morgan Grenfell, KMV Corporation, and the old Swiss Bank Corporation and Union Bank of Switzerland[6]. A model analog to CreditMetrics^{TM} is that developed internally by the Canadian Imperial Bank of Commerce and presented in Crouhy et al. (2000), CreditVaR I and II. The latter is an extension that takes into account stochastic interest rates for the case of credit-sensitive derivatives such as forwards or swaps.
- KMV's methodology by KMV Corporation.
- CreditRisk +^{TM} from Credit Suisse Financial Products (CSFP)[7].
- CreditPortfolioView^{TM} developed by Tom Wilson and proposed by McKinsey & Company.

20.2   CreditMetrics^{TM} (AND CreditVaR I)

20.2.1 Introduction

CreditMetrics^{TM} is based on credit migrations not provided by the RiskMetrics group and that can be independently developed by users or obtained from rating agencies.

---

[6]CreditMetrics is today a trademark of the RiskMetrics Group, a spinoff from JP Morgan. All the technical documentation is freely available at http://www.creditmetrics.com/research/techdocs/.

[7]Technical documentation can be found at http://www.csfp.csh.com/.

Typically, the migrations are calculated for a one-year time horizon from a rating category to another based on the rating notation of Standard & Poors: AAA, AA, A, BBB, BB, B, CCC. An additional category (eighth) represents the "default" state, D, which is an absorbing state. CreditMetrics^{TM} computes the forward distribution of values of the loan portfolio, given that the transition probabilities are estimated from historical data and that the correlation between the behaviors of the ratings classes are directly inferred from stock market data as a proxy for the assets value of the firms. Interest rates are, however, supposed to be deterministic. The CreditVaR estimate is then simply the percentile of the generated distribution for some level of confidence.

20.2.2   The Framework

The main objective of the framework is the production of a consistent forward distribution of changes in value of the credit portfolio for an arbitrary chosen one-year time horizon[8]. Consistency means that it is not justified to assume normally distributed changes of the portfolio when these are driven by credit risk. Credit returns are highly skewed and fat-tailed, and therefore we need more than the two first moments of the distribution to estimate the percentile levels (see Figure 20.1)[9]. Moreover, as we will show hereafter, with more than two credit-risky positions, the inference of the VaR result from the returns of the portfolio requires a simulation of the whole distribution.

Let us review CreditMetrics^{TM}'s framework for a single straight corporate bond first. All parts of the presentation will be presented as step procedures to ensure its clarity for the purpose of a real implementation, in the manner of Crouhy et al. (2000).

The Case of a Single Bond

Let us return to the example provided in the CreditMetrics^{TM} documentation for the purpose of *the* illustration of the different steps: consider a senior unsecured BBB rated bond with a remaining maturity of five years and offering an annual coupon rate of 6%.

Step 1 First, since the whole framework relies on a transition matrix across credit ratings, it is necessary to specify the rating system under which we want to operate: Moody's, Standard & Poors, or the internal rating system defined by the institution. Every component (transition probabilities, forward discount structures, correlations) will then be related to one of the categories of the rating scheme chosen.

Whatever the choice made, it supposes that the migration probabilities computed on historical data or any other way are available. However, because of the problem of the deterministic separation into rating classes, the use of an internal estimation of default and transition probabilities could add more relevance if computed with respect to the typical loan or bond portfolio composition of the bank. Such a matrix is provided in Table 20.1.

---

[8]This choice is not a hazard. It comes from the fact that the most frequent revision of credit ratings is at most once per year.

[9]Typically a straight corporate bond will suffer from downgrading and default, but its upper value is capped so that there is little to be expected from the upside appreciation against the downside risk borne. Again, it is related to the notion of "loss aversion" instead of the traditional "risk aversion".

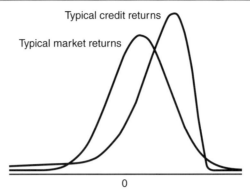

Figure 20.1 Typical distribution for credit and market risks. Adapted from CreditMetrics[TM] document

Table 20.1 Matrix of one-year transition probabilities

Initial rating	Rating at year-end (%)							
	AAA	AA	A	BBB	BB	B	CCC	Default
AAA	90.81	8.33	0.68	0.06	0.12	0	0	0
AA	0.70	90.65	7.79	0.64	0.06	0.14	0.02	0
A	0.09	2.27	91.05	5.52	0.74	0.26	0.01	0.06
BBB	0.02	0.33	5.95	86.93	5.30	1.17	1.12	0.18
BB	0.03	0.14	0.67	7.73	80.53	8.84	1.00	1.06
B	0	0.11	0.24	0.43	6.48	83.46	4.07	5.20
CCC	0.22	0	0.22	1.3	2.38	11.24	64.86	19.79

Source: Adapted from Standard & Poors' CreditWeek (April 15, 1996).

This matrix in Table 20.1 is supposed to be given by some credit risk data provider such as Standard & Poors. This matrix is typically computed from historical data.

In order to appraise the importance of the time horizon, ratings agencies also disclose tables on the cumulated default numbers on different time lengths.

Also, since these probabilities are historically estimated to be used in a framework for valuation of the "forward credit risk", the level of the probabilities could be adapted to the current conditions of the actual state of the economy. For example, matrices by business cycle, by country, by industrial sector can be built using an ordered probit technology as proposed and demonstrated in Nickell et al. (2000).

Step 2 The time horizon over which we want to calculate the credit exposure should be specified. A one-year horizon is commonly chosen because of the nature of the historical data needed for the estimation of default and transition probabilities. On one side, huge amounts of data are necessary. On the other hand, these data are not recorded frequently since credit events are expected to be, by nature, rare events.

For clarity, we will assume that a one-year risk horizon is chosen for the rest of the presentation.

Table 20.2 Forward risky discount term structures

Category	Year 1	Year 2	Year 3	Year 4
AAA	3.60	4.17	4.73	5.12
AA	3.65	4.22	4.78	5.17
A	3.72	4.32	4.93	5.32
BBB	4.10	4.67	5.25	5.63
BB	5.55	6.02	6.78	7.27
B	6.05	7.02	8.03	8.52
CCC	15.05	15.02	14.03	13.52

Source: CreditMetrics^{TM} technical document.

Step 3 The forward discount curve, for the time horizon chosen and for each category of risky counterparty, has to be entered into the system. This supposes that this input is easily estimable from market data. This will allow us to discount to one year from now, the flow of payments to be received from the counterparty from the next year to the maturity of the bond, considering all the possibilities of ending rating, except for "default", the D rating class. For this latter case, a special treatment is reserved to the so-called "recovery" value at default.

For the non-absorbing states

Table 20.2 gives a list of forward zero curves for our seven categories and for the 4-year period separating our risk horizon from the maturity of the bond.

This input is a major problem since it assumes that the institution has a clear and consistent method to derive the credit spread structures.

With regard to the proposed forward structures, it can be verified that they are consistent with a maturity-increasing spread for all rating classes except for the "CCC" class.

These forward structures are then used to compute the discounted cash-flow (DCF) price of the bond at each alternative ending rating class. As an example, the value of the bond in one year if the counterparty is then rated BB, would be

$$V_{BB} = 6 + \frac{6}{1.0555} + \frac{6}{1.0602^2} + \frac{6}{1.0678^3} + \frac{106}{1.0727^4}$$
$$= 102.02$$

For the default-absorbing state

The value of a "default" is no longer computed under an "ongoing concern" perspective[10]. It is assumed that the seniority would probably be the main determinant of the recovery rate that could be expected from the bond at the default stage. A typical table of mean recovery rates and attached standard deviations for the possible range of seniorities is shown in Table 20.3.

---

[10]This is another assumption. From earlier chapters, we have seen that some propositions assume that, even if there is a high liquidity cost, the defaulted debt still has a market value and therefore historical rates of recovery would not be required.

Table 20.3 Mean recovery rates and their standard deviation

Seniority class	Mean (%)	Standard deviation (%)
Senior secured	53.80	26.86
Senior unsecured	51.13	25.45
Senior subordinated	38.52	23.81
Subordinated	32.74	20.18
Junior subordinated	17.09	10.90

Source: Carty and Liebermann 1996, Moody's Investors Service.

Table 20.4 Distribution of the attainable value of a BBB rated par bond in one year

Year-ending rating	Probability of ending state (p_i)	Forward bond value (in $) B_i
AAA	0.02	109.37
AA	0.33	109.19
A	5.95	108.66
BBB	86.93	107.55
BB	5.30	102.02
B	1.17	98.10
CCC	0.12	83.64
D	0.18	51.13

Source: CreditMetrics™ technical document.

The final distribution of values given the ending rating is presented in Table 20.4.

Step 4   From this distribution, we can extract three different statistics: the compounded mean of changes, the standard deviation of credit quality changes, and the percentile level of our distribution corresponding to the desired confidence level (the CreditVaR)[11]:

$$\mu_B = Mean\ B = \sum_i p_i B_i = 107.09 \tag{20.1}$$

$$Std\ deviation = \sqrt{\sum_i p_i(B_i - \mu_B)^2}$$

$$= \sqrt{\sum_i p_i B_i^2 - 2\sum_i p_i B_i \mu_B + \sum_i p_i \mu_B^2}$$

$$= \sqrt{\sum_i p_i B_i^2 - 2\mu_B^2 + \sum_i p_i \mu_B^2}$$

$$= \sqrt{\sum_i p_i B_i^2 - 2\mu_B^2 + \mu_B^2 \sum_i p_i}$$

$$= \sqrt{\sum_i p_i B_i^2 - \mu_B^2}$$

$$= 2.99.$$

---

[11] Note that Crouhy et al. derive analogous statistics, but for changes in value instead of value levels.

The first percentile level which would correspond to the lowest value of the bond at a "sure" 99% confidence level, is 83.64, i.e. a loss of 23.91.

The previous standard deviation formula does not take into account any uncertainty on the recovery value at default. A modified version accounting for this would be

$$\text{Std deviation} = \sqrt{\sum_i p_i(B_i^2 + \sigma_{B_i}^2) - \mu_B^2}, \qquad (20.2)$$

where $\sigma_{B_i}^2$ takes a null value for all rating classes but "default" with a value then of 25.45. In our example, equation (20.2) would produce a value of 3.18[12].

The Case of a Loan or Bond Portfolio

Now, suppose that we want to introduce a second bond instrument in our portfolio, let us say an A rated 5% bond maturing in three years. Unless we do not want to take into account the diversification effects by assuming a null co-movement of these two bonds, we will need estimates of correlations in order to be able to derive the matrix of probabilities for the joint rating changes of these two issues.

The joint probability of a pair of rating alternatives in one year for the two bonds, in the case of no correlation, would be simply the multiplication of both individual probabilities to be at that state in one year for each bond. Suppose the A rated bond has a 2.27% chance of being upgraded to AA, then the joint likelihood of both issues being upgraded by one class would be simply

$$0.14\% = \underbrace{5.95\%}_{BBB \text{ upgraded to } A} \cdot \underbrace{2.27\%}_{A \text{ upgraded to } AA}$$

Table 20.5 provides the results of the computations for all the crossed pairs of alternatives, under the hypothesis of complete independence of the events between obligors.

It can be visually verified that, in Table 20.5, given the null correlation, the most representative probabilities lie in a small center around the value in bold. When assuming some correlation, this zone will be larger on the vertical or on the horizontal axis depending on the level estimated.

Since correlations will clearly be nonstationary because of their dependence among others on the state of the economy, a structural model that would link the default probabilities to fundamentals of the issuing firms such as Merton's model would be welcome[13]. In this respect, CreditMetrics^{TM} and KMV's model follow the same principle although their implementations differ. Given the direct unobservability of the value of the firm which is not traded, CreditMetrics^{TM} use the behavior of equity returns as a direct proxy substituted to the assets value of the firm.

Let us review briefly the principle of using the value of the firm by CreditMetrics^{TM}.

---

[12]Ratings classes except the D class have such a null value on the uncertainty of their value because it is not clear which portion of the risk attached to a rating category is really systematic, while we are discounting the cash flows leading to the different values with still a risky set of forward curves.

[13]See Chapter 3 for a presentation of Merton's methodology.

Table 20.5 Transition matrix with a null correlation between the credit events of both counterparties

		Bond issue #2 (original A)						
	AAA	AA	A	BBB	BB	B	CCC	Default
Bond issue #1 (original BBB)	0.09	2.27	91.05	5.52	0.74	0.26	0.01	0.06
AAA	0.02	0.00	0.00	0.02	0.00	0.00	0.00	0.00	0.00
AA	0.33	0.00	0.01	0.30	0.02	0.00	0.00	0.00	0.00
A	5.95	0.01	0.14	5.42	0.33	0.04	0.02	0.00	0.00
BBB	86.93	0.08	1.98	**79.15**	4.80	0.64	0.23	0.01	0.05
BB	5.30	0.00	0.12	4.83	0.29	0.04	0.01	0.00	0.00
B	1.17	0.00	0.03	1.06	0.06	0.01	0.00	0.00	0.00
CCC	0.12	0.00	0.00	0.11	0.01	0.00	0.00	0.00	0.00
Default	0.18	0.00	0.00	0.16	0.01	0.00	0.00	0.00	0.00

Source: Adapted from CreditMetrics™ document.

A threshold methodology. Under Merton's approach, the value of the assets of the firm follows a GBM such that the value of the firm at any time t is lognormally distributed, and can be expressed as

$$V_t = V_0 \exp\left\{\left(\mu_v - \frac{\sigma_v^2}{2}\right)t + \sigma_v \sqrt{t}Z_t\right\} \tag{20.3}$$

$$= V_0 \exp\{\mu_v' t + \sigma_v \sqrt{t}Z_t\} \tag{20.4}$$

by Itô's lemma, where μ_v is the drift of the instantaneous rate of return on the assets value of the firm, σ_v^2 is their variance, and $Z_t \sim N(0, 1)$. Further assumptions can be found in Chapter 3 such as time continuity, and the liability side of the balance sheet of the firm being financed by a single bond issue and equity which is also continuously traded in a perfectly efficient market and without frictions.

The existence of the bond issue makes default possible in the simple event that the value of the assets of the firm would be insufficient to honor the debt reimbursement. This idea is extended in order to have not only a threshold value to V_t that triggers default, but also thresholds for every rating class. Implicitly, this means that the distance between the assets value and the default threshold defines the rating of the bond issue of the firm. The whole distribution of possible outcomes of the change in the assets value of the BBB firm at a one-year horizon is then sliced into discrete tranches, one for every intermediate rating as Figure 20.2 shows.

These threshold values are easily computable since Z_t is normally distributed. In effect, we can revert equation (20.3) to isolate Z_t, obtaining

$$Z_t = \frac{\ln\left(\frac{V_t}{V_0}\right) - \mu_v' t}{\sigma_v \sqrt{t}} \tag{20.5}$$

$$= \frac{R_t - \mu_v' t}{\sigma_v \sqrt{t}}, \tag{20.6}$$

i.e. the normalized return on assets, over the t time horizon, which is $N(0, 1)$.

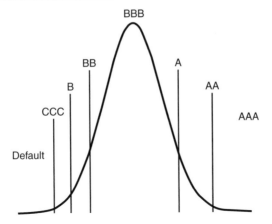

Figure 20.2 Slicing the distribution into ratings bands with thresholds. Adapted from CreditMetrics[TM] document

We are interested in the assets value falling under different critical levels, i.e.

$$P(V_t \leqslant v_i), \tag{20.7}$$

which can be translated into

$$P(V_t \leqslant v_i) \tag{20.8}$$

$$= P(V_0 \exp\{\mu'_v t + \sigma_v \sqrt{t} Z_t\} \leqslant v_i)$$

$$= P\left(Z_t \leqslant \frac{\ln\left(\dfrac{v_i}{V_0}\right) - \mu'_v t}{\sigma_v \sqrt{t}} \right)$$

$$= P(Z_t \leqslant z_i)$$

which is more useful since we know that, for a standard normal random variable, this probability is the cumulative standard normal distribution, $\Phi(z_i)$; $\Phi(\cdot)$ gives the left-hand-side probability surface from $-\infty$ up to z, the normalized "rate-of-change" version of v.

The i critical rate of change in the assets value of the firm is $r_i = \ln(v_i/V_0)$ and leads to some probability given an estimated mean and variance.

In our case, we have to return to the z_i values such that we obtain the probabilities given by the historical estimation of our rating agency (see Table 20.1). Here Φ^{-1} is the inverse cumulative function that allows us to find the implicit z_i for a required cumulative probability:

$$z_i = \Phi^{-1}(P(Z_t \leqslant \tilde{z}_i)), \tag{20.9}$$

where $\tilde{z}_i$ is the critical threshold for the corresponding normalized rate-of-change with mean 0 and variance of 1. The right-hand term of equation (20.9) allows the use of the inverse of the standard cumulative normal distribution and adapt it to our mean-variance case thereafter. To convert the threshold value z_i into the more "self-talking"

Table 20.6 Threshold values for differently rated bond issues

Rating in one year	BBB rated bond issue			A rated bond issue		
	Prob. (%)	Cum. prob. (%)	Thresholds (v)	Prob. (%)	Cum. prob. (%)	Thresholds (v)
Default	0.18	0.18	−2.91	0.06	0.06	−3.24
CCC	0.12	0.30	−2.75	0.01	0.07	−3.19
B	1.17	1.47	−2.18	0.26	0.33	−2.72
BB	5.30	6.77	−1.49	0.74	1.07	−2.30
BBB	86.93	93.70	1.53	5.52	6.59	−1.51
A	5.95	99.65	2.70	91.05	97.64	1.98
AA	0.33	99.98	3.54	2.27	99.91	3.12
AAA	0.02	100.00	$+\infty$	0.09	100.00	$+\infty$

Source: Adapted and recomputed from a CreditMetrics™ document.

critical "rate-of-change" r_i, it suffices to apply back the following change of location and scale based on equation (20.8):

$$r_i = z_i \sigma_v \sqrt{t} + \mu_v' t.$$

Let us now apply this to our case. From here on, we will assume $\mu_v' = 0$ and $\sigma_v^2 = 1$, for the sake of clarity. Moreover, for a one-year time horizon, $t = 1$, which simplifies further the previous notation. Therefore, this allows us to make no distinction between z_i and r_i. For the first threshold value of Figure 20.2, i.e. the theshold corresponding to the probability of being at default from a starting BBB rating, we just need to apply equation (20.9) to the probability of 0.18%. Assuming, we have

$$z_{\text{Def}} = \Phi^{-1}(0.18\%) = -2.9112.$$

Next, the "CCC region" has a 0.12% probability, i.e.

$$P(v_{\text{Def}} < V_t \leqslant v_{CCC}) = \Phi(z_{CCC}) - \Phi(z_{\text{Def}})$$
$$= 0.12\%.$$

Or,

$$\Phi(z_{CCC}) = P(v_{\text{Def}} < V_t \leqslant v_{CCC}) + \Phi(z_{\text{Def}})$$
$$= 0.12\% + 0.18\%$$
$$= P(V_t \leqslant v_{CCC}).$$

For the next thresholds, we only need then to apply the Φ^{-1} function on the cumulated probabilities obtained through our rating agency.

Table 20.6 shows the results for our two obligors. The threshold values should be understood as the critical values until which the rating class is defined. As an example, for a realistic standard deviation of 20% (and still a mean of 0), the default threshold of −2.91 for the BBB counterparty would mean a log-return threshold (r_i) of −60%.

The Computation of Joint Probabilities

Step 1   Joint rating probabilities   To account for correlation into the joint probabilities, we will use the thresholds for each bond issue (or firm) calculated earlier and compute back the probabilities under a bivariate normal distribution. Analogously to the assumption of standard normality of the normalized log-returns of the asset value of each firm, r_{BBB} and r_A, we will consider here their joint normal distribution, which general pdf is

$$\phi(r_{BBB}, r_A, \rho) = \frac{1}{2\pi \sigma_A \sigma_{BBB} \sqrt{1-\rho^2}}$$
$$\cdot \exp -(r_A^2 + r_{BBB}^2 - 2\rho r_A r_{BBB})/(2(1-\rho^2)).$$

For the calculation of the joint probability for each pair of ending ratings in the next table, it suffices to compute the following double integral:

$$P\{S_{BBB}^j, S_A^i\} = \int_{v_A^{i-1}}^{v_A^i} \int_{v_{BBB}^{j-1}}^{v_{BBB}^j} \phi(r_{BBB}, r_A, \rho) \, dr_{BBB} \, dr_A,$$

where S_{BBB}^j and S_A^i are the i ending rating state and the j ending rating state of the BBB rated firm and the A rated firm, respectively. The v variables stand for the threshold values calculated in Table 20.6, and the i and j subscripts refer to the line of the rating class[14]. As an example, the joint probability associated with the ending rating pair $\{BBB_{BBB}, A_A\}$, i.e. a stable credit standing for both firms, with a 20% correlation, would be obtained through the following calculation:

$$P\{BBB_{BBB}, A_A\} = P(-1.49 < r_{BBB} \leqslant 1.53, \, -1.51 < r_A \leqslant 1.98)$$
$$= \int_{-1.51}^{1.98} \int_{-1.49}^{1.53} \phi(r_{BBB}, r_A, 0.2) \, dr_{BBB} \, dr_A$$
$$= 79.37\%.$$

Step 2   Joint probabilities of default   Now that we have the entire range of joint ending ratings probabilities, it could be interesting to analyze the level of default correlation that these values implicitly suppose. In fact, the purpose is to obtain the default correlation between the two obligors from the assumed asset return correlation.

$P\{D_{BBB}, D_A\}$, the joint probability of default, can be used in the following ratio based on the probability theory and the theorem of independence, to obtain the correlation of this joint event:

$$\text{Corr}(D_{BBB}, D_A) = \frac{P\{D_{BBB}, D_A\} - P\{D_{BBB}\}P\{D_A\}}{\sqrt{P\{D_{BBB}\}(1 - P\{D_{BBB}\})P\{D_A\}(1 - P\{D_A\})}} \quad (20.10)$$

Let us consider our case from Table 20.7. We have $P\{D_{BBB}\} = 0.18\%$ and $P\{D_A\} = 0.06\%$. Moreover, let us suppose $\rho = 40\%$ with

---

[14] For the case of the "default" class, $i-1$ and $j-1$ "starting" values are $-\infty$.

Table 20.7 Matrix of transition probabilities with a 20% correlation

Bond issue #1 (original BBB)		Bond issue #2 (original A)								
		AAA	AA	A	BBB	BB	B	CCC	Default	
		0.09	2.27	91.05	5.52	0.74	0.26	0.01	0.06	Total
AAA	0.02	0.00	0.00	0.02	0.00	0.00	0.00	0.00	0.00	0.02
AA	0.33	0.00	0.02	0.30	0.00	0.00	0.00	0.00	0.00	0.33
A	5.95	0.02	0.29	5.49	0.14	0.01	0.00	0.00	0.00	5.95
BBB	86.93	0.07	1.92	79.37	4.65	0.62	0.21	0.01	0.05	86.89
BB	5.30	0.00	0.05	4.67	0.51	0.08	0.03	0.00	0.01	5.35
B	1.17	0.00	0.01	0.99	0.13	0.02	0.01	0.00	0.00	1.17
CCC	0.12	0.00	0.00	0.10	0.02	0.00	0.00	0.00	0.00	0.12
Default	0.18	0.00	0.00	0.15	0.03	0.01	0.00	0.00	0.00	0.18
Total		0.09	2.30	91.06	5.48	0.75	0.26	0.01	0.06	100

Source: Adapted and recomputed from a CreditMetrics™ document.

Table 20.8 Credit risk measures and marginal risk visualization

	BBB bond	A bond	Portfolio	
			Null correlation	20% correlation
Mean	$107.07	$105.17	$212.23	$212.43
Standard deviation	$2.99	$1.48	$3.8682	$3.4737
Percentile level (at 99% confidence)	$98.10	$103.15	$203.3856	$203.3856

$$P\{D_{BBB}, D_A\} = \int_{-\infty}^{-3.24} \int_{-\infty}^{-2.91} \phi(r_{BBB}, r_A, 0.4)\, dr_{BBB}\, dr_A$$

$$= 0.00003056.$$

From equation (20.10), it follows that $\mathrm{corr}(D_{BBB}, D_A) = 2.84\%$, i.e. 14 times smaller than the assumed asset return correlation. The statistical procedure to compute asset correlations is dealt with in section 20.3.

Credit Diversification and the Marginal Risk Measure for Management

The null-correlation matrix is not useless since it can allow us to easily verify the contribution of credit diversification. The 8×8 matrix requires 64 calculations of discounted values of both bonds in each pair of states of nature using the forward curves presented earlier.

Based on the mean and standard deviation formulas in equation (20.1), we can derive the results given in Table 20.8.

Another interesting analysis is the marginal increase to the portfolio risk when adding a new bond to it. In the case of 20% correlation, adding the A rated bond has increased the standard deviation of the portfolio by $0.4837 (= marginal risk contribution), while the stand-alone standard deviation of the A bond is of $1.49.

This results from diversification effects because of the year-end values that are imperfectly correlated. The same statement can be made on the basis of the percentile levels. The expected value of the correlated portfolio is somewhat higher than the uncorrelated case which is the perfect sum of the two individual means.

In a larger portfolio, it is no longer possible to cross the bonds multidimensionally and recourse is made to Monte Carlo simulations. The following steps are in this case necessary (directly from Crouhy et al., 2000):

1. Derivation of the asset return thresholds for each rating class.
2. Estimation of the correlations between each pair of obligors' asset returns.
3. Generation of asset return scenarios according to their joint normal distribution. A Choleski decomposition is a standard way to generate correlated bivariate normal random variables. Each scenario is characterized by n standardized asset returns, one of each of the n obligors in the portfolio.
4. For each generated scenario and for each counterparty, the normalized asset return is mapped into the corresponding rating class, following the threshold levels derived in 1.
5. The portfolio is re-evaluated along the forward spread curves introduced.
6. The procedure is repeated many times and the percentile level is directly identified on the generated empirical distribution.

Then, it is possible to compute the marginal risk contribution of each asset of the portfolio. Comparing this measure to the stand-alone standard deviation for each asset, as already shown, permits the assessment of the extent of portfolio diversification. A useful decision-making board for credit risk management is the plot of the marginal standard deviation, or better, the percentile contribution of each asset against its marked-to-market value, i.e. its importance in the portfolio, notably for the identification of concentration risk and extremes values into the portfolio, and for the determination of credit limits to specific counterparties. These limits can be thought of arbitrary horizontal and vertical lines plotted as on Figure 20.3.

The Estimation of the Capital Requirement

Let us define the following variables:

V_0	Market value of the portfolio.
ER	Expected return on the portfolio.
PR	Required return on the portfolio based on the required market spread for each component of the portfolio.
EV	Expected value of the portfolio: $V_0(1 + ER)$
FV	Expected value of the portfolio: $V_0(1 + PR)$
EL	Expected loss: $FV - EV$
$CreditVaR$	Worst scenario for the portfolio value given some confidence level $(1 - \alpha)$: the percentile levels computed earlier.

The CreditVaR number enters into the capital requirement, defined as

$$Required\ capital = EV - CreditVaR.$$

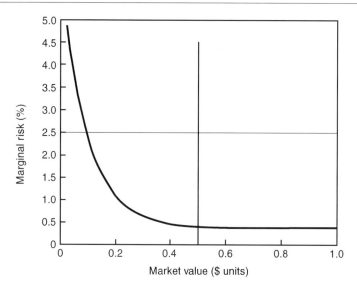

Figure 20.3 Defining limits for the management of credit risk. Adapted from a CreditMetrics™ document

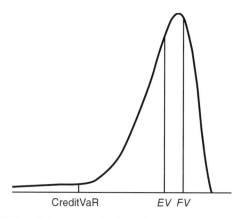

Figure 20.4 *CreditVaR* and the expected values of the portfolio. Adapted from Crouhy et al. (2000)

In parallel, the expected loss enters into the RAROC (return at risk on capital) computation.

More on Asset Correlations

Market correlations of the assets value of the firm are simply unavailable. One way to encompass this problem is to estimate them from stock market returns instead of asset returns. However, there is still a problem of dimensionality since this would mean estimating cross-correlation for all pairs of counterparties into the portfolio. CreditMetrics™ proposes, therefore, the use of a multifactor analysis where each counterparty is mapped to a country and an industry, on the assumption that the specific performance is mainly driven by this kind of factor. This relaxes somewhat the deterministic systemacy when relying on the arbitrary grid of ratings, i.e. counterparties in the same country and industry will be correlated but not necessarily perfectly, since they can still have different sensitivities with respect to these factors. Also, the user can introduce a pure "specific risk" for each counterparty independently of any factor or other counterparty.

The Specification of Exposures

In CreditMetrics^{TM}, market risks are not integrated. Although a forward structure is required for every rating class for the DCF forward pricing of bonds, as shown previously, no uncertainty on these structures is introduced. This poses some problems for some positions where

- the market exposure will in fact depend on the uncertainty of the creditworthiness as is the case with loan commitments, or
- the credit exposure can drastically change depending on the evolution of market factors such as fixed and floating interest rates, as is the case with swap contracts.

For each kind of special exposure, would it be receivables, loan commitments, financial letters of credit, swaps, forwards and others, CreditMetrics^{TM} proposes *ad hoc* procedures. Again, CreditMetrics^{TM} is a framework with some highly restrictive assumptions, but with the great advantage of proposing an implementable and easily standardizable answer to a common credit risk capital adequacy framework. Each new component to this framework is viewed by RiskMetrics Group as a challenge for a new building block that, under some minimal and reasonable assumptions, can provide at least a conservative but more dynamic picture of the entire portfolio.

20.2.3 Drawbacks of the Model

CreditMetrics^{TM} does not itself answer the question regarding the pricing of credit risk and its underlying modeling. Forward zero curves are an input to be supplied to the framework, but they are themselves the result of an estimation process of the term structure of credit spreads. Because of this, CreditMetrics^{TM} should not be considered as a model but as an integrating framework in order to provide an idea about credit portfolio diversification.

Moreover, taking forward zero risky rates allow them to ignore stochastic interest rates for pricing reasons. However, this assumption is even more restrictive in the sense that the migrating behavior is not linked to the evolution of any market risk such as interest rates.

The second main drawback is the assumption of credit homogeneity within a credit rating class. The whole framework relies on the choice of a rating scheme. Each class defines a class of systematic credit risk and two obligors, whatever is their industry, size, etc. are supposed to have perfectly the same credit behavior if in the same credit rating class. This is, however, somewhat relaxed by the computation of correlations with a multifactor analysis on equity returns.

The transition probabilities computed by rating agencies rely on statistical estimates form databases with a history of more than 20 years. During such a period, regimes could have changed. And the importance of the survivorship bias, resulting from the fact that only surviving firms remain in the sample on which the default probability is recalculated, is not specifically mentioned.

Recovery rates are fully exogenous as with all the other management models presented here and usually assumed to follow a Beta distribution (a type of bounded distribution that can take many different shapes). The state of knowledge on recovery rates is low. Recovery rates on the other hand clearly affect results. Sensitivity analyses are doable and recovery rates do appear to have a meaningful impact there notably for long-term or low-grade portfolios. But even these sensitivity analyses do not capture the true impact of a good model of recovery rates as interacting with default probabilities as they are in reality (see the Izvorski 1997 study and the chapter on empirical evidence).

Because it works mostly on the basis of simulations, CreditMetrics^{TM} is also computer intensive and faces limits on the extension it can receive (more for computer power reasons than for conceptual reasons). This appears true for the calculations of correlations for example.

As mentioned above, the methodology does not allow at today's date for good evaluation of nonlinear instruments such as swaps, credit derivatives, OTC options, etc.

Finally, and this is valid for many of the models (except for the McKinsey approach, which has nonetheless the disadvantage of being *ad hoc*) presented here, we do not have a real linkage to macro-variables, except possibly through the somewhat *ad hoc* factor decomposition of the correlations, although macro-dependent rating migrations could be used in the CreditMetrics^{TM}'s framework.

20.3   KMV CORPORATION'S MODEL

KMV has participated in the CreditMetrics^{TM}'s framework, mainly for the methodology required to estimate consistent correlations between obligors of different categories. This is a restrictive particular application of their proposed methodology. KMV's model does not start from any transition matrix between rating categories, therefore making no initial assumption on the common behavior of two counterparties belonging to the same rating class. Using a variant of Merton's model, KMV uses a structural approach to define the "distance-to-default category" (*DD*) to which the counterparty belongs. Then, relying on a huge default database, KMV is able to relate this *DD* category to an "expected default frequency" (*EDF*) for each issuer. Correlations between issuers come from an iterative method based on Merton's view of equity as a call on the value of the firm, which is, however, less simplifying than CreditMetrics^{TM}'s method that uses stock market data as a direct proxy.

Apart from the ratings simplification, CreditMetrics^{TM} also makes the strong assumption that actual default rates and historical average default rates are equivalent. KMV has shown that these two measures can differ widely from each other. Moreover, significant differences can exist in the same ratings class, with default probability ranges for each class that may largely overlap. Replicating 50 000 times Moody's study of default on the past 25 years by a Monte Carlo simulation, they have that, for a BBB counterparty and an asset correlation of 15%, the average historical default rate has a confidence interval at 95% of [4 bp, 27 bp] while the true default probability (the average computed by Moody's) was of 13 bp. The distribution obtained is right skewed, thereby having a mean default rate that overstates the modal rate for each rating class.

In the following paragraphs, we will present the main lines of the KMV method and its different applications[15].

20.3.1   The Computation and Use of the "Expected Default Frequencies" (*EDF*)

Step 1   Estimating the underlying credit risk parameters, i.e. the market asset value of the firm (V), which can trigger default, and the volatility of the relative changes of this value (σ_v), which will define the potentiality of V reaching the default boundary.

As before, V is assumed to be lognormally distributed. V also has the strong advantage that its volatility can be reasonably assumed to be stable over time. This will be important for the Merton implementation that follows.

KMV assumes that the liability side of the balance sheet of the firm is generically constituted of short-term debt (equivalent to cash), long-term debt, convertible preferred shares, and common stock. This simplified composition allows KMV to use an "augmented" Mertonian approach[16]. Broadly, the value of equity (E) is simply the value of a call on the assets of the firm[17]:

$$E = C(V, \sigma_v, K(\text{liabilities}), \text{maturities}, c, r), \qquad (20.11)$$

where K stands for the threshold level for a determined envelope of liabilities, c for the average coupon rate being paid, and r for the riskfree rate.

KMV's method consists, therefore, in solving iteratively for the asset value and then the asset volatility through two functions based on the observation of equity returns and their volatility in the market, and on equation (20.11):

$$E = f(V, \sigma_v, K(\text{liabilities}), \text{maturities}, c, r), \qquad (20.12)$$

where at the first iteration, V is extracted, making a starting guess on σ_v, and E being known from market data. Then V is introduced in

$$\sigma_E = g(V, \sigma_v, K(\text{liabilities}), \text{maturities}, c, r), \qquad (20.13)$$

σ_E also being identifiable from market data to infer σ_v, which is then reintroduced in equation (20.12), and so forth, until convergence. Expression (20.13) can be found earlier in this book and has already been presented in 1986 by Ronn and Verma, who have shown that $\sigma_E = \eta\sigma_v$, η representing the elasticity of equity to the value of the assets: $V/E \, \partial E/\partial V$, remembering that $\partial E/\partial V$ is the delta of our call option in equation (20.11).

---

[15]In part, taken from Crouhy et al. (2000).

[16]See previous chapters for an extensive presentation of the basis of this approach and its extensions through more complicated barrier option pricing models.

[17]"Augmented" and "broadly" because the procedure is sophisticated by the structure of liabilities which consists of more categories than in Merton's case. But in the final instance, the pricing approach is that of Merton.

Table 20.9 Example of calculation for the "distance-to-default"

	Nov. 97	Feb. 98
Market value of equity	$7.7	$7.3
Market value of assets	$12.6	$12.2
Book value of liabilities	$4.7	$4.9
Asset volatility	15%	17%
Threshold value	$3.4	$3.5
DD	$\dfrac{12.6 - 3.4}{0.15 \; 12.6} = 4.9$	$\dfrac{12.2 - 3.5}{0.17 \; 12.2} = 4.2$

Source: Replotted from Crouhy et al. (2000).

Step 2   Determining the normalized relative distance separating V from the default threshold value.

Taking back the derivation in equation (20.8) for the default threshold critical value, KMV has made the observation that firms default when the value of the assets reaches a level K which is roughly the value of the long-term debt plus half the short-term debt.

Setting apart specificities and frictions that can modify the final repartition rule in default, the "distance-to-default" (DD) is presented as the distance between the expected value of the assets in one year, $E(V_1)$, and the default point, K, expressed in standard deviations of future asset value, $\sigma_{\bar{v}}$, i.e. normalized[18]:

$$DD = \frac{E(V_1) - K}{\sigma_{\bar{v}}} = \frac{E(V_1) - K}{\sigma_v V_0},$$

where V_0 is the spot market value of assets.

From the lognormality assumption and by equation (20.3), this distance, for a T time horizon can be rewritten as

$$DD = \frac{\ln(V_0 / K_T) + (\mu_v - \sigma_v^2/2) T}{\sigma_v \sqrt{T}}.$$

From above, we know that the area below the default point K is straightforwardly given by $\Phi(-DD)$.

Step 3   Associating the DD value to actual probabilities of default, based on an extensive database with no prior *ad hoc* separation into ratings.

Let us take an example provided by KMV for Federal Express on two different dates (see Table 20.9). In Table 20.9 the DD value presents some deterioration. Then, these values are mapped to historical default rates from the KMV database, thereby giving the EDF values. From Figure 20.5, it appears that from all firms with a DD of 4.9 at one point in time, 0.06% of them have defaulted in 1 year. The curve shown in Figure 20.5 links all points of exhibited frequencies for the different DD values.

---

[18] $\sigma_{\bar{v}}$ is used instead of σ_v to differentiate the assets level volatility from the volatility of asset returns. $\sigma_{\bar{v}} = \sigma_v V$.

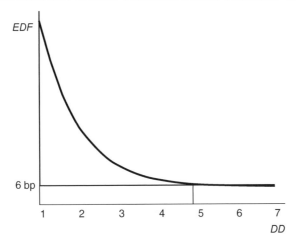

Figure 20.5 Determining the "expected default frequency" from the "distance-to-default".
Source: Replotted from Crouhy et al. (2000)

> The *EDF* for a *DD* value of 4.2 was of 0.11% at the time of the example. *EDF* values are then related to a credit rating class. An *EDF* of 6 bp would correspond to an AA^- firm and an *EDF* of 11 bp, to a A^- firm.

The Quality of EDF Values

The study of *EDFs* from 1993 show that *EDFs* seem to be quite reactive to real deteriorations. Moreover, *EDF* evolutions tend to begin to react at least one year earlier to the downgrading of the counterparties by the traditional rating agencies. This is because *EDFs* can be calculated on a regular basis on market data[19]. And *EDFs* seem not to be biased by periods of general recession or general prosperity. Note, nonetheless, that there is no published systematic and scientific study that assesses the performance of *EDFs* compared to classical ratings. It is also perfectly possible that *EDFs* do not capture the true underlying credit risk as well as ratings, even though they are more volatile. Practical studies tend to come from KMV itself and are rarely based on large samples or on valid econometric methods.

Recovering an Implicit Rating Scheme

Table 20.10 correspondence between *EDFs* and ratings from the different agencies including the internal rating scheme of CIBC, is very useful and is taken directly from Crouhy et al. (2000)[20].

Average default rates are much higher than the default rate of the typical firm because these rating classes contain groups of firms that have not been duly downgraded as yet and have much higher probabilities of default since default rates evolve exponentially when default risk increases.

---

[19]This is the kind of fact that has greatly motivated the work presented in Part II.
[20]It is important to note that while Standard & Poors ratings represent default probabilities only, Moody's takes into account the probability of loss, i.e. *EDF.LGD* (loss given default).

Table 20.10 Correspondences between the EDF scheme, and internal and public rating classes

EDF (bps)	S&P	Moody's	CIBC	Nationsbank	SBC
2–4	$\geqslant$ AA	$\geqslant$ Aa2	1	AAA	C1
4–10	AA – A	A1	2	AA	C2
10–19	A – BBB$^+$	Baa1	3	A	C3
19–40	BBB$^+$ – BBB$^-$	Baa3	4	A – BB	C4
40–72	BBB$^-$ – BB	Ba1	4.5	BBB – BB	C5
72–101	BB – BB$^-$	Ba3	5	BB	C6
101–143	BB$^-$ – B$^+$	B1	5.5	BB	C7
143–202	B$^+$ – B	B2	6	BB – B	C8
202–345	B – B$^-$	B3	6.5	B	C9

Source: Crouhy et al. (2000).

Table 20.11 EDF values for different percentiles levels as reported by KMV

Percentiles	10%	25%	50%	75%	90%	Mean value
AAA	0.02	0.02	0.02	0.02	0.10	0.04
AA	0.02	0.02	0.02	0.04	0.10	0.06
A	0.02	0.03	0.08	0.13	0.28	0.14
BBB	0.05	0.09	0.15	0.33	0.71	0.30
BB	0.12	0.22	0.62	1.30	2.53	1.09
B	0.44	0.87	2.15	3.80	7.11	3.30
CCC	1.43	2.09	4.07	12.24	18.82	7.21

Note: All numbers are in basis points.
Source: KMV Corporation as in Crouhy and Mark (2000).

Table 20.12 Matrix of transition probabilities obtained by the KMV method

Initial rating	Rating at year-end (%)							
	AAA	AA	A	BBB	BB	B	CCC	Default
AAA	66.26	22.22	7.37	2.45	0.86	0.67	0.14	0.02
AA	21.66	43.04	25.83	6.56	1.99	0.68	0.20	0.04
A	2.76	20.34	44.19	22.94	7.42	1.97	0.28	0.10
BBB	0.30	2.80	22.63	42.54	23.52	6.95	1.00	0.26
BB	0.08	0.24	3.69	22.93	44.41	24.53	3.41	0.71
B	0.01	0.05	0.39	3.48	20.47	53.00	20.58	2.01
CCC	0.00	0.01	0.09	0.26	1.79	17.77	69.94	10.13

Source: KMV Corporation as in Crouhy and Mark (2000).

Therefore, these overlappings underestimate migration probabilities, which is also a direct consequence of the infrequent revision of ratings. Of course, this does not mean that *EDF* calculations do not convey any noise. Table 20.11 shows the dispersion of *EDF* values.

Because of these considerations, KMV has constructed a matrix of transition probabilities (see Table 20.12) based on nonoverlapping ranges of *EDF* values and the subsequent accounting of *EDF* changes for each range. These ranges are then attributed to rating classes to enable comparisons with transition matrices from the rating

Table 20.13

	Component	
	Default-free	Risky component
States of nature	(A_1)	(B_1)
Default	100 (1−LGD)	0
No-default	100 (1−LGD)	100 LGD

Source: Crouhy et al. (2000).

agencies. As expected, the resulting matrix shows "nonmigrating" probabilities that are much lower than those presented in the Standard & Poors transition matrix in the first section dedicated to CreditMetrics^{TM}.

20.3.2 Discounting Cash Flows Subject to Credit Risk (DCFaCR)

In CreditMetrics^{TM}, the bond prices for each class are derived by first discounting the cash flows with a different forward discount curve for each class. Then the transition probabilities apply to generate the distribution of forward values.

KMV proposes a method based on the risk-neutral option pricing of contingent cash flows. The first objective is to separate this valuation into two components, the valuation of the default-free component and that of the component subject to credit risk.

An Example with a Single Corporate Bond Issue

Let us assume that we want to price a zero-coupon corporate bond which matures in one year from now reimbursing a face value of $100. Furthermore, assume that:

- the risk-neutral probability of default (Q) is 10%,
- the riskfree rate of return (r) is 5%, and
- the "loss given default" (LGD) is 50%.

Suppose now we separate the cash flows in each ending state (default/no-default) in two components as in Table 20.13.

Under the risk-neutral probability measure, both components can be valued today as

$$A_0 = \frac{100(1 - LGD)}{1 + r} = 47.62,$$

$$B_0 = \frac{100\, LGD(1 - Q) + 0Q}{1 + r} = 42.86,$$

$$\text{Risky bond}_0 = A_0 + B_0 = 90.48.$$

The one-year required credit spread is easily obtained through

$$cs_{0,1} = \left(\frac{100}{90.48} - 1\right) - r = 6\%.$$

The generalized formula for the discounted cash flow analysis of a coupon-bearing corporate bond with a stream of cash flows **c** comprising the reimbursement of the principal amount, is thus

$$\text{Risky bond}_0 = (1 - LGD) \sum_{t=1}^{T} \frac{\mathbf{c}_t}{(1+r)^t} + LGD \sum_{t=1}^{T} \frac{\mathbf{c}_t(1-Q_t)}{(1+r_t)^t}, \tag{20.14}$$

where Q_t is the cumulative "risk-neutral" probability of default at the horizon t.

How to Obtain the Risk-neutral EDFs?

The "risk-neutral" probability of default is simply

$$Q = P(V_T^Q \leqslant K) \tag{20.15}$$

$$= P(V_0 \exp\{(r - \tfrac{1}{2}\sigma_v^2)T + \sigma_v \sqrt{T}Z_T\} \leqslant K)$$

$$= P\left(Z_t \leqslant -\frac{\ln(V_0/K) + (r - \tfrac{1}{2}\sigma_v^2)T}{\sigma_v \sqrt{T}}\right)$$

$$= \Phi(-d_2^Q),$$

with

$$\frac{dV_t^Q}{V_t^Q} = r\,dt + \sigma_v\,dW_t,$$

where W_t is a standard Brownian motion such that $\sqrt{T}Z_T = W_T - W_0$ (variance of T), and d_2 is the traditional notation used by Black and Scholes.

Supposing that the *EDF* value is really the area below the default point K under the true probability, then

$$EDF = \Phi(-DD) = \Phi(-d_2).$$

The link between d_2^Q and d_2 is straightforward to compute, then:

$$d_2^Q = d_2 - \frac{(\mu_v - r)\sqrt{T}}{\sigma_v},$$

and, since we would compute the Q_t value from the *EDF* value mapped to the *DD* estimate with recourse to the historical database, we have that

$$Q_T = \Phi\left(\Phi^{-1}(EDF) + \frac{(\mu_v - r)\sqrt{T}}{\sigma_v}\right).$$

By the CAPM, $(\mu_v - r)$ should satisfy

$$(\mu_v - r) = \beta\pi,$$

with π standing for the market risk premium. Remembering that $\beta = \rho(\sigma_v/\sigma_M)$, σ_M as the volatility of market returns, then

Table 20.14 Percentile levels of the normal inverse probability distribution

	p	ρ	$\alpha = 0.1$	$\alpha = 0.01$	$\alpha = 0.001$	$\alpha = 0.0001$
1.	1%	0.1	1.19	3.8	7.0	10.7
2.	1%	0.4	0.55	4.5	11.0	18.2
3.	0.1%	0.1	0.98	4.1	8.8	15.4
4.	0.1%	0.4	0.12	3.2	13.2	31.7
	Normal case		1.28	2.3	3.1	3.7

Source: Adapted from Crouhy et al. (2000).

$$Q_T = \Phi\left(\Phi^{-1}(EDF) + \rho\frac{\pi}{\sigma_M}\sqrt{T}\right)$$
$$= \Phi(\Phi^{-1}(EDF) + \rho S\sqrt{T}),$$

where S is the Sharpe ratio of market returns.

Estimation of π is difficult, and the distribution of the assets return is not perfectly normal. Therefore, KMV proposes to calibrate S and θ into the following expression:

$$Q_T = \Phi(\Phi^{-1}(EDF) + \rho S T^{\theta}).$$

20.3.3 The Capital Requirement Under KMV's Methodology

With this kind of analytical framework, KMV's method is also capable of deriving analytically the loss distribution of the portfolio at some horizon without recourse to simulations.

Suppose that our time horizon, for which we want to calculate the exposure, is a time h between now and T, the general maturity of all bonds into the liability side of the balance sheet.

Following the same idea as in the last section, the portfolio loss expected at time h is just the difference between the riskless value of this portfolio at h, and its market value:

$$L^{Pf} = Pf_{h/ND} - Pf_h, \tag{20.16}$$

where $Pf_{h/ND}$ is the value of the portfolio assuming the no-default state, i.e. the riskless value, and Pf_h is the market value under the risk-neutral probability measure in the spirit of equation (20.14).

However, Pf_h is not known at time 0 and we can only rely on a distribution, which makes L^{Pf} a random variable. KMV argues that, for a well-diversified portfolio on a wide range of counterparties, and for other simplifying assumptions, the limiting distribution of the portfolio loss is a normal inverse which has the properties of high skewness and leptokurtosis.

The idea is then to determine the *capital requirement as the number of standard deviations* from the mean value of L^{Pf} by inverting the distribution in order to find the percentile corresponding to some confidence level (α-percentile), for a portfolio of bonds, with, for clarity, a unique probability of default equal to p for every bond and a constant pairwise asset correlation across the counterparties of ρ.

Table 20.14 gives some percentile levels for some αs and some combinations of p and ρ, provided in Crouhy et al. (2000). In case 3, for example, if we require a 99%

confidence level, then the required capital should be enough to cover 4.1 times the portfolio loss standard deviation. The capital requirement from the α-percentile can be refined to

α-percentile − expected spread revenue

$\qquad$ = (annualized expected revenue over funding cost) − expected loss.

20.3.4 Asset Correlations

This is the last point that remains to be discussed. As with CreditMetrics^{TM}, KMV links correlations to fundamental factors through a multifactor structural model. This conveys three main advantages:

1. With this structure, statistical errors and biases in computing simple correlations directly from historical market data is avoided.
2. The number of correlations to compute increases exponentially with the number of counterparties, and therefore, the standard mapping to fundamental factors allows the drastic reduction of this process by considering only the relationship of each counterparty with the limited number of factors.
3. And finally, using factors such as the country market index and the industrial index of the counterparty allows us to dynamically account for business cycle shocks in some part of the overall framework. As an example, correlations that are a function of the sensitivity to the economy will be able to take into account herding behaviors in recession.

The risk of firm returns is composed by systematic risk factors and specific ones, and asset return correlations come only from the common factors to all firms. The asset return generating process of any firm k is

$$r_k = \alpha_k + [\beta_{1k}\,\beta_{2k}]\begin{bmatrix} F_1 \\ F_2 \end{bmatrix} + \epsilon_k,$$

where βs are the sensitivities to the two systematic factors F_1 and F_2. Given this, it is easy then to derive the volatilities and covariances that will help us in computing the correlation parameter between two counterparties i and j:

$$\text{Var}(r_k) = \beta_k \Sigma_F \beta_k' + \text{Var}(\epsilon_k^2),$$

$$\text{Covar}(r_i, r_j) = \beta_i \Sigma_F \beta_j',$$

where β_k is the beta vector for counterparty k, and Σ_F is the variance–covariance matrix of the factors F_1 and F_2,

$$\Sigma_F = \begin{bmatrix} \sigma_{F_1} & \sigma_{F_1 F_2} \\ \sigma_{F_1 F_2} & \sigma_{F_2} \end{bmatrix}.$$

The two factors F_1 and F_2 (country and industry) are themselves split into their components: the specific risk portion of them, and global economic risk, regional risk, and sector risk components.

20.4 CreditRisk+^{TM}

CreditRisk+^{TM} relies only on default and assumes its arrival to follow a Poisson process, the severity of the subsequent loss being gamma distributed.

Basically, it is no more than a traditional actuarial model. Its advantage relies on the use of stochastic interest rates and their explanatory power for migrations as well as the analytical solutions it offers.

The actuarial approach of credit risk, in line with the reduced-form models presented earlier, does not make any fundamental conception of how default risk occurs. A counterparty i default with probability P_i or survive with a probability $(1 - P_i)$ over the time horizon specified, which can be shown to be related to a Poisson distribution function as an approximation (as there remains with the Poisson definition a small probability that there will be more defaults than the portfolio has assets). More assumptions are:

- The probability of default over a time horizon h is the same for any future time horizon of length h.

- For large portfolio, the individual probability of default of a counterparty is relatively small, and the overall number of defaults over a time length of h is independent of any other h period.

The scope of credit risk in this model is mainly represented by the probability of a certain number of defaults occurring in the portfolio over the next h period and the extent of losses for these defaults. Then, the last part of the model relies on the determination of the distribution of portfolio values given the potentiality of default and its associated losses.

Preliminary From the Poisson distribution, the number of defaults occurring in a h period of time is given by

$$P(n \text{ defaults}) = \frac{\mu^n e^{-\mu}}{n!} \quad \text{for } n = 0, 1, 2, \ldots \quad (20.17)$$

where μ is the average number of defaults during a period of time length h. The Poisson process has the advantage that the mean and variance of the random number of default are both μ. The probability of five defaults in the next year knowing that the average number per year is two, would be

$$P(5 \text{ defaults}) = \frac{2^5 e^{-2}}{5!} = 3.61\%.$$

Refinement Looking at historical average default rates (μ) and their volatility by credit rating class, it is observed that the volatility of the default rate is rarely equal to $\sqrt{\mu}$, but much higher. Thus, the Poisson process can underestimate the variability of default rates simply because it is assumed constant in the CreditRisk+^{TM} framework. Therefore, CreditRisk+^{TM} propose to adjust the mean default rate of the Poisson process and consider it in fact stochastic with mean μ and volatility σ_μ.

Step 1 The portfolio is sliced into bands of common exposure, mainly to reduce the amount of data that must be retrieved.

Table 20.15

Counterparty	Exposure	Exposure (in $200 000)	Rounding (defines the j band)
	$L_i(LGD)$	ν_i	ν_j
1	400 000	2	2
2	635 000	3.175	3
3	100 000	0.5	1
4	790 000	3.95	4
5	1 020 000	5.1	5

Source: Replotted from Crouhy et al. (2000).

Each obligor i is characterized by an associated exposure L_i (LGD), a constant probability of default P_i and an expected loss $\lambda_i = L_i P_i$. Then, each L_i exposure and λ_i expected loss is related to the unit amount of exposure chosen, let us say L:

$$\nu_i = \frac{L_i}{L} \quad \text{and} \quad \epsilon_i = \frac{\lambda_i}{L}. \tag{20.18}$$

Here ν_is are rounded to the nearest integer number, replacing L_i by the nearest L value. Depending on the initial choice of L, a number of obligors will fall into the same ν category, let us say category j, for a total number of m bands.

Table 20.15 gives an example. Each category j, or j band, is now characterized by ν_j (common exposure), ϵ_j (expected loss) and μ_j (expected number of defaults). Note that the following relationships then hold:

$$\epsilon_j = \nu_j \mu_j,$$

and therefore

$$\mu_j = \frac{\epsilon_j}{\nu_j} = \sum_{i's \text{ in } j} \frac{\epsilon_i}{\nu_i},$$

and for the whole portfolio, the expected number of defaults is

$$\mu = \sum_{j=1}^{m} \mu_j = \sum_{j=1}^{m} \frac{\epsilon_j}{\nu_j}. \tag{20.19}$$

Step 2   The "loss" probability generating function for the j band, defined in terms of an auxiliary variable z, is by definition

$$G_j(z) = \sum_{n=0}^{\infty} P(\text{loss} = nL)z^n$$

$$= \sum_{n=0}^{\infty} P(n \text{ defaults})z^{n\nu_j},$$

and since the number of default follows a Poisson process,

$$G_j(z) = \sum_{n=0}^{\infty} \frac{\mu_j^n e^{-\mu_j}}{n!} z^{n\nu_j} \tag{20.20}$$

$$= e^{\mu_j(z^{\nu_j}-1)}.$$

Step 3   The probability generating function for the entire portfolio, by our independence assumption, is

$$G(z) = \prod_{j-1}^{m} e^{\mu_j(z^{\nu_j}-1)} \tag{20.21}$$

$$= e^{\sum_{j=1}^{m} \mu_j(z^{\nu_j}-1)}.$$

Step 4   The loss probability distribution function for a loss of nL (or n units) on the entire portfolio can be derived through

$$P(\text{loss} = nL) = \frac{1}{n!} \left. \frac{\partial^n G(z)}{\partial z^n} \right|_{z=0} \quad \text{for } n = 1, 2, \ldots \tag{20.22}$$

20.4.1 Capital Requirement Calculation

Based on equation (20.22), it is straightforward to compute the unexpected loss at a 99% confidence interval which is the difference between the 99% percentile loss level minus the expected loss (ϵ) on the overall portfolio.

20.4.2 Extensions

This model can be easily extended to a multi-period framework, although with some additional computational work, and the volatility of default rates can also be related to a multifactor analysis, where factors could be the number of defaults arriving per year in the related country or industrial sector. Again relying on independence of factors and probabilities (and on the constancy of the latter), CreditRisk+[TM] framework is quite attractive in the sense that it is always capable of producing a closed-form solution for the loss distribution of the portfolio.

20.5 CreditPortfolioView[TM]

McKinsey proposes a discretized multi-period econometric model that measures only "default risk" where default probabilities depend on macroeconomic variables, some of them corresponding to financial variables acting as proxies for the state of the economy (see Ref. 21, Chapter III): the level of interest rates and forex rates, the growth rate of the economy, unemployment rates, the level of government expenses, and the aggregate savings rate. This modeling is an answer to the empirical evidence, showing that credit cycles and business cycles are cointegrated. Moreover, it has the advantage of readily available data. It is thought of as a model that applies well to speculative-grade

---

[21] In particular, a Standard & Poors study on default shows that the frequency of default increased in 1990 and 1991, which correspond to years of slowdown in the world economies.

counterparties which are more sensitive to credit cycles and their reliance on macro-variables[22].

Step 1   The default probabilities are assumed to be generated by a logit function that relates them to a "country speculative-grade specific index" which is itself related to contemporaneous and lagged macro-variables through a multifactor analysis. The default probability for a speculative debtor in industry/country j over the period t, is given by

$$P_{j,t} = \frac{1}{1 + e^{-Y_{j,t}}}, \tag{20.23}$$

where $Y_{j,t}$ is an index value described as

$$Y_{j,t} = \beta_j^0 + [\beta_j^1 \ \beta_j^2 \ \cdots \ \beta_j^m] \begin{bmatrix} X_{j,t}^1 \\ X_{j,t}^2 \\ \cdots \\ X_{j,t}^m \end{bmatrix} + v_{j,t}, \tag{20.24}$$

where β_j is the vector of coefficients (sensitivities) for industry/country j that applies to the vector of values for j of m macro-variables, $\mathbf{X}_{j,t}$. As usual, $v_{j,t}$ is the error term assumed (or required, for econometric reasons) to be independent of the realizations $\mathbf{X}_{j,t}$, and identically normally distributed, i.e. $v_{j,t}$ are i.i.d. with

$$v_{j,t} \sim N(0, \sigma_j) \ \text{ and } \ \boldsymbol{v}_t \sim N(0, \boldsymbol{\Sigma}_v),$$

where $\boldsymbol{v}_t$ is the vector of stacked index innovations $v_{j,t}$, and $\boldsymbol{\Sigma}_v$ is their $j \times j$ variance–covariance matrix.

The macro-variables are specified for each country and, when enough data are available, the vector β_j can be consistently calibrated. Moreover, in the implementation proposed by McKinsey, each of these independent variables is assumed to follow an autoregressive model of order 2 (AR(2)), such that the process $X_{j,t}^i$ has some memory. It can be written as

$$M_{j,t}^i = \gamma_{j,0}^i + [\gamma_{j,t-1}^i \ \gamma_{j,t-2}^i] \begin{bmatrix} X_{j,t-1}^i \\ X_{j,t-2}^i \end{bmatrix} + \epsilon_{j,t}^i, \tag{20.25}$$

where $X_{j,t}^i$ is the value of the ith macro-variable in the jth segment at time t, the vector of coefficients γ_j^i are the sensitivities to past information to be estimated, and again $\epsilon_{j,t}^i$ is assumed to be i.i.d. with

$$\epsilon_{j,t}^i \sim N(0, \sigma_i) \ \text{ and } \ \epsilon \sim N(0, \boldsymbol{\Sigma}_\epsilon),$$

where ϵ is the stacked vector of error terms from each of the i AR(2) equations in the jth segment, and $\boldsymbol{\Sigma}_\epsilon$ is their variance–covariance matrix.

---

[22] For any deeper scrutiny of the methodology, please refer to the two articles written by Wilson in the *Risk Magazine* (1997a,b).

While it is interesting to capture the impact of macroeconomic variables on the credit risk of companies, the choice of form proposed in this model seems *ad hoc* and does not necessarily insure its superiority toward other *ad hoc* adjustments of competing models such as modified transition matrices for CreditMetrics™.

Step 2 Equations (20.23), (20.24) and (20.25) define a system governing the joint evolution of the country/industry-specific speculative default rates and the associated macro-variables, which has to be calibrated. In particular, for the total vector of innovations

$$\mathbf{E}_t = \begin{bmatrix} \boldsymbol{v}_t \\ \epsilon_t \end{bmatrix} \sim N(0, \boldsymbol{\Sigma}),$$

with

$$\boldsymbol{\Sigma} \equiv \begin{bmatrix} \boldsymbol{\Sigma}_v & \boldsymbol{\Sigma}_{v,\epsilon} \\ \boldsymbol{\Sigma}_{v,\epsilon} & \boldsymbol{\Sigma}_\epsilon \end{bmatrix},$$

where $\mathbf{E}$ is the $(j+i) \times 1$ vector of innovations of the whole system of equations and $\boldsymbol{\Sigma}$ is the $(j+i) \times (j+i)$ covariance matrix of macro-variable forecast errors (v), and segment-specific speculative default rate shocks (ϵ). $\boldsymbol{\Sigma}_{v,\epsilon}$ is the cross-correlation matrix.

Step 3 After the calibration, the use of the Choleski decomposition[23] of $\boldsymbol{\Sigma}$,

$$\boldsymbol{\Sigma} = \mathbf{AA}',$$

allows the simulation of the distribution of joint speculative default probabilities across all segments. This is done via three suboperations:

1. The drawing of a vector of $(j+i)$ sequences of random realizations $\mathbf{Z}_t$, from $t = 1$ to T, for $(j+i)$ $N(0, I)$ random variables, where I is the identity matrix of a dimension $(j+i) \times (j+i)$.
2. The calculation of $\mathbf{E}_t$ by the expression $\mathbf{E}_t = \mathbf{A}\mathbf{z}_t$, incorporating the correlations between the macro-variables and the segment-specific default rate innovations.
3. The calculation of the $Y_{j,t}$s, and subsequently of the $P_{j,t}$, using the system of equations.

Step 4 Recovering the conditional transition matrix. Once the speculative default rates are being computed for each country/industry segment, we will be able to infer the unique Markov transition matrix for each of the segments. Several substeps will guide us to the final result:

1. The inference of the unconditional Markov transition matrix from the historical data of the rating agencies[24], let us say the matrix $\phi\mathbf{M}$.

---

[23]The Choleski factorization of a symmetric positive definite matrix is an alternative representation that is useful in regression analysis. **A** results to be a lower triangular matrix. The square roots of the squares of the diagonal of **A** are the Choleski values of **A**. This decomposition allows a fast and accurate inversion of $\boldsymbol{\Sigma}$.

[24]Unconditional because, since they are computed over a database of more than 20 years, they cover different regimes, cycles, countries, and industries.

2. From the simulated default probabilities SDP_t for each segment, we can compute their ratios with respect to their historical average ϕSDP (unconditional probability of default), $SDP_t/\phi SDP$ knowing that a ratio greater than 1 will implicitly correspond to an economic recession, with increasing downgrade migrations. In our case, the SPD_t are the generated $P_{j,t}$.

3. The powerful idea of CreditPortfolioView^{TM} is then to use these ratios to adapt the migration probabilities of matrix ϕM to obtain a transition matrix, $\mathbf{M}$, which is conditional on the state of the economy. Then

$$\mathbf{M_t} = M(P_{j,t}/\phi SDP),$$

i.e. some probability mass is shifted to downgraded and defaulted states when the ratio $P_{j,t}/\phi SDP$ is greater than 1, and vice versa, if it is less than 1.

4. The simulation can be operated over any time horizon which allows us also to generate a multi-period transition matrix of a T term horizon, by

$$\mathbf{M_T} = \prod_{t=1,\ldots T} M(P_{j,t}/\phi SDP).$$

Step 5   The same simulation methodology can be reproduced many times the conditional transition matrix to produce the distribution of the cumulated default and migration probabilities for any rating over any time horizon. Any CreditVar measure can be then extracted from this distribution, such as the 99% percentile level, the maximum possible default probability for each segment.

20.5.1 Remarks

Tom Wilson notes that, if long-run average levels of the macro-variables are used as initial conditions for simulating the AR(2) processes, then the cumulative default probability of the revised conditional transition matrix would be equal to the original unconditional transition matrix as given by Standard & Poors or Moody's. This remark shows that the impact of the credit cycle effects are well encompassed by the methodology.

One of the limitations of the model is the need of reliable (and frequent) data on the countries and for the industrial sectors within this country. Also, what is criticized is their *ad-hoc* rule to adjust the transition matrix, even though it is a powerful suggestion to be able to relate the classical ratings' approach to the ongoing economic reality. Crouhy et al. (2000) state that there is no proof that this method performs better than another Bayesian alternative that would be based on the internal expertise and appreciation of the credit department of the institution. One of the answers to this criticism is that, for regulatory purposes, we require a standardized approach. Even though the calibration and simulation techniques can be in part subjective, they rely at least on a formal methodology with defined adjustment procedures.

20.6 COMPARATIVE STUDIES AND CONCLUSION

All models presented above, except for CreditPortfolio View^{TM}, are compared with the BIS (1988) standardized approach by Crouhy et al. (2000) on a benchmark portfolio consisting of 1800 bonds, across 13 currencies, various maturities, and the entire range of credit standings.

A priori surprisingly, the main conclusion is that the four models produce CreditVaR values within a relative range of 1.5. The author thinks it is not a surprise since all these models mainly rely on "default risk" and the relevancy and reliability of the data collected is of major concern.

The standardized approach produces a lower required capital charge than any model when the portfolio contains a high proportion of bonds from OECD banks.

Gordy (2000) compares more precisely CreditRisk+^{TM} and CreditMetrics^{TM}. He shows that under restrictive assumptions each model can mathematically be mapped into the other, despite what seemed *ex ante* fundamental differences between a reduced-form analytical type of CreditRisk+^{TM} and the extensive simulation approach of CreditMetrics^{TM}. That leads to the idea that, if they are well specified, both models will lead to similar percentile levels of protection. Nonetheless, CreditRisk+^{TM} seems more sensitive to specification errors, notably on the volatility of default.

Löffler (1999) proposes a comparative study of the sensitivity to input errors of a KMV style of model and of CreditMetrics^{TM}. Two inputs that are shared by both models seem particularly problematic today: correlations and recovery rates. CreditMetrics^{TM} appears to be more sensitive to recovery rates errors, but possibly less to correlation errors. The author does not provide for systematic tests of difference although he shows that the confidence interval on results such as probabilities of default can be wide open (and overlap from rating class levels to the next), a problem that will need to be addressed in further assessment papers of the models.

Further comparative studies are required, not only to assess the validity of the models but to give a clearer idea of which environment suits each model better, as far as instruments, time horizon, and overall economic context (US versus Europe versus Asia, types of industries bank versus corporate use, risk management versus portfolio optimization) are concerned.

It should nonetheless be clear from the preceding sections that all the models have major shortcomings at present. Recovery rates are determined in an *ad hoc* way (beta distributions for most, with levels determined from US-based studies even for implementation of the models in Europe or in Asia, where bankruptcy laws differ substantially from US laws).

None of the models currently integrates some minimal form of market risks, at least via stochastic interest rates. None of the models can handle nonlinear instruments (from guarantees to swaps to credit derivatives and letters of credit or call features and OTC options). Some technical issues, such as discrete approximation of the continuous distribution, may lead to difficulties (and not only on small samples) for all of them. But fundamentally, even if these models do not yet present the advances in credit risk analysis that have been exposed in this book, they achieve the desirable advance in credit risk thinking of providing for skewed and fat-tailed distributions that make classical risk management techniques based on standard deviations obsolete.

20.7 REFERENCES

Basle Committee on Banking Supervision, 1999, *Credit Risk Modelling: Current Practices and Applications*, Basle, April, 60 pp.

Carty, Lea V. and Dana Lieberman, 1996, "Defaulted Bank Loan Recoveries, Moody's Investors Service, Global Credit Research, Special Report, November.

Crouhy, Michel, Dan Galai and Robert Mark, 2000, "A Comparative Analysis of Current Credit Risk Models", *Journal of Banking and Finance*, **24** (1–2), 59–117.

Duffie, Darrell and David Lando, 1997, "Term Structures of Credit Spreads with Incomplete Accounting Information", Preliminary Draft, September 12, 39 pp.

Gordy, Michael, 2000, "A Comparative Anatomy of Credit Risk Models", *Journal of Banking and Finance*, **24** (1–2), 119–49.

Löffler, Gunter, 2000, *Using Credit Risk Models in Practice*, Commerzbank Asset Management.

Nickell, P., W. Perraudin and S. Varotto, 2000, "Stability of Rating Transitions", *Journal of Banking and Finance*, **24** (1–2), 203–27.

21
Financial Structuring with Credit Derivatives

Most academic research on derivatives view them as an instrument for the transfer of risks from a counterparty to another. In the case of market risks, it is the transfer of generic risks, namely stock market, foreign exchange or interest rate risks. In the case of credit risk, it is the transfer of a risk on a third counterparty. This variable to which we are exposed can take the form of a market spread or the total return of a loan that one of the transferers owns against the third counterparty, or a lump-sum payment in case of default.

However, because of the redundancy of derivative products, these off-balance sheet transactions could either reduce market and credit impacts on a portfolio or they could be used to leverage and overexpose the portfolio to them.

In financial terms, as we have seen in Chapter 3 with Merton's view of the structure of the firm, redundancy implies that an arbitrage relationship exists between the underlying instrument and the derivative product. This relationship is that which makes possible the hedging of an underlying position, taking the opposite stake in derivatives. It also allows agents to make arbitrage profits, taking advantage of pricing gaps existing between the theoretical equivalency and the market price[1]. But, in many cases, agents use this substitutability to avoid investing in the underlying and to create directly the synthetic position with the derivative instrument[2]. The advantage of this replication is in part its leverage. A derivative instrument requires little capital investment, but makes a bet on an underlying variable which notionally can be substantial.

In the case of credit risk, credit derivatives also have the advantage of circumventing problems of recovery at default.

The credit derivative determines a certain payoff to be paid if some event occurs, while with a straight defaulted debt, it can be the case that the lender is given back a bunch of illiquid assets, or at least assets that require some management, to be cashed out.

Typically, if we imagine market makers dealing with credit risk instruments, they will greatly prefer dealing with credit derivatives than with traditional lending and borrowing instruments.

Summarizing, we can advance the theory that the reasons to enter into such contracts are arbitrage dealing, the transfer of credit risk (or hedging), and the use as an investment substitute to traditional lending (or exposure enhancer). The latter activity is the riskier; it requires a perfect understanding of the dynamics of the exposure with respect to the underlying market and a monitoring system capable of warning the agent about overexposures and potential losses.

The next section presents the broad categories in which we can sort credit derivatives. Once the reader is aware of the different configurations, section 21.2 will describe the

---

[1] It assumes that the reference pricing model is perfect and that any gap can be assumed to be a real market inefficiency.
[2] This is also called a noncovered position since one side of the equivalency is missing.

evolution of the market for credit derivatives. Section 21.3 approaches the use of credit derivatives in different contexts (risk transfer for corporates, for portfolio managers, investment vehicle). The last section deals with the pricing methodologies for credit derivatives.

21.1   THE MAIN CATEGORIES OF CREDIT DERIVATIVES

Before the recent rise of specific credit derivatives, companies have started issuing products with embedded credit derivatives. The groundbreaking issuance of credit-related debt by Enron Corp. is well described in Das (1997) and priced in Das and Tufano (1996) in the spirit of the Jarrow et al. paper. In June 1989, Enron Corp. issued $100 million in noncallable credit-sensitive notes with maturity in June 2001 that had a coupon linked to Enron's credit rating, as measured by either Standard & Poors or Moody's. This issue is considered to have launched the public market in CSNs and the subsequent credit derivatives market. The payment schedule assured payments slightly lower than market rates for the same rating in case of improvement in Enron's rating, but appreciably higher payments in case of downgrades than market rates for corresponding ratings. The structure allowed Enron to issue in a difficult market at a lower rate than market rates for straight fixed-income instruments. The reason for this structure is probably multiple. Possibly the risk transfer appeared favorable to investors that did not want to carry Enron's downgrade risk. An important factor in this specific structure may also have been its signalling impact as Enron somehow committed (thanks to the high cost of a downgrade to the company) to keep or improve its rating. It may also have overcome any agency costs (conflict of interest between shareholders and bondholders in this case) by protecting bondholders against a downgrade. The risk transfer dimension is the one dimension that credit derivatives have since made much easier to replicate.

The concept of the credit derivatives that appeared in the early 1990s represents an attempt by sophisticated financial institutions to apply techniques and methodologies developed in the market risk arena. In its broadest sense, a credit derivative is a customized agreement between two counterparties in which the cash flows are linked to some measure of creditworthiness of a reference credit (in isolation or in combination with some market risk dimension). Like other derivatives with market risk, credit derivatives allow the user to transfer or single out the credit risk of any given asset, possibly transforming or eliminating exposure to this risk dimension without modifying ownership of the underlying asset.

The classification of credit derivatives differs from market derivatives classification. Even the difference between forward and option-type contracts so usual in market derivatives is less clear in credit derivatives (where credit default swaps may look as much as options as swaps). There are currently three main classes of credit derivatives:

1. Spread instruments.
2. Event instruments.
3. Total return instruments.

Spread instruments, such as credit spread options, or credit spread forwards, allow users to take positions on the future spread between two financial assets, with one of them of stable credit risk as reference, such as a government bond or an interbank rate. Although conceptually interesting, these instruments have failed to truly take off, while event instruments have gained liquidity.

Event instruments, such as credit default swaps, offer user protection against a credit event prespecified in the contract by having a payoff contingent on this event (for example, default). They constitute the lion's share of the pure credit derivative markets.

Total return instruments, such as total return swaps, let users transfer the total economic performance of a credit-risky asset against a predetermined rate (e.g. LIBOR plus a spread). Some would not consider these true credit derivatives, though, as they do not isolate credit risk, while the other two types of instruments do. Many publications classify them in the credit risk area. But traders may differ in large firms.

Here is a more complete characterization of the different products. Some purists would consider only the first two classes (credit default swaps and credit spread options) to be pure credit derivatives. Indeed, only these two truly separate credit risk from market risk. Nonetheless, total return swaps (as well as credit sensitive or credit linked notes, as in the Enron deal described above) have a strong credit risk component as well, and thus can be considered as embedding credit risk derivatives.

21.1.1   Credit Default Swaps (or Default Swap, or Credit Swap, or Credit Event Swap)

The credit default swap is the security that is contractually closest to the classical letter of credit. On the "fixed" leg of the swap, the counterparty who is buying credit protection agrees to pay a periodic fixed payment over the life of the swap. In return, the counterparty who is selling credit protection agrees to make a conditional payment should the agreed-upon "reference credit" default or experience some other mutually agreed-upon credit event. This is the "floating" leg of the swap. Overall, credit default swaps look as much as options as swaps. The protection comes as a bullet payment at time of default, if default occurs, rather than as a periodic payment. The reference credit is typically a corporation or some other entity to which the buyer of credit protection has some sort of exposure. The typical payoffs of a credit default swap could thus be:

At time 0:	the event of default is defined and a senior corporate bond of a company is referenced
]0, T[:	the "protection buyer" makes periodical payments to the "seller" in basis points of the notional, for example
At credit event or at maturity (T)	if the company enters into default or in bankruptcy, the "seller" pays to the "buyer": (par — recovery rate). notional

The credit default swap (or default swap, or credit swap) is currently the most common of the true credit derivatives. It should be clear that this instrument is particularly sensitive to the documentation (the so-called "docs") defining notably the event of payment (event of defaults). Nonstandardization has created problems in the last few years, with some not receiving the protection they expected. These problems, arising from a still immature market, seem to have been overcome during the year 1999, a year of restructuring for the credit swap market and the finalization of the ISDA Master Agreement which may finally bring more standardization to the market.

21.1.2 Credit Spread Options

Credit spread options are simply options on a particular reference credit spread in the loan or bond market over a standard rate. One party pays a premium up front in return for a lump sum payment in the event that the reference credit's spread crosses a certain threshold. The payoffs of a typical European style credit spread put option would thus be:

At time 0:	payment of the option price. One-time payment or . . .
]0, T[:	. . . partitioned payments
At maturity (T):	the buyer receives:
	Max(exercise spread − spread at maturity, 0) . time to maturity . notional

This instrument, that looks promising in many ways, has not found a large market at present. It has the advantage over the credit swap of being less contract sensitive. Its payoff depends directly on another rate that reflects the credit risk. This advantage turns in a disadvantage as it may create a basis risk for the user. In that way, the credit spread option is less customizable than the credit swap, which can define any type of event as a payoff determiner. The credit spread option offers more possibilities for future standardization though, something the market for credit derivatives certainly needs at present.

21.1.3 Credit Spread Forward

Credit spread forwards are a straightforwardly understood instrument. Credit spread forwards are forwards on a particular reference credit spread over a standard rate. They are similar to market forwards except that they bear on a predefined credit risk spread.
   The typical payoffs of a credit spread forward are thus:

At time 0:	no exchange. Just a commitment to sell or buy at maturity
]0, T[:	no flow
At maturity (T):	the buyer pays:
	(forward spread − spread at maturity) . time to maturity . notional

Despite their simplicity, credit spread forwards are currently not as frequent an instrument as one could expect. This may come from the hesitation of many players to take full position on credit risk, expecially when pricing does not appear easy. Hedging techniques, though, are becoming more and more available.

21.1.4 Total Return Swaps

A total rate of return swap transfers the total economic performance of a reference asset or index, including cash flows and capital appreciation or depreciation from one party to another. The total return payer pays the total rate of return on the reference asset plus any appreciation; the total return receiver pays a floating rate plus any depreciation on the reference asset. The typical payoffs of a total return swap can thus be:

At time 0:	the counterparties (one of them, say bank X, owning a fixed rate loan, or a bond, for example) define the reference asset and the reference rate (LIBOR, etc.)
]0, T[:	bank X returns to its counterparty all the gains from the loan or the bond in exchange for LIBOR. The swap is reconsidered at differents points in time previously defined. Any position change in the market value of the loan is paid by the bank and vice versa
At maturity (T):	Any position change in the market value of the loan or the bond is again paid by the bank and vice versa

This structure allows one counterparty to hedge the risk of an asset while it remains on the books. Total return swaps are also flexible, allowing users to buy protection for, say, the last two years of a 5-year bond. Total return swaps are particularly popular among insurance companies which, for regulatory purposes, are required to hold some instruments to maturity.

21.2   THE MARKET FOR CREDIT DERIVATIVES

The market for credit derivatives, although small in size ($302 billion, 0.5% of all derivatives' notional value in the US during the first quarter of 2000 (source: Office of the Comptroller of the Currency) has become an essential market in the derivatives field. First, the OCC numbers show that the credit derivatives market has grown hugely since the OCC started to report the market size in the first quarter of 1997, growing almost tenfold in two years (see Table 21.1 and Figure 21.1).

The interest in this new market lies not only in the large margins that banks may raise with exotic, difficult-to-price instruments but more importantly in the fact that the birth of this market has truly completed (and is completing) the financial markets, creating both arbitrage opportunities on a previously poorly priced risk (credit risk) and allowing corporates and financial intermediaries to manage their credit risk exposures with an ease that was previously not possible. See Table 21.2 (source: OCC, p. 7) for market data.

Credit derivatives look like a new release in our toolbox of risk management tools. In fact, if we consider asset swaps as a kind of primary credit derivative, then we can argue that they started trading around the early 1990s. As has been shown earlier, they were constituted as parallel instruments to their analogs in the area of market risks. With the crisis of the middle 1990s and the growing interest in modern contingent products, it became clear that there was a market for credit derivatives. Credit risk is everywhere, in any contract involving bilateral flows or claims to future cash flows. Before the outcoming of such modern instruments, a long list of mitigating techniques has been developed to be able to trade financial market risks on a credit riskfree basis. Some of them are oriented to the protection of one counterparty by imposing some covenants on

Table 21.1 Derivative contracts by product ($ billions)[a]. From *OCC Bank Derivatives Report* (first quarter 2000)

	91Q4 ($)	92Q4 ($)	93Q4 ($)	94Q4 ($)	95Q4 ($)	96Q4 ($)	97Q4 ($)	98Q1 ($)	98Q2 ($)	98Q3 ($)	98Q4 ($)	99Q1 ($)	99Q2 ($)	99Q3 ($)	99Q4 ($)	00Q1 ($)
Futures & fwds	3876	4780	6229	8109	7399	8041	9550	9379	10003	11644	10918	10358	9918	10356	9390	9993
Swaps	2071	2417	3260	4823	5945	7601	9705	10060	10846	12369	14345	14610	15419	17355	17779	19666
Options	1393	1568	2384	2841	3516	4393	5754	6518	7197	8467	7592	7503	7456	7712	7361	7672
Credit derivatives							55	91	129	162	144	191	210	234	287	302
Total	7339	8764	11873	15774	16861	20035	25064	26049	28176	32641	32999	32662	33003	35658	34817	37632

[a]In billions of dollars: notional amount of futures, total exchange traded options, total over the counter options, total forwards, and total swaps. Note that data *after 1994 do not include spot fx* in the total notional amount of derivatives.
Credit derivatives were reported for the first time in the first quarter of 1997. Currently, the Call Report does not differentiate credit derivatives by product and thus they have been added as a separate category. As of 1997, credit derivatives have been included in the sum of total derivatives in this chart.
Note: Numbers may not add due to rounding.
Data source: Call Reports.

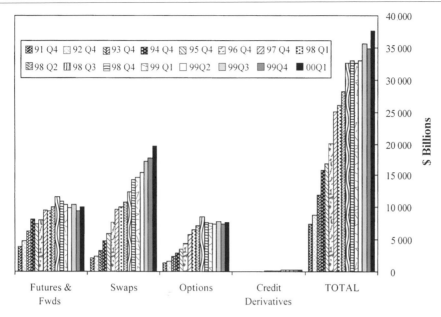

Figure 21.1   Evolution of the market for derivative contracts by product ($ billions). From *OCC Bank Derivatives Report* (first quarter 2000)

the other, while the constitution of clearing houses for standard traded derivatives is the acceptance by a third counterparty of some residual risk. But these techniques are linked to the underlying operation subject to credit risk; there are no margin calls if there are no futures contracts, for example. The possibility of trading credit risks, buying or selling them from or to a counterparty independently of their real existence through underlying operations, is one of the attractive features of credit derivatives.

The second reason for the sudden importance of these instruments is twofold. From one side, we have more and more volatile financial markets with drastic consequences on the number of distressed firms we have witnessed during these last years. From the other side, we have an ever-increasing demand for new investment areas, on standardized markets as well as on OTC markets. With the great speculative bullish market of 1997–99, with the propensity of requiring higher and higher returns, traditional high-grade investments and restriction to high rated classes for OTC trading have left a wide spectrum to emerging markets, investments in small chips and booming technology startups, acceptance of low-grade counterparties for higher spread taking, etc. The increasing exposures therefore impose monitoring, control, the responsibility of trading agents and management of credit risk. Of course, this is the good side of the coin. For others, it is a means to speculate more, or to cash in a good spread given the lack of experience of the participants. Because this market is still young and also because there is no consensus on the right way to price credit risk in the theoretical as well as on the practical field. As has been discussed in previous chapters when introducing credit risk, it is important to define which credit risk are we aware of, and this question does not have a single answer. Credit derivatives have revealed themselves to be strongly contract-dependent, and contract interpretation has been problematic in an area looking for (and getting closer to) standardization.

Table 21.2 From *OCC Bank Derivatives Report* (first quarter 2000). Notional amount of off balance sheet derivatives contracts of the 25 commercial Banks and Trust Companies with the most off balance derivative contracts, March 31, 2000, $ millions. Note: data are preliminary.

Bank	Bank name	State	Total assets	Total derivatives	Total futures (EXCH TR)	Total options (EXCH TR)	Total forwards (OTC)	Total swaps (OTC)	Total options (OTC)	Total credit derivatives (OTC)	Spot FX
1	Chase Manhattan Bank	NY	$312 205	$13 346 628	$740 376	$276 937	$2 764 805	$8 213 571	$1 324 628	$26 311	$144 483
2	Morgan Guaranty TR Co of NY	NY	$182 972	$9 338 142	$516 349	$405 135	$938 877	$4 888 491	$2 413 473	$175 818	$2 572
3	Bank of America NA	NC	$585 373	$6 465 602	$343 963	$329 830	$1 218 302	$3 593 381	$945 121	$35 005	$92 338
4	Citibank NA	NY	$337 958	$4 506 836	$137 553	$56 404	$2 259 803	$1 307 882	$699 067	$46 127	$181 948
5	Bank One National Assn	IL	$101 026	$926 773	$33 250	$384	$115 178	$556 506	$221 206	$250	$12 092
6	First Union National Bank	NC	$231 716	$899 042	$193 435	$148 206	$68 466	$265 431	$214 972	$8 532	$2 934
7	Bank of New York	NY	$72 954	$363 353	$31 042	$10 419	$56 258	$101 303	$164 006	$325	$11 740
8	Fleet National Bank	RI	$148 841	$288 520	$11 467	$39 378	$67 201	$83 817	$83 766	$2 891	$8 464
9	HSBC Bank USA	NY	$82 270	$208 792	$28 585	$16 313	$67 141	$46 430	$49 868	$456	$10 990
10	Wells Fargo Bank NA	CA	$99 155	$201 524	$68 007	$8 005	$29 733	$51 069	$44 625	$85	$710
11	Bankers Trust Co	NY	$46 280	$192 244	$0	$0	$6 155	$155 596	$29 550	$943	$0
12	State Street Bank and Trust Co	MA	$56 235	$139 246	$3 595	$0	$131 498	$2 988	$1 164	$0	$6 509
13	Keybank National Assn	OH	$75 301	$64 995	$9 332	$1 741	$3 616	$43 906	$6 386	$14	$899
14	National City Bank	OH	$34 587	$59 972	$18 318	$0	$854	$31 419	$9 265	$116	$256
15	Mellon Bank National Assn	PA	$39 321	$58 964	$6 419	$615	$25 543	$23 179	$3 208	$0	$4 561
16	PNC Bank National Assn	PA	$66 820	$55 839	$1 346	$0	$5 816	$23 340	$21 013	$4 325	$1 275
17	Lasalle Bank National Assn	IL	$46 217	$37 614	$5 377	$0	$392	$26 980	$4 864	$0	$24
18	Chase Manhattan Bank USA NA	DE	$34 340	$34 634	$32	$0	$3 324	$9 534	$21 744	$0	$0
19	Suntrust Bank	GA	$93 146	$34 229	$1 419	$0	$3 292	$21 590	$7 927	$0	$221
20	First Tennessee Bank NA	TN	$19 159	$31 532	$0	$0	$5 582	$1 522	$24 227	$202	$0
21	Wachovia Bank National Assn	NC	$64 275	$30 243	$0	$0	$4 710	$22 159	$3 053	$320	$314
22	Citibank South Dakota NA	SD	$15 313	$23 308	$7 300	$0	$0	$15 390	$618	$0	$0
23	Northern Trust Co	IL	$27 723	$20 060	$1	$0	$17 443	$2 369	$247	$0	$2 875
24	Chase Bank of Texas NA	TX	$25 359	$15 854	$95	$0	$1 586	$5 878	$8 294	$0	$918
25	Citibank Nevada NA	NV	$7 327	$14 180	$3 100	$0	$2	$9 937	$1 141	$0	$0
	Top 25 Commercial Banks & TCs with derivatives		$2 805 873	$37 358 124	$2 160 360	$1 293 367	$7 795 578	$19 503 668	$6 303 432	$301 719	$486 124
	Other 364 Commercial Banks & TCs with derivatives		$1 745 887	$273 675	$6 833	$10 191	$29 923	$161 851	$64 682	$194	$3 378
	Total amounts for all 389 Bks & TCs with derivatives		$4 551 760	$37 631 799	$2 167 194	$1 303 558	$7 825 501	$19 665 519	$6 368 114	$301 913	$489 502

Note: Currently, the Call Report does not differentiate credit derivatives by contract type. Credit derivatives have been included in the sum of total derivatives here.
Note: Before the first quarter of 1995 total derivatives included spot foreign exchange. Beginning in the first quarter, 1995, spot foreign exchange was reported separately.
Data source: Call Report, schedule RC-L.

The last reason is one of the most important. It will take on even more importance when regulators will admit standard reductions in capital requirements when credit risk is mitigated, diversified away, or transferred through credit derivatives in particular. It is important because it is linked to the main deterrent of efficient and sustainable financial markets: the illiquidity or the scarcity of liquidities. On the theoretical side, markets are efficient, they can be as volatile as they could be, but reversion is always possible. In reality, there exist some barriers under which the market will not be able to recover. It is analogous to stop-loss rules for traders on the exchange. You can assume any drawback whenever your available working capital is still sufficient to ensure the continuity of your strategy. In periods of recession, the need for cash, or, let us say, the convenience yield[3] of available cash can be really high. The lack of available inflow can induce large selling blocks, falling prices and rolling distresses that can plunge the whole market into a crash. Whenever the recognition of credit risk management by regulatory institutions can help alleviate the charges on the trading agents, it is not obvious that credit derivatives will really help to manage the endpoint of credit risk, the risk of a breakdown of the market, or a substantial number of its members due to illiquidity. This will motivate the discussion of section 21.3.

Now that the reader is aware of the potentialities of the development of this market, let us describe it with some of its participants with their typical portfolios and their motives. Owing to the specificity of this market and the difficulty in dealing with credit risk which is less tangible than any other market risk, it is obvious that the expectations of the participants, diverse in size and market power, will not be homogeneous and will therefore reflect into their motives to trade.

21.3   THE USE OF CREDIT DERIVATIVES FOR THE TRANSFER OF RISKS

Credit derivatives can make an important dimension of financial risk tradeable. They thus form an important step toward market completion and efficient risk allocation.

As they provide a specific way of valuing and transferring credit risk exposures, credit derivatives offer financial intermediaries and corporates a more customized way of managing their credit risk exposure than simple ownership transfer of assets or use of credit lines and other guarantees. In particular, credit derivatives may allow users to separate market risk from credit risk. This can be revealed to be particularly useful to corporates as well as to portfolio managers and investors.

21.3.1   The Use of Credit Derivatives for Corporates

Although still in infancy, the use of credit derivatives for corporates is promising (see Frost, 1997, for a good description that we partly follow here). Of particular interest to corporates today is the use of credit derivatives as a means to hedge cross-border credit risk and credit risk on receivables. Increasingly, credit derivatives may also be used as a synthetic form of debt buy-back. Other applications, such as using credit derivatives to

---

[3]The convenience yield is one of the major issues for oil trading, for example. You can have a claim on future oil delivery. But on periods of scarcity, the underlying is far more useful than a claim on it.

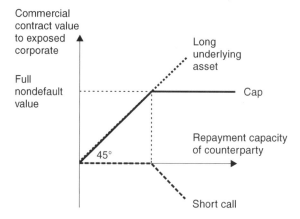

Figure 21.2 The cap

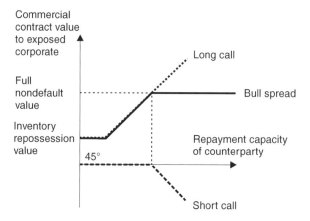

Figure 21.3 The bull spread

hedge against the credit impacts of customer business disruptions (e.g. strikes) seem further away.

Let us consider the credit risk of receivables, for example. Traditionally, corporates have been able to manage the credit risk of commercial contracts by turning to factoring or by buying insurance. Securitization of the receivables is also a viable alternative in specific situations. Most of these alternatives offer partial to full protection, but at a significant cost. Use of traditional equity derivatives is another possible alternative that does present lower costs. Depending on the original contract setup, a commercial agreement can look like a long position in the underlying combined with a short position in a call (a cap) (see Figure 21.2).

In this case, if the counterparty does well, the contract value is capped. But losses are fully taken on by our corporate. It can also look like a bull spread (see Figure 21.3), if the contract specifies conditions under which the corporate can cut its losses and recoup part of its investment, for example, via inventory repossession (it corresponds to a long position in a call with a low strike, and a short position in a call with a high strike).

In both cases, use of long and short positions on calls on the underlying allow to hedge the position. A good proxy of the underlying may be the value of the counterparty itself, thus the use of equity derivatives. Equity derivatives being generally rather liquid, the cost of the operation remains low. The major difficulties that arise are twofold. First, major basis risk may arise as the risk of the equity of the counterparty may differ from the risk of payment on the commercial contract. Second, many commercial counterparties are not traded counterparties and thus do not offer the opportunity of equity derivatives.

Credit derivatives are more expensive and less liquid, being OTC products, but they offer a more efficient means of hedging the credit component of the overall risk of the commercial contract. Current credit derivatives are very flexible financial contracts as we have seen that their payouts can be derived from loan or bond values, default or credit events, credit spreads, or credit ratings. These reference assets, in turn, can be associated with single names, baskets or indices with cash settlement or physical delivery of a relevant underlying asset or portfolio of assets. Basis risk can thus be much better controlled than when using the more liquid equity derivatives. The reference asset is obviously selected with an eye to minimizing this basis risk. This includes attempting to select assets that have equal rights to payment in a default scenario (*pari passu*). In other words, if you have a senior unsecured obligation from the company, your reference asset should also be senior unsecured. The major difficulty here lies in finding a reference asset that offers a sufficiently low basis risk.

Suppose that Star Corp. has a $50 million account receivable exposure to Sun Ltd. To hedge this, Star Corp. would first determine the most appropriate reference asset, a bank loan or publicly traded bond that would represent this receivable. Priority should be similar to the receivables in order to limit credit risk. Star would then determine with its the dealer the structure of the deal that fits best its hedging preferences. A credit swap, for example, would provide event protection that may be close to Star's desires for a one-shot deal. A total return swap may be a better structure for a continuing relationship in between Star and Sun. The credit swap is more complex to define and less secure contractually (as the event of default can have some legal ambiguity). The credit swap structure will require defining a contingent payment methodology, be it cash settlement based on the market value of the reference assets, or some other predetermined amount based on the expected recovery value of the receivables. While the total return swap is easier to define and contractually stronger, the total return swap may present more basis risk, as will be done on a reference instrument that is sufficiently liquid. The periodic payments to the swap counterparty (for credit as well as total return swaps) should typically be based on the underlying credit spread on the reference asset, the custody costs relating to the underlying assets, the cost of funding relative to LIBOR, the capital costs from the use of the counterparty's balance sheet, and credit and capital charges on the swap. Some flexibility can be built in using the definition of the credit event. The overwhelming number of contracts link the credit event or trigger to some form of default or bankruptcy scenario. However, credit events could also be structured, based on the change in market value of the reference asset (i.e. below some predetermined threshold) or in the event of a ratings downgrade. All these elements have to be taken into account by the bank in order to do the pricing of the swap. Note, though, that pricing of credit-risky instruments seems secure only when simple replication is viable. Otherwise, methodologies differ and can give somewhat different numbers as illustrated below. In general, because of the novelty and the exotic character of these instruments, as well as because of the complexity of the pricing issue, both at a theoretical and at a practical level, pricing can differ in nontrivial ways from one intermediary to another.

A major source of use for credit risk derivatives for corporates lies in the management of sovereign risk. More and more multinationals that invest in emerging markets complement other forms of insurance (such as home-country subsidized insurance structures) with credit derivatives. An engineering company that works on a large infrastructure project in a South East Asian country would be a typical user of such a deal. This use gives rise to large notional values and thus represents an important share (possibly the major share) of corporate uses of credit derivatives. For example, using a default swap, a corporate could pay a dealer a fixed period payment in exchange for a contingent payment based on a given country's equity index or specific bonds. Bonds considered would typically be sovereign bonds. Besides the basis risk problem that arises in this situation, similar to that discussed above, the necessity of having a good reference asset limits the use of credit derivatives to countries with some decently well-traded sovereign fixed-income instruments.

Although these are the two major uses of credit derivatives by corporates at today's rate, many other uses can be foreseen in the future as the markets extend and liquidity increases price reliability. It may become interesting at some point to manage counterparty risk on swap portfolios for corporates also, as the swap market opens to lower ratings and credit risk pricing becomes more efficient. In general, credit derivatives could also be used to synthetically repurchase outstanding debt. For example, the corporate could do a total return swap with a bank paying LIBOR plus a spread in return for the corporate receiving the coupon and the change in market value of its debt. This avoids defeasement or tendering the debt immediately, but locks in the current price of the bonds. It also can be done less publicly, so that the cash market is not immediately alerted to the repurchase effort, and less likely to adjust prices accordingly. Though, depending on the dealer's position in the cash market and prevailing conditions, its offsetting transactions might give some indication.

21.3.2   The Use of Credit Derivatives for Portfolio Managers and Investors

Bond investors know that a downgrade in the rating of a bond will decrease its value even when no default has occurred. On the other hand, bond issuers can see their cost of borrowing for future operations depends strongly on unanticipated events. Credit derivatives can thus be a financial institution affair as well as a corporate concern.

We have been interviewing a European financial institution which has a growing activity in the credit derivatives sector. They mainly trade puts on asset swaps and a fewer credit default swaps. It must be noted that puts on asset swaps are not credit derivatives in the sense of a direct linkage to a credit risk event (the default or the downgrading) or to the credit spread. However, many agents that trade credit derivatives trade in fact a large portion of options on asset swaps.

Overall, if we divide the trading motivations in "arbitrage", "investment vehicle", or "credit lines management", we observe that the main trading motivation is to trade credit derivatives in an investment perspective. In that case, only sovereign risk positions are considered. The "arbitrage"-driven operations are purely on corporates and the "credit

Table 21.3 Medium size European bank market in credit derivatives and uses

	Sovereign (%)	Financials (%)	Industrials (%)	Total (%)
Puts on asset swaps				
Arbitrage	0	0	11	11
Investment	89	0	0	89
Credit line management	0	0	0	0
Total	89	0	11	100
Credit default swaps				
Arbitrage	0	0	11	11
Investment	22	0	0	22
Credit line management	0	67	0	67
Total	22	67	11	100
Both Instruments				
Arbitrage	0	0	11	11
Investment	81	0	0	81
Credit line management	0	8	0	8
Total	81	8	11	100

line management"-driven operations are purely related to underlying financial firms. It appears that put on asset swaps are mainly used in the context of an investment incentive, while credit default swaps are mainly used in the case of credit line management.

It can be also mentioned that all sovereign risk are in Euros (the domestic currency) while others are in US dollar terms.

Table 21.3 summarizes the described activity.

21.4 THE PRICING OF CREDIT DERIVATIVES

21.4.1 A Caveat on the Pricing of Credit Derivatives

The credit derivative product is different from the traditional market derivatives and is less easily fitted by standard pricing models because, in the present context, their tractability is somewhat questionable. Default as an event is an absorbing state that has more complex implications than the simple exercise of an option (although the technical analogy is valid). The resolution of default is very opaque. Liquidity certainly plays an important role that pricing theories detailed below do not value. This is all the more important where the market is still in its infancy. Liquidity may be even more of a problem in the Asian markets or in Europe than in the US, where both the credit derivatives market is somewhat larger and alternatives exist that allow for replication. Note also that the definition of default is not perfectly stable itself. A credit derivative such as the credit default swap depends on the definition of the event that will trigger a payment by one of the counterparties. This requires a well-documented contract with the shortest range of interpretation by the counterparties. But, depending on the country, the type of counterparty, and the product, it can be difficult to surround the definition of the event such that, if default should happen in reality, both parties would agree that this is the event that triggers the payment. The documentation established in the past (the "docs") for these deals has not always been foolproof. These types of difficulties may supersede many technical refinements.

The fact that both counterparties would rely on the same underlying is also problematic. The reality is much more complex since counterparties negotiate a credit derivative in order to match a particular exposure, for an independent position or in the context of banking affairs. Depending on the money of reference and the regulation to which the underlying exposure is subject to, the counterparty will have some particular demand that will reflect into the price of the derivative instrument once compared to the offer of protection.

As an example, suppose you are a seller of protection: you owe some money if some event happens. As a buyer, in the pure protection perspective, you are looking at maximizing your chances to get money back at the time of the defined event, while regulations and other specifications can differ widely from your current exposures. This will result in a mismatching of recovery amount and timing.

Another example of the difficulty in matching exposures is the case of Japan's distressed firms. The credit market in Japanese industry is mainly constituted of corporate private loans which are not freely traded and therefore illiquid. How can we reasonably make use of the marking-to-market, the most popular risk mitigating technique in standard Japanese financial markets, in a default swap? The valuation of companies can be difficult and could very well provide too wide distortions to be estimated with classical techniques.

Nonetheless, as markets become more liquid, and as products become more standardized, it is clear that the benchmark provided by the theoretical models become more and more pertinent. Empirical studies, which are still lacking, will hopefully be developed. But already some companies have developed or are in the process of developing proprietary models in order to identify irrational differences in pricing and take advantage of these differences.

21.4.2 Pricing Via Replication

Although complex models such as those presented in previous chapters (structural approach, reduced-form approach) should ideally become the way of pricing credit derivatives, the complexity of the contracts and the low reliability of fitting the previous models have made more simple methodologies predominant in pricing credit derivatives. The best alternative, when possible, is to price these instruments via simple replication. Credit default swaps and total return swaps are usually priced this way. For example, buying protection via a credit default swap is functionally equivalent to shorting a floating rate note (FRN) with the same maturity, issuer, credit rating, and seniority in bankruptcy and buying a corresponding AAA FRN. The payoff on this portfolio equals a payment stream equal to the excess of the FRN coupon over the AAA FRN coupon, plus a contingent payment equal to the loss on the FRN upon default. In equilibrium, the value of the credit default swap should equal the value of the replicating portfolio.

In a more realistic institutional setup, and supposing that the cash bond that is available with the underlying credit risk is fixed rate, then the investor who wants to replicate her/his selling the protection can go through the swap markets and through

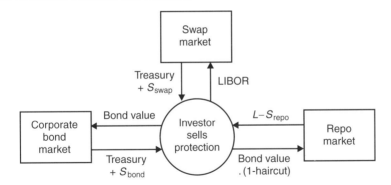

Figure 21.4 Replication of short position in credit default swap

the repo markets. Suppose, for example, that an investor sells protection via a credit default swap on MLCorp. and that there is a coupon bond of MLCorp. of the same maturity that is available on the markets. The investor can replicate her/his position by:

1. Purchasing the MLCorp. bond at a spread of Treasury + S_{bond} for par.
2. Paying fixed at a rate of Treasury + S_{swap} on a swap of the same maturity as the bond against LIBOR.
3. Financing the position in the repo market with the MLCorp. bond as collateral at a spread to LIBOR of $L - S_{repo}$.

See Figure 21.4 for illustration of the classical structure (a similar example can be found in Saunders, 1999).

If there is no haircut on the repo deal, the position exactly replicates a credit default swap. If there is a haircut, the price impact of the haircut has to be factored in (see Chapter 18 on collateralization for more on the topic).

The above replication would generally be considered an exact replication by the markets and thus be used for pricing.

The net of the flows considered in the replication is $S_{bond} - S_{swap} + S_{repo}$. This would thus give the credit default swap premium. Contract design matters first among instruments that are not yet fully standardized. Some credit default swaps may actually require payment of the premium until maturity even in case of default. This should obviously affect the pricing. (Duffie, 1999, presents a thorough discussion of good replication conditions on a similar setup.) More fundamentally, though, the replication described above works well as long as all the markets involved are efficient. Low credit risk may not get good pricing from the swap market (possibly cannot access them at all), or worse from our point of view, may access them with specific collateral requirements that are not taken into account in the pricing but that (as shown in Chapter 18 on collateralization) do affect the pricing. One possibility would be to obtain from theoretical models a price modified to take into account the presence of collateral. The swap markets remain quite efficient, but the repo markets, especially for high credit risk, may show even more inefficiencies. Haircuts may be imposed on the collateral (the investor may get less than 100% of value for the MLCorp. bond) and this will also affect the pricing. The counterparty risk of the repo deal itself cannot be neglected as defaults have occurred in the repo market as well (this would be also true for the swap, but should have less impact on the pricing). And, more fundamentally, instruments and rates may not be available to obtain a good replication: the bond with the correct maturity may not exist (and bonds of the same rating are not necessarily good substitutes as ratings do not take into account recovery risk well). Swap quotes may not be available for the investor. Worse, and more probable, the repo market may not offer a quote for that specific bond, specially for low rated bonds (or nonrated bonds). Special repos have been known to be built from credit default swaps quotes themselves, which defeats the object of our exercise. Having formal pricing models of different classes of credit derivatives thus represents a viable alternative to replication.

We present below two models for credit derivatives that can be used when simple replication is not viable (or not unambiguous). The first model is a refined structural model that frames the credit derivative problem as a compound option problem (credit risk being an option and the credit derivative being an option on the option of credit risk). It presents the nice feature of allowing for N-shaped credit spread term structure, an empirical fact not accommodated by classical structural credit risk models. The second model takes credit spreads as an exogenous process (a feature that makes fitting easy) and derives simple option pricing on these spreads, while leading to some unexpected consequences which should be of interest to practitioners.

21.4.3 A Structural Model for Credit Derivatives: Das (1995)

Das (1995) presents an evolution of the structural models that allows for pricing of credit derivatives (and credit default swaps as a special case) as compound options. The model allows for stochastic interest rates as well as stochastic exercise price. Interestingly, the Das (1995) model provides for N-shaped credit spread term structures by combining stochastic interest rates and endogenous recovery. The classical credit risk structural models (Merton, 1974, Longstaff and Schwartz, 1995b) give rise to hump-shaped credit spread term structures, as previously shown. The credit spreads rise first then fall with maturity and tend asymptotically toward a constant in the Merton model and toward 0 in the Longstaff and Schwartz model (see Wei and Guo, 1997, for further discussion). In the case of high credit risk (junk bonds) these models give a monotonic decrease of the spreads with the maturity. Fama (1987) and Wei and Guo (1997) tend to find that credit spreads take a N-shape with maturity: they first rise, then decrease, then rise again. Although theoretical discussions of the time length considered in these empirical studies would be valid, the empirical fact remains that in the medium to short term, we observe N-shaped credit spread term structures that cannot be fitted by the classical hump shape of the usual structural models. The Das (1995) model relies on the Ho and Lee (1986) term structure model and obtains N-shaped credit spread term structures and prices theoretical credit default swaps as a compound option. The Ho and Lee term structure model has the advantage of being a Markov analytically tractable model. It easily reaches exact fits of the empirical term structure. Its main weaknesses certainly are its lack of mean reversion and the simplicity of the volatility of interest rates in the model.

Consider an option in which the writer agrees to compensate the buyer for a prespecified fall in credit standing of the issuer of the underlying bond (as determined by a strike level either in ratings or in yields). The payoff of the option is the amount by which the price of the bond at the prevailing default-free rate plus the spread defined by the strike exceed the prevailing market price of the bond. With constant interest rates, it means that

$$K = Fe^{-(r+r^*)(T-T^*)}, \tag{21.1}$$

where T is the maturity of the bond, T^* the maturity of the option, and r^* the strike rate and all the other usual notations.

If we assume that the value of the firm follows a process

$$dV = \mu V dt + \sigma_1 V dz_1 + \sigma_2 V dz_2 \tag{21.2}$$

and that forward interest rates are given by

$$df(t, T) = \theta(t, T) dt + \sigma_r dz_1. \tag{21.3}$$

As the two processes (firm value and forward rates of interest rates) share the Wiener process z_1, they are correlated.

Since equity S is a call option on the value of the firm with maturity being the maturity of the debt T and exercise price the face value of the debt, debt can be valued as the difference between the value of the firm and the equity value. After some calculations, one obtains[4]:

$$D(0, T) = V(0)[1 - N(k)] + FP(0, T)N(k - \psi), \tag{21.4}$$

where $P(0, T)$ is the price of a safe discount bond at 0 maturing at T,

$$k = \frac{\log\left[\dfrac{V(0)}{FP(0, T)}\right] + 1/2\psi^2}{\psi},$$

and

$$\psi^2 = (\sigma_1^2 + \sigma_2^2)T - \sigma_1\sigma_r T^2 + 2/3 * \sigma_r^2 T^3.$$

Note that the author also gives a general form for a HJM term structure.

The simple Ho and Lee structure allows for many different shapes of the credit spread term structure, a welcome generalization of the previous models using Vasicek and limited to hump-shaped credit spread term structure. Indeed the shape of the credit spread structure is affected by the choice of the three volatility parameters σ_1, σ_2, and σ_r. σ_r, which measures the riskfree interest rate volatility, tends to affect the long maturity spreads. Here σ_1, the correlation between changes in firm value and interest rates, affects spreads at short maturities, σ_2, and the volatility of the firm value that is independent from interest rate volatility affects the spread curve across all maturities. Yield curves and spread curves of many different shapes can thus be fitted nicely with this simple structural model. N-shaped credit spread curves, as described in Fama (1987) and Guo and Wei (1997) notably, are easily obtained.

Once credit-risky debt is priced, we can follow Das into pricing options on risky debt as a compound option (as risky debt itself is an option on firm value). The buyer of the

---

[4]We have modified the result from the Das paper as there seems to have been a computational mistake in the published paper.

option receives compensation when the date T^* price of the credit-risky bond falls below the price of a bond priced at the riskless rate plus r^*, the strike credit spread. Because interest rates are stochastic, the exercise value of the bond is also stochastic. It can be written:

$$K(T^*, T, F, r^*) = F \exp(-[-(1/T - T^*) \log P(T^*, T) + r^*](T - T^*)).$$

The price of the credit derivative is then obtained by taking the expectation under the risk-neutral measure Q:

$$\text{Credit derivative value} = \int_{z_1} \int_{z_2} \max(K(T^*, T, F, r^*) - D(T^*, T), 0) \phi(z_1) \phi(z_2) dz_1 dz_2.$$

Direct computation of the double integral takes considerable computer time, but the author proposes discrete time approximations based on this methodology that reduce computation time drastically. Discrete time approximations also allow for easy extensions to coupon bonds, debt with embedded derivatives (such as convertibles or callables), alternative bankruptcy procedures and stochastic volatilities. The discrete time approach is straightforward, starting from the general continuous time presentation carried out above. Numerical analysis based on binomial trees shows (as presented in Das, 1995) that such credit derivatives tend to be valued highest at middle maturities (when a combination of both the time value of the credit risk debt and that of the derivative instrument on the credit-risky debt is considered), decrease with the volatility of interest rates and increase with the volatility of the firm.

21.4.4   A Model for Credit Spread Options: Longstaff and Schwartz (1995)

Longstaff and Schwartz (1995a) present a model in which credit spreads are supposed to follow an exogenous stochastic process. This simple structure insures that a few empirical facts are included, those that can easily be checked for credit spreads, notably the fact that credit spreads are mean-reverting. If one further assumes that they are conditionally lognormally distributed, one can model credit spreads via their logarithm (to insure spreads are positive) as

$$dL = (a - bL)dt + \sigma dZ_1, \tag{21.5}$$

where L is the logarithm of the credit spread cs.

Of course, modelizing credit spreads directly like this allows for a less good analysis (and a less good understanding of the economics behind the analysis) than using structural models. On the other hand, this simplification gives an easy fit to past data and generates interesting results, as discussed below.

We can then assume a Vasicek interest rate model:

$$dr = (\alpha - \beta r)dt + \sigma_r dZ_2 \tag{21.6}$$

with a correlation of ρ between the two Wiener processes.

The model allows for easy pricing of spread options. From standard valuation theory, we know that the price of the European option F must solve the stochastic PDE:

$$\frac{\sigma^2}{2} F_{LL} + \rho \sigma \sigma_r F_{Lr} + (\alpha - \beta r) F_r + (a - bL) F_L - rF - F_T = 0 \tag{21.7}$$

subject to the initial condition $F(L, r, 0) = H(L)$, payoff at maturity of the option.

Consider a European call on spreads $C(L, r, T)$. The payoff function of this option can be written:

$$H(cs) = \max(0, cs - K) = \max(0, e^L - K), \tag{21.8}$$

where K is the strike spread of the option.

The authors propose on the basis of Longstaff (1990) a closed-form solution (determined by using the certainty-equivalent representation):

$$C(L, r, T) = P(0, T)e^{(\mu + \eta^2/2)}N(d_1) - KP(0, T)N(d_2) \tag{21.9}$$

with

$$\mu = e^{-bT}L + \frac{1}{b}\left(a - \frac{\rho\sigma\sigma_r}{\beta}\right)x(1 - e^{-bT}) + \frac{\rho\sigma\sigma_r}{\beta(b + \beta)}x(1 - e^{-(b+\beta)T}), \tag{21.10}$$

$$\eta^2 = \frac{\sigma^2(1 - e^{-2bT})}{2b},$$

$$d_1 = \frac{-\ln K + \mu + \eta^2}{\eta},$$

$$d_2 = d_1 - \eta.$$

Other classical properties that can be derived from that point of the derivation are the delta of a call and the put–call parity. The delta of the call on credit spread is

$$\text{Delta}(L, r, T) = P(0, T)e^{(\mu + \eta^2/2)}N(d_1)e^{-bT}e^{-L} \tag{21.11}$$

and the put–call parity is

$$\text{Put}(L, r, T) + P(0, T)e^{(\mu + \sigma_r^2/2)} = \text{call}(L, r, T) + P(0, T). \tag{21.12}$$

The authors derive several counterintuitive comparative statics linked to the mean reversion of the credit spread. These results show that classical properties of equity derivatives could be misleading with credit derivatives, if the proposed model is pertinent. Among these results, we notably have:

1. The value of a call option on the credit spread can be less than its intrinsic value.
2. The call price can be a concave function of the credit spread (while calls on equity are always convex functions of the underlying). In other words, the call price can change by less than the change in the underlying.
3. The delta of a call on the credit spread decreases to 0 as maturity goes to infinity. A consequence of this property is that large maturity differences among instruments will lead to poor hedging properties.

Note that Das and Sundaram (1998) present a model for credit derivatives pricing that is arbitrage-free, accommodates path dependence, and handles a range of securities, even with American features. The basis of the computer implementation, as the model is notably interesting for its engineering implementation, is presented in the paper.

Duffie (1999) presents an application of a classical reduced-form default model to credit default swaps. Starting from a default rate of h (intensity of the corresponding

Poisson process), one can price $1 at time t if default has not yet occurred, and $1 at default if default occurred before. Assuming a recovery rate of a certain level, it is thus easy to determine the premium of the credit default swap that will insure that the value of the swap at origination is 0. The value of the credit default swap for our investor (selling default insurance) corresponds to the recovery value "discounted" as an annuity until maturity at the value of $1 when default has occurred just before, minus the premium "discounted" as an annuity until maturity at the value of $1 when default does not occur before. The premium that will insure a zero value to the credit default swap is thus the recovery value times the ratio of the discounted annuity values with and without default. This type of model suffers from the independence in the pricing of recoveries and default processes, a problem that the author stresses could be less evident in practice than expected, as estimation errors may compensate each other.

In general, and as usual, structural-form models give a more precise idea of the impact of true economic underliers to the pricing of credit derivatives and are thus more meaningful economically. Reduced-form models, on the other hand, can handle more complex structures more easily and can provide for better fitting of historical data (without always capturing the nonlinear interdependence of the variables concerned).

21.5 REFERENCES

Albanese, Claudio, 1997, "Credit Exposure, Diversification Risk and Coherent VaR", *Working Paper*, Department of Mathematics, University of Toronto, 20 pp.

Bank of England, 1996, "Developing a Supervisory Approach to Credit Derivatives", *Discussion Paper*, Supervision and Surveillance, November 1996.

Basle Committee on Banking Supervision, 1999, *Credit Risk Modelling: Current Practices and Applications*, Basle, April, 60 pp.

Crouhy, Michel, Dan Galai and Robert Mark, 2000, "A Comparative Analysis of Current Credit Risk Models", *Journal of Banking and Finance*, **24** (1–2), 59–117.

Das, S. R., 1995, "Credit Risk Derivatives", *Journal of Derivatives*, Spring, 7–23.

Das, Sanjiv, 1997, "Enron Corp. — Credit Sensitive Notes" (Harvard Case HBS #297 099).

Das, Sanjiv and Peter Tufano, 1966, "Pricing Credit Sensitive Debt when Interest Rates, Credit Ratings and Credit Spreads are Stochastic", *Journal of Financial Engineering*, **5** (2), June.

Delianedis, Gordon and Robert Geske, 1998, "Credit Risk and Risk Neutral Default Probabilities: Information about Rating Migrations and Defaults", *Working Paper*, Anderson Graduate School, July, 39 pp.

Duffee, Gregory R., 1996, "Rethinking Risk Management for Banks: Lessons from Credit Derivatives", *Working Paper*, Federal Reserve Board, April 18, 31 pp.

Duffee, Gregory R. and Chunsheng Zhou, 1996, "Bank and Credit Derivatives: Is it Always Good to Have More Risk Management Tools?", *Working Paper*, Federal Reserve Board, September, 26 pp.

Duffie, Darrell, 1999, *Credit Swap Valuation*, Association for Investment Management and Research, 73–86.

Duffie, Darrell and Jun Pan, 1997, "An Overview of Value at Risk", *The Journal of Derivatives*, Spring, 7–49.

Fama, Eugene F., 1986, "Term Premiums and Default Premiums in Money Markets", *Journal of Financial Economics*, **17**, 175–96.

Fama, Eugene F and Kenneth R. French, 1987, "Forecasting Returns on Corporate Bonds and Common Stocks", University of California at Los Angeles, Anderson Graduate School of Management Finance, *Working Paper*: 4–88, p. 26, December.

Federal Reserve, 1998, *Credit Risk Models at Major U.S. Banking Institutions: Current State of the Art and Implications for Assessment of Capital Adequacy*, Federal Reserve System Task Force on Internal Credit Risk Models, May, 57 pp.

Finger, Christopher, 1998, *Sticks and Stones*, RiskMetrics Group Publication, 10 pp.

Frost, Joyce, 1997, *Corporate Uses for Credit Derivatives*, International Treasurer.

Ho, Thomas S. Y. and Sang-bin Lee, 1986, "Term Structure Movements and Pricing Interest Rate Contingent Claims", *Journal of Finance*, **41** (5), December, 1011–29.

Holton, Glyn A., 1995, "Risk Visualization", *Research Paper Advanced Visual Systems*, 11 pp.

Hull, John, 1989, "Assessing Credit Risk in a Financial Institution's Off-Balance Sheet Commitments", *Journal of Financial and Quantitative Analysis*, **24** (4), December, 489–501.

Iben, B. and R. Brotherton-Ratcliffe, 1994, "Credit Loss Distributions and Required Capital for Derivatives Portfolios", *Journal of Fixed Income*, June.

Jamshidian, Farshid and Yu Zhu, 1997, "Scenario Simulation: Theory and Methodology", *Finance and Stochastics*, **1**, 43–67.

J P Morgan, 1997, CreditMetrics® documentation: *Introduction to CreditMetrics* (35 pp.) and *Technical Document* (199 pp.).

Kealhofer, Stephen, 1998, "Portfolio Management of Default Risk", *Net Exposure*, **1** (2).

Koyluoglu, Ugur and Andrew Hickman, 1998, "Reconciliable Differences", *Risk Magazine*, October.

Koyluoglu, Ugur and Andrew Hickman, 1998, "A Generalized Framework for Credit Risk Portfolio Models", *Working Paper*, October, 18 pp.

Longstaff, Francis and Eduardo Schwartz, 1995a, "Valuing Credit Derivatives", *The Journal of Fixed Income*, June, 6–12.

Longstaff, Francis and Eduardo Schwartz, 1995b, "A Simple Approach to Valuing Risky Fixed and Floating Rate Debt", *Journal of Finance*, **50** (3), July, 789–819.

Merton, Robert C., 1974, "On the Pricing of Corporate Debt: The Risk Structure of Interest Rates", *The Journal of Finance*, **29**, May, 449–70.

Office of the Comptroller of the Currency, Administrator of National Banks (USA), 2000, *OCC Bank Derivatives Report — First Quarter 2000*, 40 pp.

Saunders, Anthony, 1999, *Credit Risk Measurement*, John Wiley & Sons.

Toft, Klaus B. and Brian Prucyk, 1996, "Options on Leveraged Equity: Theory and Empirical Tests", *Working Paper*, Graduate School of Business, Department of Finance, University of Texas at Austin, August, 42 pp.

Toft, Klaus B. and Brian Prucyk, 1997, "Options on Leveraged Equity: Theory and Empirical Tests", *The Journal of Finance*, **52** (3), July, 1151–80.

Van Deventer, D., Samuel Chang and Sou Cheng Choi, 1999, "Credit Risk Models and Applications in Asian Markets", *Working Paper* for the 11th PACAP/FMA Finance Conference, Kamamura Corporation, July.

Van Deventer, D., Samuel Chang and Sou Cheng Choi, 1999, "The Merton Model and Jarrow Model of Credit Risk and Implications for Bank Safety and Soundness", *Working Paper*, Kamamura Corporation, July, 16 pp.

Wei, D. G. and D. Guo, 1997, "Pricing Risky Debt: An Empirical Comparison of the Longstaff and Schwartz and Merton Models", *The Journal of Fixed Income*, September, 9–28.

Wilson, Tom, 1997a, "Portfolio Credit Risk I", *Risk Magazine*, **10** (9), September.

Wilson, Tom, 1997b, "Portfolio Credit Risk II", *Risk Magazine*, **10** (9), September.

Part Seven
Appendices

Itô's Lemma[1]

22.1 INTRODUCTION

Suppose $F(X, t)$, a function of two variables. We further assume that its partial derivatives are continuous functions.

Where X_t is a differentiable function, we have

$$dF(X, t) = \frac{\partial F}{\partial X}(X_t, t)\frac{dX_t}{dt}\, dt + \frac{\partial F}{\partial t}(X_t, t)\, dt,$$

or

$$dF(X, t) = \frac{\partial F}{\partial X}(X_t, t)\, dX_t + \frac{\partial F}{\partial t}(X_t, t)\, dt.$$

Some remarks:

- F is a function of two variables, $\partial F/\partial X$ is a new function of two variables, the partial derivative with respect to the first variable, and $\partial F/\partial X\,(X_t, t)$ is the value of this new function applied to points X_t and t.

- The differential expression:

$$dF = \frac{\partial F}{\partial X}\, dX_t + \frac{\partial F}{\partial t}\, dt,$$

is equivalent to the integral formula:

$$F(X_s, s) - F(X_0, 0) = \int_0^s \frac{\partial F}{\partial X}(X_t, t)\, dX_t + \int_0^s \frac{\partial F}{\partial t}(X_t, t)\, dt.$$

Suppose now that X_t is not differentiable. We can decompose the time interval $[0, s]$ in small intervals of length Δt and obtain, through the Taylor theorem, that

$$F(X_s, s) - F(X_0, 0) = \lim_{\Delta t \to 0} \sum \frac{\partial F}{\partial X}(X_t, t)\Delta X_t$$

$$+ \lim_{\Delta t \to 0} \frac{1}{2}\sum \frac{\partial^2 F}{\partial X^2}(X_t, t)(\Delta X_t)^2$$

$$+ \lim_{\Delta t \to 0} \sum \frac{\partial F}{\partial t}(X_t, t)\Delta t$$

$$+ \lim_{\Delta t \to 0} \text{remainder}(\Delta t),$$

---

[1]Special thanks to André Dubey from Lausanne University for his clear introduction to stochastic processes.

with

$$\Delta X_t = X_{t+\Delta t} - X_t.$$

By hypothesis, X_t is a continuous function. For this function to be not differentiable, it has to be constituted by very small oscillations that are so frequent that the slope is always $-\infty$ or $+\infty$.

The variation of such a function is infinite, i.e. that

$$\lim_{\Delta t \to 0} \sum |\Delta X_t| = +\infty,$$

while

$$\lim_{\Delta t \to 0} \sum \Delta X_t = X_s - X_0.$$

The interesting case is the one where the quadratic variation of the function X_t is a continuously differentiable function, i.e. that

$$\langle X \rangle_s = \lim_{\Delta t \to 0} \sum (\Delta X_t)^2$$

is a differentiable function. Notice that some textbooks write $\langle X_s, X_s \rangle$ instead of $\langle X \rangle_s$. In this case, the remainder of the Taylor expansion above tends to 0 and, since

$$\Delta \langle X \rangle_s = (\Delta X_t)^2,$$

we can write

$$F(X_s, s) - F(X_0, 0) = \lim_{\Delta t \to 0} \sum \frac{\partial F}{\partial X}(X_t, t) \Delta X_t$$

$$+ \frac{1}{2} \int_0^s \frac{\partial^2 F}{\partial X^2}(X_t, t) d\langle X \rangle_t$$

$$+ \int_0^s \frac{\partial F}{\partial t}(X_t, t) dt.$$

The remaining limit in this expression is called the "Itô integral" and it is written as

$$\int_0^s \frac{\partial F}{\partial X}(X_t, t) dX_t.$$

In its differential form, we can rewrite the above expression as

$$dF(X_t, t) = \frac{\partial F}{\partial X}(X_t, t) dX_t + \frac{1}{2} \frac{\partial^2 F}{\partial X^2}(X_t, t) d\langle X \rangle_t + \frac{\partial F}{\partial t}(X_t, t) dt.$$

22.2   THE ITÔ PROCESS

In particular, the trajectories of the standard Wiener process W_t are nondifferentiable continuous functions. Their quadratic variation is

$$\langle W \rangle_t = t.$$

Therefore, in that case, we have

$$dF(W_t, t) = \frac{\partial F}{\partial X}(W_t, t)\,dW_t + \frac{1}{2}\frac{\partial^2 F}{\partial X^2}(W_t, t)\,dt + \frac{\partial F}{\partial t}(W_t, t)\,dt.$$

An Itô process is defined by the following differential equation:

$$dX_t = A_t\,dt + B_t\,dW_t,$$

where A_t and B_t are Markov processes with continuous trajectories. Itô's theorem shows that, under certain conditions for A_t and B_t such a process exists and it is unambiguously determined.

In particular, we have

1. $X_s = X_0 + \int_0^s A_t\,dt + \int_0^s B_t\,dW_t.$
2. If $A_t = 0$, X_t is a martingale.
3. $d\langle X \rangle_t = B_t^2\,dt.$

In this process, A_t is the time t trend and B_t is the volatility.

22.3   THE LEMMA

Applying the formula we get, for a given function $F(X, t)$,

$$dF(X_t, t) = \frac{\partial F}{\partial X}(X_t, t)\,dX_t + \frac{1}{2}\frac{\partial^2 F}{\partial X^2}(X_t, t)\,d\langle X \rangle_t + \frac{\partial F}{\partial t}(X_t, t)\,dt.$$

Thus

$$dF(X_t, t) = \frac{\partial F}{\partial X}(X_t, t)\,B_t\,dW_t + \left\{\frac{\partial F}{\partial X}(X_t, t)\,A_t\,\frac{1}{2}\frac{\partial^2 F}{\partial X^2}(X_t, t)\,B_t^2 + \frac{\partial F}{\partial t}(X_t, t)\right\}dt.$$

Itô's lemma shows, therefore, that $F(X_t, t)$ is still an Itô process and enables us to compute its trend or drift and its volatility.

A Review of Interest Rate Models

23.1 INTRODUCTION

It is important to emphasize pricing models of the term structure of interest rates since they represent the main source of market risk that is being studied in conjunction with credit risk. Most credit risk sensitive contracts are in fact interest-rate-dependent contracts. As is stressed in the present work, the difficulty of the appraisal of credit risk resides in part in the interaction existing between both sources of risk. Many of the models presented here make an assumption on the model kept for the term structure of interest rates and then they follow with their own perception of credit risk behavior. Unfortunately, the evidence would suggest that these two choices cannot be made independently of each other (see Chapter 12 for the empirical research that has been devoted to this joint behavior).

Broadly speaking, the relationship between interest rate risk and credit risk can be of different natures:

1. First, the specification of this market risk is necessary when dealing with interest rate contingent claims such as loans, corporate bonds, and in a more advanced stage, interest rate derivative products such as swaps, etc. From the earlier theories, credit risk translates, for example in the case of corporate debt, into special put options that come in diminution of an otherwise riskless debt:

   Risky debt = riskless debt − put option(s) on credit risk.

2. If we rely on structural models of credit risk where the source of risk is represented by the variability of the value of the assets of the firm, then we might be interested in the sensitivity of the activities of the firm and its capital structure to the structure of interest rates, even though we are not directly pricing interest rate dependent claims.
3. Independently from the reliance or not of credit risk on some underlying, interest rates and credit spreads can be thought as naturally covarying.
4. Finally, there is an interest in the aggregation of these two kinds of sources of risk into a common risk management system.

The present chapter presents the different choices that are available to the modeler when trying to parametrize the term structure of interest rates.

Models of stochastic interest rates have been developed in opposition to standard pricing formulas of bonds derived simply as a discounting of cash flows by an appropriate term structure of interest rates supposed to be constant across time. Indeed, a flat term structure, i.e. a unique and constant interest rate is still a common hypothesis, would it be in the case of the standard Black and Scholes or when using standard duration measures.

Term structure models can be categorized as follows:

1. Arbitrage[1] versus equilibrium models.
2. One-factor versus multifactor models.
3. Those which are fitted versus the nonfitted ones to the initial term structure.

Consistency with what is being observed in financial markets and with the AAO, would require:

- that the spot rates induced by the model should not be negative or with too high values that would be inconsistent with economic theory,

- the bond price to be a decreasing function of time to maturity with a price of 1 at maturity,

- the rates to follow a mean-reverting process in the long run which produces upward- or downward-sloping shapes,

- the interest rate volatility to be higher for shorter maturities,

- the model to provide tractable and efficient pricing and hedging of derivatives.

We do not pretend to be exhaustive here, but present some of the typical term structure modeling approaches.

23.2   ARBITRAGE MODELS

We must first identify those models whose factors are entirely specified by the model itself such as

- CIR (1985a) and Vasicek's (1977) models,

- and the two-factor models of Brennan and Schwartz (1979) and Schaefer and Schwartz (1984)

in opposition to those which are fitted to the term structure of interest rates such as the approaches of Hull and White and HJM.

23.2.1   One-factor Arbitrage Models

They rely on one sole random factor that governs the whole evolution of the term structure, on a relative pricing argument and on the assumption of the absence of arbitrage opportunities (AOA) order to give a price to zero-coupon bonds, $P(t, T)$, for all maturities T. This will further allow us to infer a term structure of interest rates $R(t, T) = -1/(T - t) \ln P(t, T)$, and develop hedging strategies based on this AOA. To enable AOA, standard continuous-time financial assumptions are required: financial markets are assumed to be complete, efficient, and frictionless, trading takes place continuously, and base factors follow diffusion processes.

---

[1]Absence of arbitrage is also called "partial equilibria".

Vasicek's Partial Equilibrium Characterization

The instantaneous spot interest rate, r, follows a continuous Markovian process[2] of the form:

$$dr(t) = \mu(r(t), t)\,dt + \sigma(r(t), t)\,dZ(t), \tag{23.1}$$

where $\mu(r(t), t)$ is the drift of the process, i.e. the mathematical expected value of the instantaneous change in r, $\sigma(r(t), t)$ is the volatility of r, $dZ(t)$ is a standard Wiener process with a normal distribution: $E(Z(t)) = 0$, $Var(Z(t)) = t$.

The price of the zero-coupon bond paying \$1 at T is completely determined by $r(t, T)$ and T:

$$P(t, T) = P(r(t), T) = P(r, \tau).$$

Now, we have to derive the expression of the dynamics of the bond price, given the form stated for the underlying spot rate. From Itô's lemma,

$$dP = P_r\,dr + P_t\,dt + \tfrac{1}{2}P_{rr}(dr)^2. \tag{23.2}$$

Substituting equation (23.1) in equation (23.2)

$$dP = [P_r\mu(r, t) + P_t + \tfrac{1}{2}P_{rr}\sigma^2(r, t)]\,dt + P_r\sigma(r, t)\,dZ,$$

and therefore the diffusion equation of the evolution of the bond price can be written as

$$\frac{dP}{P} = \underbrace{\frac{1}{P}[P_r\mu(r, t) + P_t + \tfrac{1}{2}P_{rr}\sigma^2(r, t)]}_{\alpha(r,\,t,\,T)}\,dt + \underbrace{\frac{1}{P}P_r\sigma(r, t)}_{\gamma(r,\,t,\,T)}\,dZ,$$

where $\alpha(r, t, T)$ denotes the expected instantaneous rate of return of the bond and $\gamma(r, t, T)$ denotes the unanticipated instantaneous rate of return of the bond.

We have now the dynamics of the underlying and the zero-coupon bond as a contingent claim on this underlying but no AOA context has yet been introduced. We have thus to construct a riskless portfolio to use the AOA statement that "riskless and profitable arbitrage opportunities should not exist in an efficient market", since these opportunities would be theoretically instantaneously arbitraged, leading back to the partial equilibrium. Such a portfolio (M) would require the integration of two arbitrarily chosen bonds[3] $P(r, \tau_1)$ and $P(r, \tau_2)$, in proportions x_1 and x_2.

$$\frac{dM}{M} = x_1\frac{dP_1}{P_1} + x_2\frac{dP_2}{P_2}$$
$$= [x_1\alpha(r, t, T_1) + x_2\alpha(r, t, T_2)]\,dt + [x_1\gamma(r, t, T_1) + x_2\gamma(r, t, T_2)]\,dZ.$$

For this portfolio to be riskless x_1 and x_2 should ensure that the resulting uncertainty is eliminated, i.e.

$$x_1\gamma(r, t, T_1) + x_2\gamma(r, t, T_2) = 0, \tag{23.3}$$

---

[2] Which assumes independence with respect to past evolution.
[3] n sources of risk require $n + 1$ assets, if markets are complete, to create a riskless position.

and that therefore

$$\frac{dM}{M} = r\,dt$$

which is equivalent, in a riskless setting, to

$$\rightleftharpoons [x_1\alpha(r, t, T_1) + x_2\alpha(r, t, T_2)]dt = r\,dt \tag{23.4}$$

$$\rightleftharpoons x_1[\alpha(r, t, T_1) - r] + x_2[\alpha(r, t, T_2) - r] = 0.$$

The nontrivial solution to equations (23.3) and (23.4) implies a relationship between the instantaneous excess return and the amount of risk of each security, in the sense that

$$\frac{\alpha(r, t, T_1) - r}{\gamma(r, t, T_1)} = \frac{\alpha(r, t, T_2) - r}{\gamma(r, t, T_2)} = \lambda(r, t), \tag{23.5}$$

i.e. that the unit price of risk is the same for all bond securities independently of the time to maturity since these two bonds were arbitrarily chosen. We straightforwardly obtain the expected risk–return relationship, analogous to those produced by the CAPM or the APT,

$$\alpha(r, t, T) = r(t) + \lambda(r, t)\gamma(r, t, T). \tag{23.6}$$

This formal expression permits straight comparisons among classical theories that make assumptions on the existence or absence of a risk premium and on its sign. Theoretically speaking, this generic property is also a weakness since the risk premium must be defined exogenously, therefore leading to arbitrary choices. Consequently, there is no way to verify that the risk premium is still consistent with the arbitrage condition that the model is supposed not to violate.

Admitting that a consistent risk premia can, however, be identified, we can substitute for α and γ in equation (23.6) to obtain

$$\frac{1}{P}[P_r\mu(r, t) + P_t + \tfrac{1}{2}P_{rr}\sigma^2(r, t)] = r + \frac{P_r}{P}\lambda(r, t)\sigma(r, t)$$

$$\rightleftharpoons [\mu(r, t) - \lambda(r, t)\sigma(r, t)]P_r + P_t + \tfrac{1}{2}P_{rr}\sigma^2(r, t) - rP = 0 \tag{23.7}$$

which is the required PDE that has still to be conditioned on the constraint that the bond price at maturity equals its repayment value, i.e. $P(r, T, T) = 1$, to produce zero-coupon bond prices for different maturities and consequently, the term structure of interest rates.

The precise specification and estimation of $\mu(r, t)$, $\sigma(r, t)$, and the identification of $\lambda(r, t)$ are still absent for the current framework to be implementable. The models that we will be presenting below are merely particular cases of the framework presented so far.

Vasicek's (1977) Model

It is the application of an Ornstein–Uhlenbeck process which relies on a mean-reverting behavior of the drift, into the previously presented partial equilibrium framework. The riskless rate is pushed to revert to its long run or equilibrium value b^4 with a speed of a which is proportional to the rate's current deviation from that equilibrium value. The instantaneous volatility $\sigma(r, t)$ is modeled as a constant parameter. Therefore

$$dr(t) = a(b - r(t))\,dt + \sigma\,dZ(t). \tag{23.8}$$

Under the assumption of a constant unit price of risk, λ, Vasicek proposes a closed-form solution to zero-coupon bond prices:

$$P(r, \tau) = \exp\left[\frac{1}{a}(1 - e^{a\tau})(R(r, \infty) - r) - \tau R(r, \infty) - \frac{\sigma^2}{4a^3}(1 - e^{-a\tau})^2\right] \tag{23.9}$$

with

$$R(r, \infty) = R(\infty) = \left(b - \frac{\sigma^2}{2a^2}\right) + \frac{\sigma\lambda}{a}.$$

With the additional restriction of $\lambda = 0$, which would correspond to the local expectations hypothesis, we can rewrite the previous expression as

$$P(r, \tau) = \exp\left[\frac{1}{a}(1 - e^{a\tau})\left(b - \frac{\sigma^2}{2a^2} - r\right) - \tau\left(b - \frac{\sigma^2}{2a^2}\right) - \frac{\sigma^2}{4a^3}(1 - e^{-a\tau})^2\right]. \tag{23.10}$$

Using $R(r, \tau) = -1/\tau \ln P(r, \tau)$, the term structure of interest rates can be derived through the successive application of the following equation to different maturities:

$$R(r, \tau) = \frac{1}{a\tau}(e^{-a\tau} - 1)\left(b - \frac{\sigma^2}{2a^2} - r\right) - b - \frac{\sigma^2}{2a^2} - \frac{\sigma^2}{4a^3}(1 - e^{-a\tau})^2 \tag{23.11}$$

with starting and asymptotic values of R being respectively

$$R(r, 0) = R(r, T, T) = r \quad\text{and}\quad \lim_{\tau\to\infty} R(r, \tau) = R(r, \infty) = b - \frac{\sigma^2}{2a^2}.$$

Some cons have to be mentioned about this formulation, however. First, the deterministic expression for $R(r, \infty)$ produces a constant which is completely independent of the level and the slope of the structure of interest rates. Second, it does not preclude negative nominal interest rates which causes the process to degenerate into a random walk when r gets close to 0.

CIR (1985)

With the previous Ornstein–Uhlenbeck process in Vasicek (1997), we obtain short-term interest rates that are normally distributed and that can be negative. Because of the volatility term in equation (23.8), nothing prevents the trajectory of future interest rates to reach negative levels. This latter drawback has led CIR (1985) to propose an alternative with a volatility term that is a function of $r(t)$:

$$dr(t) = a(b - r(t))\,dt + \sigma\sqrt{r(t)}\,dZ(t). \tag{23.12}$$

---

[4] It would represent the monetary target in an interventionary policy of the National Bank, whenever, $r(t)$ would diverge from b.

With the square root, whenever $r(t)$ gets near zero, the volatility term vanishes, letting the whole power to the mean reversion behavior of the drift term[5]. Bond prices in this model are obtained as

$$P(r, \tau) = A(\tau) \exp[-B(\tau)r],$$

with

$$A(\tau) = \left[\frac{2\gamma \exp[(a + \gamma)\tau/2]}{(a + \gamma)(\exp[\gamma\tau] - 1) + 2\gamma} \right]^{2ab/\sigma^2}$$

$$B(\tau) = \frac{2(\exp[\gamma\tau] - 1)}{(a + \gamma)(\exp[\gamma\tau] - 1) + 2\gamma},$$

and

$$\gamma = \sqrt{a^2 + 2\sigma^2}.$$

Hull and White (1990): Extended Vasicek's model

Hull and White generalize the specification of Vasicek, enabling the model to have time-dependent drift ($\theta(t)$), reversion speed ($a(t)$), and volatility ($\sigma(t)$), therefore nesting the standard specification of Vasicek:

$$dr = a(t)(b'(t) - r)dt + \sigma(t)dZ(t) \tag{23.12}$$

with

$$b'(t) = \frac{\theta(t)}{a(t)} + b.$$

Any interest rate contingent claim would then have an arbitrage-free price at t, that is, solution to the following PDE:

$$P_t + [\phi(t) - a(t)r]P_r + \tfrac{1}{2}\sigma(t)^2 P_{rr} - rP = 0,$$

with

$$\phi(t) = \theta(t) + a(t)b - \lambda(t)\sigma(t).$$

The bond pricing equation is then estimated to be of the form

$$P(r, t, T) = A(t, T) \exp[-B(t, T)r]. \tag{23.13}$$

Hull and White's model is a fitting model in the sense that $A(t, T)$ and $B(t, T)$ are estimated through calibration to the actual term structure of volatilities, making use of the following additional expressions: we know that

$$R(t, T) = -\frac{\ln P(r, t, T)}{T - t} = \frac{\ln A(t, T) - rB(t, T)}{T - t}$$

---

[5]It has to be noted that this is the continuous behavior of this process. Whenever it is implemented through its simple discretization, a problem arises: with noninfinitesimal steps in time, it is not possible to be sure that any trajectory will never reach negative levels (without additional refinements).

and that, by Itô's lemma,

$$\sigma_{R(t,T)} = \frac{B(t, T)\sigma(t)}{T - t},$$

which allows us to estimate $B(t, T)$ through

$$B(t, T) = \frac{(T - t)\sigma_{R(t,T)}}{\sigma(t)}.$$

Once $B(0, T)$ is determined, $A(0, T)$ can be estimated from the current term structure of interest rates since $P(r, 0, T)$ is then known, in

$$P(r, 0, T) = A(0, T)\exp[-B(0, T)r],$$

but ensuring that $A(t, T)$ satisfies

$$\ln A(t, T) = \ln A(0, T) - \ln A(0, t) - B(t, T)\frac{\partial \ln A(0, t)}{\partial t}$$

$$-\frac{1}{2}\left[B(t, T)\frac{\partial B(0, t)}{\partial t}\right]^2 \int_0^t \left[\frac{\sigma(\tau)}{\partial B(0, \tau)/\partial\tau}\right]^2 d\tau.$$

For a matter of completeness and because it will be necessary in the case of contracts contingent on the price of zero-coupon bonds themselves, the dynamics of P can be straightforwardly obtained by previous equations as

$$dP(t, T) = \mu_{P(t,T)}dt + \nu(t, T)P(t, T)dZ(t) \qquad (23.14)$$

$$= \mu_{P(t,T)}dt + \sigma(t)B(t, T)P(t, T)dZ(t).$$

23.2.2 Multifactor Models

Brennan and Schwartz (1979)

Brennan and Schwartz (1979) are the first to propose a two-factor model with a process for the short rate and one for the long rate. The short rate reverts to the long rate, and both processes are interrelated. The market risk premia of the long-term rate is elegantly identified through the fact that we know from actuaries the price of a consol bond. If l is the long rate, $1/l$ is the price of this bond. We do not reproduce here the derivations of Brennan and Schwartz, since part of them have been taken back by Schaeffer and Schwartz in order to obtain then an analytical solution.

Schaefer and Schwartz (1984)

By the liquidity preference theory and the expectations hypothesis, the long-term bond yield reflects the anticipations of economic agents on the future level of the short-term interest rate. The long-term rate, l, thus contains relevant information, and the distortions of the term structure can simply be captured by the evolution of the spread between the long-term and the short-term interest rates, $s = r - l$. This idea has been developed by Schaefer and Schwartz making use of the empirical evidence at that time showing that these two factors are orthogonal[6]. As in Brennan and Schwartz (1979), using the fact that the price of a consol bond should also satisfy the same partial differential equation (PDE) and that this price, observed on the market, is simply the inverse of the long-term rate, the risk premia linked to the long-term factor is directly identifiable. Based on the following definition of the stochastic processes for the two factors:

$$ds = m(\xi - s)dt + \gamma dz_1,$$

$$dl = f(s, l, t)dt + \sigma\sqrt{l}dz_2,$$

Schaefer and Schwartz (1984) present an approximate valuation equation that has the advantage of having an exact analytical solution where a constant $\hat{s}$ is used in place of s in the coefficient of P_l of the derived PDE[7]. The yield on a pure discount bond with maturity τ can therefore be valued as

$$R(s, l, \tau) = -\frac{1}{\tau}\ln[P],$$

$$\cong s_x - F(\tau)(s_x - s) + G(\tau) + \frac{1}{\tau}[B(\tau)l - \ln(A(\tau))],$$

where

$$s_x = \xi - \frac{\lambda_1\gamma}{m} - \frac{1}{2}\frac{\gamma^2}{m^2},$$

$$\lambda_1 = \text{spread risk premia (constant)}.$$

$$\alpha = \sqrt{\hat{s}^2 + 2\sigma^2}$$

$$A(\tau) = \left[\frac{2\alpha e^{(\hat{s}+\alpha)\tau/2}}{(\hat{s}+\alpha)(e^{\alpha\tau} - 1) + 2\alpha}\right]$$

$$B(\tau) = \frac{2(e^{\alpha\tau} - 1)}{(\hat{s}+\alpha)(e^{\alpha\tau} - 1) + 2\alpha)}$$

$$F(\tau) = \frac{1 - e^{-m\tau}}{m\tau}$$

$$G(\tau) = \frac{\gamma^2}{4m^3\tau} \cdot (1 - e^{-m\tau})^2$$

Ho and Lee (1986)

Ho and Lee proposed in 1986 a model in the form a binomial recombining tree of bond prices. The two parameters are mainly the volatility of the short-term interest rate and the market price of risk. It can be shown that their discrete modelization is equivalent to the following continuous characterization of the short-term interest rate process:

---

[6]It seems today that this can be a restrictive assumption.
[7]The specification of this constant obeys to some reconciliation between the exact valuation equation and the approximate one.

$$dr(t) = \theta(t)\,dt + \sigma\,dZ,$$

where $\theta(t)$ is chosen so that the parameters fit the initial (evidenced) term structure, since the model is a model of bond prices and not of the short interest rate directly; σ is the now standard volatility of $r(t)$; $\theta(t)$ defines the average trend of r and it is defined as a function of the initial term structure and it is not a function of r:

$$\theta(t) = \frac{\partial f(0,\,t)}{\partial t} + \sigma^2 t,$$

where $f(0,\,t)$ is the instantaneous forward rate. What is interesting to remark is that we obtain bond prices at a future time t for bonds maturing at time T based on today's bond prices and the short rate prevailing at t. Therefore, in the following notation, we will differentiate time 0, t and T, without the use of τ.

The resulting price of the bond maturing at time T at any date t, $t \leqslant T$, is

$$P(r,\,t,\,T) = A(t,\,T)\exp[-r(t)(T - t)],$$

where

$$\ln A(t,\,T) = \ln\frac{P(r,\,0,\,T)}{P(r,\,0,\,t)} - (T - t)\frac{\partial P(r,\,0,\,T)}{\partial t} - \frac{1}{2}\sigma^2 t(T - t)^2.$$

Heath, Jarrow & Morton (1992)

Interest rates can be seen from two different perspectives: either at one date we look at the shape of the term structure, or for a given maturity, we look at the history or forecast values of one of this rate among the whole structure. All previous modeling articulates around the timely evolution of one or two of these rates, the model expressing the whole shape as a function of these starting variables. But, in fact, series of forward rates are continuously available on the market for the most important currencies. Why do we not calibrate then a model over the whole structure rather than just to some of the rates? This would avoid the problem of letting the model do the hard work of giving us the recipe of the whole structure based on these sole factors. That was the idea of HJM with forward rates based term structure model.

They take into account the entire forward curve and derive back the dynamics of the whole structure simultaneously and not only one or two aspects of it. It allows the user to take into account as many points as s/he would require. Their motivation resides, therefore, in the fact that, in a factor model, the drifts of the factors are unknown under the risk-neutral probability measure. Drifts are then inferred from prices, and the more factors you have the better match you will obtain. But this method of choosing drifts is computationally intensive and subject to econometric problems. Also, the expected rate of change of a discount bond under the risk-neutral probability measure is the short rate which has strong implications for yields and forward rates.

The main advantages of HJM is that the drifts of forward rates under the risk-neutral probability are entirely determined by their volatilities. Since these volatilities are the same as those under the actual probability, they can normally be estimated from historical data on forward rates. Second, the current forward rate curve can be input as an initial condition so that the model matches actual prices at the origin.

Technically speaking, it is a methodology based on the equivalent martingale measure. It takes as given an initial forward rate curve and a family of potential stochastic processes for its subsequent movements. The no-arbitrage condition restricts the family of processes to a single number, allowing consistent pricing of interest-rate-dependent contingent claims.

The yield curves out from a collection of discount bonds or from the instantaneous forward rates through the following relationships:

$$P(0, T) = \exp\left[-\int_0^T f(0, s)\, ds\right] \qquad f(0, T) = \frac{-\partial \ln P(0, T)}{\partial T}. \tag{23.15}$$

Note that the spot rate at time t is the instantaneous forward rate at time t for maturity t: $r(t) = f(t, t)$.

For clarity of presentation, we firstly consider a one-factor case worked out from the discount bond price. Straight generalization through the forward curve is presented in the next subsection.

Suppose, then, a one-factor framework with a single Brownian motion and a constant volatility parameter: $\sigma_1(t, T, \omega) = \sigma > 0$. It is shown, by no arbitrage, that the forward drift is conditioned to the volatility of the factor through[8]:

$$\alpha(t, T) = -\sigma\phi(t) + \sigma^2(T - t). \tag{23.16}$$

The forward rate stochastic process would be given by

$$f(t, T) = f(0, T) + \sigma^2 t(T - t/2) + \sigma Z(t) \tag{23.17}$$

which would lead to the following process for the spot rate:

$$r(t) = f(0, t) + \sigma^2 t^2/2 + \sigma Z(t). \tag{23.18}$$

It should be noted that expression (23.18) does not exclude spot rates from being negative. Bond prices are obtained by the straight use of equation (23.15):

$$P(t, T) = [P(0, T)/P(0, t)]e^{-(\sigma^2/2)Tt(T-t)-\sigma(T-t)Z(t)}. \tag{23.19}$$

HJM Forward Rate Process Formulation

We have previously presented the results for the HJM approach worked out from the discount bond price instead of the forward curve. But the two approaches will be shown to be equivalent. Also, the present section is not restricted to a one-factor framework.

If the rolled-up money market account is taken as numeraire, all assets, under the equivalent martingale measure, instantaneously grow at the riskless interest rate. For discount bond prices, we therefore obtain

$$dP(t, T) = r(t)P(t, T)\, dt + v(t, T, P(t, T))\, dZ(t),$$

---

[8] This is an important insight into the modeling of the term structure. The HJM model implicitly nests all other one-factor and two-factor previous approaches. This means that, in any standard one-factor or two-factor model, the drift(s) cannot be estimated separately from the volatility parameter(s) without verifying this condition.

where $\nu(t, T, P)$ is the time t volatility for a bond of maturity T. The drift component is such that equation (23.16) holds. The specification of the volatility, however, is very general and admits all types of structures for the volatility.

Let us specify

$$y(t, T) = \ln P(t, T).$$

Then, by Itô,

$$dy(t, T) = d(\ln P(t, T)) = \left[r(t) - \frac{\nu(t, T, P)^2}{P(t, T)^2} \right] dt + \frac{\nu(t, T, P)}{P(t, T)} dZ.$$

Thus,

$$d(\ln P(t, T_2) - \ln P(t, T_1)) = \frac{1}{2} \left[\frac{\nu(t, T_1, P)^2}{P(t, T_1)^2} - \frac{\nu(t, T_2, P)^2}{P(t, T_2)^2} \right] dt$$

$$+ \left[\frac{\nu(t, T_2, P)}{P(t, T_2)} - \frac{\nu(t, T_1, P)}{P(t, T_1)} \right] dZ.$$

Knowing that the continuously compounded time-t forward rate for the period $[T_1, T_2]$ is given by

$$f(t, T_1, T_2) = - \frac{\ln P(t, T_2) - \ln P(t, T_1)}{T_2 - T_1},$$

and with

$$\xi(t, T, P) = \nu(t, T, P)/P(t, T),$$

we obtain

$$d(f(t, T_1, T_2)) = \left[\frac{\xi(t, T_2, P(t, T_2))^2 - \xi(t, T_1, P(t, T_1))^2}{2(T_2 - T_1)} \right] dt$$

$$+ \left[\frac{\xi(t, T_1, P(t, T_1)) - \xi(t, T_2, P(t, T_2))}{T_2 - T_1} \right] dZ.$$

Moving to the limit as $T_2 \to T_1$, the discrete forward rate tends to the instantaneous forward rate

$$f(t, T) = - \frac{\partial \ln P(t, T)}{\partial T},$$

and remembering that

$$\frac{\partial (f(x)^2)}{\partial x} = 2 f(x) \frac{\partial f(x)}{\partial x},$$

we obtain

$$df(t, T) = \xi \left[\left(\frac{\partial \xi}{\partial T} \right)_P + \left(\frac{\partial \xi}{\partial P} \right)_T \frac{\partial P}{\partial T} \right] dt + \left[\left(\frac{\partial \xi}{\partial T} \right)_P + \left(\frac{\partial \xi}{\partial P} \right)_T \frac{\partial P}{\partial T} \right] dZ,$$

where $(\partial f(x, y)/\partial x)_y$ is the partial derivative with respect to x, irrespective of y. This is a very general expression for the forward rate process. In a multifactor framework, the generalization of the previous equation would give the *family of forward rate processes*. In particular, the previous equation shows that

- using the money market account as numeraire, forward rates are not martingales;
- there must exist a link between ν and the drift of forward rates in a risk-neutral world, should no arbitrage be required.

Only the definition of the no-arbitrage framework has been presented so far. The next step would be to choose a volatility function. For instance, in the previous subsection, the example was provided with a constant volatility.

23.3   REFERENCES

Brennan, M. J. and E. S. Schwartz, 1979, "A Continuous-Time Approach to Pricing Bonds", *Journal of Banking and Finance*, **3**, July, 133–55.

Brennan, M. J. and E. S. Schwartz, 1982, "An Equilibrium Model of Bond Pricing and a Test of Market Efficiency", *Journal of Financial and Quantitative Analysis*, **17** (3), September, 301–29.

Cox, J. C., J. E. Ingersoll and S. A. Ross, 1985a, "A Theory of the Term Structure of Interest Rates", *Econometrica*, **53**, 385.

Gibson-Asner, Rajna, 1990, *Obligations et Clauses Optionnelles*, Presses Universitaires de France, Paris, 243 pp.

Heath, David, Robert Jarrow and Andrew Morton, 1992, "Bond Pricing and the Term Structure of Interest Rates: A New Methodology for Contingent Claims Valuation", *Econometrica*, **60** (1), January, 77–105.

Ho, Thomas S. Y. and Sang-bin Lee, 1986, "Term Structure Movements and Pricing Interest Rate Contingent Claims", *Journal of Finance*, **41** (5), December, 1011–29.

Hull, John and A. White, 1990, "Pricing Interest Rate Derivative Securities", *Review of Financial Studies*, pp. 573–92.

Rebonato, Riccardo, 1996, *Interest-Rate Option Models*, John Wiley and Sons, UK, 372 pp.

Schaefer, Stephen and Eduardo Schwartz, 1984, "A Two-Factor Model of the Term Structure: An Approximate Analytical Solution", *Journal of Financial and Quantitative Analysis*, **19** (4), December, 413–24.

Vasicek, O., 1977, "An Equilibrium Characterization of the Term Structure", *Journal of Financial Economics*, **5**, 177–88.

24
General Bibliography

Abken, Peter A., 1993, "Valuation of Default-Risky Interest-Rate Swaps", *Advances in Futures and Options Research*, **6**, 93–116.

Aghion, Philippe and Bolton, Patrick "An Incomplete Contracts Approach to Financial Contracting", *The Review of Economic Studies*, **59** (3), 473–94.

Albanese, Claudio, 1997, "Credit Exposure, Diversification Risk and Coherent VaR", *Working Paper*, Department of Mathematics, University of Toronto, 20 pp.

Alessandrini, F., 1998, "Credit Risk, Interest Rate Risk and the Business Cycle", Master's Thesis, Master of Science in Economics, HEC, Lausanne University, n. 98, November, 62 pp.

Alessandrini, F., 1999, "Credit Risk, Interest Rate Risk and the Business Cycle", *Journal of Fixed Income*, September.

Altman, E. and D. L. Kao, 1992, "Rating Drift in High-Yield Bonds", *Journal of Fixed Income*, March.

Altman, Edward and Vellore Kishore, 1996a, "Defaults and Returns on High Yield Bonds: Analysis through 1995", New York University Salomon Center *Special Report*.

Altman, Edward and Vellore Kishore, 1996b, "Almost Everything You Wanted to Know about Recoveries on Defaulted Bonds", *Financial Analysts Journal*, November/December, 57–64.

Altman, Edward and Anthony Saunders, 1996, "Credit Risk Measurement: Developments Over the Last 20 Years", *Working Paper 96–40*, New York University, Salomon Center, September, 38 pp.

Anderson, R. F and A. Friedman, 1977, A Quality Control Problem and Quasi-Variational Inequalities, *Archive for Rational Mechanics and Analysis*, pp. 205–52.

Anderson, Ronald and Suresh Sundaresan, 1996, "Design and Valuation of Debt Contracts", *The Review of Financial Studies*, Spring, **9** (1), 37–68.

Anderson, Ronald and Suresh Sundaresan, 2000, "A Comparative Study of Structural Models of Corporate Bond Yields: an Exploratory Investigation", *Journal of Banking and Finance*, **24** (1–2), 255–69.

Anderson, Ronald W, Suresh Sundaresan and Pierre Tychon, 1996, "Strategic Analysis of Contingent Claims", *European Economic Review*. **40** (3–5), April, 871–81.

Artzner, Philippe and Freddy Delbaen, 1995, "Default Risk Insurance and Incomplete Markets", *Mathematical Finance*, **5** (3), July, 187–95.

Asquith, P., 1995, "Convertible Bonds are not Called Late", *The Journal of Finance*, **4**, 1275–89.

Bank of England, 1996, "Developing a Supervisory Approach to Credit Derivatives", *Discussion Paper*, Supervision and Surveillance, November.

Bank for International Settlements, August 1996, *International Banking and Financial Market Developments*, 41 pp.

Basle Committee on Banking Supervision, 1999, *Credit Risk Modelling: Current Practices and Applications*, Basle, April, 60 pp.

Baz, Jamil, 1995, "Three Essays on Contingent Claims", Harvard PhD Thesis, August.

Beneish, M. D. and E. Press, 1995, "Interrelation Among Events of Default", *Contemporary Accounting Research*, Summer.

Benjamin, Daniel K, 1978, "The Use of Collateral to Enforce Debt Contracts." *Economic Inquiry*, **16** (3), 333–59, July.

Bensoussan, A. and Lions, J. L., 1973, "Nouvelle formulation de problèmes de contrôle impulsionnel et applications", *C.R. Acad. Sci. Paris*, **276**, 1189–92.

Bester, Helmut, 1994, "The Role of Collateral in a Model of Debt Renegotiation", *Journal of Money, Credit & Banking*, **26** (1), 72–86, February.

Bhattacharya, A. K., 1990, "Synthetic Assets Swaps", *Journal of Portfolio Management*, **17** (1), Fall, 56–64.

Black, Fisher and John C. Cox, 1976, "Valuing Corporate Securities: Some Effects of Bond Indenture Provisions", *The Journal of Finance*, **31** (2), 351–67.

Brennan, M.J., and E. S. Schwartz, 1979, "A Continuous-Time Approach to Pricing Bonds", *Journal of Banking and Finance*, **3**, July, 133–55.

Brennan, M. and E. Schwartz, 1980, "Analyzing Convertible Bonds", *Journal of Financial and Quantitative Analysis*, **15**, 907–29.

Brennan, M. J. and E. S. Schwartz, 1982, "An Equilibrium Model of Bond Pricing and a Test of Market Efficiency", *Journal of Financial and Quantitative Analysis*, **17** (3), September, 301–29.

Briys, Eric and François de Varenne, 1997, "Valuing Risky Fixed Rate Debt: An Extension", *Journal of Financial and Quantitative Analysis*, **32** (2), June, 239–49.

Briys E., M. Bellalah, H. M. Mai and F. de Varenne, 1998, *Options, Futures and Exotic Derivatives: Theory, Application and Practice*, John Wiley and Sons Ltd, 1st edn, 459 pp.

Broadie, M., P. Glasserman and S. Kou, 1997, "A Continuity Correction For Discrete Barrier Options"; *Mathematical Finance*, **7** (4), 325–49, October.

Cantor, Richard, and Frank Packer, 1996, "Determinants and Impact of Sovereign Credit Ratings", December, pp. 76–91.

Cantor, Richard, Frank Packer and Kevin Cole, 1997, "Split Ratings and the Pricing of Credit Risk", December 1997, pp. 72–82.

Chan, K. C., Andrew Karolyi, Francis Longstaff and Anthony Sanders, 1992, "An Empirical Comparison of Alternative Models of the Short-Term Interest Rate", *Journal of Finance*, **47** (3), July, 1209–27.

Chang, Ganlin and Suresh Sundaresan, 1999, "Asset Prices and Default-Free Term Structure in an Equilibrium Model of Default", *Working Paper*, Graduate School of Business, Columbia University, March, 49 pp.

Chen, Andrew and Arthur Selender, 1995, "Determination of Swap Spreads: An Empirical Analysis", *Working Paper*, Southern Methodist University, Edwin L. Cox School of Business, Dallas, Texas, February.

Chen, Y., J. F. Weston and E. Altman, 1995, "Financial Distress and Restructuring Models", *Working Paper*, Stern Institute, New York University, May.

Chesney, M. and R. Gibson, 1994, "The Investment Policy and the Pricing of Equity in a Levered Firm: A Reexamination of the Contingent Claims' Valuation Approach", *Working Paper*, Groupe HEC, Paris, May, 35 pp.

Chowdhry, Bhagwan and Mark Grinblatt, 1995, "Information Aggregation, Security Design and Currency Swaps", The Anderson School, University of California, Los Angeles, CA 90024-1481, #19-94, October 1994, revised April 1995.

Claessens, Stij and George Pennacchi, 1996, "Estimating the Likelihood of Mexican Default from the Market Prices of Brady Bonds", *Journal of Financial and Quantitative Analysis*, **31** (1), March, 109–26.

Clark, Corolyn, Paul Foster and Waqar Ghani, 1997, "Differential Reaction to Bond Downgrades for Small vs. Large Firms: Evidence from Analysts' Forecast Revision", *The Journal of Fixed Income*, December, 94–9.

Coleman, Thomas S., Lawrence Fisher and Roger G. Ibbotson, 1992, "Estimating the Term Structure of Interest Rates from Data that Include the Prices of Coupon Bonds", July, Yale *Working Paper*.

Cook, D. and L. Spellman, 1991, "Federal Financial Guarantees and the Occasional Market Pricing of Default Risk: Evidence from insured deposits", *Journal of Banking and Finance*, **15**, 1113–30.

Cooper, Ian A. and Antonio S. Mello, 1991, "The Default Risk of Swaps", *Journal of Finance*, **46**, 597–620.

Cossin, D., 1997, "Credit Risk Pricing: A Literature Survey", IGBF *Working Paper*, University of Lausanne.

Cossin, D. and F. Aparicio, 1999, "Control of Credit Risk Collateralization using Quasi Variational Inequalities", IGBF *Working Paper*, University of Lausanne.

Cossin, D., and F. Aparicio, 2000, "Optimal Control of Credit Risk, Security Collateralization, Deposit Insurance and Other Financial Guarantees", Advances in Computational Management Science-series (AICM), Kluwer Academic, forthcoming.

Cossin, D. and T. Hricko, 1999, "Pricing Credit Risk With Risky Collateral: A Methodology for Haircut Determination", HEC, University of Lausanne, *Working Paper*.

Cossin, Didier and Hugues Pirotte, 1997, "Swap Credit Risk: An Empirical Investigation on Transaction Data", *Journal of Banking & Finance*, **21** (10), 1351–73, October.

Cossin, D., and H. Pirotte, 1998, "How Well Do Classical Credit Risk Models Fit Swap Transaction Data?", *European Financial Management Journal*, **4** (1), March, 65–78.

Cox, J. C., J. E. Ingersoll and S. A. Ross, 1985a, "A Theory of the Term Structure of Interest Rates", *Econometrica*, **53**, 385.

Cox, J. C., Ingersoll, J. E. and S. A. Ross, 1981, "The Relation between Forward Prices and Futures Prices", *Journal of Financial Economics*, December **2**, 321–46.

Cox, D. R. and H. D. Miller, 1965, *The Theory of Stochastic Processes*, Chapman & Hall, reprinted in 1995, 398 pp.

Cox, J. and M. Rubinstein, 1985, *Options Market*, Prentice-Hall, Englewood Cliffs, NJ.

Crouhy, Michel and Dan Galai, 1997, "Credit Risk Revisited: An Option Pricing Approach", May, *Working Paper* 97-2, Canadian Imperial Bank of Commerce/Market Risk Management/Global Analytics, 18 pp.

Crouhy, Michel, Dan Galai and Robert Mark, 2000, "A Comparative Analysis of Current Credit Risk Models", *Journal of Banking and Finance*, **24** (1–2), 59–117.

Dai, Q. and K. Singleton, 1998, "Specification Analysis of Affine Term Structure Models", *Working Paper*, Graduate School of Business, Stanford University.

Das, S., 1994, *Swap and Derivative Financing*, Probus Publishing, Chicago, Ill.

Das, S. R., 1995, "Credit Risk Derivatives", *Journal of Derivatives*, Spring, 7–23.

Das, Sanjiv, 1997, "Enron Corp.- Credit Sensitive Notes" (Harvard Case HBS # 297 099).

Das, Sanjiv and Peter Tufano, 1996, "Pricing Credit Sensitive Debt when Interest Rates, Credit Ratings and Credit Spreads are Stochastic", *Journal of Financial Engineering*, **5** (2), June.

Davis, M. H. A., 1993, *Markov Models and Optimization*, Chapman & Hall, pp. 188–204.

Delianedis, Gordon and Robert Geske, 1998, "Credit Risk and Risk Neutral Default Probabilities: Information about Rating Migrations and Defaults", *Working Paper*, The Anderson School at UCLA, July, 38 pp.

Duan, J. C. and J.-G. Simonato, 1998, "Maximum Likelihood Estimation of Deposit Insurance Value with Interest Rate Risk", *Working Paper*, November, 21 pp.

Duffee, G. R., 1995a, "On Measuring Credit Risks of Derivative Instruments", *Working Paper*, Federal Reserve Board, February.

Duffee, G. R., 1995b, "The Variation of Default Risk with Treasury Yields", *Working Paper*, Federal Reserve Board, January.

Duffee, Gregory R., 1996, "Estimating the Price of Credit Risk", *Working Paper*, Federal Reserve Board, n. 96-29, 42 pp.

Duffee, Gregory R., 1996, "Rethinking Risk Management for Banks: Lessons from Credit Derivatives", *Working Paper*, Federal Reserve Board, April 18, 31 pp.

Duffee, Gregory, 1998, "The Relation Between Treasury Yields and Corporate Bond Yield Spreads", *The Journal of Finance*, **53** (6), December, 2225–42.

Duffee, Gregory, 1999, "Estimating the Price of Default Risk", *The Review of Financial Studies*, **12** (1), Spring, 197–226.

Duffee, Gregory R. and Chunsheng Zhou, 1999, "Credit Derivatives in Banking: Useful Tools for Managing Risk?", *Working Paper*, Federal Reserve Board, September, 38 pp.

Duffie, Darrell and Ming Huang, 1994, "Swap Rates and Credit Quality", Graduate School of Business, Stanford University, August 17, 37 pp.

Duffie, Darrell and Ming Huang, 1996, "Swap Rates and Credit Quality", *Journal of Finance*, **51** (3), July, 921–49.

Duffie, Darrell and Rui Kan, 1996, "A Yield-Factor Model of Interest Rates", *Mathematical Finance*, **6** (4), October, 379–406.

Duffie, Darrell and Jun Pan, 1997, "An Overview of Value at Risk", *The Journal of Derivatives*, Spring 1997, pp. 7–49.

Duffie, D., J. Pan and K. Singleton, 1999, "Transform Analysis and Asset Pricing for Affine Jump-Diffusions", *Working Paper*, Graduate School of Business, Stanford University, September, 44 pp.

Duffie, Darrell and David Lando, 1997, "Term Structures of Credit Spreads with Incomplete Accounting Information", Preliminary Draft, September 12, 39 pp.

Duffie, D., M. Schroder and C. Skiadas, 1996, "Recursive Valuation of Defaultable Securities and the Timing of Resolution of Uncertainty", *Annals of Applied Probability*, **6**, 1075–90.

Duffie, D. and K. Singleton, 1994, "Econometric Modeling of Term Structures of Defaultable Bonds", *Working Paper*, Graduate School of Business, Stanford University, November.

Duffie, Darrell and Ken Singleton, 1999, "Modeling Term Structures of Defaultable Bonds", *Review of Financial Studies*, Special 1999, **12** (4), 687–720.

Duffie, D. and T. Sun, 1990, "Transactions Costs and Portfolio Choice in a Discrete-Continuous-Time Setting", *Journal of Economic Dynamics and Control*, **14**, 35–51.

Duffie, Darrell, 1999, *Credit Swap Valuation*, Association for Investment Management and Research, pp. 73–86.

Durbin, J., 1992, "The First-passage Density of the Brownian Motion Process to a Curved Boundary", *Journal of Applied Probability*, June.

Eastham, J. F. and K. J. Hastings, 1988, "Optimal Impulse Control of Portfolios", *Mathematics of Operations Research*, **13** (4).

Ellis, David, 1997, "Different Sides of the Same Story: Investors' and Issuers' Views of Rating Agencies", *Working Paper*, Finance Division, Babson College, August, 18 pp.

Ericsson, Jan and Joel Reneby, 1995, "A Framework for Valuing Corporate Securities", *Working Paper*, Stockholm School of Economics, November, 35 pp.

Ericsson, Jan and Joel Reneby, 1996, "Stock Options as Barrier Contingent Claims", *Working Paper*, Stockholm School of Economics, November, 38 pp.

Fama, Eugene F., 1984, "Term Premiums in Bond Returns", *Journal of Financial Economics*, **13**, 529–46.

Fama, Eugene F., 1986, "Term Premiums and Default Premiums in Money Markets", *Journal of Financial Economics*, **17**, 175–96.

Fama, Eugene F. and Kenneth R. French, 1987, "Forecasting Returns on Corporate Bonds and Common Stocks", University of California at Los Angeles, Anderson Graduate School of Management Finance *Working Paper*: 4-88, p. 26. December.

Fan, Hua and Suresh Sundaresan, 1997, "Debt Valuation, Strategic Debt Service and Optimal Dividend Policy", *Working Paper*, Graduate School of Business, Columbia University, March, 47 pp.

Federal Reserve, 1998, *Credit Risk Models at Major U.S. Banking Institutions: Current State of the Art and Implications for Assessment of Capital Adequacy*, Federal Reserve System Task Force on Internal Credit Risk Models, May, 57 pp.

Finger, Christopher, 1998, *Sticks and Stones*, RiskMetrics Group Publication, 10 pp.

Flood, R. P. and P. M. Garber, 1989, "The Linkage between Speculative Attack and Target Zone Models of Exchange Rates", NBER *Working Paper*, no. 2918.

Franks, J. R. and W. Torous, 1989, "An Empirical Investigation of US Firms in Reorganization", *The Journal of Finance*, **44**, 747–69.

Franks, Julian R. and Torous, Walter N., 1994, "A Comparison of Financial Recontracting in Distressed Exchanges and Chapter 11 Reorganizations", *Journal of Financial, Economics*, **35** (3), June, 349–70.

Fridson, Martin, Christopher Garman and Sheng Wu, 1997, "Real Interest Rates and the Default Rate on High-Yield Bonds", *The Journal of Fixed Income*, September, 29–34.

Frost, Joyce, 1997, *Corporate Uses for Credit Derivatives*, International Treasurer.

Geman, H. and M. Yo, 1993, "Bessel Processes, Asian Options and Perpetuities", *Mathematical Finance*, **4** (3).

Geman, H. and M. Yo, 1996, "Pricing and Hedging Double-Barrier Options: A Probabilistic Approach", *Mathematical Finance*, **6** (4).

Geman, H., N. El Karoui and J. C. Rochet, 1995, "Changes of Numeraire, Changes of Probability Measure and Pricing of Options", *Journal of Applied Probability*, **32**, 443–58.

Geske, Robert, 1977, "The Valuation of Corporate Liabilities as Compound Options", *Journal of Financial and Quantitative Analysis*, pp. 541–52.

Geyer, Alois L. J. and Stefan Pichler, 1999, "A State-Space Approach to Estimate and Test Multifactor Cox–Ingersoll–Ross Models of the Term Structure", *The Journal of Financial Research*, **22** (Spring), 107–30.

Gibson-Asner, Rajna, 1990, *Obligations et Clauses Optionnelles*, Presses Universitaires de France, Paris, 243 pp.

Glowinski, R., J. L. Lions and R. Trémolières, 1981, *Numerical Analysis of Variational Inequalitites*, North-Holland.

Gordy, Michael, 2000, "A Comparative Anatomy of Credit Risk Models", *Journal of Banking and Finance*, **24** (1–2), 119–49.

Grinblatt, Mark, 1994, "An Analytic Solution for Interest Rate Swaps Spreads", *Working Paper*, UCLA AGSM, June.

Grossman, S. J. and G. Laroque, 1990, "Asset Pricing and Optimal Portfolio Choice in the Presence of Illiquid Durable Consumption Goods", *Econometrica*, **58**, (1), 25–51.

Hamilton, James D., 1996, *Time Series Analysis*, Princeton University Press, 799 pp.

Harbonn, Claude and Peter Keller, "Optimal Capital Structure, the Case of Nestlé". Master's Thesis, MBF, University of Lausanne.

Harris, Milton and Arthur Raviv, 1991, "The Theory of Capital Structure", *The Journal of Finance*, **46** (1), March, 297–355.

Harrison, M. and D. Kreps, 1979, "Martingales and Arbitrage in Multiperiod Security Markets", *Journal of Economic Theory*, **20**, pp. 381–408.

Harrison, M. and S. Pliska, 1981, "Martingales and Stochastic Integrals in the Theory of Continuous Trading", *Stochastic Processes and Their Applications*, **11**, 215–60.

Harrison, J. M. and S. R. Pliska, 1983, "A Stochastic Calculus Model of Continuous Trading: Complete Markets", *Stochastic Process. Appl.*, **15**, 313–16.

Harrison, J. M., T. Selke, and A. Taylor, 1983, "Impulse Control of Brownian Motion", *Mathematics of Operations Research*, **8**, August, 454–66.

Harrison, Michael J., 1985, *Brownian Motion and Stochastic Flow Systems*, Wiley Series in Probability and Mathematical Statistics, John Wiley & Sons, New York.

Heath, David, Robert Jarrow and Andrew Morton, 1992, "Bond Pricing and the Term Structure of Interest Rates: A New Methodology for Contingent Claims Valuation", *Econometrica*, **60** (1), January, 77–105.

Hindy, A. and C. F. Huang, 1992, "Intertemporal Preferences for Uncertain Consumption: A Continuous Time Approach", *Econometrica*, **60** (4), 781–801.

Hirtle, B., "The Growth of the Financial Guarantee Market", *FRBNY Quarterly Review*, Spring, 10–28.

Hite, Gailen and Arthur Warga, 1997, "The Effect of Bond-Rating Changes on Bond Price Performance", *Financial Analysts Journal*, May/June, 35–47.

Hlavácek, I., J. Haslinger, J. Necas, and J. Lovísek, 1988, *Solution of Variational Inequalities in Mechanics*, Springer-Verlag.

Ho, Thomas S. Y. and Lee, Sang-bin., 1986, "Term Structure Movements and Pricing Interest Rate Contingent Claims", *Journal of Finance*, **41** (5), December, 1011–29.

Hogg, Robert V. and A. T. Craig, 1995, *Introduction to Mathematical Statistics*, Prentice-Hall, 5th edn, Englewood Cliffs, NJ.

Hsieh, S-J., A. H. Chen and K. R. Ferris, 1994, "The Valuation of PBGC Insurance Premiums Using an Option Pricing Model", *Journal of Financial and Quantitative Analysis*, **29** (1), 89–99.

Hübner, Georges, 1997a, "A Two-Factor Gaussian Model of Default Risk", *Working Paper* 97/23/FIN, INSEAD, Paris and University of Liège, Belgium, 84 pp.

Hübner, Georges, 1997b, "The Analytic Pricing of Asymmetric Defaultable Swaps", *Working Paper* 97/24/FIN, INSEAD, Paris and University of Liège, Belgium, 52 pp.

Hull, John, 1989, "An Analysis of the Credit Risk in Interest Rate Swaps and Currency Swaps", *Recent Developments in International Banking & Finance*, Khoury-Gosh published by McGraw-Hill, New York, pp. 109–30.

Hull, John, 1989, "Assessing Credit Risk in a Financial Institution's Off-Balance Sheet Commitments", *Journal of Financial and Quantitative Analysis*, **24** (4), December, 489–501.

Hull, John and A. White, 1990, "Pricing Interest Rate Derivative Securities", *Review of Financial Studies*, **3**, 573–92.

Hull, J., and A. White, 1995, "The Impact of Default Risk on the Prices of Option and Other Derivative Securities", *Journal of Banking and Finance*, **19**, pp. 299–322.

Iben, B. and R. Brotherton-Ratcliffe, 1994, "Credit Loss Distributions and Required Capital for Derivatives Portfolios", *Journal of Fixed Income*, June, 6–14.

Iben, Th. and R. Litterman, 1991, "Corporate Bond Valuation and the Term Structure of Credit Spreads", *Journal of Portfolio Management*, **17** (3), Spring, 1991, 52–64.

Ingersoll, Jonathan E., Jr, 1987, *Theory of Financial Decision Making*, Rowman and Littlefield Studies in Financial Economics Totowa, N.J.: Littlefield, Adams; Rowman and Littlefield, pp. xix, 474.

Ingersoll, Jonathan, 1977, "A Contingent Claims Valuation of Convertible Securities", *Journal of Financial Economics*, **4**, 289–322.

Izvorski, Ivailo, 1997, "Recovery Ratios and Survival Times for Corporate Bonds", International Monetary Fund *Working Paper*, Research Department, WP 97/84, July, 32 pp.

Jamshidian, Farshid and Yu Zhu, 1997, "Scenario Simulation: Theory and Methodology", *Finance and Stochastics*, **1**, 43–67.

Jarrow, R. and Stuart Turnbull, 1991, "A Unified Approach for Pricing Contingent Claims on Multiple Term Structures: The Foreign Currency Analogy", Working Paper.

Jarrow, R. and Stuart Turnbull, 1992, "Lecture Notes: Recent Advances in the Pricing of Options on Financial Assets with Credit Risk", 34 pp.

Jarrow, R. and Stuart Turnbull, 1995, "Pricing Derivatives on Financial Securities Subject to Credit Risk", *Journal of Finance*, **50** (1), March, 53–85.

Jarrow, Robert A. and Stuart M. Turnbull, 2000, "The Intersection of Market and Credit Risk", *Journal of Banking and Finance*, **24** (1–2), 271–99.

Jarrow, Robert, David Lando and Stuart Turnbull, 1997, "A Markov Model of the Term Structure of Credit Spreads", *Review of Financial Studies*, **10** (2), Summer.

Jensen, M. and J. Meckling, 1976, "Theory of the Firm: Managerial Behavior, Agency Cost and Ownership Structure", *Journal of Financial Economics*, **3**, 305.

Johnson, H. and R. Stulz, 1987, "The Pricing of Options with Default Risk", *Journal of Finance*, **42** (2), June, 267–80.

Jones, E. P. and S. P. Mason, 1980, Valuation of Loan Guarantees, *Journal of Banking and Finance*, **4**, 89–107.

Jones, E. Philip, Scott P. Mason and Eric Rosenfeld, 1984, "Contingent Claims Analysis of Corporate Capital Structures: An Empirical Investigation", *The Journal of Finance*, July 1984, **39** (3), 611–27.

Morgan, J. P., 1997, CreditMetrics® documentation: *Introduction to CreditMetrics* (35 pp.) and *Technical Document* (199 pp.).

Karatzas, I. and S. Shreve, 1988, *Brownian Motion and Stochastic Calculus*, Springer, Berlin, Heidelberg, New York.

Kealhofer, Stephen, 1998, *Portfolio Management of Default Risk*, Net Exposure 1 (2) (http://www.netexposure.co.uk), March/April, 22 pp.

Keenan, Sean C., 1998, "Historical Default Rates of Corporate Bond Issuers, 1920–1997", *Moody's Special Comment*, Moody's Investors Service, Global Credit Research, February, 61 pp.

Koyluoglu, Ugur and Andrew Hickman, 1998, "Reconciliable Differences", *Risk Magazine*, October.

Koyluoglu, Ugur and Andrew Hickman, 1998, "A Generalized Framework for Credit Risk Portfolio Models", *Working Paper*, October, 18 pp.

Lando, David, 1994, "On Cox Processes and Credit Risk Bonds", *Working Paper*, Institute of Mathematical Statistics, University of Copenhagen.

Lando, D., 1998, "On Cox Processes and Credit-Risky Securities", *Review of Derivatives Research*, **2**, 99–120.

Lardic, S., and E. Rouzeau, 1999, "Implementing Merton's model on the French corporate bond market", *Working Paper*, Crédit Commercial de France, Direction de la Recherche et de l'Innovation, May, 32 pp.

Lehrbass, Frank, 1997, "Defaulters get intense", *Credit Risk Supplement*, Risk Publications, Financial Engineering Ltd, July, pp. 56–9.

Leland, Hayne E., 1994, "Corporate Debt Value, Bond Covenants and Optimal Capital Structure", *Journal of Finance*, **49** (4), September, 1213–52.

Leland, Hayne E., 1998, "Agency Costs, Risk Management, and Capital Structure", Presidential Address presented at the AFA meeting in Chicago (December 1997), 43 pp.

Leland, H. E. and K. B. Toft, 1996, "Optimal Capital Structure, Endogenous Bankruptcy and the Term Structure of Credit Spreads", *Journal of Finance*, **51** (3), July, pp. 987–1019.

Li, Haitao, 1996, "Pricing of Swaps with Default Risk", *Working Paper*, Yale School of Management, New Haven, 38 pp.

Litzenberger, Robert H., 1992, "Swaps: Plain and Fanciful", *Journal of Finance*, **47** (3), July, 831–50.

Löffler, Gunter, 1999, *Using Credit Risk Models in Practice*, Commerzbank Asset Management.

Longstaff, Francis, 1990, "Pricing Options with Extendible Maturities: Analysis and Applications", *Journal of Finance*, **45** (3), July, 935–56.

Longstaff, F. and E. Schwartz, 1994, "A Simple Approach to Valuing Risky Fixed and Floating Rate Debt and Determining Swap Spreads", *Working Paper* (#22-93), Anderson Graduate School of Management, University of California, April.

Longstaff, F. and E. Schwartz, 1995a, "Valuing Credit Derivatives", *Journal of Fixed Income*, June, 6–12.

Longstaff, Francis and Eduardo Schwartz, 1995b, "A Simple Approach to Valuing Risky Fixed and Floating Rate Debt", *Journal of Finance*, **50** (3), July, 789–819.

Lucas, D.J. and J. Lonski, 1992, "Changes in Corporate Credit Quality 1970–1990", *Journal of Fixed Income*, **2**, March, 7–14.

Madan, Dilip, 1998, "Default Risk", in *Statistics in Finance*, ed. by D. Hand, Ch. 12.

Madan, D. and H. Unal, 1993, "Pricing the Risks of Default", *Working Paper*, College of Business, University of Maryland.

Madan, Dilip and Haluk Unal, 1995, "Pricing the Risks of Default", *Working Paper*, September, 68 pp.

Marcus, A. J. and I. Shaked, 1984, "The Valuation of FDIC Deposit Insurance Using Option-pricing Estimates", *Journal of Money, Credit, and Banking*, **16** (4), 446–60.

Margrabe, W., 1978, "The Value of an Option to Exchange One Asset for Another", *Journal of Finance*, **33**, March, 177–87.

Mason, Scott and Sudipto Bhattacharya, 1981, "Risky Debt, Jump Processes and Safety Covenants", *Journal of Financial Economics*, **9**, 281–307.

Mella-Barral, P. and W. Perraudin, 1997, "Strategic Debt Service", *The Journal of Finance*, **52** (2), June, 531–56.

Merton, Robert C., 1973, "Theory of Rational Option Pricing", *Bell Journal of Economics and Management Science*, **4**, 141–83.

Merton, Robert C., 1974, "On the Pricing of Corporate Debt: The Risk Structure of Interest Rates", *The Journal of Finance*, **29**, May, 449–70.

Merton, Robert C., 1977, "On the Pricing of Contingent Claims and the Modigliani–Miller Theorem", *Journal of Financial Economics*, **5**, 241–9.

Merton, Robert C., 1994, "Pricing and Hedging Contingent-Claim Securities When the Underlying Security is Not Continuously Traded or Observable", *Class Teaching Notes*.

Merton, Robert C., 1994, *Continuous-Time Finance*, Blackwell Publishers, 732 pp.

Merton, R. C. and Z. Bodie, 1992, "On the Management of Financial Guarantees", *Financial Management*, **22**, Winter.

Minton, B., 1994, "Two Essays on Interest Rate Swaps", PhD Dissertation 9509, University of Chicago.

Moody's report by Keenan, Sean C., 1998, "Historical Default Rates of Corporate Bond Issuers, 1920–1997", *Moody's Special Comment*, Moody's Investors Service, Global Credit Research, February, 61 pp.

Musiela, Marek and Marek Rutkowski, 1997, *Martingale Methods in Financial Modelling*, Springer-Verlag, 512 pp.

Myers, S. and M. Majluf, 1984, "Corporate Financing and Investment Decisions When Firms Have Information that Investors Do Not Have", *Journal of Financial Economics*, **13**, 187–222.

Nickell, P., W. Perraudin and S. Varotto, 2000, "Stability of Rating Transitions", *Journal of Banking and Finance*, **24** (1–2), 203–27.

Office of the Comptroller of the Currency, Administrator of National Banks (USA), 1999, *OCC Bank Derivatives Report — Third Quarter 1999*, December 9, 27 pp.

Pearson, N. D., and T.-S. Sun, 1994, "Exploiting the Conditional Density in Estimating the Term Structure: An Application to the Cox, Ingersoll and Ross Model", *The Journal of Finance*, **49**, 1279–304.

Pirotte, H., 1999a, "Implementing a Structural Valuation Model of Swap Credit-Sensitive Rates", *Working Paper*, Institute of Banking and Finance, Ecole des HEC, University of Lausanne, December, 32 pp.

Pirotte, H., 1999b, "A Structural Model of the Term Structure of Credit Spreads with Stochastic Recovery and Contractual Design", *Working Paper*, Institute of Banking and Finance, Ecole des HEC, University of Lausanne, December, 85 pp.

Plaut, Steven E., 1985, "The Theory of Collateral". *Journal of Banking & Finance*, **9** (3), 401–19, September.

Ramaswamy, K., and Suresh Sundaresan, 1986, "The Valuation of Floating-Rate Instruments", *Journal of Finance*, **17**, February, 251–72.

Rebonato, Riccardo, 1996, *Interest-Rate Option Models*, John Wiley and Sons, Chichester, UK, 372 pp.

Rendleman, Richard, Jr., 1993, "How risks are shared in Interest Rate Swaps", *Journal of Financial Services Research*, **7** (1), 5–34.

Rich, Don, 1994, "The Mathematical Foundations of Barrier Option-Pricing Theory", *Advances in Futures and Options Research*, **7**, 267–311.

Rich, Don, 1996, "The Valuation and Behavior of Black–Scholes Options Subject to Intertemporal Default Risk", *Review of Derivatives Research*, **1**, 25–59.

Risk Magazine, 1997, "Credit Risk: A Risk special supplement", *Risk Publications*, Financial Engineering Ltd, July, 65 pp.

Ronn, Ehud and Avinash Verma, 1986, "Pricing Risk-Adjusted Deposit Insurance: An Option-Based Model", *The Journal of Finance*, **41** (4), September, 871–95.

Rubinstein, Mark, 1991, "Exotic Options", Finance *Working Paper* no. 220, Institute of Business and Economic Research, University of California at Berkeley, December, various papers.

Rubinstein, M. and Reiner, E., 1991, "Breaking down the Barriers", *Risk Magazine*, **4**, 28–35.

Saá-Requejo, Jesús and Pedro Santa Clara, 1997, "Bond Pricing with Default Risk", *Working Paper*, John E. Anderson Graduate School of Management, UCLA, Los Angeles, 23 pp.

Samant, Ajay A., 1992, "Corporate Liability Choice under Asymmetric Information: A Theoretical and Empirical Study of Interest Rate Swaps", PhD, Indiana University.

Sarig, Oded and Warga, Arthur, 1989, "Some Empirical Estimates of the Risk Structure of Interest Rates", *Journal of Finance*, **44** (5), 1351–60, December.

Saunders, Anthony, 1999, *Credit Risk Measurement*, John Wiley & Sons, Chichester, UK.

Schaefer, Stephen and Eduardo Schwartz, 1984, "A Two-Factor Model of the Term Structure: An Approximate Analytical Solution", *Journal of Financial and Quantitative Analysis*, **19** (4), December, 413–24.

Schönbucher, P., 1997, "The Term Structure of Defaultable Bond Prices", *Working Paper*, University of Bonn.

Shalev, Jonathan, 1997, "Loss Aversion Equilibrium", *Working Paper*, CORE, Université Catholique de Louvain-la-Neuve, Belgium, 26 pp.

Sharp, Keith, 1987, "Bond and Bond Option Prices Dependent on n Correlated Stochastic Processes", *Working Paper in Actuarial Science*, Department of Statistics and Actuarial Science, University of Waterloo, Ontario, 11 pp.

Shimko, David, Naohiko Tejima and Donald Van Deventer, 1993, "The Pricing of Risky Debt When Interest Rates are Stochastic", *The Journal of Fixed Income*, September, 58–65.

Sorensen, Eric H. and Thierry F. Bollier, 1994, "Pricing Swap Default Risk", *Financial Analysts Journal*, **50** (3), May–June, 23–33.

Stulz, René and Herb Johnson, 1985, "An Analysis of Secured Debt", *Journal of Financial Economics*, **14**, 501–21.

Sun, Tong Sheng, Suresh Sundaresan and Ching Wang, 1993, "Interest Rate Swaps: An Empirical Investigation", *Journal of Financial Economics*, **34** (1), August, 77–99.

Sundaresan, S., 1991, "Valuation of Swaps", *Recent Developments in International Banking & Finance*, Khoury.

Sussman, Oren and Joseph Zeira, 1995, "Banking and Development", Centre for Economic Policy Research, Financial Economics and International Macroeconomics, n. 1127, February, 42 pp.

Titman, Sheridan and Torous, Walter N., 1989, "Valuing Commercial Mortgages: An Empirical Investigation of the Contingent-Claims Approach to Pricing Risky Debt", *Journal of Finance*, **44** (2), 345–73, June.

Toft, Klaus B. and Brian Prucyk, 1997, "Options on Leveraged Equity: Theory and Empirical Tests", *The Journal of Finance*, **52** (3), July, 1151–80.

Van Deventer, D., Samuel Chang and Sou Cheng Choi, 1999, "Credit Risk Models and Applications in Asian Markets", *Working Paper* for the 11th PACAP/FMA Finance Conference, Kamamura Corporation, July.

Van Deventer, D., Samuel Chang and Sou Cheng Choi, 1999, "The Merton Model and Jarrow Model of Credit Risk and Implications for Bank Safety and Soundness", *Working Paper*, Kamamura Corporation, July, 16 pp.

Vasicek, O., 1977, "An Equilibrium Characterization of the Term Structure", *Journal of Financial Economics*, **5**, 177–88.

Wall, Larry D., and John J. Pringle, 1988, "Interest Rate Swaps: A Review of the Issues," *Federal Reserve Bank of Atlanta Economic Review*, **73** (November/December), 22–37.

Wei, D. G. and D. Guo, 1997, "Pricing Risky Debt: An Empirical Comparison of the Longstaff and Schwartz and Merton Models", *The Journal of Fixed Income*, September, 9–28.

Weiss, L. A., 1990, "Bankruptcy Resolution: Direct Costs and Violation of Priority of Claims", *Journal of Financial Economics*, **27**.

White, H., 1980, "A Heteroscedasticity-Consistent Covariance Matrix Estimator and a Direct Test for Heteroscedasticity", *Econometrica*, **48**, 817–38.

Wilson, Tom, 1997a, "Portfolio Credit Risk I", *Risk Magazine*, **10** (9), September.

Wilson, Tom, 1997b, "Portfolio Credit Risk II", *Risk Magazine*, **10** (9), September.

Zhou, Chunsheng, 1997, "A Jump-Diffusion Approach to Modeling Credit Risk and Valuing Defaultable Securities", *Working Paper*, Federal Reserve Board, Washington, 47 pp.

Index

Index compiled by
Indexing Specialists, Hove